A326 Empire: 1492–1975

The Open University

Block 1
What are empires?

Block 2
How do empires begin?

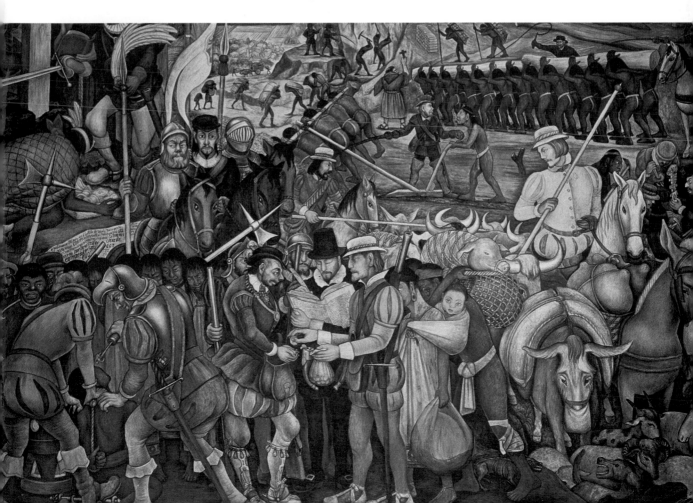

This publication forms part of an Open University course A326 *Empire: 1492–1975*. Details of this and other Open University courses can be obtained from the Student Registration and Enquiry Service, The Open University, PO Box 197, Milton Keynes MK7 6BJ, United Kingdom: tel. +44 (0)845 300 60 90, email general-enquiries@open.ac.uk

Alternatively, you may visit the Open University website at http://www.open.ac.uk where you can learn more about the wide range of courses and packs offered at all levels by The Open University.

To purchase a selection of Open University course materials visit http://www.ouw.co.uk, or contact Open University Worldwide, Michael Young Building, Walton Hall, Milton Keynes MK7 6AA, United Kingdom for a brochure. tel. +44 (0)1908 858793; fax +44 (0)1908 858787; email ouw-customer-services@open.ac.uk

The Open University
Walton Hall, Milton Keynes
MK7 6AA

First published 2008

Edited and designed by The Open University.

Typeset in India by Alden Prepress Services, Chennai.

Printed and bound in the United Kingdom by Bell & Bain Ltd., Glasgow

ISBN 978 0 7492 1710 5

1.1

CONTENTS

Block 1
What are empires?   **5**

Introduction to Block 1   6

Unit 1   Mapping empires in history   12

Unit 2   Tools and terms for studying empires   41

Unit 3   Empires of the mind   79

Conclusion to Block 1   111

Block 2
How do empires begin?   **113**

Introduction to Block 2   115

Unit 4   The beginning of Atlantic empires: Spain in the New World   120

Unit 5   Pirates, pilgrims, plantations and pigs: the beginnings
          of the British Atlantic empire 1497–1660   156

Unit 6   Empires of trade? The Portuguese and the Dutch in east Asia 1580–1670   194

Unit 7   The expansion of Russia 1500–1725   227

Conclusion to Block 2   262

Glossary   **263**

Acknowledgements   **270**

Index   **271**

BLOCK 1
WHAT ARE EMPIRES?

Introduction to Block 1   **6**
Learning outcomes   6
References   11

Unit 1
Mapping empires in history   **12**
Aims   12
Introduction   12
Reading maps   12
An overview of empires   18
Conclusion   36
References   39

Unit 2
Tools and terms for studying empires   **41**
Aims   41
Introduction   41
Definitions of empire   42
Types of colonies and of rule   46
Empires as systems   62
Conclusion   76
References   77

Unit 3
Empires of the mind   **79**
Aims   79
Introduction   79
Debating empire   80
Empires and popular culture   90
Individual experiences of empire   100
Conclusion   108
References   109

Conclusion to Block 1   **111**

INTRODUCTION TO BLOCK 1

Paul Lawrence

Learning outcomes

When you have completed your study of this block, you should:

- be aware of the broad contours of the history of empires from 1492
- be able to demonstrate knowledge and understanding of the main theories and concepts involved in the study of empires
- be able to engage critically with a variety of debates about the significance of 'culture' in relation to empire.

On 9 March 1623, local Dutch authorities executed twenty men on the small Pacific island of Amboyna. Amboyna (now Ambon) is a mountainous tropical island that currently forms part of Indonesia (see World map 3 in the Visual Sources Book). At the start of the seventeenth century, it was part of the Moluccas (controlled mainly by the Dutch) and was known as a place where spices such as nutmeg and cloves could be obtained. Ten of those executed were English, employees of the East India Company (EIC),[1] a venture set up to exploit the wealth of the Indies; nine were Japanese mercenary soldiers (*samurai*), who had previously been in the pay of the Dutch East India Company (Verenigde Oost-Indische Compagnie or VOC); and one was Portuguese. Before being executed, the men were tortured. Normal torture practice in the Dutch East Indies was to wrap cloth around the head of the man being interrogated, and then repeatedly to douse this with water, producing partial asphyxiation (see Figure i). The victims ended up both swallowing and breathing in large amounts of water, which led to their internal organs becoming painfully bloated. When they lost consciousness, they were made to vomit up the water. As soon as they were breathing again, the procedure was repeated. If the prisoner still refused to talk, burning candles might be held under his armpits (Milton, 2000). The men had been charged by the Dutch authorities with treason and, according to Dutch records, they all eventually confessed their guilt – with or without being tortured. Accordingly, on 9 March, they were decapitated. The head of the English merchant and sea captain Gabriel Towerson was stuck on a pole for public display.

The immediate circumstances that precipitated this minor but intriguing incident are fairly clear. The Dutch East India Company had established a trading post on Amboyna in 1609 by the simple expedient of forcibly driving out the Portuguese, who had got there before them. They built an impressive

---

[1] In 1600 this was chartered as the 'Company of Merchants of London trading to the East Indies'. It was at first specifically chartered by the English state, but from the Act of Union in 1707 it was in effect a British Company.

Figure i   Frontispiece from Skinner, J. (1624) *A True Relation of the Uniust, Cruell, and Barbarous Proceedings against the English at Amboyna ... Also the copie of a pamphlet, set forth first in Dutch and then in English, by some Neatherlander; falsly entituled, A True Declaration of the Newes that Came Out of the East-Indies ... Together with an answer to the same pamphlet,* London, printed by H. Lownes for Nathanael Newberry. British Library, London, T 39928 (c)–(e). By permission of the British Library. The engraving depicts the torture of English East India Company employees on Amboyna.

fortification (Fort Victoria), which was manned by 200 soldiers (Chancey, 1999, p. 585). In 1619, the English East India Company had set up a trading station (known as a **factory**) on the island. The executed Englishmen were drawn from among the twenty residents of this factory. The Dutch governor of the island, Herman van Speult, believed that Towerson and nine others had been planning to seize control of Fort Victoria – an unlikely supposition given that they had no stockpile of weapons and would have been outnumbered at least ten to one. Before being executed, the English merchants went to great trouble to recant the confessions they had made while being tortured. Several, for example, left a note affirming their innocence in an account book that a servant managed to smuggle past their Dutch captors. As Chancey notes, 'they went to their deaths protesting their innocence' (1999, p. 586).

Knowledge of these basic facts, however, gives us only the most meagre comprehension of this event. How, as historians, can we interpret and understand this incident more fully? What historical forces, both personal and impersonal, led these merchants to their gruesome deaths over 7,000 miles away from their homes and families? Given the nature of this course, a fairly safe answer might be 'it's all about empire, isn't it?' This is true. This incident can be read as one small part of the history of empire, touching (as it does) on the expansion of overseas influence of Britain, Holland and Portugal. But it is also instructive in highlighting the different ways in which the history of empire can be considered, and the different skills required by the historian of empire.

In the first place, and most obviously, it is impossible properly to understand this incident without knowing more of the historical context. In other words, we need to know the before and the after – the framework of imperial development into which this event fits. The suspicions of the Dutch and the executions of these men are much more comprehensible when we know, for example, that although a treaty of 1619 had given the English East India Company the right to a one-third share of the spice trade of the Moluccas, this treaty was widely ignored in the region. In addition, it is helpful to know that the Dutch administration of the East Indies was notoriously suspicious of English merchants.

The aftermath of the incident, which became what we would now call a 'diplomatic incident', is also interesting. James I rapidly came under pressure from the EIC, who petitioned him to seek redress from the Dutch for their losses in the incident (their factory on Amboyna had also been destroyed). The Dutch, in turn, began a propaganda campaign with the publication, in 1623, of an anonymous tract entitled *A True Declaration of the Newes that Came Out of the East Indies*. This detailed account of events claimed (among other things) that Towerson had admitted his guilt and explained that his actions had been motivated by 'the desire of Honour and Profit' (Anon, 1624, p. 6). While the VOC denied any part in the publication of the pamphlet, this claim was derided in England as the company's stockholders had helped to distribute it there. The EIC then published its own version of events, as part of a wider publicity campaign. The event also gripped the public imagination. Numerous ballads and pamphlets were produced lamenting the events (as evidenced by John Skinner's 1624 pamphlet, from which the engraving in Figure i is drawn).

Thus, with the benefit of this wider historical context, the Amboyna massacre becomes one point of contact in the developing rivalry of two early modern countries seeking to develop trading empires. You will learn more about the early development of the British and Dutch empires in Block 2. Before that, however, the first unit of this block will provide you with an overview of the broad, interconnected histories of imperial expansion (and contraction) over the *longue durée*. This is the first prerequisite for analysing individual incidents such as Amboyna, but also for a broader understanding of the question 'what are empires?' It is impossible to understand the nature or development of any one imperial power in isolation. However, a broad historical knowledge, while vital, is not all that is required to understand empires. As historians of empire, we also need to think about empires on an analytical and theoretical level.

For example, the small 'factories' of the East Indies, run by private joint-stock companies, are perhaps not what we might expect an empire to be built on. When we think of 'empires', we are more likely to think of the stereotype of a powerful state controlling lots of territory. In fact, however, large empires were often composed of many different 'types' of colonies. This point is perhaps best illustrated comparatively. At around the same time as the EIC was attempting to muscle in on Dutch trade in the East Indies, the Plymouth Colony was founded in America. A group of religious separatists fleeing persecution (who had first moved to Amsterdam, then Leiden) set sail on the *Mayflower* and the *Speedwell* with the intention of building a new life in America. This type of 'settler' colony was clearly very different in its aims and outcomes from the 'trading enclaves' maintained by the EIC in the East Indies. The British (and indeed, the Dutch) aim in the East Indies was not the permanent settlement of citizens abroad, nor dominion over vast swathes of land, still less was it the maintenance of direct rule over the indigenous inhabitants of the region. Rather, both countries sought (through the involvement of the joint-stock companies set up by Royal Charter for the purpose) to control trade and natural resources for profit.

The early settler colonies of America and the trading outposts in the east were both component aspects of the nascent British empire, but were very different in their aims and in their interactions with the **metropole** (the mother country). It is thus only by analysing these initiatives at an abstract level, by comparing their essential characteristics, that the internal workings of the empire can be analysed. As you work your way through the course, you will encounter many different types of empires, which functioned in different ways, and were made up of very different component parts. To think coherently about the comparative history of empires, we thus need some kind of theoretical or analytical framework to enable comparison across time and place. This will be the subject of the second unit in this block. Thinking about empires in terms of broad, conceptual categories is another way of analysing individual events and of answering the big questions, such as 'what are empires?'

There is a final piece of the puzzle to consider, however. As historians we also need to give some consideration to the motivations, opinions and experiences of the individuals involved in the events we study. Arguably, it is no use knowing all the retrospective 'facts' of empire (the bare bones of 'what happened'), and having an overview of all the relevant explanatory theories, if we do not at least consider what those participating in empires thought about them. Enquiring as to what those involved in the histories of empires *thought* they were doing can thus provide us with yet another possible answer to the question 'what are empires'?

On a personal level, the analysis of key individuals can be useful to our understanding of empires. Jan Pieterszoon Coen (the Dutch governor of the Dutch East Indies), for example, hated the English, and was waging a very brutal armed campaign against the indigenous inhabitants of the Banda Islands when news of the 1619 treaty between Holland and Britain reached him (see ~~Plate 2.11 in~~ the Visual Sources Book). Clearly, he was a servant of the Dutch state in some ways, but he also had his own individual ambitions and motivations, and was a man inured to acts of extreme violence. Gabriel Towerson, by contrast, had a much more tenuous connection with the British state, certainly at the time of the massacre. A wily survivor, he was now living permanently in the east, on private means, and was on very cordial terms with the Dutch administration on Amboyna. Thus, we might argue from this that Towerson was unlikely to be leading a conspiracy with the aim of bolstering British relations in the region, and that Coen was very likely to use the idea of a conspiracy for his own ends despite the lack of evidence.

[handwritten margin note: Plate 2.13]

Stepping back from the individual level, however, it is also important to consider public opinion and attitudes to imperial events in the metropole. The immediate aftermath of the massacre has already been mentioned, but the event wormed its way deep into the public psyche in Britain. Although the Dutch had paid compensation at the end of the first Anglo–Dutch war in 1654, the memory of the Amboyna massacre was such that the poet John Dryden still used it as the subject for (and title of) a propaganda play during the third Anglo–Dutch war in 1673 (Markley, 1998). The analysis of public opinion is another way of answering the question 'what are empires?'

One thing is still missing here, however – the voices and experiences of the indigenous people of the region. Clearly, armed conflict between European and local troops was a feature of the period. However, oppression and violence were not the sole defining factors of the indigenous experience. Trade was also pursued, on occasion, and Fort Victoria (the objective of the alleged Amboyna conspiracy) was protected by a force of 400 locally recruited *mardiker* (landless labourers for hire). Thus Amboyna reveals the complexities and diversities of experience even among those on the receiving end of empires. While often hard to obtain, a consideration of the experiences, thoughts and opinions of individuals involved in empires is just as important in understanding what empires are and how they function as the consideration of historical context and a knowledge of relevant theories. However, we will leave the Amboyna massacre here – a dramatic, but relatively minor, episode in the history of empire. You can, if you wish, take a look at some of the documents relating to it by searching for 'Amboyna' in your primary source database (accessible from the course website). We will now spring from this toehold into the first of the big questions around which this course is structured – 'what are empires'?

REFERENCES

Anon (1624) *A True Declaration of the Newes that Came Out of the East Indies.*

Chancey, K. (1999) 'The Amboyna massacre in English politics, 1624–1632', *Albion*, vol. 30, no. 4, pp. 583–98.

Markley, R. (1998) 'Violence and profits on the Restoration stage: trade, nationalism, and insecurity in Dryden's Amboyna', *Eighteenth-Century Life*, vol. 22, no. 1, pp. 2–17.

Milton, G. (2000) *Nathaniel's Nutmeg. How One Man's Courage Changed the Course of History*, London, Sceptre.

UNIT 1
MAPPING EMPIRES IN HISTORY

Robin Mackie

AIMS

- To give you an overview of the history of empires between 1492 and 1975 as context for the later units.
- To raise some of the key questions about empires that will be discussed in greater detail later in the course.
- To use maps both as a framework for this overview and to introduce you to an important way that empires were represented and imagined.

INTRODUCTION

As the aims explain, the main purpose of this first unit is to give you a brief overview of the history of the world's major empires in the last 500 years. This will provide a context for the more detailed accounts in later units and should also raise questions relevant to the study of empires. We hope too that the overview will link together your own prior knowledge of topics in world history, since, for all of us, some periods and some countries are likely to be more familiar than others. Inevitably, the unit contains a great deal of information – far more than you will need to remember. The goal is to consider the period as a whole; later, you may find this unit, together with the associated maps in the Visual Sources Book and the datechart on the course website, a useful point of reference.

This overview is supported by maps and it is with maps that the unit starts. Before proceeding to the overview in later sections, the first section looks at two historic maps (Plates 1.1 and 1.2 in the Visual Sources Book) to explore some of the issues surrounding their use in studying history. This section will ask you to consider the context in which maps are made and how this shapes the way that they transmit knowledge.

READING MAPS

The Piri Reis map

Look at Plate 1.1 in the Visual Sources Book (located after the collection of ten world maps, which we will turn to shortly). If you are not used to looking at old maps, you may find this one quite difficult to decipher. It may help to start in the top right-hand corner (the northeast, since it has a north orientation like most maps we use), where one can make out the coasts of Spain and Portugal, and to the south of them the curve of the West African coast. The map shows the central and south Atlantic (you may find it helpful to compare it with one of the world maps earlier in the Visual Sources Book). Having identified Europe and Africa, it becomes clear that the line of the left of the map must be the eastern coast of the Americas (the Caribbean and Brazil to be precise) and the groups of islands in the northeast, the various archipelagos of Atlantic islands: from north to south, the Azores, Madeira, the Canaries and the Cape Verde Islands.

The map also has many design features with which we are not familiar, such as the **compass roses and rhumb lines** (the grid of circles and linking lines) and others that may seem inappropriate for a map, such as the pictures of animals and ships. Even if we concentrate on the lines that represent geographical features there are a number that are confusing. The Caribbean islands, for instance, seem badly distorted, and the prolongation of the coastline south of Brazil suggests that the American continent sweeps round to the south of Africa. Our natural reaction on seeing an old map such as this one is to compare it with what we know, to check how 'accurate' it is. This is fair enough, so long as it does not lead us to dismiss maps of the past simply as inferior to those we produce today. A map is not a mirror of nature; it communicates knowledge through representation. We need to think both about the knowledge that is being transmitted (including how accurate it is), and the process by which this is done. J. B. Harley argues that the process is 'culturally and historically specific: the rules of cartography vary in different societies'. It is important that we understand these rules or conventions, which are both technical and cultural (Harley, 1992, pp. 232–3).

Another way of saying this, which will be familiar to you if you have studied history before (for instance, the Open University course A200 *Exploring history*) is that maps are texts created by an author, in a context, for a purpose. As you know, historians subject contemporary documents (often referred to as primary sources) to analysis, using questions such as the following:

- What kind of document is it? Who wrote (or created) it? When? Who was the intended audience?
- What do we know of its context? Are there special features to note?

Even if we cannot find answers to all such questions, we need to ask them; only then are we really in a position to evaluate how much the document, whether it be a written text, or an image, or some other object, will help with our enquiry. Moreover, if we find new evidence about the document, it is necessary to review the analysis. Assessing a source is not a one-off process, but a developing one, which goes hand-in-hand with a developing knowledge of the subject under study. In all this, maps are no different from other sources – they too need to be evaluated and placed in context. As with many other sources, an important part of this process of evaluation is understanding the rules of the genre: the contemporary conventions surrounding representation in this type of text.

So what do we know about the map in Plate 1.1? Perhaps you noted the date in the caption. The map was produced in 1513 – just 21 years after Columbus crossed the Atlantic. It is a fragment (the only surviving one) of a larger map that appears to have covered the whole world as known in Europe at the time. However, it was the writing in Arabic script on the map that first caught my attention.

Relatively little is known about the origins of the map, and almost all of that from the map itself: from the texts on the map or what can be deduced from the way lands are presented. It was created by an Ottoman naval commander, known as Piri Reis (although Reis simply means sea captain) and was presented to the Ottoman emperor, Sultan Selim I, shortly after his conquest of Egypt in 1517. One of the texts tells us something about its making:

> No such map exists in our age. Your humble servant is its author and brought it into being. It is based mainly on twenty charts and *mappa mundi*, one of which is drawn in the time of Alexander the Great, and is known to the Arabs as Caferiye [*dja'grafiye*]. This map is the result of comparison with eight such [*dja'grafiye*] maps, one Arab map of India, four new Portuguese maps drawn according to the geometrical methods of India and China, and also the map of the western lands drawn by Columbus; such that this map of the seven seas is as accurate and reliable as the latter map of this region.

> (quoted in Brotton, 1997, p. 108)

In the early 1500s, the Ottoman empire was a dynamic and expanding power: Constantinople had been captured in 1453, and the Ottoman armies reached the gates of Vienna in 1529 and conquered Baghdad in 1533. Nor were they only a land power: they had needed a fleet to stop Constantinople being supplied from the sea and went on to push the Venetians out of many of their bases in the eastern Mediterranean. When they conquered Egypt, they built a navy on the Red Sea, captured Aden in 1549, and laid siege to Hormuz in the Persian Gulf in 1552 (many of these places are shown on World maps 1 and 2 in the Visual Sources Book). But the Portuguese discovery of a route round Africa threatened to undermine the value of these conquests: no longer did all trade between Europe and Asia need to pass through the Middle East. Hormuz was in fact held by the Portuguese and Piri Reis, who commanded the eastern fleet, was beheaded in 1554 for his failure to take it (Soucek, 1992, p. 269).

Knowledge of the discoveries of Columbus and Vasco da Gama (who pioneered the sea route round Africa to India in 1498) spread rapidly in Europe and forced contemporaries to revise the way they imagined the world. A number of maps made in the early sixteenth century that incorporate the new knowledge have survived. Most famous is perhaps the Waldseemüller map (Primary Source 1.4 in the primary sources database), created in Strasbourg in 1507, which was the first to give the name America to the newly discovered western continent. We tend to think of Christian Europe and the Islamic Middle East as confronting each other in this period, and indeed they were frequently in armed conflict. Yet, at the same time, trade and ideas flowed back and forth across the Mediterranean. Arab, Genoan and Catalonian cartographers worked within a shared tradition and this is evident if the Piri Reis map is compared with contemporary European ones such as the Cantino map in Plate 1.3 in the Visual Sources Book.

Exploring the historical origins of the Piri Reis map therefore reveals it as more than a romantically inaccurate old map of the Atlantic. As the text on the map reveals, Piri Reis drew on a wide range of sources from both the Islamic and Christian worlds. Much of the interest in the map has centred on his knowledge of America. It now seems most likely that he used a captured Spanish map that had been drawn during Columbus's second expedition of 1493–94, from which no original charts have survived (McIntosh, 2000, pp. 135–6). Based in the Middle East, Piri Reis 'had access to one of the most comprehensive collections of geographical information available to any scholar or pilot active in the early modern world' (Brotton, 1997, p. 100). With the knowledge available to him, he was able to create a map of a dramatically changing world: a world that created new opportunities – and threats – for rival Christian and non-Christian empires.

Cook's first map of New Zealand

The second map I would like you to look at is Plate 1.2 in the Visual Sources Book, an engraving based on charts drawn by Captain James Cook during his first expedition to the Pacific in 1768–71 (for Cook's route, see World map 5). A number of journals were meticulously kept during the expedition and these provide a great deal of background information on the making of the charts, so, in this respect, the map stands in complete contrast to the Piri Reis one.

EXERCISE

Two documents (Primary Sources 1.1 and 1.2) relating to the voyage are available on the course website. Primary Source 1.1 is a section from the instructions Cook was given before he set out, and Primary Source 1.2 consists of extracts from his journals. Using these two documents and the map in Plate 1.2, answer the following two questions:

1   What was the purpose of Cook's expedition?
2   How does Cook's map present New Zealand?

SPECIMEN ANSWER

1   Cook was sent to the Pacific with clear instructions on what to do after observing the transit of Venus in Tahiti (the primary purpose of the expedition). He was to explore whether a southern continent existed and, if not, to locate and map New Zealand, which had been sighted and named by the Dutch explorer Abel Tasman.

2   The map of New Zealand is quite recognisable. There are a few mistakes: Banks's Island is in fact a peninsula, while Cape South is on a separate island. The only features shown are physical ones; no settlements have been marked. This creates the impression of a newly discovered island: a pristine – and unclaimed – world. This is reinforced by the inclusion of the route of the *Endeavour*, and by the names, which, with the exception of the names of the two main islands, are mostly English.

View of the North Side of the Entrance into Poverty Bay, & Morai Island, in New Zealand.
1. Young Nicki Head.
2. Morai Island.

Figure 1.1   R.B. Godfrey probably after Parkinson, 'View of the North Side of the Entrance into Poverty Bay, & Morai Island, in New Zealand', engraving, from Parkinson, S. (1773) *A Journal of a Voyage to the South Seas, in His Majesty's Ship, the Endeavour. Faithfully transcribed from the papers of the late Sydney Parkinson, draughtsman to Joseph Banks, Esq.*, London, Stanfield Parkinson. British Library, London, L.R.294.c.7. By permission of the British Library.

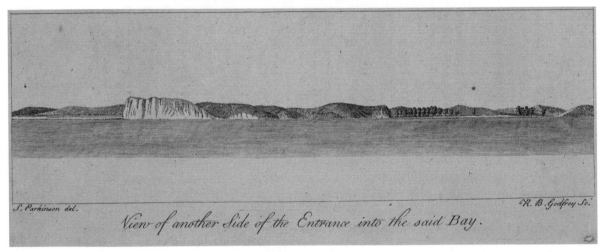

S. Parkinson del.   R. B. Godfrey Sc.

View of another Side of the Entrance into the said Bay.

Figure 1.2   R.B. Godfrey after Parkinson, 'View of another Side of the Entrance into the said Bay', engraving, from Parkinson, S. (1773) *A Journal of a Voyage to the South Seas, in His Majesty's Ship, the Endeavour. Faithfully transcribed from the papers of the late Sydney Parkinson, draughtsman to Joseph Banks, Esq.*, London, Stanfield Parkinson. British Library, London, L.R.294.c.7. By permission of the British Library.

DISCUSSION

Cook's map, together with the journals and detailed small-scale charts and drawings (see two of the drawings in Figures 1.1 and 1.2), were made in fulfilment of his brief. Cook's route, the map he made, and the names given are closely linked. As Cook explains in the final section of the journal, his mapping of New Zealand was based on where he went. It was at times difficult to get close enough to the coast; hence the errors round South Island (Toai Poonamoo on the map). Moreover, although he does not say this, since the mapping was largely done from the sea, it is a map of the coastlines. Although several landings were made on North Island (Ea Heinom Auwe), the expedition only landed at the very north of South Island. Not surprisingly, the interior is shown in much less detail.

The names also tell the story of the journey (Carter, 1987, pp. 4–9). Many are linked to the progress of the voyage itself: the journal entry for the 11 October, for instance, explains the choice of the names Poverty Bay and Young Nicks Head, and their last sight of New Zealand was Cape Farewell (Beaglehole, 1974, p. 225). Other features are named after members of the crew (as well as the Cook's Straits, there are islands named after Joseph Banks and Daniel Solander, two scientists on the *Endeavour*) or after patrons in Britain, such as Cape Palliser. Very few Maori names are given. Yet Cook and his crew did communicate with the local population. The entry for the 31 January shows them questioning an old man as to whether New Zealand was one or two islands and finding out the names of the islands (although Cook later reveals that he is not entirely sure that the name (given here as Tovy-poenammu) refers to the whole of South Island). Communication was possible through Tupaia, a Polynesian priest who had sailed with the *Endeavour* from Tahiti. To the surprise and pleasure of Cook and his companions, Tupaia was able to talk to the Maori, since their languages were closely related.

We talk of putting something 'on the map' and this describes rather nicely what Captain Cook's map did. It created knowledge of New Zealand: before Cook's voyage, almost nothing was known in Europe about the islands. The expedition came during a new eighteenth-century age of discovery in which Europeans explored much of the Pacific and began to investigate the interior of Africa (if you studied A207 *From Enlightenment to Romanticism c.1780–1830*, you will recall Mungo Park's journey to the Niger). In contrast to the age of Columbus and Magellan, the emphasis was more on the accumulation of knowledge than of riches and Cook's expedition was very much a scientific one. In the journal extracts, he mentions the work of Charles Green, who had been in charge of the observation of the transit of Venus, while Banks and Solander investigated plants and wildlife: the *Endeavour* returned home with a large collection of plants from the South Pacific. Cook himself was a skilled mapmaker and his map of New Zealand has been recognised as a great achievement (Beaglehole, 1974, p. 221).

Cook had been instructed, 'with the Consent of the Natives to take possession of Convenient Situations in the Country in the Name of the King of Great Britain' and the entry for the 31 January describes one such ceremony. You may have noted that Cook did ask for consent before erecting his post and that the ceremony was witnessed by an old Maori man. What he would have made of this event is hard to know. Anne Salmond suggests that it would probably have been interpreted in terms of ritual communication with ancestors and as such was not seen as a threat (Salmond, 1991, p. 251). As the encounters at Poverty Bay showed, the Maori were quite prepared to fight invaders. The way Cook explained the event is in itself revealing: the purpose was to 'set up a mark upon the Island in order to shew to any ship that might put into this place, that we had been here before' (Primary Source 1.2, pp. 4–5). The rival claim to the land that the post was meant to fend off came not from the Maori inhabitants but from other European explorers.

In many ways, however, it was not the post, but the map that was the real basis to the British claim. In the eyes of Cook and his companions, they were creating new knowledge of the islands that was separate from and better than the existing knowledge of the Maori. Cook makes clear that his notes are solidly based on his own observations and those of his companions. He is quite dismissive of the geographical knowledge of the Maori inhabitants: 'I am inclinable to think that they know'd no more of this land than what came within the limets of their sight' (Primary Source 1.2, p. 6). In fact, we may suspect that his notes incorporate some information obtained from the Maori. Cook and Banks were always keen to ask questions through Tupaia, and their account of Australia (where they went next), where Tupaia was unable to understand the people, is much sparser (Williams, 2005). At other times, they probably misunderstood what they were being told or discarded information that did not fit their ideas, for instance information that incorporated religious elements (Salmond, 1991). The ability to dispassionately observe and record was seen by eighteenth-century Europeans as evidence of their superior civilisation (Edney, 1997, pp. 48–53, 308–16). Knowing and claiming could be linked. In the final extract from his journals, Cook moves seamlessly from a description of the islands to an assessment of their value for settlement. The map is thus both a tool – allowing New Zealand to be found again and ships to navigate its shores – and a representation of British ownership. It proclaimed Cook's discoveries, and the naming conventions symbolised British possession. Most of the names given by Cook are still in use. Eventually, the process set in motion by Cook's expedition was to lead to the occupation and settlement of the islands (there is more on New Zealand in Unit 13).

AN OVERVIEW OF EMPIRES

Examining the Piri Reis and Cook maps will, I hope, have demonstrated the importance of considering the context in which maps were created, what they were designed to show, and how they show it. Maps do not simply reflect the world; they convey knowledge through representation. And, as the Cook map of New Zealand reveals, they can wield real power by shaping the way we imagine the lands they show.

In the next and principal section of the unit, we will be using two types of map to support the overview of the history of empires that is at the heart of this unit. Some are historical maps, like the Piri Reis and Cook ones. Although they will not be discussed in the same depth, they should be approached in the same way. You will need to consider their origins, purpose and context, and how this links to how they represent territories: how they construct and transmit knowledge. The other type of map that the unit uses is a series showing the major empires of the world at different dates from 1490 to 1970 (World maps 1–10). These ten maps are present-day representations of the world and were produced specifically for the course. Take a quick look through these maps now: you will find them at the beginning of the Visual Sources Book.

In this unit we will use these maps in a different way from the historic maps: the focus will be on the evidence they provide about the development of the world's major empires. Nevertheless, before we use them, we still need to think about the implications of how they represent empires. A first point to make is that they are produced within a European tradition of cartography. As with most maps of the world that we use, they present the globe with north at the top, Europe in the centre and America on the left – as was the case in the full Piri Reis map. Although the ten maps use a **projection** that does something to correct for the shape of the globe, they still exaggerate the importance of Europe. They also use many names bestowed by European explorers, from America to New Zealand. Even the units into which we divide the world may have imperial roots. Matthew Edney shows how the European idea of 'India' as an area stretching from the Himalayas to the Indian Ocean emerged during the eighteenth century (Edney, 1997, pp. 3–9). How we conceive of the world is greatly influenced by European exploration and mapmaking in the last five centuries.

EXERCISE

Turn now to World maps 1–10, which present information on empires. Only a few details have been given so as to keep the maps uncluttered. Can you identify ways that this might affect how empires are represented? Think about how the maps show empires, but also consider what is left out. Do not spend more than 10–15 minutes on this: all I am expecting are some general ideas.

DISCUSSION

My question is very general and, rather than give a specimen answer, I will discuss and develop some issues you might have spotted.

Starting with how the maps show empire:

- The maps show empires in spatial terms: as blocks of territory in the same colour or (when territories are just bases) with the initial of the country they belong to. This may seem rather an obvious point, but this emphasis on land, and on size, may be misleading. Domination over people may be more important than land. And, as we will see, some colonies were far more important than others.

- The maps show all empires in the same way. In fact, empires varied enormously. In some cases, they might constitute a unified state; in others, a collection of territories held together by little more than a common ruler. Some colonies, indeed, were officially governed by an independent body, such as a chartered company. The way the maps present empires misleadingly suggests uniformity.

- To show empires, the maps need to show frontiers. Yet frontiers too might vary. In some parts of the world, boundaries were precise and agreed frontiers between neighbouring states. Elsewhere, particularly where societies beyond the frontiers were not organised in formal states (such as was long the case in North America), boundaries were far more vague. Where space allows, we have blurred the edges of such frontiers, but the scale of the maps makes this relatively imprecise.

And what about what they do not show?

- Most obviously, there is a lot of blank space. The maps do not show what exists beyond the frontiers of the empires, but this does not mean there were not organised states or even states called, at the time or since, empires. To make these maps, a choice was made as to which empires to show.

- The maps do not show a great deal of detail within empires. This suggests a greater unity than was always the case. By the early twentieth century, major empires, such as the British empire, consisted of a wide range of territories held in very varied ways, from virtual self-government to direct rule from the metropole.

Now for the overview of the history of empires.

1500–1680

The first two of the specially drawn maps (World maps 1 and 2) show the world in 1490, on the eve of Christopher Columbus's epic voyage to America, and in 1535, after Francisco Pizarro's defeat of the Incas.

EXERCISE

Compare the two maps and answer the following questions:

1   What has changed in the Americas?
2   What has changed in the Indian Ocean? How does the Portuguese empire in the Indian Ocean compare with that of the Spanish in America?
3   Look at the southern parts of Asia (the area from the eastern Mediterranean to the China Sea). Do you see more change or continuity here?

SPECIMEN ANSWER

1   The most dramatic changes on the world map between 1490 and 1535 occurred in the Americas. In 1490, the only major states in America were those of the Aztecs in Mexico and the Incas in the Andes. By 1535, both had been conquered by the Spanish, who had created an empire stretching from the Gulf of Mexico in the north to the central Andes in the South. There were also small Portuguese settlements on the coast of Brazil.

2   In 1490, there were Portuguese toeholds along the west coast of Africa but there were no Portuguese colonies in the Indian Ocean, although Bartolomeu Dias had rounded the Cape of Good Hope. By 1535, the Portuguese were established on the coasts of the Indian Ocean in east Africa, the Persian Gulf, India, and in southeast Asia. In contrast to the Spanish empire in the Americas, however, these were simply coastal bases. The Portuguese did not conquer large territories.

3   The 1535 map (World map 2) shows four empires in south Asia – from east to west, in China, north India, Persia (now Iran) and the eastern Mediterranean. In the last three cases, the empires have the names of their ruling dynasties: the national names we use as shorthand to describe western European states and their empires are inappropriate for such multi-ethnic entities. Of these empires, the Safavid and Mughal empires do not figure on World map 1, while the Ottoman empire has grown dramatically since 1490.

Starting the course around 1500 means starting with one of the most dramatic events in world history: the European discovery of the Americas. Prior to Columbus's voyage, the world's two major landmasses were almost entirely isolated from each other. Norsemen had crossed the north Atlantic to Greenland

and North America around 1000, but their explorations had been of minimal significance to Europe and were largely forgotten. Columbus's journey was quite different. By the fifteenth century, Europeans knew something about the societies of south and east Asia from trading contacts and from the reports of travellers such as Marco Polo, and great profits were made from the trade of some high-value goods, particularly spices. There was therefore much interest in exploring new routes to Asia that would bypass the Muslim states of North Africa and the Middle East, which controlled trade with the east. One route that seemed possible was to circumnavigate Africa. Gradually improving shipbuilding techniques and navigational skills enabled Iberian seafarers to explore the eastern Atlantic and the west coast of Africa, reaching the Azores by the 1380s, Cape Verde in 1445 and the Cape of Good Hope in 1488.[2]

As is well known, Columbus's voyage was based on an alternative idea: since the world was a globe, it should be possible to reach China and east Asia by sailing west. In this, of course, he was disappointed, but his discovery of a new continent (even if it was not at first realised that this was what it was) provoked enormous interest. As we have seen from the Piri Reis map, within two decades of his first trip, long stretches of the western shore of the Atlantic had been explored and mapped. Sailors from other European nations crossed the Atlantic: John Cabot, sailing from Bristol, reached Newfoundland in 1497, while the Portuguese, under Pedro Alvares Cabral, accidentally discovered Brazil in 1500. Their routes are shown on World map 2 in the Visual Sources Book.

The landing in Brazil was made on a voyage to India: Cabral was the leader of the second Portuguese expedition around Africa to the Indian Ocean. In 1497–98, Vasco da Gama, building on the work of earlier Portuguese navigators, had successfully sailed up the east coast of Africa and across to Calicut in south India. As a voyage of exploration, this was very different from Columbus's crossing of the Atlantic. Although da Gama's voyage took much longer, once he had reached the ports of east Africa, he was able to tap into existing trade networks, and indeed took a pilot to guide him across the Arabian Sea to India (Winius, 1995). As in the Americas, once the first journey had been made, others followed, and the Portuguese soon reached the Persian Gulf and Red Sea in the west and Indonesian archipelago and China in the east. In 1519–21, less than 30 years after the first landing in America, the first journey round the world was made as Ferdinand Magellan (and, after his death, Juan Sebastián de Elcano) sailed round South America, across the Pacific to the Philippines and back by the Cape of Good Hope.

The years around 1500 therefore saw a tremendous increase in European knowledge about the world. In many areas, discovery was followed by conquest, and the expeditions of Columbus, da Gama and others led to the

---

[2] All the dates given in this unit are listed in the datechart on the course website. At this stage, you will probably find it more useful to concentrate on the text, but you will find the datechart and unit chronologies useful reference tools later in the course.

creation of maritime, **transoceanic** empires by Spain and Portugal. The origins of these empires predate 1490: as can be seen in World map 1, the Spanish had already conquered the Canary Islands, while the Portuguese held other islands in the Atlantic and a few bases on the African coast. But the empires established after 1500 were of a completely different order. The peoples of the Americas proved unable to resist the Spanish invaders, who rapidly conquered the Caribbean islands and then moved on to the more sophisticated, and therefore lucrative, civilisations of the mainland. Hernando Cortés's conquest of Aztec Mexico in 1519–21 and Francisco Pizarro's invasion of the Inca empire in 1531–35 are among the most astonishing imperial triumphs in history. Unit 4 explores why the Spanish conquest was so rapid and successful. Portugal also established an overseas empire, but in Africa and Asia it was very different from the Spanish one. In both continents the Portuguese faced local peoples and states who, on land, were well able to resist them. Portuguese success depended on their naval superiority and on deals with local rulers: deals that benefited both parties because of the potential trading benefits. If the Spanish empire depended on conquest, the Portuguese was built on their control of trade (Subrahmanyam, 1993). The Portuguese empire in the Indian Ocean is explored in Unit 6.

Five centuries of Portuguese empire

The Portuguese route round Africa led to a great increase in European knowledge about the world. The 'Cantino Planisphere' (Plate 1.3 in the Visual Sources Book) was produced within a few years of da Gama's journey and reveals not only the new knowledge of the coasts of Africa and the Indian Ocean, but also of Brazil. Portuguese ships sailing to the east were issued with nautical charts and these were collected on their return at the Armazém da Guiné e Indias (storehouse of Guinea and the Indies), which collated new data onto master maps, the Padreo Real (Buisseret, 2003, p. 77). This was partly a matter of fitting together information from diverse sources, which was a complex process – the Armazém together with its Spanish equivalent have been called 'Europe's first scientific institutions' (Turnbull, 1996, p. 7). But it was also about controlling knowledge – a royal charter forbade the production and sale of nautical charts of the new sea route (Harley, 1988, p. 61). Most of the records of the Armazém were destroyed in the Lisbon earthquake of 1755. The Cantino map, which appears to be based on one smuggled out of Portugal by Alberto Cantino, an agent acting for the duke of Ferrara in Italy, is probably the closest surviving copy of the early Padreo Real maps. Both the story of its creation and the richness of its decoration indicate the value attached to such maps. Pictures and texts on the map describe the riches of the newly discovered lands (Brotton, 1997, pp. 22–4).

The Cantino map reveals the importance of the route to India to the developing Portuguese empire. Most Portuguese colonies were near this route: islands and bases in and on the coasts of the South Atlantic (including Brazil on the western shore), up the east coast of Africa and scattered across south Asia. The voyages of da Gama and his successors established an empire that was the most long-lasting of those of western European states. If you look ahead for a moment to World map 10, you will see that some of these colonies were still held in 1970. For a small country on the periphery of Europe this empire was a major achievement and, not surprisingly, it had a significant impact on the mother country, perhaps greater than was the case for any of the other European maritime states. Yet, this empire was always under threat. Its success in India depended on alliances with local rulers, and some of the *feitorias* ('factories') in India, and later in China and Japan, only existed by local permission and were abandoned when this was withdrawn. During the seventeenth century, as will be explored below, many of the most valuable bases were lost to Asian or European rivals, while others became backwaters as trade routes were diverted. If the Portuguese empire survived, it was because a new empire emerged from defeat. In the late seventeenth and eighteenth centuries this happened in Brazil, which became by far the most important colony. Sugar and other plantation crops, farmed by slaves, were the first exports; later, after around 1700, gold and other minerals were mined (Scammell, 1989, pp. 35–8). In the late nineteenth century, after Brazilian independence in 1822 and the gradual ending of the Atlantic slave trade, attention turned to the exploitation of the natural resources of the African colonies. In the twentieth century, Angola also became a magnet for settlers. Thus, the striking survival and continuity of the Portuguese empire was based on change (Winius, 1995).

It is easy to allow the dramatic development of the European transoceanic empires to dominate our view of this period. But, as we noted above, the core of the Eurasian landmass, the area between the Mediterranean and the China Sea, in which more than half the world's population lived, was dominated by non-Christian land empires. Of these, by far the most powerful in 1500 was China, or Zhongguo, 'the Central Kingdom', as it styled itself, ruled since the fourteenth century by the Ming dynasty. In the early fifteenth century, they had sent great fleets into the Indian Ocean, but, as China came under increasing pressure from the nomadic peoples to the north, these expeditions ceased. Chinese efforts were focused on ensuring calm around its periphery. When Europeans came into contact with China in the 1520s, relations were perceived in the same way: contact was to be managed on the frontier.

The three great Asian empires to the west of China were far newer. Much of central and southwest Asia had been disrupted by the last of the great Mongol invasions at the end of the fourteenth century. At this time, settled societies had few military answers to nomadic armies able to move swiftly and fight effectively on horseback (Black, 1998, p. 12). Even in the early sixteenth century, such mobile tribally organised peoples were able to win dramatic victories. Between 1501 and 1510, Türkmen nomads from the area between the Black and Caspian seas invaded and conquered Persia, creating the Safavid empire (Morgan, 1988). Only a few years later, Muhammad Babur crossed the Hindu Kush from central Asia to invade northern India and found the Mughal empire (Richards, 1993, pp. 6–8). The Ottomans were also of central Asian descent but belonged to an earlier wave of migrations. As we have seen, they captured Constantinople in 1453 and turned the city, which had long been the centre of Orthodox Christian Byzantium, into their capital. In 1490, however, the Ottoman empire was as much a European as an Asian one, controlling only the Balkans and what is now Turkey. Only with the conquests of Egypt and the Levant in the first decades of the sixteenth century did it achieve control of trade between Asia and the Mediterranean. Thus, in 1535, south and southwest Asia were dominated by powerful and expanding Muslim-ruled empires – empires whose wealth and power inspired great admiration in the west.

EXERCISE

Turn now to World map 3, which shows the world over 100 years later, in 1650. How does this compare with World map 2 (1535)? Consider in particular:

1   the Americas
2   Africa south of the Sahara and the shores of the Indian Ocean
3   the mainland of Asia.

SPECIMEN ANSWER

1   Despite the longer time span, there was less change in the Americas than in the period between 1490 and 1535. The Spanish and Portuguese frontiers in South America expanded, as did the northern border of Spanish control in Mexico. There were greater changes in the Caribbean and North America, where a number of colonies belonging to England, France and Holland are shown both in the smaller Caribbean islands and on the east coast of North America.

2   The European colonies in Africa and on the coasts of the Indian Ocean were mostly still small and coastal, and even where larger territories are shown, their boundaries are blurred, since they were little more than claims. Such territories were no longer just Portuguese. Spain claimed the Philippines and there were a few small bases held by France and England. However, the main rivals to the Portuguese were the Dutch.

3   South Asia was still dominated by the Chinese, Mughal, Safavid and Ottoman empires, and the second and last had grown. The Mughal empire now extended across all north India and the Ottoman empire deep into Europe, almost encircling the Black Sea. The greatest change, however, was in the north of the continent, where Russia, which in 1535 was confined to northeast Europe, by 1650 stretched eastwards to the Pacific.

The great success of Spain and Portugal, and the enormous wealth they derived from their overseas empires, encouraged other European states to challenge them. Competition was also stimulated by political and religious rivalries. In particular, the Protestant states of northern Europe did not feel bound to respect the territorial claims of Catholic Spain and Portugal. The chief Protestant challengers were England and the United Provinces (usually referred to by the name of the most powerful province, Holland). The Dutch had rebelled against Spanish rule in 1565, but it was Portugal, united with Spain by a union of crowns from 1580 to 1640, whose empire suffered the brunt of their attacks. This rivalry is explored in Unit 6. Other European states also tried to establish colonies. Although not shown on the map, there were attempts by Sweden, Denmark and Prussia to establish colonies in North America or trading forts in West Africa. More significant were the colonial ventures of Catholic France in Canada, the West Indies, West Africa and India.

Although I have used the names of countries as shorthand, in many cases empire building overseas was not carried out by the states themselves, but by trading or settlement companies set up specifically for that purpose. This was particularly the case for the Dutch and the English. The two great Dutch trading companies, the Dutch East India Company or VOC (founded in 1602) which you will remember from the block introduction, and the West India Company (1621) had official monopolies of trade with Asia and the Atlantic, respectively. The English also had their East India Company (the EIC, 1600). Although relations with government were close, and these companies wielded state-like powers, their priorities were trade and profit. English expansion in America is explored in Unit 5. Here, too, the initiative was often taken by powerful individuals or small groups operating as a company with a Royal Charter. Overseas possessions were managed in this way because they were primarily seen in economic terms. Colonies were usually seen as serving various specific purposes – trade or the cultivation of spices in Asia, the slave trade in West Africa, plantation crops in the Caribbean, settlement along the eastern shore of North America, and the fur trade in the far north.

In answer 3 above, we noted the expansion of Russia in the north of Asia. Until the 1550s, Russian expansion eastward was held back by the Tatar **khanates** on the Volga. Once this was overcome, the Russian advance into sparsely populated Siberia was rapid, since European weaponry gave them a similar advantage to that enjoyed by Europeans in North America (Darwin, 2007, pp. 65–73). The Russian empire is considered in Unit 7. Further east, the middle of the seventeenth century was a time of turmoil in China as the Ming dynasty came under pressure from internal unrest and external threat. In 1644, Manchu invaders from beyond China's northern frontier invaded the empire and captured Beijing. A new dynasty, the Qing dynasty, was founded, which gradually extended its rule throughout south China.

1680–1830

World maps 4 and 5 show the world after two major treaties between the European powers, the Treaty of Utrecht at the conclusion of the War of Spanish Succession, between Britain[3] and Holland on the one hand, and France and Spain on the other (1713), and the Treaty of Paris after the Seven Years War, in which Britain and France were again the major antagonists (1763). The choice of dates decided by European treaties is significant: rivalry between European powers and, in particular, between Britain and France, led to repeated wars between 1689 and 1815. These wars were fought not only in Europe but also in their empires, especially in North America and India. The rivalry between these two powers is the theme of Unit 8.

---

[3] The Act of Union in 1707 led to a common government for England and Scotland. From this date on, one can refer to Britain and a British empire.

EXERCISE

1   What do the two maps suggest was the main outcome of the conflicts between Britain and France up to 1763?

2   Comparing the two maps with that for 1650 (World map 3), what other major changes do you note?

SPECIMEN ANSWER

1   World map 4 (1713) shows French claims to huge territories in North America, stretching from Quebec on the St Lawrence river to New Orleans at the mouth of the Mississippi, and surrounding the main British colonies on the eastern American seaboard. By 1763, most of these territories were British. Less evident on the map, because the territories were smaller, were British gains in India, largely at the expense of the Mughal empire, which had granted control of Bengal to the East India Company by 1763.

2   In fact, both maps show considerable continuity from 1650. Some changes include: the territories shown as Spanish and Portuguese in South America are again larger; the Portuguese lost territories in Africa and Asia, while the Dutch presence in the East Indies grew. In Asia, the major changes came between 1713 and 1763. World map 4 shows gains for Russia, China and the Ottoman and Mughal empires, the last two of which reached their greatest extent in the late seventeenth century. By 1763, however, the Safavid empire had disappeared while the Mughal territories were greatly reduced (World map 5).

In colonial terms, the Franco-British wars up to 1763 were a great success for Britain. With the fall of Quebec in 1759, the French were driven out of North America, and France and its allies were defeated in India too. At the battle of Plassey, the British EIC, defeated the **nawab** of Bengal and won control of this rich province, although it formally remained part of the Mughal empire. A major factor in these victories was British naval strength, which gave Britain dominance of the seas, isolating French forces overseas. Plassey was also significant as the first major land victory by European forces in Asia. Yet the impact of the battle should not be overestimated. If the Mughal empire struggled to maintain control of its territory, this had more to do with internal divisions and pressure from other Indian states or invaders from central Asia, such as the raid on Delhi by Nadir Shah in 1739. The Safavid dynasty in Persia collapsed under a similar combination of internal unrest and external pressure, and the Ottoman empire also struggled to retain control of rich outlying provinces. Thus the gains of British or other European powers were often the result, rather than the cause, of decay in the great Muslim empires (Bayly, 1989). In the Far East, the Qing dynasty had established its rule in China and went on to conquer vast new areas in central and northern Asia, driving back the Russians in the 1680s (Black, 1998, pp. 72–3). Despite their gains, it was by no means the case that European empires yet possessed a decisive military advantage on land.

The rise and fall of the Ottoman empire

If reconfiguration and renewal are features of the Portuguese imperial experience, that of the Ottoman empire might seem to fit more easily into a pattern of 'rise' and 'fall'. From small beginnings in World map 1 (and really from 1354 and the first Ottoman conquests in Europe) it expanded until reaching its maximum extent around 1680 (see World map 3). It then began a long period of shrinkage, until finally disappearing during the First World War (see World maps 8 and 9). In discussing the Piri Reis map (Plate 1.1), we encountered the Ottoman empire as a naval power and, indeed, during the sixteenth century it challenged European maritime power in the Mediterranean, driving Venice and Genoa out of their island bases in Greece and Cyprus. Yet, the Ottoman empire was always primarily a land empire and most of its growth was due to the conquests made by its armies.

As a land empire, the distinctions between the centre and the **periphery** were far less clear-cut than in maritime empires such as that of Portugal. For a start, if the Ottomans originated in Anatolia (the Asian part of modern Turkey), this became something of a backwater as the empire expanded. Constantinople, once conquered, became the capital of the empire, while some of the richest provinces, such as Egypt, were distant from the centre. Moreover, whereas ethnic and racial differences played a major role within maritime empires, the Ottoman empire was a multi-ethnic one, in which religious and local loyalties were far more important in defining identities. Islam helped unite the empire, but non-Muslim minorities were significant, particularly in the economic sphere. It is easy to see this heterogeneity as a source of internal weakness, but in fact historians now stress the continued vitality of the Ottoman empire, certainly up to the middle of the eighteenth century (Darwin, 2007, pp. 138–43). If, by the nineteenth century, the empire was under attack, demands for national independence were only really a factor in the European provinces, and were complicated here by the complex mix of peoples. Just as it would be anachronistic to see the Ottoman empire as 'Turkish' for much of its history, it would be wrong to assume that nationalism would inevitably undermine a multi-ethnic land empire, at least until the twentieth century.

Although the British victory over France in 1763 was an important one, its extent should not be exaggerated. France retained major colonies, particularly in the West Indies, where sugar-producing St Domingue (now Haiti) was a far more valuable possession than Canada. Moreover, Franco-British rivalry did not stop in 1763. France and Spain supported the Americans in the War of Independence and, in defeat, Britain lost territories to both. Only a few years later, the French Revolution of 1789 plunged Europe into a series of wars that were to last until 1815. These wars and their aftermath had a dramatic impact on the colonial empires of the European powers. This period of crisis between 1780 and 1820 was not, however, confined to Europe. In Asia, too, the period saw major changes. Christopher Bayly, in particular, has argued that the world underwent its first age of global crisis – the 'wreck of nations', which saw old empires overthrown and new ones established (Bayly, 1989).

EXERCISE

World map 6 shows the world in 1830, after this period of violent upheaval. In which continent has this had the most impact on empires?

SPECIMEN ANSWER

Change is most evident in the Americas, where the European empires largely disappeared between 1763 and 1830 except in the far north and the Caribbean. In Africa, most colonies were still small, although the British now had a growing presence in South Africa, as did the French in Algeria. By 1830, there were a number of major European colonies in Asia, including the British in India and the Dutch in the East Indies. The Mughal empire had disappeared. On the other hand, the Ottoman and Chinese empires still held very similar territories, while the Russian empire had expanded, even crossing into America with its annexation of Alaska.

The ending of the colonial empires in America was a dramatic process, equal in rapidity to their original conquest. It began, of course, with the American War of Independence. We tend to see the loss of the American colonies as an isolated event, but within 40 years Spain had lost most of its American empire, Brazil was independent, and France had abandoned its major American colony, the Caribbean island of St Domingue. In most cases, independence followed local rebellions, but it was the upheavals of the Napoleonic Wars that provided the catalyst. War with Britain also prevented France from sending troops to St Domingue to put down the rebellion. In the Spanish and Portuguese colonies, control from Europe was lost during the French occupation, and after the wars it proved impossible to reassert it, not least because of British refusal to support intervention. In 1815, Britain enjoyed unrivalled naval supremacy.

By preventing the re-imposition of Spanish power, Britain therefore played the role of liberator in Latin America. Elsewhere too, for instance in Greece, Britain supported rebellions against empires in the early nineteenth century. The decades following the American Revolution saw major debates in Britain about the value and role of its empire, both in terms of the possibility of retaining control of British settlements overseas and of the political and moral consequences for Britain of the despotic rule over peoples of different races. Growing industrial production in Britain and the success of British exports also led many to question the economic case for empire. Nor were these debates only about the British empire. During the Napoleonic era and its aftermath, empires in Europe came to be associated with autocratic and backward-looking rule, and liberals, fired partly by the ideals of the French Revolution and partly by national resistance to French rule, supported liberation movements. During the nineteenth century, nationalist movements came increasingly to challenge the multinational land empires of eastern Europe, such as Austria and Russia. The ideology of liberation also proved useful in Latin America, although the new states were dominated by **creole** elites descended from European settlers. More problematic to Europeans was whether the rhetoric of emancipation also applied to non-European peoples. Although European protests against the slave trade and slavery increased in this era, relations between Europeans and non-Europeans were more often defined in terms of tutelage than equality.

Despite these early nineteenth-century setbacks and doubts, most empires, as can be seen in World map 6, survived the turbulent era of the 'wreck of nations' and some, such as the British and Russian, emerged greatly strengthened. The years between 1780 and 1805 saw the consolidation of

British dominance in India, and British territory in the subcontinent continued to expand in the following decades. New colonies were added in Australia and South Africa. The Ottoman and Qing empires also demonstrated great resilience. In particular, China, the dominant power in east Asia, continued to set the terms for its relations with the west. Unit 11 considers the Chinese empire around 1800, and, in particular, its relations with Britain, the dominant European and maritime imperial power.

1830–1914

EXERCISE

World maps 7 and 8 move forward with snapshots of the world empires in 1878 at the time of the Congress of Berlin (a conference of the European powers that attempted to settle the future of the Ottoman empire in Europe) and on the eve of the First World War (1914).

1   Using World maps 6 and 7, identify some major changes and continuities between 1830 and 1878.

2   Looking now at World map 8, compare 1914 with 1878 (World map 7). How does the extent of change compare with the earlier period?

3   Which new imperial powers can you identify in World map 8? Have any disappeared?

SPECIMEN ANSWER

1   Continuity is more striking than change in the period between 1830 and 1878. The period was chiefly marked by the consolidation and extension of existing colonies. Changes included the extension of British rule in India, Canada, Australia and South Africa, and Russian expansion into central Asia. Relatively few large new colonies were established in this period – two worth noting are the British colony of New Zealand and the French in Indochina. In the northwest of the map, Alaska has passed from Russia to the USA.

2   Change is far greater. By 1914, most of the world had been divided up by the imperial powers – even if effective control took longer to establish. Whereas in 1878 European colonies in Africa were still largely confined to the coast, by 1914 the only independent states left were Liberia and Abyssinia (now Ethiopia). Southeast Asia, with the exception of Siam (now Thailand) and the Pacific had also been divided up. In the Middle East, the Ottoman empire had largely been pushed out of Africa and Europe.

3   The 1914 map shows the empires of a number of countries that had not previously held colonies. These include Germany (colonies in Africa and the Pacific), Italy, Belgium (both with colonies in Africa), Japan (Korea and some Pacific islands), and the USA (as well as territories that now form part of the USA, Puerto Rico in the Caribbean and the Philippines in east Asia). No imperial powers disappeared completely.

The maps show the outcomes of two quite distinct imperial periods. The middle of the nineteenth century was marked by British economic and naval dominance following the end of the Napoleonic Wars. British frontiers did continue to expand, particularly in India and in areas of British settlement, where pressure to grab new land came from the settlers. Elsewhere, however,

Froude lived this though 'an aggressive Protestant'

the British government was often reluctant to acquire large new territories. In economic terms, it was argued, Britain had more to gain from free trade than from direct rule, and new acquisitions could be restricted to ports and coaling stations. In those areas of the world where Britain was able to prevent other European powers extending their empires (and perhaps imposing restrictions on trade), it preferred non-intervention. With regards to the remaining Asian land empires, Britain was keen to open them to trade (going to war twice with China to force it to allow trading access, particularly for opium), but at the same time was anxious to preserve their territorial integrity. British naval supremacy meant that other countries were only able to extend their empires with British support or at least toleration (the Dutch in the East Indies and the French in Indochina), or in regions where naval power was irrelevant (the Russians in central Asia) (Wesseling, 2004). This period of British dominance is considered in Unit 9.

The second French overseas empire

Maps were widely used in imperial propaganda. Plate 1.4 in the Visual Sources Book shows a poster from the 1890s, advertising a publication about 'the war in Madagascar', where France was engaged in a campaign to subdue the island. By this period, there was a public appetite for tales of colonial adventure and the poster uses simple and instantly recognisable images (a colonial soldier planting the French flag) to sell papers. Plate 1.5 in the Visual Sources Book is more complex. Produced during the Second World War in Vichy France, it shows all the territories that had ever been owned by France, distinguishing between those lost before 1940 (in yellow) and those lost since 1940 (in red). Only Tunisia and Indochina (in blue) are shown as still held by France. The text claims that all the French colonies had been taken by the USA and England and the map was clearly designed to mobilise opinion against the Allies.

This map is interesting in that it combines in an unusual way two French empires: an eighteenth-century empire in America and India (largely in yellow on the map and with rather exaggerated frontiers – compare with World map 5) and a nineteenth-century empire, mostly in Africa, southeast Asia and the Pacific (shown in red and blue – compare with World map 9). As a result of the Napoleonic Wars, France lost almost all its overseas empire, retaining only a few islands and coastal bases. In the nineteenth century, however, a new and very different empire was established. In some places, this second empire developed out of the remaining French colonies or other French interests. Thus, Dakar in West Africa became the centre for French expansion into the interior, while the first French military intervention in Indochina was to protect French missionaries. However, the key event was the invasion of Algeria in 1830. This eventually led to the conquest of the whole country and, later, **protectorates** over Tunisia (1881) and Morocco (1912) (Aldrich, 1996).

There were major debates in France about the wisdom of this renewed French expansion overseas. There were many who argued that overseas expansion was a dangerous distraction from recovering Alsace-Lorraine, lost to Germany in the Franco-Prussian war of 1870–71. On the other side of the debate was a powerful colonial lobby, associated particularly with the navy, who saw the empire as contributing to France's moral regeneration and economic strength. Expansion, moreover, was often initiated not from the centre but by French colonial officers. In West Africa, for instance, the governors of Senegal played a key role in pushing the frontiers inland. This could lead to conflict with the agents of other imperial powers, especially Britain, also often acting with little control from above. The result was a series of colonial crises, only settled by government-level negotiations. Imperial expansion, therefore, was at times a process happening almost independently on the frontier, and at others one caught up in internal debates and international controversy. Public opinion became a significant factor, and imperial propagandists sought to mobilise support for expansion (for an example from the British Empire, see Plate 1.6). The result – and this was not only true for France – was an empire with little coherence, containing many colonies of dubious value. Much of the large area of red in northwest Africa in Plate 1.5 is the Sahara.

The late nineteenth century was very different from the period before 1878. This was partly because of a renewed belief in the value of imperial possessions, both in countries that had long possessed empires, such as Britain and France, and in those that had not previously held overseas territories, such as Germany and the USA. Growing international competition was itself a factor. Thus, the division of Africa (sometimes called the 'scramble for Africa') came about because Britain was no longer able to prevent other countries carving out new territories, and so preferred to seize those areas it considered essential. With more participants, imperial expansion was more fraught, but, in fact, the established imperial powers of Britain and France secured not only the largest but also the most valuable areas of Africa, including Egypt and South Africa (Britain), and Algeria (France).

This European advance was frequently resisted both before and after European occupation, and in a few cases, such as the French invasion of Algeria or the Indian Mutiny-Rebellion of 1857,[4] resistance or rebellions greatly alarmed European rulers. However, by the middle of the century a clear 'weapons gap' between Europe (and its overseas offshoots) and other states was emerging. In Africa and the Pacific, in particular, European invaders often encountered peoples with significantly less-advanced military technology. So, although these peoples sometimes won astonishing victories against the European invaders – such as the Zulu defeat of a British army at Isandhlwana in 1879 and the Ethiopian defeat of the Italians at Adowa in 1896 – in most cases European victory was inevitable. By 1900, this 'weapons gap' threatened the survival of all remaining non-European states, including the great empires of Asia. To counter this European advantage,

---

[4] For reasons of recognition, most of the names used in this unit are those commonly used in Britain and Europe to describe the wars of invasion and rebellions against European rule, although these names perpetuate contemporary European assumptions. Not surprisingly, such names are contested in former colonies: thus the events usually known in Britain as the Indian Mutiny are in India more likely to be referred to as the Rebellion of 1857.

non-European states needed to engage in a process of 'defensive modernisation' in which they adopted western technology and forms of organisation (Curtin, 2000). In some cases, this was sufficient to stave off European occupation, and in the case of Japan the process allowed it to successfully compete as an imperial power. Japan, however, was a highly homogenous society and the modernisers were able to call on a strong sense of national identity. In the Ottoman and Chinese empires, too, nationalist modernisers seized power in the years before 1914. In 1908, a group of reformers known as the Young Turks took over the running of the Ottoman empire, while in China the empire was overthrown and a republic declared in 1911. Yet, for multi-ethnic land empires, such as the Ottoman empire, but also the Russian and Austro-Hungarian empires, appeals to nationalism were risky, since they threatened imperial unity. Particularly in eastern Europe and the Balkans, the years before the First World War were marked by inter-ethnic conflicts. This is explored for Austria-Hungary in Unit 18.

If European expansion was frequently resisted, it also led to tensions between imperial powers. In Africa, these tensions, although at times dramatic, never led to wars between imperial powers. In other parts of the world, however, the two decades preceding 1914 saw a number of small wars, such as the Spanish-American war of 1898 (in which Spain lost its last American colonies and the Philippines), or wars between Japan and first China and then Russia in 1895 and 1904–05. Such wars, and the very public disagreements between European states, were long seen by historians as evidence that imperial differences were contributing to mounting international tension leading up to the First World War. More recently, historians have tended to find the causes of the war in Europe. Nevertheless, the fact that by 1914, with the exception of the Americas, the world was largely divided between empires meant that war, when it came, was global.

1914–2000

World map 9 shows the world after the Peace Treaties that followed the First World War (the Treaty of Versailles, between Germany and the Allies, was the most significant, but not the only, postwar treaty).

EXERCISE

Comparing World maps 8 and 9, is change or continuity more marked?

SPECIMEN ANSWER

This depends on whether we focus on Europe and the Middle East or on the wider world. We usually think of the First World War as destroying an old imperial order, and this is certainly true for Europe. As a direct result of the war, four empires – Hohenzollern Germany, Habsburg Austria-Hungary, Romanov Russia and Ottoman Turkey – disappeared, to be replaced by many new states. In Europe and the former Ottoman empire, frontiers were redrawn. In Africa, south Asia and the Pacific, however, the map shows far less change. Germany lost its colonies, but other overseas empires retained largely unchanged boundaries. Indeed, the two major maritime empires of Britain and France both acquired new territories, even if these were formally held in trust as **mandates** of the League of Nations. Even Russia lost territories in Europe rather than in Asia.

The collapse of the great dynastic empires left a zone of conflict in eastern Europe and the Middle East that lasted well into the 1920s. The new states tried to establish favourable frontiers, Russia was convulsed by civil war, and the British and French faced resistance in their new Arab mandates (Darwin, 2007, pp. 382–9, 399–402). If the postwar settlement, Soviet victory in the Russian civil war, and the defeat by Britain and France of rebellions in Egypt, Syria and Iraq created some stability by 1926, this was to prove temporary and the region remained at the centre of international conflicts throughout the twentieth century.

Elsewhere, however, the First World War was less of a watershed. This was not only in terms of territory. If there was change in the postwar years, it was not towards the collapse of imperial rule but towards its intensification. Before 1914, many territories claimed by Europe, particularly in Africa and southeast Asia, had barely been conquered. For these territories, it was the interwar years that saw the beginning of a more systematic exploitation as ports and railways were built, export crops planted and mineral deposits exploited. For most Europeans, retreat from empire remained inconceivable. If debates were increasingly framed in terms of the duties of imperial rule, as well as the benefits, colonial peoples were still seen as needing western government. This was not greatly altered either by the growing importance of two powers, the USA and the Soviet Union, which defined themselves as anti-imperial, or by the emergence in many colonies of nationalist organisations that sought independence for their countries as nation states.

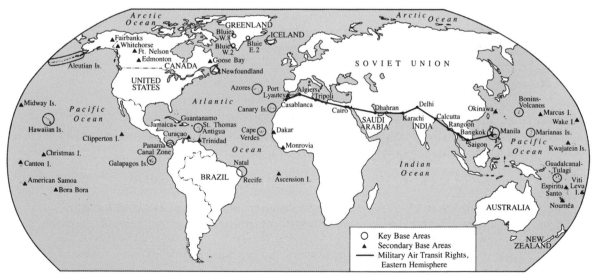

Figure 1.3   US military base requirements, from Leffler, M.P. (1992) *A Preponderance of Power: National Security, the Truman Administration, and the Cold War*, Stanford, CA., Stanford University Press, p. 57. © 1992 by the Board of Trustees of the Leland Stanford Jr. University. All rights reserved. Used with permission of Stanford University Press, www.sup.org. The map shows US requirements in 1945 as defined by the Joint Chiefs of Staff.

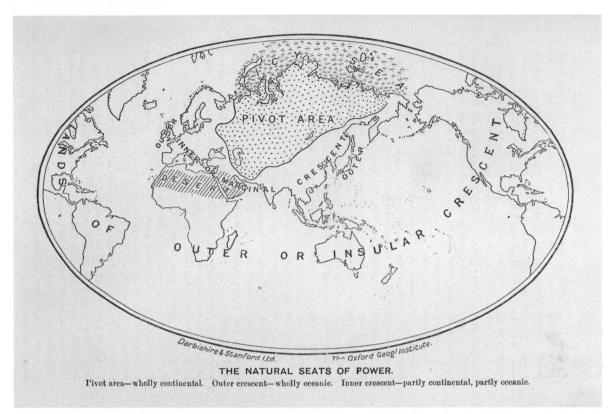

THE NATURAL SEATS OF POWER.

Pivot area—wholly continental.   Outer crescent—wholly oceanic.   Inner crescent—partly continental, partly oceanic.

Figure 1.4   'The natural seats of power', from Mackinder, H.J. (1904) 'The geographical pivot of history', *The Geographical Journal*, vol. 23, no. 4, p. 435. Cambridge University Library, T690.c.3.1-. Reproduced with permission.

The Unites States of America: an imperial power?

We do not usually think of the USA as an imperial state, partly because its origins lie in an anti-imperial rebellion and because opposition to empires (and the hierarchical social and political structures that were seen as linked) came to be part of American identity. Yet, there are three senses in which the USA might be seen as imperial and is sometimes so defined. First, its western expansion within North America in the nineteenth century was very similar to the expansion of Canada or Australia. Should this process not be regarded as imperial? Secondly, and more obviously, from 1898 on the USA, as can be seen in World map 8, possessed an overseas empire in the Caribbean and the Pacific similar to that of the European powers.

Yet, when we debate whether the USA is an empire, it is usually with the third meaning in mind: the rise of American **hegemony** over much of the world in the twentieth century. In a recent book, a leading British historian, Niall Ferguson, argues that the USA after the Second World War came to fill a similar role to that occupied by Britain in the nineteenth century (Ferguson, 2004). In this, the key years are seen as the decade following the Second World War in which American leaders responded to the perceived threat of Soviet expansion by a policy of 'containment' – surrounding the Soviet Union with a ring of political allies and military bases. Figure 1.3 shows the bases identified by military leaders in the summer of 1945 as necessary to American security requirements in the postwar world (Leffler, 1992, p. 56).

In defining these requirements, American policy was strongly influenced by 'geopolitics' – a way of thinking about strategy shaped by map-based understandings of the world. In particular, the ideas of the British geographer, Sir Halford Mackinder, were influential. In an article published in 1904, he used the map in Figure 1.4 to argue for the importance of 'the pivot area' at the heart of the Eurasian landmass: the changing balance of land and sea power, he argued, could give the advantage to 'the pivot state, resulting in its expansion over the marginal lands of Euro-Asia, [which] would permit of the use of vast continental resources for fleet-building, and the empire of the world would then be in sight' (Mackinder, 1904, p. 436). To counteract this threat, 'the peripheral states' of the 'outer crescent' would need continental 'bridge heads' supported by naval forces (p. 436).

EXERCISE

Now consider World map 10, which shows the world in 1970. The changes here are dramatic: does this represent the end of empires?

SPECIMEN ANSWER

In one sense, there is no doubt that the 25 years following the Second World War saw major changes. Most maritime empires, including the largest of them – Britain and France – were reduced to rumps. Only Portugal retained nearly all its colonies in 1970. On the other hand, one might argue that, in territorial terms, some of the former empires survived. Indeed, the Soviet Union extended its boundaries westwards into Europe while the frontiers of China remained largely unchanged.

"land empires" evolved to counter the threats of revolution & nationalism.

There is no doubt that the collapse of the European overseas empires was one of the major developments of the postwar years. In 1945, the leaders of most European states expected to continue to rule overseas empires for decades, even if many in Britain recognised that withdrawal from India was inevitable. In the event, it proved impossible to maintain European rule in most of the areas in east Asia that had been overrun by the Japanese during the Second World War. By 1949, the Dutch recognised that they were unable to control the East Indies, and the islands became the independent state of Indonesia; after bitter fighting, the French withdrew from Indochina in 1954. The British also rapidly conceded independence to their colonies in south Asia, starting with India and Pakistan in 1947. The process was even faster in most of the Middle East. Nor did the retreat from empire stop there: Ghana became independent in 1957 and within a decade all Africa, with the exception of the Spanish and Portuguese colonies, was either independent, or well on its way towards that status. Units 19 and 20 explore this process of decolonisation. Unit 19 looks at the case of the British retreat from the Indian subcontinent, the most significant example of negotiated independence, and one that in many respects set the pattern for other countries. Unit 20, in contrast, looks at two of the most bitter of the anti-colonial wars, in Algeria and Angola.

By the 1960s and 1970s, as the Caribbean and Pacific islands also moved towards independence, it seemed as if the process of decolonisation was largely complete. When Angola and Mozambique finally achieved independence in 1975, all that remained of the great European maritime empires were a few scattered outposts, most with little economic or strategic value. However, as the new states that emerged from empires struggled to overcome deep-seated economic and political problems, it was argued that formal domination by the imperial powers may have ended, but that former colonies were still tied into dependent **neo-colonial** relationships. Was the end of empire more apparent than real? Moreover, in the 1990s came the break-up of the Soviet Union. Was this part of the same process of imperial disintegration? Much of the territory of the Soviet Union, had, after all, been conquered under the tsars. Yet, officially it was an anti-imperial power and all citizens enjoyed equal rights. The territory of much of the former Soviet Union was also ethnically mixed, with significant Russian populations in many of the newly independent states, and other non-Russian minorities within Russia itself (Lieven, 2000). In such circumstances, how useful is the distinction between colony and metropole? And might the process continue? Would other states, welded into nation states in the nineteenth and twentieth centuries, prove less united than they once seemed?

CONCLUSION

This rapid survey of the history of empires in the last 500 years has, no doubt, left you slightly breathless. I hope it has also raised many and varied questions. This final section of the unit will look at these questions and explain where they will be addressed.

Organising the survey chronologically and using maps has highlighted questions relating to time and place. You might, for instance, have noted how different was the chronology of European rule in the Americas, where the imperial era lasted from approximately 1500 to 1800, and in Africa, where for much of the continent European rule lasted only from around 1880 to 1960. Why was the experience so different? Or else you might have noted the contrast between periods of rapid change, such as the decades between 1490 and 1540, or 1780 and 1830, and others, such as between 1830 and 1870, where rather less seems to have happened.

Starting from such questions leads into others relating to causes and effects, contrasts and similarities, and about the validity of comparisons. You will also recall that, before starting on the overview, we looked at some of the issues raised by the use of maps. You might therefore be asking how the way the history of empires has been presented here has shaped the way issues are formulated.

Many of the questions fit into the following broad areas.

How do empires begin?

At the beginning of the survey, we discussed two empires that were launched by specific events – Columbus's crossing of the Atlantic and da Gama's journey to India. But seeing the Spanish and Portuguese empires solely as the result of these events is clearly too simple. Why did these voyages take place? And why were the consequences so far-reaching? After all, Cabot crossed the Atlantic only five years after Columbus, but it took over a century for England to establish its first colony in America. Moreover, as we have seen, other empires started in very different ways – think of Babur's sudden emergence into north India or the growth of the Ottoman empire. What about those that started in very different periods, such as the German empire? Can comparisons be made across space and time? Furthermore, to what extent has the choice of a starting date for the survey shaped our answers? Was 1500 a key moment in the emergence of a new sort of maritime, global empire, qualitatively different from previous ones? How empires begin is discussed in Block 2.

[handwritten margin notes: What did they do:? look for the East Indies, a sea route to the spices. land route blocked by Persia/Mongol hordes. Travellers "found" new continents.]

How do empires 'work'?

As has become clear, some empires were more long-lived than others. Compare the Chinese and Mughal empires in Asia, or Britain and Holland in North America. You will also have noted examples of renewal: countries defeated and stripped of colonies re-emerge in a later map with new empires. Even empires superficially as resilient as China underwent periods of disruption and rebirth. Questions must therefore be asked about maintenance, survival and renewal: what forces held empires together? One might think of this in military terms, but it was clearly also an economic issue, and a political one – how were armies paid for and colonies administered? Ideology and culture also play a role: empires need to mobilise support and retain unity. But changing ideas also affect how empires develop. Such questions are explored in Block 3.

Why do empires end?

The overview highlights the dramatic end of many European empires in the postwar period. But this was not the only time when empires disappeared – the period round 1800 saw the dissolution of most of the European empires in the Americas. In both cases, the end came suddenly. Other empires took longer to disappear – Turkey was described as 'the sick man of Europe' from the middle of the nineteenth century on, but it survived until the disasters of the First World War; while Portugal was widely regarded as the weakest of the European empires throughout the nineteenth century but in fact proved to be the most durable. Why did some empires disappear so quickly and others survive so long? One way we explain the end of empire is in terms of the rise of nation states. Many states that have emerged from empires, from the USA on, celebrate their independence as a struggle of liberation from foreign oppression. How useful is this as an explanation? Was the defeat of empire linked to the rise of nationalism? How empires end is discussed in Block 5.

What are empires?

The questions above, and indeed the preceding survey, imply that there is a category of state called empires that can be compared and contrasted. This is reinforced by the set of ten maps (World maps 1–10), which require a sharp distinction between 'empires' and other forms of state or social organisation. But is this valid? In discussing China and Portugal together are we comparing similar phenomena? Note, for instance, how I have described different empires: I have talked about the Ottoman empire, but not of the Bourbon or the Stuart empire. Was there a fundamental divide between dynastic and national empires? Or between land empires and maritime ones? Even when comparing European empires, there were important differences between Spain and Holland; while in Asia, it is difficult to compare any state with China. Nor did empires stay the same over time – we have noted how the Portuguese empire evolved and that of France was reborn in the nineteenth century. If comparisons are to work, we need to agree on definitions and typologies that allow us to identify what they have in common and what distinguishes them. These issues become still more pressing as one approaches the present. Is the age of empires over or do they continue in different forms today? How empires are defined is tackled in Unit 2, while Block 6, the course conclusion, considers the continued impact of empires today.

How were empires experienced?

A focus on the broad sweep of history – as in these maps of the world and in the accompanying text – has created a history that highlights key figures and events and focuses on the size and power of empires. But empires are more than material constructs, and how they are perceived and understood are important in shaping their development. Although we have to think of imperial ideologies, it is also necessary to consider the many and varied experiences of empire. In particular, you may feel that what has emerged from this survey is a rather sanitised version of history in which words we associate with empire, such as oppression, exploitation or violence, are conspicuously lacking. What did empire mean for the people caught up in the events described so briefly in this chapter, be they conquerors or conquered, or the many groups who found themselves somewhere in between?

Ideas about empire and the experience of imperial rule are introduced in Unit 3 of this block, and explored more fully in Block 4. But I hope the use of maps in this brief introduction to the history of empires has also suggested that it is not easy to separate their reality from perceptions and representations. The tools we need to describe empires may be sanitised, but they are not neutral. The maps used in this unit were created in very varied circumstances and for different purposes. Some were created to share (and shape) knowledge of newly discovered lands, others to mobilise popular enthusiasm or define strategic objectives. In the case of the ten maps at the centre of this unit (World maps 1–10), they were designed as props to focus a historical overview. The maps have also been used in different ways. Yet, in each case, the authors made conscious and unconscious decisions about what to include and how to present it, and, as with all other historical sources, it is important to think about their choices at the same time as we consider the information conveyed.

REFERENCES

Aldrich, R. (1996) *Greater France. A History of French Overseas Expansion*, London, Macmillan.

Bayly, C.A. (1989) *Imperial Meridian. The British Empire and the World, 1780–1830*, London, Longman.

Beaglehole, J.C. (1974) *The Life of Captain James Cook*, London, Adam & Charles Black.

Black, J. (1998) *War and the World. Military Power and the Fate of Continents, 1450–2000*, New Haven and London, Yale University Press.

Brotton, J. (1997) *Trading Territories. Mapping the Early Modern World*, London, Reaktion.

Buisseret, D. (2003) *The Mapmaker's Quest. Depicting New Worlds in Renaissance Europe*, Oxford, Oxford University Press.

Carter, P. (1987) *The Road to Botany Bay. An Essay in Spatial History*, London, Faber & Faber.

Curtin, P.D. (2000) *The World and the West. The European Challenge and the Overseas Response in the Age of Empire*, Cambridge, Cambridge University Press.

Darwin, J. (2007) *After Tamerlane: The Global History of Empire*, London, Allen Lane.

Edney, M.H. (1997) *Mapping an Empire. The Geographical Construction of British India, 1765–1843*, Chicago, University of Chicago Press.

Ferguson, N. (2004), *Colossus. The Rise and Fall of the American Empire*, London, Allen Lane.

Harley, J.B. (1988) 'Silences and secrecy: the hidden agenda of cartography in early modern Europe', *Imago Mundi*, vol. 40, pp. 57–76.

Harley, J.B. (1992) 'Deconstructing the map' in Barnes, T.J. and Duncan, J.S. (eds) *Writing Worlds. Discourse, Text and Metaphor in the Representation of Landscape*, London, Routledge.

Leffler, M.P. (1992) *A Preponderance of Power: National Security, the Truman Administration, and the Cold War*, Stanford, Stanford University Press.

Lieven, D. (2000) *Empire. The Russian Empire and its Rivals*, London, John Murray.

Mackinder, H.J. (1904) 'The geographical pivot of history', *Geographical Journal*, vol. 23, no. 4, pp. 421–44.

McIntosh, G.C. (2000) *The Piri Reis Map of 1513*, Athens, GA, and London, University of Georgia Press.

Morgan, D. (1988) *Medieval Persia, 1040–1797*, London, Longman.

Richards, J.F. (1993) *The New Cambridge History of India,* vol. 1.5, *The Mughal Empire*, Cambridge, Cambridge University Press.

Salmond, A. (1991) *Two Worlds. First Meetings between Maori and Europeans, 1642–1772*, Honolulu, University of Hawaii Press.

Scammell, G.V. (1989) *The First Imperial Age. European Overseas Expansion c.1400–1715*, London, Unwin Hyman.

Soucek, S. (1992) 'Islamic charting in the Mediterranean' in Harley, J.B. and Woodward, D. (eds) *The History of Cartography,* vol. 2, book 1, *Cartography in the Traditional Islamic and South Asian Societies*, Chicago, University of Chicago Press, pp. 263–92.

Subrahmanyam, S. (1993) *The Portuguese Empire in Asia, 1500–1700. A Political and Economic History,* London, Longman.

Turnbull, D. (1996) 'Cartography and science in early modern Europe: mapping the construction of knowledge spaces', *Imago Mundi*, vol. 48, pp. 5–24.

Wesseling, H.L. (2004) *The European Colonial Empires, 1815–1919*, Harlow, Pearson.

Williams, G. (2005) '"Far more happier than we Europeans": reactions to the Australian aborigines on Cook's voyage' in Williams, G. (ed.) *Buccaneers, Explorers and Settlers. British Enterprise and Encounters in the Pacific, 1670–1800*, Aldershot, Ashgate Variorum.

 Winius, G.D. (ed.) (1995) *Portugal the Pathfinder. Journeys from the Medieval to the Modern World, 1300–ca.1600*, Madison, Hispanic Seminary of Medieval Studies.

UNIT 2
TOOLS AND TERMS FOR STUDYING EMPIRES

Karl Hack

AIMS

- To provide you with tools for defining, analysing, comparing and contrasting empires and their major components.
- To construct a typology of colonies.
- To construct a model of empires as systems.

[handwritten margin notes: EMPIRE: has :— 1. types of colonies 2. types of rule 3. systems of control]

INTRODUCTION

Unit 1 gave an overview of empires from 1500 to 1975. It provided an essential framework for the course, but perhaps also an embarrassment of riches. You might well fear such kaleidoscopic variety could become more infuriating than fascinating. Only the bravest of scholars would attempt to tackle, as you must, both land empires (Chinese, Austro-Hungarian and Russian) and overseas empires (British, Dutch, French and Iberian); and empires both early modern and modern. How can you generate meaningful comparisons within and across empires and periods?

The task is daunting, but don't worry. Just as a carpenter has a toolkit tailored for the task and mathematicians have a common set of terms, we too will assemble a topic-specific set of tools and terms. And by breaking empire down into its parts – types of colony, types of rule and systems of control – we will be in a better position to recognise and compare similar situations across time and space.

It goes without saying that the definitions we discuss will not be universally accepted. The concept of empire has been used to mean many different things. This so exasperated empire historian Sir Keith Hancock, that he declared 'imperialism is no word for scholars' (Hancock, 1940, p. 1). Many 'empires' had alternative names, such as *France d'Outre-Mer* (France overseas) or Japan's Greater East Asia Co-Prosperity Sphere. Queen Victoria only took the title empress of India in 1877 (see Figure 2.1). When you use words such as empire, remember you are translating – sometimes literally – past terms into a language that makes sense to us today. Some historians have responded by not bothering to define key terms. But that would not do for a third-level Open University student. So this unit will provide definitions as *working models*, which are **heuristic**. By this, I mean they are models used to help us think about the past, by simplifying and clarifying. But they remain just that, useful models, which need to be set out clearly, and may be contested and adapted.

The rest of this unit divides into three main sections, namely: 'Definitions of empire'; 'Types of colony and of rule'; and 'Empires as systems'.

Figure 2.1   Queen Victoria with two Indian servants, Mustafa and Chidda, 1896. Photographed by Gunn & Stuart. The Royal Collection, RCIN2105779. Photo: The Royal Collection © 2006 Her Majesty Queen Elizabeth II. This photograph was taken close to the Diamond Jubilee of 1897, which was marked by a procession of imperial forces in London. A written inscription, verified as being in Victoria's hand, identifies each of the sitters and provides the date.

DEFINITIONS OF EMPIRE

What is empire? An internet search would uncover talk of property empires, of cultural and economic empires, and of a modern, colony-less 'American empire'. By using the term, authors associate some aspects of units historically labelled as empires – size, acquisitiveness, aggression – to things that may not themselves be empires. This is fine if the word is being used metaphorically, but it is problematical if meant literally. Can you have 'cultural empire' with no central control? Can you have empire without territorially defined colonies? Empire might come to mean little more than a powerful body able to project influence. Indeed, it might come to mean less, since 'cultural empire' does not even require a conscious attempt by one organisation to exert power over others. Culture, as in 'American culture', for instance, can transfer by osmosis.

Now, whether or not you agree with concepts such as 'economic empire', we clearly need to define empire if our study is to have limits. The first step is to be aware of your assumptions about empire. You might like to consider for a moment what these are and where they come from. Do you assume empires are usually good or bad (normative or value judgements), or strong or weak? You might, for instance, assume empire is not right, or not sustainable. Yet these assumptions would be questionable. Unit 1 showed that empires could last hundreds of years, with millions accepting them as legitimate. Resource concentration, internal peace, and the reduction of barriers to movement and trade, can all be public benefits. It is by no means clear that a nation state (which rules over a group with a shared identity or equal citizenship rights) will be better placed to deliver such public goods than an empire, which rules over many peoples and places.

If you want to enter the world of pre-1750 empires, and to a lesser extent that of 1750 to 1917, you must recognise that there were very different notions about what was 'natural' in relations between societies. M. I. Finley (1976, 1978) insists on the 'naturalness' of empire from Athens and Rome, until the American War of Independence (1776–83) and the French Revolution (1789) boosted contrary ideas of the 'naturalness' of freedom, equality, and the rights of all men (if not women) to choose their own form of government. According to Finley:

> Underlying [empires] ... was hierarchy: domination was 'natural', whether of men over women, of the free over the slaves, or of some communities over others. 'We have done nothing extraordinary,' Thucydides (1.76.2) has an unnamed Athenian say in Sparta in defence of the Athenian Empire [fifth–fourth century BCE], 'nothing contrary to human practice, in accepting an empire when it was offered to us and then in refusing to give it up. It has always been a rule that the weak should be subject to the strong.'
>
> (Finley, 1978, p. 5)[5]

Finley notes that Greeks and Romans found it a 'fine thing' to rule over other peoples. Europeans studied ancient empires, taking Rome as the supreme

---

[5] The Athenian League started as an alliance, but some cities offered money rather than forces, or found Athens intervening to ensure they remained, like it, democracies: 'League' became 'Empire'.

example of a land empire and Athens as the archetype of a maritime (overseas) empire (Doyle, 1986, pp. 51–103). Sixteenth-century European colonisers of the Americas (as discussed in Unit 4 on the beginnings of Spanish empire) cited the Greek thinker Aristotle to justify arguments that men of lesser civilisation might be dominated for their own good, or might be 'natural' slaves.

Nor were thinkers who argued for individual rights at home necessarily against such domination abroad. British official and writer John Locke (a favourite of later Liberals) argued in the late seventeenth century that there was a 'natural' right to property, which he defined as land improved by labour. Land not 'improved' was 'waste'. What he meant by this, as a supporter of overseas settlement, was that it could be legitimately colonised. By this thinking, indigenous peoples who attacked settlers moving onto 'waste' lands such as forests were denying the latter's 'natural' rights. Here lay the roots of an attitude that saw much of North America, and then Australasia, treated as *terra nullius*, 'empty' or 'waste' land, as a justification for its seizure and more intensive development (Arneil, 1994). There were, it is true, also occasions when consent was sought or given by local inhabitants, as Unit 1 shows happened in New Zealand in 1770, but even that limited rather than prevented Maori losses in the decades afterwards.

In short, notions that there were hierarchies of social classes, and between whole societies and economies, eased the way to empire throughout most of our period. Before 1750, and to a lesser extent afterwards, it was not assumed that a local community, even one as coherent as an ethnic-based nation, should seek 'independence' from such domination. There were often counter-arguments, for instance that expansion might dissipate metropolitan resources, or that settlers did not treat indigenous peoples as various churches felt they should, but hierarchy was an entrenched principle.

Now we have established that empires were for long simply seen as the largest form of organisation of communities into hierarchies, headed by an emperor, monarch or 'king of kings', we can work on detailed definitions. Here is one attempt by a political scientist:

> I define 'empire' in political terms, as a relationship of domination and subordination between one polity (called the metropole) and one or more territories (called colonies) that lie outside the metropole's boundaries yet are claimed as its lawful possessions.

(Abernethy, 2000, p. 19)

So far, so good. Few would dispute the need for a dominating **core** or metropole, and for dominated territories or 'colonies'. The problem comes when we push this a little further, and try to define what is, and what is not, a 'core' and a 'colony'.

EXERCISE   Read Secondary Source 2.1 on the course website. Summarise Motyl's definition of 'empire', and then of 'core', and 'periphery'. What key characteristics does he think each must have?

"CORE" and "PERIPHERY"

MOTYL

Motyl's definition portrays an empire as consisting of linked parts, namely 'a core and ... a periphery ... both core and periphery ... situated in geographically bounded spaces inhabited by culturally differentiated elites and populations'. Here he echoes Abernethy's definition given above. Both emphasise that there must be a dominant core, and territorially and culturally distinct peripheries. But Motyl then goes on to prescribe that a *core* and a *periphery* must also have very specific characteristics.

The core. According to Motyl, the core must have a centralised decision-making authority. This is common sense, since it is difficult to control several territories without developing a centralised state, even if empire can be acquired by tribal conglomerations such as the Mongols. If no centralised machinery is developed, the death of a conqueror such as Alexander the Great will be followed by a division among regional generals and officials.

The periphery. Motyl further insists that the imperial core must 'direct the finances of peripheries; they appoint peripheral governors or prefects; and they are not accountable to the periphery, which, in turn, has no legal basis for influencing the appointment of core officials and the choice of core policies.' Here Motyl gives us a demanding set of characteristics for defining a periphery or colony. It is not just dominated but directed, financially and in its appointment of high officials. It also has no legal basis for influencing policy making in the core.

These definitions properly concentrate on the central characteristic of empires: the coercive or undemocratic direction of peripheries, of other peoples, by a dominant core.

If political: undemocratic.

Now you have answered the first exercise, you may well feel Motyl's use of political science terms seems unnecessarily complicated. Why make a meal out of something so obvious? But his approach does have a strength. His dual criteria for empire – it must have *both* a complex core dominating peoples it is not accountable to *and* several culturally and administratively distinct peripheries – are vital to defining what is 'not empire'. Most states (as he shows on p. 2) fail to qualify on one of these two criteria.

Cultural empires fail to qualify because they lack a central, directing core. By contrast, the USA fails to qualify because its central, dominating core is accountable to the citizens of its component fifty states of the Union. These cases fail the test of having a dominant, directing core that does not answer to its component parts.

States such as pre-2003 Iraq, meanwhile, fail Motyl's test on having culturally and administratively distinct peripheries. Despite being a multinational dictatorial state with Kurds, Shias and Sunnis, Iraq was also a unitary state. In short, empire requires both domination, and culturally and administratively distinct territories.

Abernethy suggests one further requirement: the weaker state or territory should be recognised as less than sovereign by major states. Why? Well, some people have been tempted to describe relations between superpowers such as the USA and some weaker 'client states' as imperial. Abernethy's definition, by contrast, excludes relations between merely unequal states where the stronger state exerts 'marked influence', but the weaker retains enough control to be treated by other states as sovereign. He is attempting to exclude merely unequal power relations. After all, almost all international relations bring together states of unequal power, since no two states can be exactly the same.

Together, these definitions are good starting points, though if taken too far they might exclude situations that some academics do accept are 'imperial'. In particular, some historians would argue that a territory can be a colony even if control is only surrendered over a limited sector, say foreign policy, while internal policy is hardly affected. For instance, take a local khanate (a territory ruled by a khan) that is subject to the expanding power of the Russian tsar (Unit 7), but largely autonomous in internal policy. Is this a periphery? If we exclude such territories, we might also have to exclude, say, early twentieth-century British dominions, such as Australia and Canada. These colonies had come to have almost total control over internal policy, and some control over external policy as well. But few people would want to deny that they were, in some sense, still peripheries in a British imperial system.

For the moment, let's put aside the difficulty over how strict to make our criteria for being a colony. Let's define them in a way that leaves open the question of whether internal, as well as external, policy needs to be dominated. Excluding this, political scientists tend to agree on three requirements. First, a colony is dominated as a unit that is administratively distinct from the ruling power's core territory. Secondly, there is a lack of explicit consent from the population ruled. Thirdly, the majority of the colonial territory's population feels culturally distinct from the core (Hack and Rettig, 2006, p. 3).

The best way of exploring this problem further is to construct a typology of colonies. This is the next logical next step towards categorising empires, since all our definitions of empire mention three main variables: core, periphery, and a system for maintaining the hierarchical relationship between the core and its peripheries. In short, an empire consists of its component parts (a dominant core or metropole and dominated colonial territories) and a system that relates the core to its peripheries.

This suggests empires will differ according these two main constituents. First, they will differ according to the number and type of peripheries. Each empire is a shifting portfolio of types of territory and of styles of rule. So in the next section 'Types of colonies and of rule', we construct a typology of territories, and then of styles of rule, from which a portfolio might be constructed. Secondly, empires will differ according to the type of system put in place to bind the colonies and maintain the core's ability to dictate their internal or external policies. This system is a composite of politics, force, ideology and relationships, and we deal with it in the section 'Empire as systems'.

TYPES OF COLONIES AND OF RULE

If empires are shifting portfolios of different types of colonial territory, arranged around a core, then it makes sense to begin by making a list of the different types of colonial territory: a typology. This section will, therefore, begin by getting you to construct a typology of colonies, before moving on to talk about different styles for ruling these colonies.

A typology of colonies

You have already come across a number of types of colonial territory in Unit 1, for instance settler colonies such as New Zealand. If you were asked, you might be able to think of more. But you might also be slightly unsure of the best way to label and define each type. The next exercise is intended to give you a typology that can describe most types of colony you will come across.

EXERCISE

Read Secondary Source 2.2 on the course website. Use this to answer two questions:

1   What types of colony does Fieldhouse name?
2   What are his main criteria for distinguishing one type of colony from another?

SPECIMEN ANSWER

1   Fieldhouse mentions five main types of colony: mixed; occupation; plantation; 'small tide-water trading settlements and naval bases containing little territory and few permanent settlers'; and settlement. *'enclave'*

2   The difference he most consistently mentions is the population balance between settlers and others. How many people from the metropole are there in the colony, relative to the local population? Though he does mention other criteria, for instance function or aim, which for small settlements with little territory and few settlers is seen as trade or security.

DISCUSSION

When Fieldhouse talks of 'small tide-water trading settlements and naval bases containing little territory and few permanent settlers', he is at root describing how a small slice of a peripheral state is dominated for specific functions, as an **enclave**. The second part of the source ('Europeans in the East before 1815') depicts one empire, the Portuguese (the origins of which you will revisit in Unit 6), mainly as a commercial trading empire, focused on a string of enclaves from Portugal, around Africa and India, to Goa in India and Macao in China. In the rest of the unit, therefore, I will use the term 'enclave' to represent one of Fieldhouse's five types of colony.

In order to demonstrate why the balance between settlers and indigenes in the population is so important, I will now zoom in and focus on the categories mentioned or described by Fieldhouse, starting with commercial enclaves and settler colonies.

Enclaves are more significant than size alone might suggest. They often formed the centre of inkspots of influence, which permeated outwards over time. They might begin life as coaling stations, naval bases, **entrepôts**, or factories. As you saw in the block Introduction and in Unit 1, 'factories' here means bases where traders (factors – those who transact business on another's behalf) resided, setting up a factory where they could trade between visits of their company's ships. Some of the enclaves were obtained outright (as was Singapore between 1819 and 1824, and Hong Kong in 1842 – see Figure 2.2). Others were held on lease from or by agreement with a still-sovereign local power (as with Portuguese Macao on the China coast).

VIEW OF VICTORIA TOWN — ISLAND OF HONG-KONG.

Figure 2.2   B. Clayton after Piqua, 'View of Victoria Town – Island of Hong-Kong', lithograph, from Corner, J. (1846?) *The History of China and India*, London, Dean & Co. Photo: Time & Life Pictures/Getty Images. Formally acquired in 1842, Hong Kong became one of a string of enclaves along the China coast where Europeans either controlled cities or enjoyed extraterritorial privileges in parts of them. The most notable included Guangzhou (Canton) and Shanghai.

In the latter case, the right to rule was ceded for a small area, typically a coastal city. Alternatively, European companies and traders were granted exemptions from local law in a specific area. This was most famously the case in the capitulations in the Ottoman empire, and from 1842 in the **extraterritorial privileges** granted in China's coastal and riverine cities (Osterhammel, 1999). Or, as with the Imperial British East Africa Company, company agents signed agreements with local rulers, paving the way for later penetration inland. So enclaves might start as little more than a speck in an indigenous state whose leader the Europeans were clients of, or paid rents to. But ultimately many of them spawned larger colonies, or alternatively grew into cities at the forefront of 'globalisation'.

At the latter extreme, Shanghai by the 1920s – where the majority of the city always remained under Chinese control – had become the epitome of enclave success. It had not one but two foreign enclaves. There was a modest French settlement, but above all it possessed a multinational 'foreign settlement', heavily dominated by the British and with full civic organisation, including its own police (Bickers, 2003). It was this foreign settlement that gave Shanghai its historic waterfront, the Bund, which still survives today in the midst of the city's rebirth since the 1980s as a global centre.

Fieldhouse's types move from such enclaves at one extreme, where permanent settlers might be all but non-existent, to settler colonies at the other. In his eyes, quantitative differences in settler numbers translate into qualitative differences in colonial rule. Generally speaking, the bigger the proportion of non-indigenous population, the more radical the impact on indigenous structures. In an enclave such as Shanghai, outsiders dominated only a tiny proportion of the host state – in this case a fraction of a city. Despite the large number of such foreign 'treaty ports' opened from 1842, China survived as a sovereign state, much of its interior scarcely ever seeing a foreigner. At the other extreme, in the pure settlement colony, through battle, disease and design, "settlers" came to dominate almost all the most fertile space, marginalising indigenous peoples, and pushing the latter into reservations, if not destroying, enslaving or absorbing them. Such was the fate of aboriginals in Australia. Most of these settler colonies were in temperate zones (or zones where niches came close to temperate conditions, such as in coastal Algeria, and parts of South Africa and the highlands of Kenya). Here 'neo-metropoles', '**neo-Europes**' or 'neo-Mediterraneans' (see Unit 4 on the Spanish Americas) could be created, replicating home – an aim witnessed by names such as New Amsterdam, New Spain and Plymouth in Massachusetts.

These settler colonies and neo-Europes frequently involved 'ecological imperialism' (Crosby, 1986), transplanting culture, flora, fauna and ecological, economic and social practices from Europe to 'new worlds' (see Figure 2.3). The resulting marginalisation of local populations is also what Hitler – more deliberately – intended for the western parts of Poland from 1939: their 'cleansing' of non-Germans by whatever means necessary to provide *Lebensraum* (living room).

If settler colonisation could devastate indigenous populations and social structures, plantation colonies were scarcely less devastating. Here the settlers were a more modest proportion of the population, but they often imported large numbers of labourers (indentured and slaves), whose presence transformed demographics and land use.

In between these extremes of enclave and settler colony, there is Fieldhouse's "occupation colony". The defining characteristic of this sort of colony is the thinness of the layer of permanent settlers. Such colonies could be acquired by any number of means, including inheritance or treaty, of which conquest was perhaps the most common. In an occupation colony, then, a thin ruling layer of colonial officials meant changes to local society were more restricted. After all, in areas such as French Indochina, the ratio of military to population (around 1:1000 there) was considerably lower than that found in many European states (as high as 1:100 – Hack and Rettig, 2006, p. 57). The relative lack of manpower often dictated very limited levels of interference outside the main cities or towns, and high levels of reliance on local elites to help rule.

Is this Froude's "Australia"

Is this Froude's "South Africa"

Figure 2.3   Unknown artist, *The res[idence] of W[illia]m Cunningham Esq, Lot 20, Range 5, Godmanchester Tp, Huntingdon Co[unty], P[rovince of] Q[uebec]*, c.1850, lithograph. Photo: Mary Evans/Grosvenor Prints. Settler colonies transplanted people, fauna and flora across continents, sometimes transforming new lands in the image of the old. Take away the caption details, and this could almost be an English county, rather than what it really is: a farm in Quebec.

Fieldhouse does also mention the function of a colonial territory as a criteria; for instance, his enclaves are 'to organize a lucrative trade ... a commercial ... empire'. But his main criteria remains the balance between original peoples (indigenes, aboriginals), transplanted peoples (colonisers, bonded labourers, slaves) and new peoples (**mestizo** or **mulatto** mixes such as Hispanic–Native American and European–African, respectively).

Fieldhouse has now given us five types of colony. But you may be able to remember one more, when Unit 1 discussed 'The second French overseas empire' (p. 30). This talked about French *protectorates* over Tunisia (1881) and Morocco (1912). Such protectorates may agree to subordinate only a limited part of their sovereignty to a dominant power, in this case foreign relations, in return for protection or other assistance. There could, at the extreme, be few or no permanent representatives from the imperial power in such a periphery. There might be little interference in internal policy, the latter remaining under a cooperative or intimidated peripheral elite: sometimes called a collaborating elite.

There is a good case for saying protectorates have to be incorporated in any typology of colonies. They are numerous, often a first step towards fuller domination (if only because they are cheap), and highlight the fact that state sovereignty is not always an all-or-nothing situation: you can lose partial control. With some protectorates being over company possessions, such as British protection of the North Borneo Chartered Company (1888), this also points towards another messy category of domination: the area penetrated not

[handwritten margin note: Fieldhouse 'five' empires with "balance between original peoples" + new peoples]

directly by a powerful state, but by autonomous institutions. This leads us to our next exercise.

EXERCISE

Read Secondary Source 2.3 on the course website. As described by Fieldhouse, what were the main characteristics of European 'empire' in the east up to 1759? See also Figure 2.4.

SPECIMEN ANSWER

Fieldhouse emphasises the relative lack of presence by European states: 'Until 1769 ... no North European state owned colonies in the east ... [this was] the heyday of the chartered companies'. Empire as practised by private companies shared a number of characteristics.

First, it was overwhelmingly commercial. It involved pooling merchant capital in the likes of the English East India Company (1600) and the Dutch United East India Company (VOC). These, and similar French companies, were controlled by a court or board of directors, appointed by holders of capital. The companies were designed to reduce competition for trade between a specific area and their home company, and as such sought charters from their governments giving them monopolies, hence 'chartered companies'.

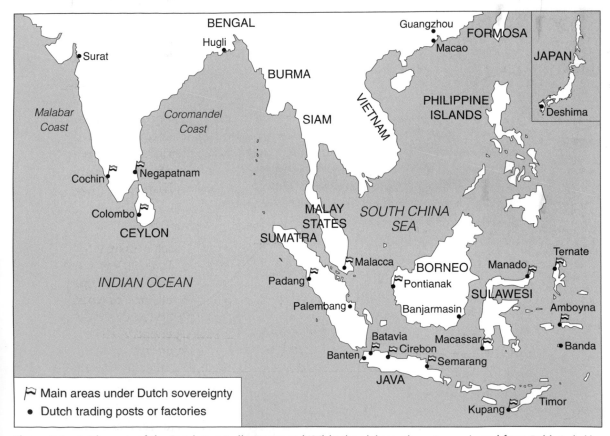

Figure 2.4   Settlements of the Dutch East India Company (VOC) in the eighteenth century, adapted from Reid, A. (ed.) (1996) *Encyclopedia of Indonesian Heritage: Volume 3: Early Modern History*, Singapore, Archipelago Press, p. 73. Empire was often a matter not of inland conquests, but of strings of trading ports. A classic example of this are the various European East India companies, such as the English East India Company and the VOC. The map shows the latter's trading posts from which it secured goods, such as pepper, to trade to Europe.

Secondly, such empire sought trade not territory. For instance, the early eighteenth-century East India Company had three main bases – Bombay, Madras and Calcutta (the last two held by permission of local rulers), and innumerable 'factories'. Chartered companies' power was based on trade, sea power, alliances with local rulers and the few fortified bases they could muster, such as the VOC's Malacca and (in Java) Batavia (see Figure 2.4).

Thirdly, local agents, whether **viceroys** or individual traders, often enjoyed considerable autonomy, and scope for initiative, if not for corruption as well.

DISCUSSION

Fieldhouse is talking only of 'North European' states. From southern Europe, Spain did control the Philippines – the islands south of China named after King Philip of Spain. Its capital, Manila, was one of the largest European bases in east Asia until the nineteenth century. However, it looked more to the Spanish empire in the Americas, than to the rest of the east. The 'Manila Galleon' took American precious metals to the Philippines, where these paid for Chinese goods to ship back to Acapulco, in New Spain. Similarly, the Portuguese state owned territories, but only the insignificant island of East Timor, tiny Macao on the China Coast, and various small footholds in India.

Overall, however, Fieldhouse is right to emphasise companies, which were also important in the west. The French empire in the Americas originated with seventeenth-century companies, whose interests the state eventually took over. Britain's first successful colony on the American mainland, in seventeenth-century Virginia, was started by a company and later taken over by the state.

In the nineteenth century, in a slightly different form, companies would spearhead the European drive into parts of Africa.

There was often a close relationship between such companies and their home government, which allowed the company to act as a quasi-state in specified areas. Thus these areas' potential was tapped at little or no cost to the company's home state. Hence the VOC was empowered by the Dutch **States General** and the States of Holland to enter treaties, wage war, set up courts of law and coin money in the East Indies. Why take on expensive duties if a company will do it for you?

This is not a new category of colony. Chartered companies could set up enclaves, settler colonies or occupation colonies just as a state could. But it is important to note that the European state was not always the main player locally, as opposed to such sub-imperialists and sectoral institutions. Transnational institutions, such as chartered companies and missionary organisations, were vital across our period.

So protectorates are a separate category, and sub-imperialists, whether church institutions, adventurers or chartered companies, did much legwork in paving the way for more direct imperial control by European states.

Abernethy (2000, pp. 35–8) further argues that the vitality and partial autonomy of sub-imperialists was one of two main factors that made post-1500 'European' imperialism more transformative than previous types. If the state stalled, sub-imperialist transnational actors, such as companies and

[handwritten margin note: Countries didn't have the money, borrowed from wealthy companies – shareholders were the great + good of aristocratic society]

missionaries, might press on. The other factor was Europe's overarching culture, combined with multiple, competing states. Competition fuelled individual state development, while inter-state rivalry encouraged further expansion. He argues that, for many non-European empires, by contrast, constant state support was vital. For instance, the withdrawal of state support led to the end of China's huge maritime fleets going to southeast Asia from 1405 to 1433 under Admiral Zheng He (Cheng Ho) – fleets and ships larger than anything Portugal managed in the following century.

EXERCISE

We now have Fieldhouse's five types of colony, plus protectorates as a sixth, and a distinction between state actors and sub-imperialist actors. This is a good point at which to visualise a full typology of colonies.

Read Secondary Source 2.2 again. Using Fieldhouse's five categories and our discussion of protectorates, draw up a typology of colonies. By typology I mean a list of types, with each ascribed its main characteristics, and one or more examples. What I suggest is that you create a box with three columns. List the types of colony Fieldhouse identifies in the first. In the second, produce a very short description for each type: basically a list of its defining characteristics. For the last column, think of a couple of examples of each type. The result will be a table that visually organises types of colony. To help you, we include a blank table to be filled in (Table 2.1). It does not matter if your final typology is incomplete or crude. Alternatively, if you think of types or characteristics I do not mention below, you may be running ahead of me. Any typology is a simplification. But credible simplification is vital if we are to establish tools for analysis. So this exercise is practise in turning text into a visual representation, and creating a typology.   *practice*

Table 2.1   Blank typology table

Typology	Description	Examples
1 Settlement		
2 Mixed		
3 Plantation		
4 Occupation		
5 Enclave		
6 Protectorate		

SPECIMEN ANSWER See Table 2.2.

Table 2.2   A six-fold typology of colonial territories

Typology	Description	Examples
1 Settlement	Settlers take large tracts of space, often separating settler from indigenous lands to form a racial frontier of exclusion. Introduction of private property rights in land where they had never existed.	New England type settlements, such as in North America, Canada and Australia. Parts of Siberia.
2 Mixed	Settlers have lower relative numbers and a higher requirement for indigenous labour. There may also be a significant mixed population.	African type settlement colonies, such as Algeria. South American type settlements, such as Brazil.
3 Plantation	A small, dominant settler core, often using slaves and bonded labour.	Caribbean type colonies, such as Jamaica.
4 Occupation	Dominated by small numbers of non-resident military and civilian personnel.	India, Philippines.
5 Enclave	Dominated by small numbers of non-resident military and civilian personnel. Small scale. Trading settlement, factory or military base.	'Factories'. International settlements held by treaty, such as Shanghai. Military bases as in US rights over Diego Garcia on British Indian Ocean Territory. Directly ruled micro-territories, often ports, such as Portuguese Goa and Macao.
6 Protectorate	Few metropolitan officials, sometimes a single Resident. Imperial power has treaty rights over limited functions, such as foreign relations.	French protectorates over Tunisia (1881) and Morocco (1912). Some transmute into or overlap characteristics of occupation over time.

DISCUSSION I hope my specimen answer in Table 2.2 is self-explanatory. The first five types are those Fieldhouse mentions. The sixth type is the protectorate. In the second column, types are distinguished mainly by the balance between occupiers and rulers on the one hand, and the indigenous population on the other, but with some mention also of aim, size and the degree of rights the core exercises.[6]

---

[6] After 1919, some colonies were transferred from defeated to victorious powers as 'mandated territories' of the League of Nations. This meant they were held in trust, with a view to development and eventual independence, with regular reports made to the League. Nevertheless, such 'mandated territories' could still be classified under 1–5 in Table 2.2. Hence German East Africa became British-run Tanganyika, an occupation colony held as a 'mandated territory'.

Can this typology be applied across the full range of empires? The answer is 'almost', and that is the best we can hope for. Fieldhouse mainly had Europe's overseas empires in mind, and clearly it works best for them. But equally clearly he thought it could be applied to some land empires, as he himself does for Russia (Fieldhouse, 1982, pp. 334–41). Consequently, we can pick out his types of colony in several of the big land empires, such as the Ottoman, the Russian and the Chinese. Ming China (1368–1644) had settler colonies, using farmer-soldiers to colonise borderlands. Nineteenth-century Russia had protectorates in the Caucasus. The Ottoman empire treated some of its European conquests as occupation colonies. That is, it imposed a thin layer of new officials and Ottoman landowners on a Christian majority. Dynastic land empires such as the Habsburg (which you will meet again in Unit 18) – a collection of territories splattered across Europe and assembled by marriage, inheritance and conquest – fit the model less easily. But even here, a ruler gaining a new territory might treat it like a protectorate, leaving local cities and representative assemblies with considerable autonomy, but controlling foreign and military policy. Or they might treat it more like an occupation colony, imposing a thin, new layer of officials and some additional taxation from an 'imperial' centre. In short, though far from perfect, our typology can be stretched to cover a gratifying range of imperial sins.

There is, however, one big imperial sin this typology does not cover well. This is the 'empire' where a 'foreign' ruling elite lord it over the core territory's population as well as over peripheries. A good example of this is Manchu rule over Han Chinese in the Qing dynasty of 1644–1911 (see Figure 2.5).[7] The Qing Chinese empire did have occupation colonies and protectorates outside of its core territory – Tibet for instance – but it also represented a dual-faced type of empire, where there was dominance by a foreign dynasty over the centre as well. This latter sort of domination is so distinct, and so problematic in terms of any usable definition of empire, that I am not going to attempt to integrate it into our system. For now, all you need to know is that the peripheral areas of the Chinese empire can be incorporated, and that the internal aspects will be discussed as a special case of 'bureaucratic empire' in Unit 11 on China.

I am relaxed about this limitation, and you should be too. As we emphasised at the beginning, no toolkit can cover every situation. In the meantime, our typology covers as much as any 'heuristic' device is ever likely to, for such a diverse phenomenon as empires. Because it is a heuristic device, or working model, we have to keep a couple of additional points in mind when using it.

First, the categories given are 'ideal types'. They isolate certain characteristics as defining each type of colony, and use these to describe a pure form. In reality, changing populations and aims could mean types overlapped, forming a continuum. An area might move from one category to another over time.

---

[7] The Manchu came from Manchuria, to the northwest of the Chinese empire they conquered, and once in power maintained separate Manchu, Mongol and Han 'banners' or sections to their army.

Figure 2.5   William Alexander, *The Approach of the Emperor of China to his Tent in Tartary to Receive the British Ambassador*, 1799, watercolour, 56 × 79 cm. Royal Asiatic Society, London. Photo: © Royal Asiatic Society, London. Lord MacCartney, representative of Britain and its powerful maritime empire, found in the 1790s (see Unit 11 on China) that the gifts he brought to China were received with little evident enthusiasm. The Qianlong Emperor (ruled 1736–95) had recently conquered the steppe land to China's north-east, and the emperors regarded China as the 'central kingdom' to whom others should offer tribute. <u>Chinese emperors ruled their vast territories through a centrally controlled bureaucratic system. Ottoman, Qing, Russian and Mughal land empires were arguably far more powerful than the West European maritime empires right up to the middle of the eighteenth century</u> (Darwin, 2007).

Secondly, we could have devised an alternative with more types, or fewer. One of the types we could have included, for instance, is the neo-colony. A neo-colony is independent or decolonised. For that very reason, it seems reasonable for us to exclude it from our main typology. But, at the same time, we cannot totally ignore it.

To understand why neo-colonies are significant, you need to understand how imperial dominance is exercised. One way is as a series of hierarchic relationships between elites. Put bluntly, a central elite dominates elites in other places. Now ask yourself what happens if, one day, the core elite hauls down its flag and pronounces a colony independent. Does the peripheral elite automatically escape dominance? Perhaps, but equally, perhaps not.

For instance, after full independence in 1946, the Philippines remained tied to the USA militarily. Its elite's scope for economic policy was also severely constrained by both its own, and its country's, heavy reliance on exports to the

USA. Was the 1950s–60s Philippines and its elite truly 'independent', or in some senses a 'neo-colony' or semi-colonial?

The argument here is that sometimes, despite formal independence, the neo-colony's elite continues to serve the interests of a former colonial power, or of capitalists from a 'core region'. The elite acts as *compradors* – collaborators – deriving security or taking a slice of profits from dealings with outsiders, in return for subordinating the neo-colony's wider interests. You could envisage this domination as happening along an axis as follows:

becomes a "dependency" after (nominally) gaining independence

metropolitan elite (*m*) ↔ metropolitan representatives in periphery (*mr*) ↔ peripheral elite (*p*)

Using this model, it seems obvious that some elites might continue to act as metropolitan representatives (*mr*) within their own state after 'independence'. They might find themselves locked in subordinate (and profitable) relationships with the elites of a former metropole, or remain reliant on outside support to keep power. These ideas of continuing exploitation of postcolonial states through a relationship between core and *comprador* elites made neo-colonies and neo-colonialism major themes of the 1970s to 1980s (Wallerstein, 1974).

In short, imperialism can live from beyond the grave.

There is a complex historiography on all this, but for now it is important you studiously ignore that, and stick to the six-fold typology above. It is enough to note the following. First, there is an additional, hotly disputed, category of neo-colonies. Secondly, the *m–mr–p* relationship shapes the nature of imperialism. Thirdly, the *mr* can include local elites (rulers, business elites and others) with interests in 'collaboration': interests that may persist after formal independence (Robinson, 1972).

EXERCISE

Now, back to our main, six-fold typology. Unless we can put such devices to work, they will remain academic fluff and nonsense. So let's try our typology out. I want you to use the typology and table above to identify what type of colony predominated in the Portuguese empire at three different times:

1   sixteenth century
2   eighteenth century
3   twentieth century.

Remember, you are not trying to list all the colonies or types. For each period, just write down which of our six types of colony was predominant within the Portuguese empire, and give one, or at most two, examples of that type.

To complete this exercise, you should re-read the section on 'Portugal and Spain' in Secondary Source 2.2, and 'Five centuries of Portuguese empire' on pp. 22–3 in Unit 1. If you wish, you could also look up the entries on Brazil and the Portuguese empire in Secondary Source 2.4 on the course website (this is optional). See also Figures 2.6a and b.

This exercise will help you later in the course, when you look at the beginnings of the Portuguese empire in Unit 6, and its end in Unit 20.

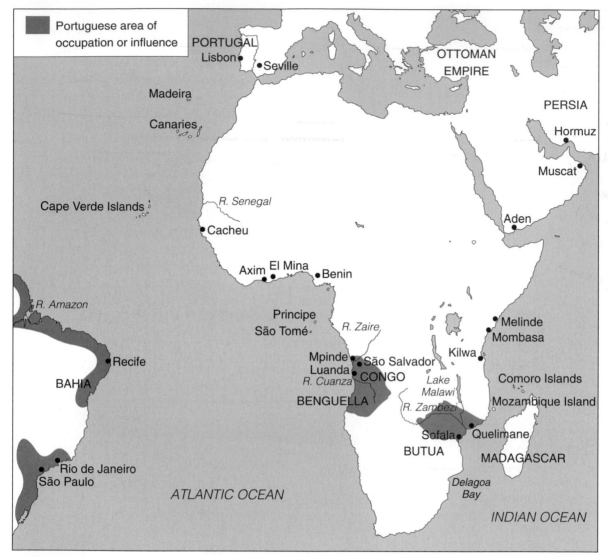

Figure 2.6a   Portuguese influence in Africa and South America, adapted from Newitt, M. (2005) *A History of Portuguese Overseas Expansion 1400–1668*, Oxford, Routledge, maps 2 and 5. This map and Figure 2.6b show territories the Portuguese came to dominate at various times between the late fifteenth and nineteenth centuries. Some territories were lost over time. Others, such as Brazil and Angola, expanded from mere coastal settlements in the fifteenth and sixteenth centuries to become colonies with considerable hinterlands at later periods.

SPECIMEN ANSWER

1   Portugal's sixteenth-century empire centred on a string of commercial enclaves and bases that took its ships around Africa, across the Indian Ocean and into Asia (as shown in Figures 2.6a and b). There are many possible examples, such as: São Tomé, El Mina, Sofala, Mombasa, Aden, Muscat, Goa and Malacca.

2   By the eighteenth century, the enclaves had been eclipsed by British, French and Dutch chartered companies. Portugal's plantation and mixed colonies now took centre stage. These originated in 1418, from when Portugal 'discovered' the Atlantic islands off the north and west of Africa, namely Madeira, the Azores and the Cape Verde group. On these, sugar was farmed using peasant share-croppers and imported African labour. The plantation and mixed models peaked when

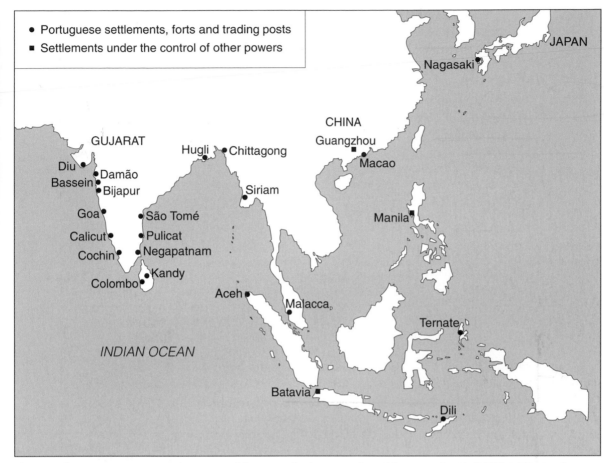

Figure 2.6b   Key Portuguese settlements and fortresses in the east, adapted from Newitt, M. (2005) *A History of Portuguese Overseas Expansion 1400–1668*, Oxford, Routledge, maps 3 and 4. Individual settlements sometimes changed status several times. In the seventeenth century some of the most important fell to other European powers. For instance, all European trade with Nagasaki ceased in 1640. The Dutch took control of Malacca in 1641, the Sri Lankan ports in the middle of the century, and Cochin in 1667. Despite this decline, Portuguese presence in the east technically outlasted the British, only finally ending with the transfer of Macao to China as a 'special administrative region' in 1999.

extended to Brazil, for sugar in the seventeenth century, for gold and diamond mining, and finally coffee. By the eighteenth century Brazil was the world's biggest slave importer.

3   Brazil's creole (local-born descendants of the Portuguese) elite, under Prince Dom Pedro, had become independent in 1822. In the twentieth century, Portugal's most significant territories were the mainland African colonies of Angola and Mozambique. There the original trading enclaves had seeded occupation colonies. Apart from in a few towns, Portuguese, Portuguese–Africans and Portuguese–Asians formed a thin layer over an indigenous majority.

DISCUSSION

Analysing Portuguese empire as a shifting portfolio of types of colony suggests three Portuguese empires: a first dominated by state-supported trade from enclaves; a second dominated by plantation and mixed colonies; and a third dominated by occupation colonies in Africa. Hence our typology does allow us to describe dramatic shifts in emphasis within Portuguese imperialism over time.

So far in our section on 'Types of colonies and of rule', then, we have constructed a useable typology of colonies. This gives us six unproblematical types of colony, plus one (neo-colony) for debate.

Types of rule in colonies

Within any single 'type' of colony, however, there can also be varying styles of rule. So you now need to look at the different types of rule that could be applied in colonies. Most notably, there is a continuum between totally **direct rule** and totally **indirect rule**.

Direct rule implies a near monopoly over key functions of state, such as use of force, and legal and tax-raising activities. Indirect rule implies key state functions are left with semi-autonomous leaders. Such semi-autonomous agents might be local or European.

In military terms, direct methods of rule include raising regular troops and police paid from central funds, under the command of centrally appointed officers down to low levels. Indirect methods might include demanding local levies, raised, commanded and perhaps even paid for by indigenous leaders, or taking payment in lieu of troops.

In fiscal terms, direct rule might mean the collection of tax by salaried bureaucrats of the central state. Indirect methods might mean collecting tribute from semi-autonomous local rulers, or 'farming' taxes (selling the right to collect specific taxes to the highest bidder).

In legal terms, direct rule might mean courts under salaried state officials. Indirect rule might mean local populations continuing under local laws and officials. These latter authorities were often declared to be traditional 'native' representatives: sultans, rajas, chiefs, *ulama* (learned Islamic men), or village heads.

The two types of rule could be used on a pick and mix basis. For instance, in French Algeria (whose settlement is covered in Unit 13 and whose decolonisation is covered in Unit 20), Europeans and assimilated locals (Arabs and Berbers who had both assimilated French culture and chosen to forsake trial by Islamic courts for personal law) were '*citoyens*', with full political rights and tried by state-salaried officials according to French law. Non-assimilated locals (the majority) were '*sujets*', lacked political rights and were tried by Islamic officials (for family and inheritance law) or under the *indigénat*. The latter law code allowed more discretion to officials.

The reason the above discussion may sound abstract is that it is difficult to say one colony was ruled by direct means, another by indirect. Colonial rule might begin with indirect forms of rule. Then, as the colonial state generated extra taxation, it could pay for more salaried officials, and so rule more directly.

Nor was one or the other approach better in itself. Direct rule promised quicker change and economic advance, but higher disruption. Indirect rule was cheaper and less likely to provoke opposition (see Figure 2.7 for indirect rule in

Malaya). Some saw the latter as a way of gently inducting 'traditional' societies into a 'modern' world, for instance by slowly 'modernising' established leadership groups, through advisers, oversight and the education of their sons. Schools for chiefs, or education for elites in metropolitan-style schools, were a core part of any 'civilising' project.

Figure 2.7   The first Malay Durbar (Ceremonial Meeting of Rulers) at Kuala Kangsar, 1897. Unknown photographer. Museum Negara, Malaysia. In Africa, India and Asia, European empires often exerted influence through local rulers, such as the princes who ruled about a third of the Indian subcontinent up to independence. Here British 'residents' and 'advisers' are seated next to the nine sovereign Malay sultans they 'advised', in what was sometimes termed 'British Malaya'. Note that some of the sultans (second row seated) retain 'traditional' Malay dress, while others adopt European dress.

Lord Lugard (1858–1945), after service in east Africa and Nigeria, famously rationalised a 'dual mandate', to modernise gently, while 'protecting' 'native' populations from over-rapid change. Hence, in early twentieth-century Nigeria, only the city of Lagos was technically a colony with its own representative assembly. The rest of Nigeria was divided into a protectorate of the north and a protectorate of the south. In the north, Lugard preserved the rule of the Fulani sultan of Sokoto and the emirs: a well-established Islamic system. In the southwest, the non-Muslim Yoruba city states provided indirect rulers. But the Ibo of the southeast were acephalous (meaning without higher level leaders), so the British 'invented' indirect rulers: the so-called warrant chiefs. In short, Nigeria had areas of direct and indirect rule, the latter under both 'customary' and 'invented' local authorities (Lugard, 1922; Buell, 1928, pp. 645–727; Nicolson, 1969).

Beyond the direct/indirect distinction, ultimate decision-making power could be vested in a single executive figure as ruler or governor, for instance the son or appointee of a central king. More likely, the highest representative of the metropolis would be bound to consult local interest groups, whether powerful merchants, creoles (local-born descendants of settlers) or indigenous populations. Typically, there might be an advisory or executive council, and sometimes a representative council: the former to make policy, the latter to make laws and vote on government policies. Within both, power might differ according to the balance between officials (in government pay or office) and non-officials (representing outside interests and without government office). Non-officials could be nominated in various ways: directly by the governor to represent specific groups; by specific groups such as merchants; or by election from general constituencies.

As colonies developed – meaning a narrowing gap between metropolitan and peripheral power and wealth – one of two tendencies was likely. On the one hand, power might be feudalised, becoming more indirect, with more offices and rights farmed out or permanently granted to prominent men. Alternatively, local elites (creole and indigenous) gradually achieved more representation in the colony's councils. The former tendency was evident in Spanish colonies in the Americas, underpinning creole revolutions from 1807 to 1824. The latter was evident in British settler dominions, where governors more and more submitted to **responsible government**. This meant the governor accepted an obligation to submit policies to votes in executive council, and executive council policies to votes in legislative assemblies. The British attempt to limit this loss of central power, by imposing taxes and trade restrictions without a local vote, precipitated the loss of the American colonies in 1783. Unit 19 of this course will show, by contrast, how successive grants of responsible government to the white settler dominions and India culminated in full self-government.

Now, having looked at types of colony and styles of rule, we are finally in a position to start analysing empires as a whole. What 'glue' or 'system' held together the core and these varied sets of colonies and styles of rule?

EMPIRES AS SYSTEMS

In this section, you will look at the 'glue'. First, you will examine empires as systems for binding together the core and its colonies. Secondly, you will look at empires as even broader international power systems.

Empires as systems: systems for controlling colonies

EXERCISE

Read Secondary Source 2.5 on the course website. The reason we are using the political scientist Alexander Motyl is that he offers a model that will allow us to visualise empires as systems. Read all the pages through once before starting to tackle the questions below. Don't worry if it seems complex; you will be guided to specific pages to answer the three questions that follow.

First: how does Motyl describe the relationship between the components of an empire, both in writing and visually? Read 'Concepts' (pp. 1–2) and 'Constructing empire' (pp. 3–4) again, noting in particular the figure on p. 4.

Motyl (p. 1) describes empire as 'a hierarchically organized political system with a hublike structure – a rimless wheel – within which a core elite and state dominate peripheral elites and societies by serving as intermediaries for their significant interactions and by channelling resource flows from the periphery to the core and back to the periphery.'

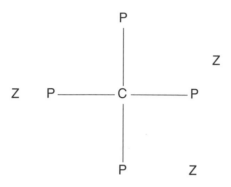

Note: C = core; *P* = peripheries; *Z* = nonimperial polities

Figure 2.8 'The structure of empire', from Motyl, A.J. (2001) *Imperial Ends: The Decay, Collapse, and Revival of Empires*, New York, Columbia University Press, p.16.

That quote sounds very complicated as text, but is clear when visualised as in Figure 2.8 above. In short, a number of peripheries have at least some categories of interaction, such as foreign policy or trade policy, channelled through one dominant core. They are not free to conduct these functions among themselves, or have to do so under conditions laid down by the core. Hence Motyl's description of a 'rimless wheel' with the spokes only joined at the centre. Note that this does not necessarily mean, for instance, that one empire's colonies would not trade with each other. The emphasis was seldom on controlling all trade, but rather on the core having control over trading rules or over the flow of key products. Alternatively, trade might be left free, and another area, such as foreign policy, be coordinated through the centre.

The answer and discussion above described the components in an empire, and their spatial arrangement. But what does Motyl, in Secondary Source 2.5, pp. 1–4, argue glues these things together?

Motyl does not mention the things we might first think of as the glue of empire – military force, common origins of settlers and metropolis, ideology, royal legitimacy, or distribution of patronage to local elites. He portrays empire as a dynamic relationship between core and peripheries, especially between their elites. For him, the glue is the way this relationship involves a sustained subordination of some aspects of the peripheries' internal or external policy to the core: what Motyl calls 'significant interactions'.

Now let's go beyond the immediate answer, and ask what the implications of Motyl's approach are. What 'significant interactions' each empire channels may differ, and we can differentiate on this basis. It could be periodic tribute from otherwise independent polities, or it might not include much of an economic aspect at all. For instance, for European maritime empires from 1500 to the early nineteenth century, the 'significant relations' they most valued were economic. In a system termed **mercantilism**, each metropole attempted to channel the most lucrative parts of its colonies' trade to Europe through the imperial centre. Hence Spain sought to channel American gold and silver to itself. Portugal's Estado da India channelled eastern spices to Lisbon, and Dutch and British East India Companies directed spice, tea, textiles and ceramic flows through Amsterdam and London. In theory, England's American colonies should have sent their trade to and from Europe through Britain, in British and colonial ships. This British mercantilist system, institutionalised by the 1651 Navigation Act, was only fully repealed in 1849. In the mercantilist model, empire existed primarily as the flows of directed trade along the spokes of Motyl's ~~axis.~~ wheel .

Of course, it would be an exaggeration to say there was an entirely 'rimless wheel'. It is virtually impossible to stop trade even in a few products seeping between empires at the periphery. But it certainly is true to say that these mercantile empires tried to control and pattern key parts of the trade between their colonies and Europe along spokes leading to a core.

Many theories of imperialism have been claims that the most 'significant relations' channelled along Motyl's spokes were indeed economic. Hence economic theories were once popular in explaining the 'new imperialism': the late nineteenth-century 'scramble for Africa' and for new tropical possessions. The Liberal J. A. Hobson's *Imperialism* (1965 [1902]) saw this 'new imperialism' as a deficit exercise, generating little new trade for high costs. He claimed it only profited particular groups. It was propelled by the greed of generals, aristocrats and professionals, and by capitalists needing to invest 'surplus profits'. That is, capitalists paid metropolitan workers so little that the workers could not afford the extra goods the capitalists could potentially generate from reinvesting high profits. Instead of paying higher wages to boost demand, these groups sought virgin fields abroad for the 'surplus investment'. For Hobson, imperialism was thus the selfish policy of a military–industrial–aristocratic complex, resulting in 'a debasement ... of genuine nationalism, by attempts to overflow its national banks and absorb the near or distant territory of reluctant and unassimilable peoples' (Hobson, 1965 [1902], p. 6).

Lenin's *Imperialism: The Highest Stage of Capitalism* (1916) made a similar case, emphasising the monopolistic habits of 'finance capitalists'. He saw the export of capital by them as a structural necessity if mature capitalism were not to destroy itself. Merged bank and industrial groups were supposedly producing a 'monopoly capitalism' by the late nineteenth century. They monopolised whole sectors of the domestic market, generating super-profits that could not be profitably invested at home. Hence between 1870 and 1914, as the transition to monopoly capitalism happened, each European country supported the search for new investment fields. The race for new areas became so frenzied that, in 1884–85, the Berlin Conference was called to regulate it for Africa. Some of you will have touched upon these events and the Berlin Conference in A200. The conference dictated that '**effective occupation**' was required before any area could be claimed: planting a flag was not enough. When the world was fully carved up by this 'new imperialism', European states then turned on each other to seek a redivision of the spoils in 1914, in the First World War. This Lenin saw as the apocalyptic end of capitalism in an 'imperialistic' war to redivide investment fields.

Much ink has been spilt over such theories. While it is true that economics must underpin empire to some extent – even if only by paying for armies (Kennedy, 1989) – such theories over-emphasise single causes. Only some empires, some of the time, have heavily prioritised any one type of wealth, as opposed to a mix of different types of wealth, and of status, security, emigration, religious conversion and cultural interchange. In addition, Hobson's and Lenin's theories fail on economic grounds. From 1870 to 1914, the majority of European investment and trade went to other European countries, or to now-independent settler empires and to India. In 1914, less than 5 per cent of European investment was in territories conquered since 1870.

Political

Economic

Military

Social

Cultural

It is just as convincing to argue that the 'scramble for Africa' happened for a very different sort of economic reason: namely that African countries were now more behind Europe economically than ever. Industrialising Europe and its neo-Europes so outpaced the rest of the world after 1750, that by the middle of the nineteenth century a cycle of improvements in industrialisation, medicine (quinine's use to prevent malaria was perfected in the 1850s), transport (steam ships whose efficiency multiplied by the decade from the 1820s, and which could penetrate up-river) and communication (the Suez Canal in 1869, telegraph cables) made conquest easier and cheaper (Headrick, 1988). Far more was passing between European and undeveloped areas, faster, and at less cost. The tropics were not seized as structurally necessary (Lenin, 1916), or because key elites (Hobson, 1965 [1902]) or gentlemanly capitalists, overlapping and intermarrying groups of financiers, aristocrats and decision makers (Cain and Hopkins, 1993) manipulated governments. But they were seized so rapidly because of far-reaching economic changes. Western industrialisation meant these African and Asian economies were now so small, in relative terms, as to be easily overcome by the wash from vastly larger and faster-moving European economies. Vast flows of emigrants, traders and investment from Europe and neo-Europes eroded weak peripheral governments. These flows sometimes precipitated crises. The increased levels of European investment and presence at the periphery then made European governments less reluctant to back the outrageous claims of local representatives (Hack and Rettig, 2006, pp. 39–72; Locher Scholten 1995; Robinson, 1972).

(out)

In short, economics and empire are natural bedfellows throughout our period, *(Hack)* but some specific economic theories do over-prioritise one type of flow along Motyl's spokes. That is, they over-emphasise only one type of wealth (as opposed to a variety of tribute, wages, investment returns, labour force and troop provision). In short, they indulge in gross over-simplification.

Motyl's model of spokes on a wheel is useful here. It suggests we are free to select a more sophisticated range of 'significant relations' as being most important in particular places and periods. One key question for any imperial system will always be: what flows or policies does it insist on coordinating through the centre?

Motyl's model may also be useful in explaining the weakening of empire. He argues that as the spokes or peripheries develop a rim – that is, as colonies start dealing with each other and third parties directly for significant relations such as trade rules, rather than through the core state – empire weakens. Its power to control flows of policy, information and wealth decline. This decreases its resources, while increasing the ability of peripheries to resist control: the benefit of empire declines and its costs rise. You will have a chance to test how far this is true in Block 5, 'Why do empires end?'

For now, however, we need to look at how Motyl attempts to use his model, to describe different types of imperial system.

1   How does Motyl describe the differences between the main types of empire?

2   What major divisions or types of empire does Motyl use his model to illustrate?

You need to use Secondary Source 2.5 again, paying particular attention to the figure on p. 5.

1   Motyl's approach to describing the difference between empires is spatial and diagrammatic. While not literally mapping reality to scale, he uses diagrams to show the interrelationships between components, like many transport maps, such as the London underground map. In this way, his model not only suggests we ask what 'significant relations' are channelled and how, but also provides a way of visualising different types of system.

2   Motyl uses this model to describe the differences between what most historians call maritime or seaborne (French, British, Dutch, Portuguese) and land (Russian, Ottoman, Chinese) empires. In his diagram, which follows (Figure 2.9), C is the core, and each P a periphery.

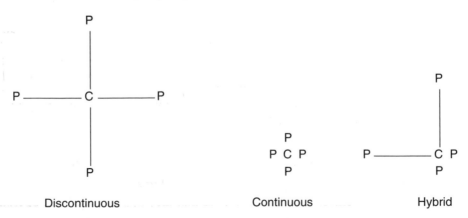

Figure 2.9   'Types of empires', from Motyl, A.J. (2001) *Imperial Ends: The Decay, Collapse, and Revival of Empires*, New York, Columbia University Press, p. 19.

While most historians would say 'maritime' and 'land' empire, Motyl favours 'continuous' and 'discontinuous'. Hence:

> As the defining characteristic of greatest relevance to us is structure, it makes sense to make structural variation the key to an imperial typology. One obvious structural feature is the length of the spokes. Some empires are territorially concentrated, whereas others, consisting of far-flung, even overseas, possessions, are not. That is, the imperial wheel can be small, with short spokes, or large, with long ones ...

> A second, equally obvious, feature is the number of spokes – that is, of core–periphery relationships. That number can range anywhere from two ... I term empires with few, short spokes *continuous* and those with many, long spokes *discontinuous* ... In general, continental, or territorially contiguous, empires tend to be continuous ... whereas overseas, or maritime, empires are almost invariably discontinuous. Empires may also be both continuous and discontinuous, or *hybrid,* thus resembling a 'noncircular' wheel. The Habsburg Empire was highly continuous, the British Empire was discontinuous, and the [Second] German Reich, with imperial possessions in Europe, the Pacific, and Africa, was a combination.

DISCUSSION

There are cases where use of continuous/discontinuous makes more sense than a strictly maritime/land division. For instance, Algeria (a French colony 1832–1962 and discussed in Units 13 and 20) was closer to France than Siberia was to Moscow. France viewed it not as an alien, overseas place, but as an integral part of itself. Parts of Algeria, notably the coastal regions, were made into metropolitan French departments in the middle of the nineteenth century, able to return deputies to the metropolitan French assembly.

On the other hand, Motyl's terminology might obscure something different about modern (post-1500) European 'maritime' empires. This difference lay not simply in them being discontinuous or 'overseas', but in their being transoceanic systems. They linked different continents, ecologies and economies, integrating these into politico-economic systems characterised by direct links.

For instance, before the advent of transoceanic European empires, spices were produced by means more or less unchanged over centuries. They were traded through a series of linked but separate economic actors, zones and polities as they went from the 'East Indies' (the eastern islands of contemporary Indonesia), through Indian Ocean intermediaries, to Ottoman Turkey, hence to Venice or Genoa, and from there to their final destinations. By contrast, oceanic empires meant that by 1700 spices could sail in one ship from the East Indian spice island of Amboyna to Amsterdam. By the eighteenth century, the so-called 'Atlantic system' also saw eastern textiles, cutlery and weapons shipped from Europe to Africa, exchanged for slaves bound for the West Indies, from where plantation sugar returned to Europe. This triangular trade of a new 'Atlantic world' was an example of maritime empires pioneering a first phase of 'globalisation', albeit mainly in high-value goods.

In the context of this first phase of 'globalisation', the likes of the seventeenth-century English, Dutch and French East Indies companies were proto-multinationals. 'Multinationals' in that they had property and operations in different regions of the world, linked into one company headquarters, and often pooled capital and risk, but 'proto-' in the sense that they were granted

Figure 2.10   Unknown artist, *View of Canton [Guangzhou] in 1822*, oil on canvas, 18.5 × 24.5 cm. Tropenmuseum, Amsterdam, 2034-1. Photo: Tropenmuseum, Amsterdam. The island of Jongsin-Seeluan is situated on the north side of the Pearl River. The *factorijen* (tradehouses) of eight Western countries were built here in the eighteenth century. The common Chinese translation of *factorijen* was 'Hong', but every *factorij* had a specific name; for instance, 'Hong of Justice' was the common name for the *factorij* of Holland and 'Peace Keeping Hong' was the common name for the *factorij* of England. Trade from these was not initially free, but rather had to be conducted with specified Chinese businessmen. These tradehouses subsequently burned down in the great fire of 1822.

monopolies of trade between their home country and prescribed areas. They were mercantilist rather than free-trade multinationals: merchants with arms and attitude, relying on monopolies and cannons rather than free markets (see Figure 2.10 on Western commercial interests in Guangzhou (Canton)).

Thus, while the largest land empires dominated the largest land masses and populations, and commanded the greatest resources until the middle of the eighteenth century (Darwin, 2007), it was the largest maritime empires that created a first 'globalisation'. Once these new empires had become established, they further boosted transoceanic shipping, and so made possible the transoceanic projection of metropolitan flora, fauna and culture to distant territories. Now, in the seventeenth to eighteenth centuries, empires could replicate the homeland in 'neo-Europes'. The years 1750 to 1850 saw growing maturity for many of these children of European maritime empires – the neo-Europes concentrated in temperate zones in South America, the USA, South Africa, Australasia, coastal Algeria and South Africa. The population of what became the USA alone ballooned from less than 2 million to over 23 million

1750 – 1850

between these dates. By the latter point, most neo-Europes had already asserted self-government.[8] It was the relations between Europe and the neo-Europes (plus perhaps India) that was the most dynamic aspect of the eighteenth to nineteenth centuries. This made the west increasingly 'a single economic space', creating the conditions for Europeans, for the first time, to assert global predominance from 1850 to 1914 (Clark, 1936; Darwin, 2007 p. 238).

Another reason for this dynamism, and for the suffering and destruction these neo-Europes caused, was that the European maritime empires were more radical in their impact than most land empires. Where land and continuous empires frequently sought to maximise revenue from existing social relations and methods of production – they did *not* necessarily seek much interference in the internal policy of peripheries – transoceanic empires introduced new crops, methods of production and social relations. Hence quasi-industrialised sugar production was transplanted from the North Atlantic Canary Islands and Madeira to the West Indies in the sixteenth century, with methods of plantation, slave labour and monoculture also transplanted to colonies such as Virginia. Transoceanic empires not only directly joined different world regions, they transformed the productive capacity of conquered areas.

Motyl does note this qualitative difference in Europe's transoceanic empires in another area. He argues that empires wrongly tend to be seen as involving the domination – political, cultural and economic – by one nation and its culture over peripheries. This makes sense, he allows, when dealing with nation states such as nineteenth-century Britain and France, where a core people shared citizenship and culture, and attempted to transmit elements of the latter in a 'civilising mission'. 'Cores that were nation states tended to make fewer concessions to the culture of the colonised, once established'. But, along with other historians of land empire, Motyl objects that imperial powers such as Russia and Ottoman Turkey were not, initially, nation states. These land empires viewed their core populations not as equal citizens, but as culturally diverse subjects of a monarch, divided by class, status, race and area. Hence empire did not, initially, mean one nation and its culture dominating others.
Dominic Lieven, a historian of Russia, writes that:

> In some cases pre-modern empires were also created by nations: Rome is the obvious example. More often, however, they were the creation of some variety of aristocratic, warrior elite whose sense of solidarity with subordinates even of similar ethnic origin could be anything from weak to non-existent. On the other hand these elites might well accept, assimilate or cooperate with the aristocracies of the initially peripheral regions of the empires. Many aristocratic empires exploited the population of their core territories more ruthlessly than

---

[8] For the same dates the figures of some core imperial powers are: Great Britain 7.4m to 20.8m, France 21.0m to 35.8m, Portugal 2.3m to 3.8m, Spain 8.2m to 15.5m and Russia 28.0 to 68.5m (Cook and Stevenson, 1987, p. 216).

the peripheral regions because it was politically safer and logistically easier to do so.

(Lieven, 2000, pp. xii–xiii)

In the case of China, Mongol and Manchu Qing emperors assimilated much of Chinese culture, and used the pre-existing imperial bureaucracy and Confucian codes. In short, land empires were less likely than mature transoceanic empires to attempt radical economic and social restructurings of local society, and more likely to assimilate to local patterns, or to assimilate local elites into their own system. They were also more likely to treat peripheries as protectorates or occupation colonies, relatively lightly ruled. With some horrific exceptions, notably the Third Reich, the initial destruction of conquest was normally followed by relatively restrained rule.

Peripheral elites might assimilate to the centre in many land empires, or develop an ability to operate in two worlds and languages, those of the centre and of the periphery. Ottoman Turkey developed 'patrimonial' relations with some local elites, by which the centre distributed position and benefits in order to retain loyalty. Other Christians, by converting, were able to pursue careers up to the top post of grand vizier. Hence what passed along Motyl's spokes towards the centre were troops, taxes, a tribute in children and loyalty, and what passed the other way were security, position and shares in tax revenue and other benefits. Land empires might manage their peripheries by patron–client relationships, and (as in British India) with relatively small numbers of centrally appointed officials, working through local officials or aristocracies.

Motyl's approach, then, gives us a way of representing different types of empire. Diagrammatically it distinguishes continuous/contiguous land empires from discontinuous/maritime empires, and both from hybrids. It also makes us focus on empire as a series of relationships, asking what passed along the spokes as domination, as central coordination or (as in patrimonial systems) as mutual benefit between the centre and collaborating elites.

So far, defining an empire has seemed reasonably easy: it is a metropole dominating culturally and territorially distinct peripheries, including the latter's external, and sometimes internal, policies. If a metropole has at least two colonies, it is an empire, and we can analyse it according to its particular portfolio of colonial types, its particular styles of rule in the colonies, and what significant relationships along its spokes it emphasises.

The results might be varied, and there might be debate about whether neo-colonies are really 'colonies', but for the most part we can be clear what is and what is not an empire. For instance, a power exercising extensive influence over other national elites might be hegemonic (overbearingly influential), but would not be an 'empire' unless it possessed, directed and governed colonies. But is it this simple?

Empires as systems: international power systems

EXERCISE

Read the following definitions of imperialism, and of empire at least a couple of times before tackling these questions.

1 How do their definitions of imperialism (Osterhammel) and empire (Lieven) differ from those given above?

2 What are the implications if we accept these definitions?

> *'Imperialism'* ... comprises all forces and activities contributing to the construction and the maintenance of *transcolonial empires*. Imperialism presupposes the will and the ability of an imperial center to *define* as imperial its own national interests and enforce them worldwide ... Imperialism thus implies not only *colonial* politics, but *international* politics ...
>
> (Osterhammel, 1997, pp. 21–2)

> [E]mpire is, first and foremost, a very great power that has left its mark on the international relations of an era. I also mean a polity that rules over wide territories and many peoples ... the most interesting and important empires have been those liked to some great religion and high culture, thereby leaving a major impact on the history of world civilisation.
>
> (Lieven, 2000, pp. xi, xii)

SPECIMEN ANSWER

Lieven and empire

1 These definitions differ from those that preceded in that they make sheer size and the ability to project power on a global stage necessary characteristics of an empire. Hence empire must involve a **transcolonial** system for the international projection of power. Lieven goes even further, and talks of empires including only those powers that had 'a major impact on world civilisation', preferably backed by a high culture or religion.

2 Osterhammel and Lieven are describing, perhaps even exaggerating, one aspect of empires. But in so doing they highlight a question we do need to ask: in what particular ways does each empire project power? Why is it able to overcome enemies even at great distances? The 'transcolonial' and 'international' aspect requires something bigger than the sum of all parts. These definitions suggest we should emphasise not just portfolios of territories, but the 'systems' or infrastructure, such as financial, labour and communications, which allow power to be projected, and grand aims and ideologies (free trade, universal religion, democracy), to be propagated worldwide.

DISCUSSION

What elements might constitute an international system of imperial power in this sense? Finance is one aspect; others include allies and associated auxiliary troops, marines, ships, aircraft, bases and military agreements that impinge on the sovereignty of host states. For instance, contrast the way Figure 2.11 presents the British empire – as a network of naval bases – with maps of the British empire in Unit 1, which emphasise territories. Organisational ability – a combination of knowledge, skills and practices – could also give an edge even where technologies were not greatly dissimilar: well-drilled professionals, for instance, being far more effective with muskets. Beyond these, power is more likely to prove durable if there are 'colonial' or transcolonial forces. This means the ability to raise forces or military payments from a variety of territories. Hence the British East India Company's Indian soldiers – **sepoys** – numbered up to 160,000 in the late nineteenth century, with less than 80,000 British alongside. Both British and Indian troops were paid for out of Indian taxes, and deployed as far apart as Hong Kong, Burma, Mesopotamia (Iraq), South Africa and Europe. French, Dutch and British empires all selected certain groups – often minorities – as 'martial races', favouring them and deploying them across their empires (see Figure 2.12). Land empires tended to demand levies, or payments, and in the case of the Ottoman empire even levied young Christian boys, who were trained as the famous – later infamous – corps of janissaries (Hack and Rettig, 2006, p. 8–38; see also 'The rise and fall of the Ottoman empire' in Unit 1).

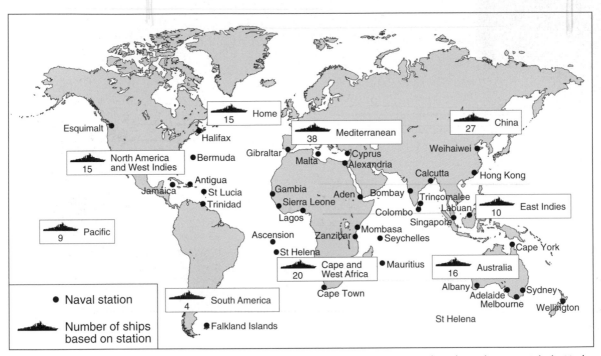

Figure 2.11   British imperial naval stations around 1898, adapted from Ferguson, N. (2003) *Empire: How Britain Made the Modern World*, London, Penguin, p. 245. We are used to mapping territories, but empire can also be thought of as an interconnected set of bases, treaties, alliances and forces which enable the projection of power.

This idea of power projection touches on another problem. The exercise of power is cheaper if it includes the ability to persuade others to comply without formal rule, and this touches on the controversial distinction between formal empire (dominion over colonies) and informal empire. By informal empire we mean domination of the effective sovereignty of other states without actual rule. Was the main strength of the nineteenth-century British empire (one of Lieven's examples of empire as great power) not continental swathes of territory (often red on the maps but underruled in reality) but a string of ports and military bases? Think of a different kind of map, with lines connecting ports, and circles scaled to military presence. Was not twentieth to early twenty-first century American influence likewise predicated on a power projection system that included a worldwide web of treaties and bases, together with long-range aircraft and carrier-based task forces?

Figure 2.12   Dutch Marechaussee in Aceh (present-day Indonesia), 1890s. Unknown photographer. Royal Netherlands Institute of Southeast Asian and Caribbean Studies, Leiden, KB 552. Photo: Collection of the KITLV, Leiden, The Netherlands. Indian sepoys, French Tirailleurs Sénégalais, Russian Cossacks and the colonial soldier in general, were crucial to imperial expansion and rule. This photograph shows members of the Dutch-raised Marechaussee, who have just stormed a stockade in Aceh. Companies of 12–15 men, with one European officer, one local and one European sergeant, were armed with European carbines (short rifles) and local short swords. In contrast to the more cumbersome regular colonial army, this allowed them to fight local-style to combat guerrilla resistance in jungle and hill terrain. But rulers also feared such troops might one day turn. In an attempt to guarantee against this, they tended to promote and favour minorities – such as India's Gurkhas – as so-called 'martial races'.

The classic statement of the case for informal empire was not based, however, merely on military might and bases, but on economic motives as well. Before 1953, many thought Britain had undergone a mid nineteenth-century period of 'anti-imperialism', after it banned slave trading (1807) and slavery (1834), dropped mercantilism in favour of free trade, and in the 1860s considered getting rid of some west African colonies. Hence the debate on why there was a 'new imperialism' after the 1870s. Gallagher and Robinson (1953) argued that, in fact, post-mercantilist British imperialism showed a continuity of motive in the 'official mind'. This focused on 'the imperialism of free trade' plus (after 1882) the linked protection of the Suez Canal trade route and its hinterland (Gallagher and Robinson, 1953; Robinson and Gallagher, 1961). The nineteenth-century British aim was to exert sufficient influence to ensure open markets and trade worldwide, and to protect investments. If an area provided open markets and security itself, this was best. If a treaty would do, fine. Failing these, however, the Royal Navy could be sent to intimidate or, as a last resort, an area would be conquered. The policy was one of 'minimum force' in the service of globalisation. As Gallagher and Robinson put it:

> Imperialism, perhaps, may be defined as a sufficient function of this process of integrating new regions into the expanding economy ...
>
> The usual summary of the politics of the free trade empire as 'trade not rule' should read 'trade with informal control if possible; trade with rule when necessary'.

(Gallagher and Robinson, 1953, pp. 5, 13)

Hence in the 'imperialism of free trade', Britain supposedly manipulated notionally independent South American countries as part of informal empire, using a series of financial, naval and other levers. The same could be said of British attempts to influence much of the Middle East in the early twentieth century.

But is such informal empire really empire? Or is it hegemony, that is, preponderant influence? Your own answer will depend on whether you adopt a 'hard' definition of a colony – it must involve the ability to direct internal policy and choose local leaderships – or a soft one – it need merely involve the ability to direct some significant aspect of another territory's sovereignty. Regardless of whether each component – formal empire, informal empire and hegemony – is 'imperial', imperial systems of power can mix all three. Table 2.3 below gives one model for distinguishing the categories.

Table 2.3   Imperial systems of power: a typology

	Peripheral government	Peripheral internal and external policy	Examples
Formal empire	Core controls local government formation, or which powers to delegate to whom in the periphery.	Core controls internal and external policy, with local participation limited.	British India. Algeria.
Informal empire	Core influences local government formation through indirect means, such as finance, protection.	Core influences limited aspects of policy, for instance concerning investment, or foreign policy, in collaboration with a peripheral elite it supports and which relies on the core for power, wealth or survival.	British and then US influence in parts of Central and South America, and in parts of the Middle East.

	Peripheral government	Peripheral internal and external policy	Examples
Hegemony	Core has no significant power or influence over local government formation.	Core influences external policy, often in collaboration with peripheral elites, who identify an overlap of interests and possibly culture, but who do not require core support to maintain power or wealth.	NATO allies of the USA, 1949–1980s.

Either way, the idea of empires as power projection systems that involve different types of relations of domination with a range of types of territory is useful. I suggest that we use the term 'imperial system of power' to describe the military–political–economic–diplomatic matrixes that project dominance on an international scale.

Taking all of our previous sections together, we can now summarise the most fundamental ways of differentiating imperial situations. Below, I represent domination as varying along two axes, those of direct/indirect and of **formal/informal methods of rule** (Figure 2.13).

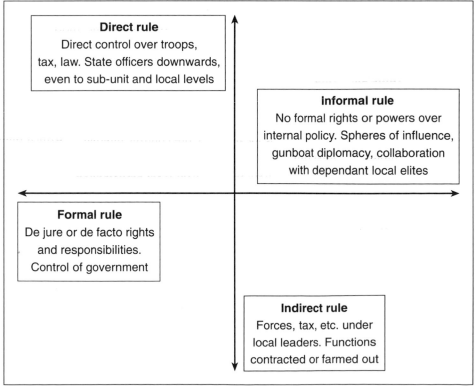

Figure 2.13   Types of imperial power. © Karl Hack and Tobias Rettig.

When we bring this all together, we have a series of tools for labelling, comparing and analysing empires, ranging from seeing them as portfolios of our six or more types of colony and varied styles of rule, to understanding how they map typologically, mix formal and informal imperialism, and construct global power projection systems.

CONCLUSION

Empire from 1500 to 1975 is such an all-encompassing topic, taking in empires early modern and modern, land and maritime, that any set of tools will be deficient. Yet though the task is impossible, my hope is that in trying to assemble a usable toolkit I, and you, have achieved three things.

First, we have some workable tools that enable us to talk to each other, and more importantly to disagree with each other, starting from a common language. You can now conceptualise empire as a core dominating a portfolio of different types of colony, using a variety of styles of rule, bound together by a wider system of power. You can label different types of colony in ways we will all recognise.

Secondly, I hope you take away an analytical approach to 'empire' and the imperial situation. This will involve being self-consciously aware of the meaning of the terms you use, and repeatedly asking how other people define their key terms. It also means using some of the tools from this unit to begin, however tentatively, to make comparisons across time and empire.

Thirdly, I hope you are ready to begin using the tools we have discussed to generate questions to ask about each empire and unit that follows. You might ask, for instance, what types of colony predominated in a particular empire at a particular time, and how this empire's treatment of them compares with other empires' treatment of similar types of colony. You might ask how the colonies were ruled, whether with preference for direct or indirect means.

You can go on to ask what 'glue' held each metropolis and its portfolio of colonies together. In Motyl's terms, what flows or key rules did the metropolis most seek to control: wealth, troops, loyalty, culture, religion?

Beyond this, you may sometimes be able to ask questions about what constituted an imperial system of power. Did this rest more on cultural links and blood ties between mother country and settlers or conquistadores, or on a military and fiscal system? What balance of formal empire, informal empire and hegemony was used? Did the empire construct transcolonial systems and forces, or merely use the leftovers from its mainstream navy and army to police empire? Block 3 on 'How do empires work?' tackles these problems head-on, with units on military, economic, cultural and bureaucratic power.

You can also ask questions about the nature of the relationship along the m–mr–p axis. Who were the main representatives of the metropolis in each colony? What was the nature of their relationship to the periphery, and downward to local subjects? Obviously, though the centre dominates, changes at the peripheries may sometimes be the motor for change, whether by collapse or resistance, and ideas can pass both ways. Throughout this course you will see references to three major types of influence on empires: metropolitan, peripheral and international (Darwin, 1991, pp. 4–7).

The tools you have so far, and these questions, will stand you in good stead when tackling later units. But you are not yet quite ready. First, you need one final set of tools: tools for analysing how culture, and individuals, interacted with empires. Equipping you with these is the job of Unit 3.

REFERENCES

Abernethy, D. (2000) *The Dynamics of Global Dominance: European Overseas Empires 1415–1980*, New Haven, Yale University Press.

Arneil, B. (1994) 'Trade, plantations, and property: John Locke and the economic defence of colonialism', *Journal of the History of Ideas*, vol. 55, pp. 591–609.

Bickers, R. (2003) *Empire Made Me: An Englishman Adrift in Shanghai*, London, Allen Lane.

Buell, R.L. (1928) *The Native Problem in Africa*, London, Macmillan.

Cain, P.J. and Hopkins, A.G. (1993) *British Imperialism: Innovation and Expansion 1688–1914*, 2 vols, Harlow, Longman.

Clark, G. (1936) *The Balance Sheets of Imperialism: Facts and Figures on Colonies*, New York, Columbia University Press.

Cook, C. and Stevenson, J. (1987) *The Longman Handbook of Modern European History*, Harlow, Longman.

Crosby, A. (1986) *Ecological Imperialism: The Biological Expansion of Europe, 900–1900*, Cambridge, Cambridge University Press.

Darwin, J. (1991) *The End of the British Empire: The Historical Debate*, Oxford, Basil Blackwell/Institute of Contemporary British History.

Darwin, J. (2007) *After Tamerlane: The Global History of Empire*, London, Allen Lane.

Doyle, M. (1986) *Empires*, Ithaca, Cornell University Press.

Ferguson, N. (2003) *Empire: How Britain Made the Modern World*, London, Allen Lane.

Fieldhouse, D.K (1982) *The Colonial Empires: A Comparative Survey from the Eighteenth Century*, Basingstoke, Macmillan.

Finley, M.I. (1976) 'Colonies: an attempt at a typology', *Transactions of the Royal Historical Society*, 5th series, vol. 26, pp. 167–88.

Finley, M.I. (1978) 'Empire in the Greco-Roman World', *Greece and Rome*, vol. 25, no. 1, pp. 1–15.

Gallagher, J. and Robinson, R. (1953) 'The imperialism of free trade', *Economic History Review, Second Series*, vol. 6, no. 1, pp. 1–15.

Hack, K. and Rettig, T. (eds) (2006) *Colonial Armies in Southeast Asia*, London, RoutledgeCurzon.

Hancock, W.K. (1940) *Survey of British Commonwealth Affairs*, vol. 2, part 1, Oxford, University Press.

Headrick, D.R. (1988) *The Tentacles of Progress: Technology Transfer in the Age of Imperialism, 1850–1914*, Oxford, Oxford University Press.

Hobson, J.A. (1965 [1902]) *Imperialism: A Study*, Ann Arbor, University of Michigan Press.

Kennedy, P. (1989) *The Rise and Fall of the Great Powers*, London, Fontana.

Lenin, V.I. (1916) *Imperialism: The Highest Stage of Capitalism*.

Lieven, D. (2000) *Empire: The Russian Empire and its Rivals*, New Haven, Yale University Press.

Locher Scholten, E. (1995) 'Dutch expansion in the Indonesian archipelago around 1900 and the imperialism debate', *Journal of Southeast Asian Studies*, vol. 25, no. 1, pp. 91–112.

Lugard, F.D. (1922) *The Dual Mandate in British Tropical Africa*, Edinburgh, William Blackwood.

Motyl, A. (2001) *Imperial Ends: The Decay, Collapse, and Revival of Empires*, New York, Columbia University Press.

Nicolson, I.F. (1969) *The Administration of Nigeria, 1900–1960: Men, Methods, and Myths*, Oxford, Oxford University Press.

Osterhammel, J. (1997) *Colonialism: A Theoretical Overview*, Princeton, Wiener.

Osterhammel, J. (1999) 'Britain and China, 1824–1914', in Porter, A. (ed.) *The Oxford History of the British Empire*, vol. 3: *The Nineteenth Century*, Oxford, Oxford University Press, pp. 146–69.

Robinson, R. (1972) 'The non-European foundations of European imperialism: sketch for a theory of collaboration', in Owen, E.R.J. and Sutcliffe, R. (eds) *Studies in the Theory of Imperialism*, Harlow, Longman.

Robinson, R. and Gallagher, J., with Denny, A. (1961) *Africa and the Victorians: The Official Mind of Imperialism*, Basingstoke, Macmillan.

Wallerstein, I. (1974) *The Modern World System*, vol. 1, New York, Academic Press.

UNIT 3
EMPIRES OF THE MIND

Paul Lawrence

AIMS

- To introduce you to the idea that empires have always been contentious, through a consideration of debates in England, France and Spain.

- To encourage you to consider the significance of 'culture' as a mechanism of imperial domination: a topic that is discussed in greater detail later in the course.

- To use four individual case studies as a means to debate the variable salience of race and class in the consideration of empire.

INTRODUCTION

The title of this unit is drawn from a speech made by Winston Churchill in 1943. While being awarded an honorary degree at Harvard University, in the midst of the Second World War, he declared that 'the empires of the future will be empires of the mind' (Garay, 1988). He made this comment at the end of a speech on the value of the English language, in which he advocated the spread of 'Basic English' (a kind of stripped-down version of English with only 650 nouns and 200 verbs).[9] The promotion of 'Basic English' around the world would, Churchill felt, help to disseminate English patterns of thought and hence have more effect than any form of propaganda ever could.

This quotation from Churchill is interesting in a number of ways. In the first place, it shows that (as a keen imperialist) Churchill was well aware of the significance of thoughts, ideas, propaganda and ideology in the maintenance of imperial rule. Secondly, of course, it seems to imply that, whereas prior to the 1940s empires had been structures of military might, political power and economic influence, they would in future be more subtle – based on the power of thought rather than outright conquest. Here, however, Churchill was wrong. While the 'big processes' that you have already encountered in Unit 1 – economic development, political will, military ambition and so forth – have always had an important role to play in the setting up and maintenance of empires, empires have also always been 'empires of the mind'.

What I mean by this is that it is impossible to understand empires without considering how those involved thought about them. While the first two units of the course have given an overview of empires in the *longue durée*, and equipped you with some of the tools you need to analyse them, many of the

---

[9] Basic English was developed by Charles Ogden during the late 1920s to serve as a universal language, along much the same lines as Esperanto and the other artificial languages developed between 1875 (Volapük) and 1922 (Novial).

most interesting questions about empires are not factual or theoretical. What, for example, did the people involved in empires, from both above and below, actually *think* about them? How were empires experienced at different times and in different places? This unit will give you an introduction to some of the perceptions, views and experiences of empire – both from the top and the bottom – that you will encounter later in the course.

In the first section of this unit, you will learn that empires have always been contentious. Debates about their moral value and economic worth have been widespread. In the second section, we will consider public perceptions of empires. Again, these have varied considerably. At certain points in time, for example, there seems to have been a lot of public support for the British empire; at other times, there was far less. Historians have also debated how much the home populations of imperial nations knew about their country's empire. Part of the reason for this debate is that there is, of course, no single 'experience of empire'. Individuals participated in empires in various ways, and opinions of empire were often determined by the success or failure of an individual's own imperial endeavours. This is equally true of those on the receiving end of an empire – the members of colonised countries. Hence, the third section of the unit will consider some individual experiences of empire, and assess just how useful they can be to the study of imperial history.

" DEBATING EMPIRE "

You may perhaps be familiar with the often-quoted epithet that England, or rather the English, acquired their empire 'in a fit of absence of mind'. Do you, however, know the origins of the idiom? The phrase is drawn from *The Expansion of England*, a series of lectures published by the Cambridge University historian Sir John Seeley in 1883.[10] The book was so popular that it sold more than 80,000 copies in two years, and was reprinted 10 times before 1899. For those of you unfamiliar with the world of academic publishing, this is *extremely* unusual, and perhaps helps to account for the ubiquity of some of Seeley's ideas. The phrase itself, however, is often used rather uncritically by those who wish to imply that England's acquisition of an empire was somehow haphazard and unplanned – 'nothing to do with me, guv; I've no idea how that got there!' as Bernard Porter puts it (Porter, 2004, p. xviii).

EXERCISE

Because Seeley's phrase crops up in so many publications, I would like you quickly to read a few pages from the original *Expansion of England* (Primary Source 3.1, available on the course website). Read this excerpt and consider the following question. What is the main point Seeley is making here about the British and their empire? You should allow 20 minutes for this exercise.

---

[10] For more information on John Seeley, see his entry in the *Oxford Dictionary of National Biography*, available online from the Open University library website. There is a link directly to the dictionary on the course website. As you study the course, you will find entries relating to most British individuals mentioned.

Seeley's remarks about the English acquiring their empire 'in a fit of absence of mind' have often been misunderstood. They are frequently quoted as meaning that the British empire was assembled without conscious design, almost as a by-product or side-effect of various wars, political rivalries and economic developments. In fact, as becomes obvious even from this short extract, far from purporting to explain the causes of British expansion overseas, this sarcastic remark was referring to the contemporary neglect of imperial history in the public psyche. Seeley felt that there was not enough recognition of the empire and its place in the development of domestic English history, and he aimed in his course of published lectures to imbue a sense of future purpose and pride in England's imperial possessions.

Froude does the same but distinguishes between

S.A. and Australia

A number of other points are worth noting about Seeley's *Expansion of England*, not all of which are apparent from the extract you have just considered. In the main, Seeley's investigation into the empire can be characterised as 'justificatory' or perhaps even 'celebratory'. Clearly, for Seeley, the empire was a 'good thing', both for the British and for those they ruled. He sought, for example, to justify English rule in India as beneficial to Indians themselves, and as something relatively unobtrusive – a contention now strongly refuted by many historians (see, for example, Dirks, 2006). He also sought to shape future policy through his reading of the past. He made a distinction between self-governing settler empire (not really empire at all, he claimed) and dependencies proper. Arguing that 'since the future grows out of the past, the history of the past of England ought to give rise to a prophecy concerning her future', he advocated a form of 'imperial federalism', and sought the integration of white settler colonies into a 'Greater Britain' (Seeley, 1895, p. 2).

Thus, while Seeley did not believe that the English had acquired an empire by accident, he did imply that the expansion of England was something that had happened without much conscious recognition or reasoned debate. But was this really the case? Here's a clue – the short answer is 'no'. As we will see, the subject of empire has always been one of heated intellectual debate, both in England and elsewhere. In this section of the unit we will consider just a few of the many intellectual, philosophical and political debates that empires have inspired, starting with some examples from the British case, and then moving further afield. In the main, debates about and within empires have historically revolved around the questions 'Are empires (in the abstract) a good or a bad thing, morally speaking?' and 'Is it a good idea for our country to have an empire?'

Wider Significance of ~~Imperialism~~

(+ where Froude's sympathies lie.)

British debates about empire

Throughout the history of the British empire, there have been debates about its moral value and economic utility. At all times, arguments have been made both for and against. It has never been the case that intellectual opinion was either wholly in favour of, or wholly opposed to, the idea of empire. However, it is possible to argue that, at different times, the strength of opinion in favour of (or against) the imperial project has waxed and waned. For example, as you know from Unit 1 (and as you will find out in more detail in Block 2), the seventeenth century was the period during which imperial expansion began in earnest for England, with the development of what is often referred to as the 'first empire' towards the end of the century.[11] This 'first' empire was primarily an Atlantic one, based on North America and the West Indies, which lasted until the American War of Independence (1776–83). It is usually depicted both as a slave-based 'plantation' empire, producing high-value commodities (such as sugar and tobacco) and as an empire of British settlement overseas. Despite some voices raised against, it is probably fair to say that justificatory arguments (such as those of Locke mentioned in Unit 2) were the norm during this period. However, by the time of the American War of Independence – and particularly in its aftermath – very different types of debate were beginning to emerge. As Sankar Muthu notes:

> in the late eighteenth century, a number of prominent European political thinkers attacked imperialism, not only defending non-European peoples against the injustices of European imperial rule, as some earlier modern thinkers had done, but also challenging the idea that Europeans had any right to subjugate, colonize, and 'civilize' the rest of the world.

(Muthu, 2003, p. 1)

In Britain, anti-imperial arguments were advanced by some of the foremost thinkers of the period, often intertwining the themes of the morality of empire, and its cost/benefit. A good example of this is provided by the writings of the political economist and moral philosopher Adam Smith (*c.*1723–1790), who criticised European empires for violating **natural rights**, for the injustices they wrought on colonised peoples and, additionally, for the disastrous economic, political and cultural effects they had on the conquering nations.

Smith was an extremely influential figure in late eighteenth-century thought. His work laid the foundations for the modern discipline of economics, and *The Wealth of Nations* (one of the most significant works of economics ever published) is indelibly linked to the defence of the free market and capitalism. However, he was also one of the eighteenth century's most innovative and sophisticated theorists of societal development.[12] Smith believed that modern, commercial societies (such as that of England at the time) enabled the best possible mode of living for citizens. However, as Jennifer Pitts has argued, he also 'articulated a moral and social theory that was broad-minded in its analysis of unfamiliar societies and practices and careful to avoid presumptions of European cultural or moral superiority' (Pitts, 2005, p. 25). Essentially, Smith outlined a theory of progress that delineated a number of stages of advancing sophistication through which societies would pass. This type of

---

[11] Although the 'planting' of Ireland, which some historians now see as a forerunner of American colonisation, had taken place during the sixteenth century (Marshall, 1999, p. 45).

[12] You can find out more about Smith's life and work by following the link to the *Dictionary of National Biography* on the course website.

thinking was common to many apologists of empire. However, Smith (unlike many others) felt that the change from one stage to another was a complex thing that could not be imposed. In other words, empire could not be justified as bringing a higher stage of development to savages. He also (again, unusually) did not seek to rank societies. While European societies might be more 'advanced' according to his ideas, they were not necessarily 'superior'. A subtle point, but a vital one.

Smith also objected to British imperial endeavours on sophisticated economic grounds, believing that the colonial trade monopoly led to England's economic system being unbalanced and inefficient (see Figure 3.1). His identification of the first British empire with a system of commercial regulation has been extremely influential in framing the subsequent historiography. The extract reproduced below gives a flavour of these debates. On the operation of tariffs (taxes) to ensure favourable rates of trade for the metropole with the colony, for example, he argued:

> The exclusive trade of the mother countries tends to diminish, or, at least, to keep down below what they would otherwise rise to, both the enjoyments and industry of all those nations in general, and of the American colonies in particular. It is a dead weight upon the action of one of the great springs which puts into motion a great part of the business of mankind. By rendering the colony produce dearer in all other countries, it lessens its consumption, and thereby cramps the industry of the colonies, and both the enjoyments and the industry of all other countries, which both enjoy less when they pay more for what they enjoy, and produce less when they get less for what they produce. By rendering the produce of all other countries dearer in the colonies, it cramps, in the same manner the industry of all other countries, and both the enjoyments and the industry of the colonies. It is a clog which, for the supposed benefit of some particular countries, embarrasses the pleasures and encumbers the industry of all other countries; but of the colonies more than of any other.
>
> (Smith, 1776, vol. 4. ch. 7, p. 95)

Thus Smith published an array of detailed arguments opposing the British empire as it existed during the eighteenth century. It is possible to dissect such writings in purely intellectual terms, to view them perhaps as an offshoot of the development of Enlightenment rationalism – the main tenets of which we might summarise as the belief that human beings deserved more freedom than they actually had, that men were intrinsically rational beings and that they should not be subject to tyrannical monarchic, political or social constraints. Smith was certainly a key Enlightenment figure. However, to view the anti-imperial writings of the late eighteenth century purely in intellectual terms would be a mistake. It is impossible to divorce ideas from their social context (although it would undoubtedly make their analysis much simpler if we could). This is something for you to consider whenever you encounter intellectual writings on empire during the course. It seems more than likely that

Figure 3.1   Gold ducat of the Dutch East India Company (VOC), 1755, gold, diameter: 23 mm, weight: 3.47 g. British Museum, London, CM 1839, 1123.3. Photo: © The Trustees of the British Museum. During the early modern period, companies like the VOC and the British East India Company became monopolistic trade organisations (as you saw in Unit 1) – something that Smith, among others, objected to. In addition, both were given powers of rule over their dominions and both issued coins for trade. The coin pictured here bears the VOC monogram and the date of issue.

international events and the fortunes of various colonial endeavours had an impact on Smith (and other authors who opposed aspects of the British empire for different reasons), and hence informed their thinking. Specifically, the loss of the American colonies (and the growth of new, different colonies in Asia) meant that theorists could no longer consider the British empire 'free' – that is, constituted primarily from willing colonists arriving in largely empty territory. The notion of empty territory being fair game employed as a justification in earlier periods became unavailable. Thus, as Pagden claims, 'by 1800 most of enlightened Europe had been persuaded that large-scale overseas settlement of the kind pursued, in their different ways, by Spain, Britain and France in the Americas could ultimately be only destructive to the metropolis itself' (Pagden, 1995, p. 6).

However, if we jump forward in time a little to the latter half of the nineteenth century, we find many of the same debates over the cost and moral value of British empire still being played out. At this time however, it is probably fair to say that, while both positive and negative views of the British empire are available, the positive are in the ascendancy (perhaps unsurprisingly, given that the empire was arguably at the apogee of its power and range at this point). One of many intellectuals with firm views about the British empire was John Stuart Mill (1806–1873).

The case of Mill is particularly interesting. A philosopher, political economist and member of parliament, Mill was one of the most influential liberal thinkers of the nineteenth century, and was closely associated with such liberal causes as the emancipation of women. Much of his work reflected on the optimum way to achieve the maximum amount of freedom for the most people. In

On Liberty (Mill, 1859), for example, one of his most widely read works, he outlined a persuasive case for individual freedom, contending that 'over himself, over his own body and mind, the individual is sovereign'. He also delineated here his famous 'harm principle': that people should essentially be able to do whatever they liked, as long as it did not harm anyone else. However, as Pitts notes

> in *On Liberty,* most famously, Mill qualified his scheme for minimal interference in individuals' lives by the state or by other people with the proviso that it was not to apply to children or young persons, but 'only to human beings in the maturity of their faculties'.

(Pitts, 2005, p. 143)

This qualification was important, as Mill (a long-time employee of the British East India Company) further claimed that the members of societies less well-developed than those of Europe could be said to be intellectually immature. Hence, the rules he outlined did not apply. Further, he argued, it could actually be beneficial to members of these less well-developed colonial societies to be brought into an empire, as this would speed their intellectual and social development. In other words, as far as Mill was concerned, progressive despotism was acceptable in the case of 'savages'. In other works, too, he elaborated on this theme. In his *Considerations on Representative Government* (1861), for example, he again outlined his belief in a 'hierarchy' of nations and his contention that 'less-civilised' nations (such as India) would benefit from rule by higher nations such as the English.

Mill also made some quite sophisticated economic and political arguments in favour of the British empire. Essentially, his economic arguments revolved around a belief that the settler colonies served as a market for British capital and as suppliers of cheap agricultural products. His political arguments, boiled down, were that imperialism increased Britain's power and prestige and, because England was the most civilised nation on earth, this state of affairs necessarily increased the sum of human happiness (Sullivan, 1983). He thought that international free trade also promoted intellectual commerce between nations and a more pacific 'international society'.

Thus, by the time we near the end of nineteenth century (back, in fact, to the publication of Seeley's *Expansion of England* in 1883) it is readily apparent that the current of intellectual opinion was again largely, although obviously not entirely, in favour of the maintenance of imperial prestige. As already noted, Seeley's *Expansion of England* in fact sought to recast the preceding several centuries of English history as primarily informed by gradual imperial expansion. Looking back from this point, we can thus trace, in the English/ British context, a series of fluctuating debates about empire. A variety of views were expressed at all times, but uncertainty and pride were in the ascendant at different points. Such debates were not, of course, unique to the British Isles.

Spanish and French debates about empire

Spain had an extensive early modern empire. You will learn more about its origins in Unit 4, but, as you already know from Unit 1, the Spanish empire was the first truly global empire, and one of the biggest in history. As one might expect, such an undertaking generated considerable pride on the part of influential Spaniards. However, it also produced some formidable opposition. Bartolomé de Las Casas (1484–1566), for example, was a Dominican priest and a New World colonist himself. He was galvanised into opposition to Spanish expansionism by witnessing 'the boldness and the unreason of those who count it as nothing to drench the Americas in human blood and to dispossess the people who are the natural masters and dwellers in those vast and marvellous kingdoms, stealing treasures beyond compare' (Las Casas, 1992 [1552], p. 7). His work *A Short Account of the Destruction of the Indies*, published in 1552, was a damning critique of the mass slaughter, slavery and torture involved in Spanish conquest (see Figure 3.2). Consider, for example, the following short extract detailing Spanish actions on Hispaniola in response to indigenous resistance.

> They forced their way into native settlements, slaughtering everyone they found there, including small children, old men, pregnant women, and even women who had just given birth. They hacked them to pieces, slicing open their bellies with their swords as though they were so many sheep herded into a pen. They even laid wagers on whether they could manage to slice a man in two at a stroke, or cut an individual's head from his body, or disembowel him with a single blow of his axe ... They spared no one, erecting especially wide gibbets on which they could string their victims up with their feet just off the ground and then burn them alive thirteen at a time, in honour of our Saviour and the twelve Apostles.
>
> (Las Casas, 1992 [1552], p. 15)

Although he always believed that the Spanish crown was the legitimate ruler of the Americas (because they had been 'donated' by the pope on condition that the Catholic kings would ensure the Christianisation of the Indians), Las Casas's *Short Account* (which you will encounter in more detail in Unit 4) was at least partly responsible for new laws of 1542 prohibiting Indian slavery and restricting the ways in which settlers could use Indian labour (although these were later suppressed in 1545). More broadly, it inspired many subsequent anti-imperial writers, and does at least provide evidence of significant debate over the imperial project from within Spain. That said, it should be noted that Las Casas's *Short Account* did not really do much to blunt the imperial ambition of King Philip II, who, in 1583, had a medal struck that bore the inscription *non sufficit orbis* (the world is not enough) (Parker, 2001).

In France, too, the whole notion of empire was similarly contested at times. At the same time as Smith was writing in England, around the end of the eighteenth century, similar anti-imperial sentiments were being advanced in France. Denis Diderot (1713–1784), for example, again drew on Enlightenment

Writers challenged the notion of 'empire' on purely intellectual terms.

Figure 3.2 R. Gaywood, frontispiece from Las Casas, B. de (1656) *The Tears of the Indians: being an historical and true account of the cruel massacres and slaughters of above twenty millions of innocent people; committed by the Spaniards in the islands of Hispaniola, Cuba, Jamaica, etc. as also, in the continent of Mexico, Peru, & other places of the West-Indies, to the total destruction of those countries*, London, J.C. for Nath. Brook. British Library, London, E.1586.(1.). By permission of the British Library.

principles of common humanity in denouncing European imperial ventures. Writing ~~the year after the French Revolution~~, Diderot argued that European explorers in 1780

> arrive in a region of the New World unoccupied by anyone from the Old World, and immediately bury a small strip of metal on which they have engraved these words: *This country belongs to us*. And why does it belong to you? ... You have no right to the natural products of the country where you land, and you claim a right over your fellow men. Instead of recognizing this man as a brother, you only see him as a slave, a beast of burden. Oh my fellow citizens!
>
> (cited in Pitts, 2005, p. 1)

Diderot is also credited with part of the production of one of the fiercest and most widely read condemnations of European imperialism – *A Philosophical and Political History of the Settlements and Trade of the Europeans in the East and West Indies*, published in 1770 by the French writer and editor of the periodical *Mercure de France*, Abbé Raynal (1713–1796). The *History of the East and West Indies* (as it is usually known) denounced European cruelty to indigenous peoples and blamed this on religious intolerance and the excesses of absolute power. Such was the impact of the work that, in 1781, Raynal was ordered into exile, only being allowed back into Paris in 1790.

EXERCISE

I would like you now to read an extract from Raynal's *History of the East and West Indies* (Primary Source 3.2 on the course website). This is from the section that deals with the French imperial endeavour. As you read, consider the following questions:

1   What is Raynal's view on expansion overseas?
2   What has, in his view, tainted the French imperial effort?

You should allow about 30 minutes for this exercise.

SPECIMEN ANSWER

1   It is apparent that Raynal is not necessarily opposed to the idea of imperial expansion *per se*. He notes at length the advantages that 'would have' accrued, both to France and to the inhabitants of Madagascar, had the French project been successful. These included a system of legislation that would have rivalled that of Europe, peace for the island's inhabitants and the introduction of 'civilisation' (brought about by intermarriage). He claims that it would have been best for land to have been purchased equitably from the indigenous inhabitants. Thus, noting that it would have been foolish to try to seize land by conquest, he seems to have envisaged a harmonious relationship of mutual advantage.

2   When considering the second question, however, it is clear that Raynal believed that this prospect of happy cooperation between French colonists and the inhabitants of Madagascar was destroyed by the actions of officials from the French East India Company, authorised by the crown to work there. They wasted money, were dishonest and behaved poorly towards the original inhabitants – so much so that 'they were massacred two years after'. Thus Raynal focused his criticism (at least in this passage of the work) on specific abuses rather than on the whole notion of imperial expansion.

So, there were clear criticisms of empire in France towards the end of the eighteenth century. Just as in England, however, other strands of thought were also in evidence – after all, why would Raynal's work have been banned were this not the case? However, again as in England, it is possible to discern a rise in more positive evaluations of empire in the period after around 1830. In the middle of the nineteenth century, French liberals such as Alexis de Tocqueville argued in favour of the conquest of non-European peoples. He, and others, believed that the liberal politics appropriate for European countries were not suitable in less-developed societies, where more despotic, paternalistic modes of rule were more apposite. However, as with Mill in England, Tocqueville's thinking on empire is multifaceted. He was certainly not simply an apologist for the domination of non-European societies. He had visited Algeria to learn about the colonial project at first hand, and was in fact considered an expert on the topic in the French Chamber of Deputies (the lower house of parliament). One of his main political aims was to sustain a liberal regime in France, and he felt that the involvement of the masses in the political life of the nation was the only way to guarantee the survival of the republican ideals of liberty, equality and brotherhood. To this end, Tocqueville advocated the maintenance of an empire as necessary for French internal political solidarity. In other words, he felt that the glory of imperial adventures would heighten national prestige and ensure the people of France participated fully in the maintenance of the Republic. Thus, while Tocqueville defended liberty and democracy within France, he was still able to support the crop burnings and other repressive measures undertaken by French forces in Algeria in the 1840s, claiming in 1841 that 'in order for us to colonize to any extent, we must necessarily use not only violent measures, but visibly iniquitous ones' (cited in Pitts, 2005, p. 203). His concern for French society and prestige trumped any concern for the rights of indigenous peoples. In the end, France held on to Algeria until 1962. The Algerian War of Independence and French decolonisation from North Africa will be addressed in one of the final units of the course.

In summary, I would like to recap on two important points that I hope have become apparent from this brief sketch of changing debates about empire. First, 'empire' has always been a contested subject. As far as intellectual and political debates (often entwined) are concerned, there was never a consensus one way or the other – either wholly in favour or entirely against. Contrary to Seeley's maxim, the topic of empire is one on which intellectuals and thinkers of all hues have historically expended much time and thought debating. The second point to note is that some awareness of the debates conducted about empires is vital to you, as students of empire. Debates such as those outlined above informed the context of imperial expansion (and often provided vital justification). Without a broad understanding of what people where thinking and debating at the time, it is impossible to understand the course of imperial development.

However, you might at this point be saying 'Hold on a minute, isn't this all a bit highbrow?' Some of you might perhaps be thinking 'So what if a lot of intellectuals got steamed up about the notion of empire? You've already told us that many had very little traceable impact on anyone in power. What about the man or woman on the street? What did ordinary people think about empires? Did they even care?' These are valid questions – which raise a number of interesting points about the historiography of empire. Traditionally speaking, the historiography of empire (at least until the middle of the twentieth century) was focused on constitutional and political events, and on decisions taken in the metropole and their effects overseas. However, in the latter part of the twentieth century, just when some thought that imperial history might be fading away and losing its relevance, there was a sudden rise in interest in the cultural facets of imperial history. In particular, historians began to consider the role of empire in metropolitan culture and, more broadly, to focus on the analysis of empires themselves as cultural phenomena, rather than as simply bureaucratic or military structures. We will explore some of these ideas in a bit more detail in the following section.

EMPIRES AND POPULAR CULTURE

The early professional historiography of the British empire (for we will again consider Britain first, before moving on to some comparative examples) was not particularly concerned with notions of popular culture as we would now understand the term, or with the broader impact of the empire at home. A lot was written about the empire during the period 1850–1950, but much of this was largely empirical, being based on observable facts and direct personal experience, and often very technical. On subjects as diverse as ethnography and forestry, books tended to be written by those working in official capacities within the empire. Moreover, as far as works on the *history* of the British empire are concerned, again there were close links between those involved in running the empire and the writing of its history. Partly because the empire was still a fact of contemporary life at the time, and partly because of a dearth of historians willing to write about colonial matters, there were often close links between scholarly and political approaches to the empire (Howsam, 2005). For example, Lionel Curtis, who held the Beit Lectureship in the History of the British Commonwealth at Oxford from 1912, was a member of the Round Table movement – a society dedicated to the strengthening and eventual unification of the British empire. Similarly, Reginald Coupland, Beit Professor at Oxford from 1920, sponsored the Ralegh club – an undergraduate society that debated colonial issues. From this, Coupland sought to recruit the best Oxford students into the service of the empire, and indeed he himself worked in a 'semi-official' capacity as a member of a government commission on Palestine (Louis, 1999, p. 24). Thus, the historiography of the British empire was intimately linked to the practice and politics of empire in the first half of the twentieth century and consequently, as Simon Potter has argued, 'was seldom discussed in a dispassionate manner' (2000, p. 1). Writing on the British empire during the first half of the twentieth century was thus very much focused on what we might now call the 'formal' empire – the visible political and economic structures of governmental dominion.

However, during the latter half of the twentieth century, just when some were thinking that imperial history might fade away, losing its relevance with the passing of the empire, a number of historians developed new approaches to the study of imperial history. These looked at issues other than the diplomatic, legal, political and economic factors hitherto seen as significant; an example is the pioneering work of Robinson and Gallagher on the concept of 'informal empire', which you encountered in Unit 2. However, the trend that concerns us first here is the growing interest at that time in the idea that empire was not just something which happened 'over there', but had a significant formative effect on British culture during the nineteenth and early twentieth centuries. In other words, in the latter half of the twentieth century, historians began increasingly to be interested in the question we posed in the preceding section of the unit – 'What did ordinary people think about empires?'

Popular perceptions of the British empire

One of the foremost names in this field is that of John MacKenzie. In both his own research, and as an editor of the 'Studies in Imperialism' series produced by Manchester University Press, he has sought to expound on the idea that 'imperialism as a cultural phenomenon had as significant an effect on the dominant as on the subordinate societies' (MacKenzie, 1989, p. i[13]). MacKenzie and a number other historians have argued that, as a mass-produced, commercial popular culture developed in Britain during the late nineteenth century, images of empire (such as in Figure 3.3) wormed their way into the fabric of British cultural life, bringing with them certain attitudes towards those from the colonies. MacKenzie argued that such images, and also similar cultural markers, could be found in a wide range of places – including children's literature, school textbooks, the cinema, music-hall songs, games and recreational pursuits. Moreover, rather than ending with the First World War, as scholars had often previously assumed, this popular enthusiasm for imperialism continued into the interwar period (MacKenzie, 1989). Perhaps the best way to illustrate this type of history and this type of cultural focus is with a concrete example.

EXERCISE

I would like you to read a chapter from a children's adventure story published in 1894 (Primary Source 3.3 on the course website). The book was entitled *Stirring Tales of Colonial Adventure* and the chapter is called 'Captured by natives – to be slaughtered on the morrow'. The story is set in the Australian outback. Consider the following while you read.

1   How are the indigenous aboriginal inhabitants of Australia depicted here?
2   What do you think the effect of such stories might have been on young English readers?

You should allow approximately 20 minutes for this exercise.

---

[13] This quotation is drawn from MacKenzie's preface to the Manchester University Press 'Studies in Imperialism' series.

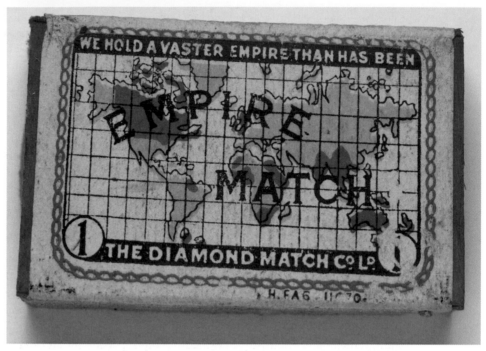

Figure 3.3   Matchbox produced by the Diamond Match Company Ltd for 'Empire Matches', early twentieth century. National Museums Scotland, H.MGP 42. © National Museums Scotland. Licensor: www.scran.ac.uk. As MacKenzie and others have argued, the empire wormed its way into popular consciousness in England through seemingly mundane routes, such as the design of a box of matches.

SPECIMEN ANSWER

1   Although initially cowardly ('a little more frightened of us than we were of them'), the indigenous aboriginal inhabitants of Australia are portrayed in this extract as aggressive and primitive. They are in some ways impressive. The author admits that he has 'always been accustomed to look down upon our aboriginal population, owing to the sorry specimens of the race I had seen in New South Wales', but goes on to note the agility and power of their dancing. However, that said, he does also liken this to a 'troop of drunken gorillas' (p. 4). Overall, the portrait given is one calculated to engender initial excitement but then a feeling of superiority. Clearly, despite the cliff-hanger ending to the chapter, the protagonists do escape and by portraying the indigenous actors in the story as fierce and savage, the courage and resolve of the white author in escaping is thus emphasised.

2   The effects of this type of writing on the reader are, of course, virtually impossible to gauge. There is little surviving evidence which can show how such material was received. However, what is clear is what the author might have intended the reaction to be. Aimed largely at the middle-class schoolboy, adventure stories such as these sought to inculcate a number of character traits such as loyalty, comradeship and confidence in one's own resilience and superiority.

DISCUSSION

While not so much in evidence in this extract, honour and fair play are also virtues typically displayed by the protagonists of adventure stories such as these. Overall, this type of literature can be seen as reinforcing for readers of an impressionable age the indomitability and superiority of the British (wherever they might find themselves). The white protagonists (generally male) in these stories usually acted in

a rational and humane manner, and compared favourably with the irrational and
savage behaviour of other peoples (and, often, the dishonourable actions of other
white Europeans). It seems likely that cultural artefacts such as these may have
played a part in persuading Britons to venture forth into the imperial arena, but
this is virtually impossible to prove. There is an online essay on the subject of
imperialism and British children's fiction available to you through the Empire
Online Database. A link is provided on the course website.

MacKenzie and others have concluded that the impact of the British empire on
the cultural life of the British Isles was significant. While interesting, and
certainly influential in the field, can you think of any ways in which work of
this type of public opinion and imperial culture might be criticised? One point
that might have occurred to you is that it is very difficult to be sure of the
reception of this type of material. It is one thing to spot particular imperial
motifs in books and on the stage, but how do we know that anyone actually
took any notice of them? In addition, there has been a debate on precisely how
'popular' MacKenzie's popular culture was. Bernard Porter, for example, has
claimed that 'whatever else it may have been, the British empire in the early
and mid-nineteenth century was not a "people's empire"' (Porter, 2004,
p. 115). Rather, he argues, the impact of empire, while greater during the
nineteenth century than previously, was still mainly confined to the upper and
middle classes. For Porter, there is no direct evidence that the working classes
supported the empire, took an interest in it, 'or were even aware of it for most
of the century' (Porter, 2004, p. 115). In addition, he has criticised historians
of the MacKenzie school over the issue of context, claiming that while it is
possible to garner plenty of individual cultural references to the British empire
if you trawl through thousands of newspapers and books of the period, these
need to be contextualised. For example, while there might be plenty of
discussion of the empire in newspapers, when the output of any *single*
newspaper is considered, it is really a very minor theme.

The critique of the MacKenzie school raised by Porter and others has been strong
enough to throw doubt on the idea that the British empire was enthusiastically
supported by most nineteenth-century Britons (see Figure 3.4). A chapter from
Porter's *Absent-Minded Imperialists* (Chapter 7, 'Culture and imperialism' –
Secondary Source 3.1) can be found on the course website. The role of
propaganda and ideology in the maintenance of empires is something that you
will consider in more detail in Block 3. We might simply note for now that many
historians currently believe that we need to have a plural understanding of the
experience of empire, which acted on different social groups in different ways,
and that 'the empire's impact, far from being forceful and aggressive, was often
subtle and unobtrusive' (Thompson, 2005, p. 241). Even when the British empire
was arguably at its apogee, it is hard to say for certain just how much impact it
had on the lives of most people living in Britain. It probably did shape the culture
of the United Kingdom in some fairly significant ways, but it did so unevenly
across time and place. But what about other empires during the same period? To
what extent does the debate outlined above apply elsewhere?

Figure 3.4   Frank E. Pape, *Smoke Empire Tobacco*, displayed 1929, poster issued by the Empire Marketing Board, 152.5 × 101.5 cm. National Archives, Kew, CO956/92. Photo: National Archives, Kew. The Empire Marketing Board was formed in 1926 to promote inter-empire trade. Is this evidence of the significance of the empire for the metropole? Or is the fact that a marketing campaign was required evidence of a lack of interest in the empire?

Perceptions of empire in France

In France, even during the Revolution of 1789, rebels in the plantation colony of St Domingue raised the question of whether the **Declaration of the Rights of Man** applied also to the colonies as well as to the metropole (Dubois, 2000, p. 22). But to what extent did France's empire really impinge on popular consciousness in mainland France? It was once generally accepted that, with the exception of a few brief stirrings of public outrage, in the late nineteenth and twentieth centuries the French empire enjoyed little popular support and generated no great mass enthusiasm. The French empire, so the argument ran, was 'even more of an elite affair' than the British (Chafer and Sackur, 2002, p. 1). It is certainly true that 'colonial expansion and the affairs of empire seldom became the preoccupation of the French' (Aldrich, 1996, p. 234). During the nineteenth century, a significant proportion of French expansion resulted not from official policy but simply from the enthusiastic or self-interested initiatives of French officials in the colonies themselves, and the French parliament was often indifferent to imperial expansion at the end of the nineteenth century. However, this picture has undergone considerable modification. Studies of the popular press show that papers such as the *Petit Journal* and later the *Petit Parisien* enjoyed wide circulation and were generally enthusiastic about empire (Schneider, 1982, pp. 6–8). More recently, Tony Chafer and Amanda Sackur have argued that, while there was never mass *enthusiasm* for imperialism in France, the public's perceptions of empire were more significant than previously believed.

For Chafer and Sackur, the significance of the French empire lies in its role as a key constitutive element of French identity for many citizens, particularly those on the right. The role of the colonies, they argue, was to bolster a belief that France was a great power, despite a mass of evidence to the contrary. That this belief in 'greater France' existed alongside a fantastic level of indifference and ignorance about what actually went on in the colonies is, for them, beside the point. What was important about the French empire in France was not its actual impact on the economic and political life of the nation, but rather the diversion it provided from the problems in these areas (particularly during the 1920s and the 1930s), and the role it thus played in bolstering a sense of pride in French national identity.

The idea of a French 'civilising mission' may also have linked the notions of citizenship and empire for many in mainland France. As Alice Conklin notes, while all European powers claimed to be bringing European civilization to their colonies, 'only in France was this claim elevated to the realm of official imperial doctrine' (Conklin, 2000, p. 2). During the latter part of the nineteenth century, the notion developed that the ideals of the Revolution (liberty, equality and brotherhood) and the finest elements of French republican culture would be of benefit to others, and hence should be exported across the globe through the imperial project. This 'civilising mission' became an important part of the French conception of empire, and again enabled public pride in the empire even if actual engagement with the empire was limited.

In fact, it is possible to argue that the empire wormed its way into French public consciousness in many spheres. In literature, novels such as Pierre Loti's *Le Roman d'un spahi* (1881) was 'a panorama of colonial life written in overwrought prose and packed with adventure, danger, sex and "local colour"' (Aldrich, 1996, p. 239). In the art world, too, a number of painters (including Gauguin and Matisse – see Plate 1.7 in the Visual Sources Book) drew on their experiences of the colonies. Colonial cinema was also an obvious vehicle for the transmission of imperial pride. One of the first pieces of film shot by a collaborator of the Lumière brothers in 1897 depicts French women in the Vietnamese province of Annam (Slavin, 2001).

Thus, in the case of France, as in Britain, there is an ongoing debate over the significance of empire to the metropolitan population. Certainly there is evidence that the empire impinged on popular consciousness in France, perhaps to the extent of shaping French national identity, but the exact extent of this influence is very hard to gauge. Moreover, as you may have noticed, these discussions of empire and popular consciousness are very 'metropolitan'. In other words, they are focused on what those in the home countries (France and Britain) thought about their empires. It is also important, of course, although rather harder, to consider the attitudes and opinions of the indigenous populations of the colonies. In other words, how was the French empire and its 'civilising mission' perceived by those on the receiving end?

Questions such as this are really very difficult to answer with any certainty. There are a number of reasons for this. In the first place, as we have just discussed, it is simply very hard to assess public opinion accurately. In addition, however, there is much less surviving evidence of opinion from colonial contexts. This is because the dominant discourse was usually provided by the metropolitan culture. In other words, those running the show published all the books and retained all the records. Also, while there was only one metropole, as we have seen in Unit 2, there were many different types of colony. Each, potentially, had a different culture and a different set of perceptions of the metropole, depending on their relationship with it.

There is, of course, quite a bit of circumstantial evidence about colonial perceptions of the French empire. France had many colonial troops in its armies, for example. Mostly volunteers, they fought and died in significant numbers for France. It seems unlikely that they would have done this had their perception of France been entirely negative. Similarly, the French empire required the assistance of large numbers of colonial employees to run smoothly. Again, would it have been possible to employ members of the local population if they had been entirely hostile to the empire? This type of evidence, however, does not really get us any closer to what colonial populations actually *thought* about the empire. For this, it is often easiest to turn to individual examples.

As one way into thinking about the French empire from below, we might consider the life and ideas of Frantz Fanon. Fanon was born in 1925 in the French colony of Martinique. He fought for France in the Second World War and stayed on in France after the war to study medicine and psychiatry in Lyon. Because of his schooling and upbringing, Fanon felt himself to be French. However, the racism he experienced as a black intellectual in metropolitan France, and more particularly the sense of difference imposed on him by those he met in France, led him to turn against French culture. As Ehlen notes, although Fanon wished 'only to belong, only to lose himself in Frenchness – in all those aspects he had been taught were superior and beautiful', in fact he was constantly made aware of his difference (Ehlen, 2000, p. 88). In *Peau noire, masques blancs* (*Black Skin, White Mask,* 1952), Fanon outlined his belief that in speaking French he had been coerced into accepting French culture. Because this culture was, at the time, inherently racist, he argued that he had been left with an unhealthy disjunction between his appearance (black) and his cultural consciousness (the 'white mask' he was forced to assume).

In the early 1950s, Fanon left mainland France to work in Algeria, and subsequently resigned his hospital post to work actively for the Algerian independence movement. In a later, more famous, work, *Les Damnés de la Terre* (*The Wretched of the Earth*, 1961), Fanon argued that to overcome the binary western cultural system (in which black was bad and white was good), an entirely new world order needed to come into being. This could not be achieved either by the former imperial powers simply relinquishing their hold on their colonies, or by the efforts of bourgeois intellectuals like Fanon – in both of these instances, the western culture itself would be bound up in the

"revolution"

solution. Rather, what was necessary was for the peasantry of colonised nations to rise up, violently overthrow their oppressors and forge an entirely new cultural identity for themselves.

Thus, Fanon's life story provides us with a useful insight into the way in which many in the colonies did indeed feel themselves to be French, but also highlights how the perceived betrayal of the promise of assimilation eventually contributed to the movements that resulted in decolonisation. In addition, however, thinking about Fanon can help us to consider the role of 'culture' and 'knowledge' in the maintenance of empire more broadly.

EXERCISE

I would like you now to watch Chapter 1 of the course DVD, 'Frantz Fanon'. This is an excerpt from a documentary film made in 1996 and is a mix of archive footage, interviews and acting. As you watch the montage, which provides an overview of Fanon's life and ideas, consider the following question: What can we learn about the significance of 'culture' as a mechanism of imperial domination from Fanon's life and ideas?

SPECIMEN ANSWER

Fanon left Martinique at the age of 18 to fight for the Free French forces in the Second World War. Martinique was, at the time, under the authoritarian administration of Admiral Robert (appointed by the leader of the Vichy regime in mainland France, Marshal Pétain), and Fanon felt he needed to help 'defend freedom' (as his brother puts it). Colonial subjects like Fanon were not coerced into enlisting. Rather, having been brought up to believe himself French, he was culturally conditioned to think of himself as part of 'Greater France'. On his arrival at the front, he thus felt disillusioned that the indigenous French 'peasantry' seemed not to share the same passionate ideals.

For Fanon, this illusion of being part of 'Greater France' was shattered further when he arrived in Paris to study medicine. The issue was not just the outright racism he experienced (as when the female patient would not let him examine her). Rather, as Stuart Hall notes, because Fanon had been 'formed in relation to France, with a French education' he arrived in Paris 'expecting to be accepted'. Instead, he found that he was seen as an 'other' – not French. In writing *Black Skin, White Mask*, Fanon thus detailed his experiences as a 'black man who has grown up wearing a white mask for himself'. In other words, he felt he had been tricked into adopting an alien culture as if it were his own.

Fanon then travelled to Algeria. When the struggle for independence began, he resigned his hospital position in order to aid the freedom fighters, and wrote another book – *The Wretched of the Earth*. He advocated an armed struggle for independence on the part of colonial peoples. As the interviewees on the DVD note, Fanon felt that the inhabitants of the colonies had been 'brainwashed' into accepting the culture of the imperial power. As Stuart Hall points out, Fanon believed that, if the imperial power voluntarily granted independence, the colonial subjects would be somehow still in the cultural sway of the oppressor. Only an armed conflict allowed the colonial subjects, at last, to assert their own cultural identities. For Fanon, therefore, the dissemination of the culture of the metropole (which encourages colonial subjects to identify with the imperial power) is a key mechanism by which imperial rule is maintained.

These discussions about the interaction between empire and popular culture in the metropole point us in the direction of some interesting broader debates about empires as 'systems of culture'. From the late 1960s onwards, some theorists began to think that the analysis of culture might be the key to understanding how empires functioned and sustained themselves. In other words, what was important when considering any particular empire was not really the military might of the conquering nation (which could not be exerted indefinitely) or the bureaucratic machinery of imperial rule (after all, there were only just over a thousand British men in the Indian Civil Service in 1901, supposedly 'controlling' a population of around three hundred million). Rather, so the theory went, empires could (and should) be analysed primarily as 'states of mind' or 'systems of knowledge'. In other words, what made the European empires of the nineteenth century tick was a complex set of beliefs in their own superiority, expressed through literature and popular culture, but also through science, medicine and the social sciences. The dominance of these 'systems of knowledge' also had the effect that colonised nations were unable to assert their own true identities, and were forced to play the roles assigned to them by 'western' culture.

"systems of knowledge"

One of the most prominent authors associated with this approach was literary theorist Edward Said, whose book *Orientalism* (1978) was perhaps the most significant precursor of what has been called 'the cultural turn' (simply, the development of ways of analysing societies that consider the role of culture). Said scrutinised a range of authoritative texts from (mainly nineteenth-century) European writers concerning the 'Oriental' (Islamic) world. As Thornton puts it, using close analysis of these texts Said sought to show how, 'through rhetorical devices, linguistic conventions, and narrative structures, these texts represented Oriental subjects in arbitrary, demeaning, and inferiorizing ways, while claiming to speak in the name of objective science and universal truth' (Thornton, 1999, p. 597). In other words, the systems of knowledge produced about imperial subjects were not (even in the case of scientific and medical knowledge) neutral. They were constructed in such a way as to legitimise imperial rule.

Consider, for example, the following excerpt from a speech given to the House of Commons by the former prime minister Arthur Balfour in 1910.

> Western nations as soon as they emerge into history show the beginnings of those capacities for self-government ... having merits of their own ... You may look through the whole history of the Orientals in what is called, broadly speaking, the East, and you never find traces of self-government. All their great centuries – and they have been very great – have been passed under despotisms, under absolute government. All their great contributions to civilisation – and they have been great – have been made under that form of government. Conqueror has succeeded conqueror; one domination has followed another; but never in all the revolutions of fate and fortune have you seen one of those nations of its own motion establish what we, from a Western point of view, call self-government. ... Is it a good thing for

these great nations – I admit their greatness – that this absolute
government should be exercised by us? I think it is a good thing.
I think that experience shows that they have got under it far better
government than in the whole history of the world they ever had
before, and which not only is a benefit to them, but is undoubtedly a
benefit to the whole of the civilised West. ... We are in Egypt not
merely for the sake of the Egyptians, though we are there for their
sake; we are there also for the sake of Europe at large.

(A. Balfour quoted in Said, 1979, pp. 32–3)

This is a fairly crude, brief example, but it does show the way in which a
particular set of assumed knowledge about 'the orient' was used to justify
imperial rule. 'Orientalism', according to Said, set up a category of 'the other'
in western thought. This 'other' was seen to be culturally very different from
Europe, but also inferior in some important ways. Hence, the west felt able to
decide both what the east was, and what it needed. As you can see from
Balfour's speech, he is working on the assumption that a clear cultural
distinction can be made between east and west and on the assumption that the
west knows what is best for the east. There is no need to ask Egyptians if they
feel they are better off under the British – the set of cultural beliefs informing
Balfour's speech makes this unnecessary. Arguably, this certainty that they
were 'doing the right thing' was a key component of the will to rule on the
part of the British and other imperial nations.

Said's work has been subjected to some sustained criticism, usually on the
basis that he claimed too much from sources, used them out of context or made
basic errors of historical method (Loomba, 1998, p. 48). Despite this, however,
his work inspired a whole host of subsequent debates about the significance of
culture and particular modes of thought in the maintenance of empires, some of
which you will learn more about in Unit 10 and throughout Block 4. It has also
inspired academics of many disciplines to attempt to unearth the social,
political, economic and cultural practices that arose in response and resistance
to colonialism, and to recover the cultures of those subjected to colonisation.
This field is normally referred to as 'postcolonial studies'. Postcolonialism also
considers the persistence of colonial forms of power in the contemporary
world. However, an introductory unit is not the place for a full discussion of
these interesting but (at times) dense and acrimonious debates. It will perhaps
suffice for now to note that a major focus of the recent historiography of
empire, and one you will encounter again later in the course, has been the way
in which systems of knowledge such as science and medicine frequently
functioned to sustain imperial rule rather than for the benefit of the colonised
population (despite the ardent belief of many of those involved to the contrary).

To summarise this section of unit, then, we might say that the role of culture in
empires is one that has attracted a great deal of scholarly attention but produced
rather less consensus. The role of empire in shaping metropolitan culture in
Europe continues to attract attention – with the focus of much research pointing
to the way in which different social groups related to empires in different ways,

and participated to very varying degrees. Broader debates within postcolonial studies also continue to be lively. One of the key questions still generating discussion is the 'agency' (or otherwise) of the colonised subject or 'subaltern'. To what extent do the individuals on the receiving end of an empire play an active role in subverting or accommodating the intentions of the imperial power? These are all themes you will encounter in greater detail later in the course.

However, something you may have noticed while working through this section of the unit is that many of the debates discussed centre very much on the *second* British empire (particularly from the nineteenth century onward) and on other *modern* empires. The early modern period, while certainly not ignored, is much less discussed in the historiography of empire and culture. There is, perhaps, a fairly obvious reason for this. The further back one peers into the early modern period, the harder it becomes to speak authoritatively about popular perceptions of empire and the diffusion of culture more generally. Not impossible, just more complex. The early modern period lacks some of the accoutrements of mass culture with which we are now familiar – newspapers, national education programmes and the cinema, for example. Given this, historians looking to uncover early popular perceptions of empire often consider individual accounts of imperial engagement, of which many survive. However, it can be hard to judge just how representative these individual accounts are. We have already considered intellectual debates on empire (what might be considered 'high culture'), and have just reflected on mass, public perceptions of empire (popular culture). The final section of the unit, therefore, will consider some *individual* experiences of empire, and how useful they might be in the study of empire.

INDIVIDUAL EXPERIENCES OF EMPIRE

In this section, I will ask you to consider the experiences of some of those participating in empires (both willingly and otherwise), as recounted by themselves. Empires are, after all, shaped by the myriad decisions and actions of individuals as much as by large-scale, long-term social and economic processes. We will assess just how useful one individual's perceptions can be for the study of empire, and will also use a number of individual case studies to explore further some current debates in the historiography of empire.
To start with, let us consider two imperial case studies: first, Joseph Pitts.

Case Study 1: Joseph Pitts (*c.*1663–1739)

During the seventeenth century, the Mediterranean was a focal point for European trade and rivalry. Following the acquisition of Tangier by Charles II in 1661, the English state built fortifications there and began an unprecedented colonial enterprise. However, English troops and settlers were forced to abandon the colony in 1684, falling prey to armies from Morocco. Hence, this case study is not of a Briton participating successfully in a British empire.

Instead, it is of a British subject falling prey to the imperial influence of another empire.

The Mediterranean at this time was under the influence of the powerful Ottoman empire. As Lynda Colley (2003, p. 35) notes, 'the Ottomans regarded the Mediterranean as peculiarly their own'. Fleets of corsairs from the Ottoman regencies of Algiers and Tunis (essentially state-sponsored pirates) preyed for centuries on European shipping, as did ships from Morocco, which was independent but under Ottoman influence. These corsairs also, at times, raided the coastal regions of western European countries – including Spain, Portugal, France and England – seizing goods and people to sell as slaves. Slaves were captured, for example, on the south coasts of England, Ireland and Wales. Thousands of British subjects were held as slaves in North Africa during the seventeenth and early eighteenth centuries. While some were eventually ransomed back by the government, many were not. Little direct action was taken as the English state was apprehensive of attracting Ottoman ire. As Figure 3.5 (which shows a white slave held captive by a turbaned master, bottom right) demonstrates, this was a topic of concern to the English public.

Pitts was a young cabin boy from Exeter, Devon. He was captured by Barbary (North African) corsairs and taken to Algiers (an Ottoman province) in 1678. Here he was sold, in chains, at a slave market. He was told by his captors that pink people of his sort resembled pigs – unclean animals. He eventually converted to Islam (under duress, he claimed), learnt Arabic and Turkish and became interested in the teachings of Islam. Despite this, he remained as a slave until his eventual escape and return to England in 1693. On his return he published his story, an excerpt of which you will consider below.

In contrast to Pitts, we can juxtapose a second case study – an individual with a very different experience of empire – the British slave overseer Thomas Thistlewood. In doing so, we jump forward in time to the middle of the eighteenth century and cross to the other side of the world.

Case Study 2: Thomas Thistlewood (1721–1786)

In 1750, Thomas Thistlewood, aged 29, the somewhat unsuccessful second son of a tenant farmer from Lincolnshire, arrived in Jamaica aboard the *Flying Flamborough*. In his luggage was a 'Marble cover'd book for a journal' (Burnard, 2004, p. 2). He was to record his experiences on Jamaica in thirty-six of these books, leaving a remarkable record of his life and times.

Within a few hours of arriving in Westmoreland Parish in the southwest corner of the island, he had been offered (and had accepted) a job as an overseer of slaves on a sugar plantation. At this time, Jamaica was very much a black world. Thistlewood only saw white people three or four times between November 1750 and February 1751. It was also a society ruled by naked force. Just a few weeks into the job, already convinced that his slaves were 'a Nest of Thieves and Villains', he gave one of them 150 lashes. In his first year he whipped nearly two-thirds of the male slaves on the plantation, and half of the

Figure 3.5   Frontispiece from Ogilby, J. (1670) *Africa, being an accurate description of the regions of Aegypt, Barbary, Lybia, and Billedulgerid, the land of Negroes, Guinee, Aethiopia, and the Abyssines,* London, printed by Tho. Johnson for the author. British Library, London, 457.f.13. By permission of the British Library.

women. Also during his first year on the island he slept with thirteen slave women on fifty-nine occasions, whether they wanted to or not. During his 'career', Thistlewood devised a system of cruel and unusual punishments (usually involving extreme violence and degradation) to ensure order on his plantation.

Thistlewood remained on the island until his death, seldom travelling far from the town of Savanna-la-Mar. Yet he certainly achieved more for himself in Jamaica than he would have done in England, securing moderate wealth and some status as a magistrate and a commissioned lieutenant. In his diary he faithfully recorded details of all his interactions with slaves. These were mainly of a violent, commercial or sexual nature (despite maintaining a stable relationship with a slave housekeeper, he slept with numerous other slaves – often describing these sexual interactions in Latin). He lived through Tacky's revolt of 1760 – when slave rebels attempt to eliminate the whites and establish an African kingdom – and the hurricane of 1780 – the most violent to strike the Caribbean in recorded history.

EXERCISE

What I would like you to do now is to consider some the experiences of Pitts and Thistlewood, as told in their own words. First read Primary Source 3.4 on the course website, an extract from Pitts's *A True and Faithful Account of the Religion and Manners of the Mohammetans* (1704). The extract includes two passages from Pitts's book. The first is drawn from the early part of the book, and details his capture and sale into slavery. The second passage, from later in the text, gives an account of his conversion to Islam. Next, read Primary Source 3.5 on the course website, an extract from Thistlewood's diaries, written during 1750s, which contains explicit detail of the brutal nature of the slave regime in Jamaica at the time.

As you read, try to critique the extracts by considering the following questions.

1   How reliable do you think they are as historical sources?
2   Given the very different circumstances of their production, can they reveal anything about the history of empires more generally?

ask these Q: in TMA 01

You should allow at least 45 minutes for this exercise.

SPECIMEN ANSWER

1   The reliability (or otherwise) of any historical source is a question of key significance. Both of the sources presented here have question marks over their utility to the historian (in this instance, us). Pitts's *Account* is the recollection by an individual of many outlandish adventures. We thus, of course, only have Pitts's word that many of the events actually happened. Moreover, even if we accept that the encounters related are broadly correct, it is still hard to judge how accurate Pitts's memory was, or whether he perhaps had hidden agendas in writing his book (see discussion below). When considering a published work, it is always hard to assess the extent to which authors, even of supposedly 'factual' works, tweaked their narratives (consciously or unconsciously) to appeal to their intended audience.

Thistlewood's diaries, of course, were not intended for publication. They are, in fact, startlingly candid about all aspects of his life – from the brutal (even sadistic) treatment of the slaves under his command, to his sexual relations with slaves (although he tended to render these passages in Latin). That said, the diary entries are also rather brief and, if anything, too factual. Little is written which indicates much about his motivations or personality.

2   Clearly, then, these extracts are very different from one another. One is public, the other private. One detailed, the other terse. Both, however, can tell us quite a lot about the British empire, if we interrogate them appropriately. When we also consider the background we have on Pitts, for example, it becomes fairly obvious that his account of his capture and experience as a slave can be used as evidence of how tentative British power was at the time. On a deeper level, his obvious fascination with certain aspects of Islamic culture demonstrates that individuals caught up in the ebb and flow of imperial influence did not always engage with empires as we might at first assume. Far from acquiescing to the role of powerless captured subject, Pitts's conversion to Islam, knowledge of the languages of the region and eventual escape to England demonstrate the agency of individuals in shaping their own destinies, regardless of context.

Thistlewood's diary is also very much indicative of its time, in that it demonstrates clearly the brutal and degrading nature of both slavery and imperial rule in the West Indies. This region was immensely profitable for the British, but the diary entries reveal the price paid for this wealth by non-white participants.

DISCUSSION

As you may have guessed from the tone of the latter part of the Pitts extract, his book was in part a justificatory account of his experiences. In other words, it would appear he was not simply seeking (despite his assertions in the preface) simply to give a factual account of his travels. Rather, because conversion away from Christianity was such a serious matter in the seventeenth century, he wrote it 'to justify the Algerian segment of his life to his Exeter non-conformist neighbours' (Colley, 2003, p. 123). When considering any historical source intended for publication, the impression the author might have wished to give the reader is of crucial significance.

While I do not expect you to be able to read much more into these extracts at this stage of your studies, these do in fact raise some other interesting points about individual perceptions of empire. One thing you might perhaps have noticed is that Pitts and Thistlewood had somewhat different social backgrounds – the one a seaman, the other a son of a tenant farmer. The difference in their status might not have been that great (Thistlewood arrived in Jamaica with only £15 in cash, a promissory note for £60 from his older brother, some furniture and wine, and an impressive selection of clothes). However, thinking back to our discussions in the second section of this unit 'Empires and popular culture', how do you think their class might have coloured their perceptions of empire?

It seems likely that those higher on the social scale in the seventeenth century (such as wealthy traders and government officials) would have had a somewhat different experience of empire from that of the likely victims of corsairs, such as Pitts. Equally, Thistlewood's perceptions of the British empire were probably different from those of men working on ships plying the long and stifling passage between Britain and the West Indies. For those seamen, the empire was perhaps more an arduous way of making a living than any kind of passport to land and riches.

Empires are, of course, dissected by lines of both class and gender (and, in some cases, religion). These are all important variables to consider when studying empire. In other words, we must not assume that, just because race is perhaps the facet of empire that appears most significant to us, it was necessarily at the forefront of the minds of those we study. Some historians have recently considered this issue of class, and concluded that it was in many ways just as significant as race in the running of the British empire. David Cannadine, for example, has argued that upper-class Britons did not necessarily view non-European societies solely in terms of racial difference. Rather, because they viewed their own society in terms of social hierarchies (class), this was a key component of their interactions with the empire.

"class" not "race"

As an illustration of this he quotes the example of a dinner party given in 1881 to which King Kalakaua of Hawaii (visiting England), the prince of Wales (the future Edward VII) and the German crown prince (the future Kaiser, and brother-in-law to the prince of Wales) were all invited. The prince of Wales insisted that the Hawaiian king should take precedence over his relative the German crown prince in the seating arrangements. The charming justification he apparently gave for this was 'Either the brute is a king, or he's a common or garden nigger; and if the latter, what's he doing here?' (Cannadine, 2001, p. 8). Aside from demonstrating a casual racism we now find extremely offensive, this quote is interesting in that it demonstrates how class (or perceived social status, at least) had a significant role to play in the hierarchies binding the empire together.

The significance of class and gender in framing individuals' experiences of empire is something that you will consider in more detail in Block 4. I hope this exercise has demonstrated how important it is not to take our contemporary assumptions with us when we study the past. The individuals whose writings we may consider were often complex characters. Even Thistlewood, for example, as well as being an aggressive and brutal overseer of slaves, was also a keen gardener who read Enlightenment philosophy and fancied himself as a bit of an amateur scientist. There is no such thing as a typical imperial trajectory or 'experience of empire'. We will discuss this more below. First, however, I would like you to consider two more individual experiences of the British empire, both dating from towards the end of the nineteenth century.

Case Study 3: Vernon Lee Walker (1857–1887)

Vernon Lee Walker was a British trader travelling in the South Seas during the 1870s and 1880s. He was, in many ways, an extremely ordinary individual. But for the fact that a number of his letters home to his mother and other family members have survived we would probably have never heard of him. His correspondence was written variously from Melbourne and Sydney and from small trading boats travelling between the various Melanesian islands. Walker's trading ventures were never particularly successful – something he complained about often in his letters home – and he was jealous of his more successful brother Howard.

His letters are fragmentary and, at times, semi-literate. He described himself as 'an awfully bad hand at letter writing', and it is hard to contest this assessment (Thomas and Eves, 1999, p. 16). In his letters to his mother, for example, who was of course entirely unfamiliar with the Pacific, he rarely gives any details of the astounding scenery that he undoubtedly saw. He spends much time dwelling on the discomforts he experienced during his lengthy travels and on the boredom of his daily routine.

The period in which Walker was writing was perhaps the height of the 'scramble for Africa' – a period often seen by historians as the start of the confident 'new imperialism'. In the South Pacific, however, the reach of European colonial governments was decidedly limited. The role and place of white Europeans in the region was uncertain and this is reflected in Walker's letters, which relate setback after setback. His correspondence is, in many ways, a catalogue of failure and minor hardships, punctuated by an unchanging racism and a curious obsession with cannibalism. He often refers to the inhabitants of Fiji as 'niggers', at a time when the term 'natives' would have been much more common among Europeans. In December 1887, his brother Howard wrote to their mother to inform her that 'Lee' had been shot dead, and then hacked to pieces and burnt, by 'natives' when landing on the island of Pentecost to buy yams.

Case Study 4: Dadabhai Naoroji (1825–1917)

Naoroji was born near Bombay to a poor Parsi priest and his wife. He was educated at Elphinstone College in Bombay, where he subsequently taught, becoming the first Indian professor there. In 1855 (two years before the Indian Uprising) he moved to England. He became a professor of Gujarati at University College London, as well as a partner in the first Indian firm to open a branch in England. During the same period he was active in the reform movement in India. He persuaded Indian princes to fund the East India Association, which campaigned to open the Indian Administrative Civil Service to Indians. In *Poverty and Un-British Rule in India* (1901) he argued that British rule was a drain on the financial resources of India.

In England, he was elected to the House of Commons for Central Finsbury (London) by the barest of margins in 1892 – partly helped by public sympathy when the prime minister (Lord Salisbury) declared that he doubted that a British constituency 'would elect a black man'. In India, he helped to found the Indian National Congress in 1885, and was elected as its president in 1886 and again in 1906. While Naoroji was a staunch moderate within the Congress, the INC became one of the leading forces in the fight against British rule. By the time of his death, Naoroji had become known as 'the Grand Old Man of India' and was a mentor to Mahatma Ghandi, one of the authors of Indian independence in 1947.   Gandhi

Once again, we have here two very different individuals, from different
continents and different centuries even, connected only by the relationship they
both had to the British empire. One was 'on the receiving end' of the British
empire, a colonial subject, and the other was a white colonist from the
metropole. As before, I would like you to read some extracts of the works they
themselves produced.

EXERCISE

First read a letter written by Vernon Lee Walker to his mother on 19 January 1878,
posted from Melbourne (Primary Source 3.6 on the course website). In it, he details
his experiences on a recent trip to Fiji. Then read the extract from a speech delivered
by Dadabhai Naoroji in 1901 (Primary Source 3.7 on the course website). Here
Naoroji considers the impact that being part of the British empire has had on India.

As you read these two extracts, which are again very different from one another in
both style and content, and bearing in mind what you have read in the case studies
above, jot down answers to the following questions.

1   What strikes you about the attitudes of each author towards the British empire?
2   What can each of these extracts tell us about the nature of the British empire
    during the late nineteenth century?

SPECIMEN ANSWER

1   These sources reveal much about both the attitudes and the relationships of
    individuals to the British empire, but in very different ways. Walker's views on
    the subject are not particularly overt. After all, given the nature of the source
    (a letter home) he is hardly likely to write expressing a succinct opinion on
    British imperialism. However, it would appear that he is in some ways a
    moderately contented part of the imperial system. He likes the weather, he likes
    the food, he is fond (at least on one level) of the employed members of the
    indigenous population and hopes to make some money by trading. That said, he
    is also in other ways rather discontented with his lot. It is often too hot, he had
    an unpleasant fever over Christmas, and it can be quite dangerous working on
    the trading ships. What is interesting in considering a source such as this is the
    way in which it reveals that individuals like Walker (who were, essentially,
    helping to extend the British empire) did not necessarily conceive of themselves
    as doing so. Rather, they were primarily simply pleasing themselves and
    extending British influence only as a by-product of this.

    "making a living"

    Naoroji's views of the British empire are much clearer, as would be expected
    given the nature of the source. Although technically an 'imperial subject', he
    explicitly notes that Indians are 'grateful for a good many things' about the
    British empire – including education, free speech and an end to outdated
    traditions. That said, he is also a clear critic of many aspects of British policy in
    India (particularly the 'bleeding' out of money back to the metropole), which he
    discusses in a very lucid manner. For him, aspects of British imperial rule
    amount simply to the 'plundering' of India.

2   This is a trickier question to answer. Perhaps the clearest point to draw from
    these two extracts is that to conceive of imperialism as simply the domination of
    one nation by another is very short of the mark. Empires were much more
    complex entities. Naoroji, for example, was essentially a colonial subject.
    However, his life story, as outlined in the case study, and the extract from the
    speech amply demonstrate his agency (ability to act). He had significant
    influence (political and social) in both the metropole and in India. Walker, on

the other hand, despite being a British citizen (and hence theoretically an imperial 'ruler') was in fact rather hapless, and even a bit of a failure. Although his indigenous servants call him 'master', he was clearly anything but. Riddled by fever, unable to succeed in business, he ended up hacked to death on a beach thousands of miles from his home while attempting to buy yams.

We should remember, of course, that both of these individuals were atypical in many ways. The fact that they left a clear written legacy sets them apart from the vast majority of colonial subjects. However, what the two case studies you have just read do show is that the imposition of force or influence from above is not *all* that empires ever were. It is important to realise (and this is something which will be developed more in Unit 4 and Block 3) that empires were principally complex systems of *interaction*. Empires can be viewed not simply as something that some people or regions imposed on others less favoured, but rather as global systems, moving people, goods, money and ideas around, constantly changing and developing. Obviously, it would be facile to claim that the metropole/colony relationship was ever an equal partnership but (as many units in the course will show) empires were criss-crossed by complex webs of relationships. One way of illuminating this type of cultural interchange is by using individual's accounts of their own imperial journeys.

every reaction has an equal reaction

"evolving"

CONCLUSION

This unit has sought to introduce you to some of the more intangible facets of empire. Hopefully it has become clear that, in addition to the hard 'facts' of imperial rule, the realm of ideas, attitudes and experiences has much to offer when considering the nature of empires.

This 'cultural' side of empire functions on a number of levels. As has been shown, there has always been considerable intellectual debate in imperial nations about the advisability or otherwise of actually having an empire. It seems likely that a changing philosophical milieu may have contributed something to the enthusiasm for rule, or otherwise, among imperial elites. Equally, at the popular level, it is fascinating to unpick the various ways in which empires wormed their way into the psyches of metropolitan populations. Finally, at an individual level, the case studies presented in the final section of the unit enable a brief glimpse into just a few of the varied experiences of empire, highlighting the extent to which personal imperial trajectories often depended as much on class (and possibly gender) as on race or nationality.

All the themes introduced in this unit will be developed in more detail later in the course. Unit 10, in particular, considers the way in which culture functions to sustain imperial rule, while all the units in Block 4 consider the 'experience' of empire, attempting to judge how far this can be adequately reconstructed from individuals' life-stories and testimonies.

Use 3.8 for TMA 01 ?

REFERENCES

Aldrich, R. (1996) *Greater France: A History of French Overseas Expansion*, Basingstoke, Macmillan.

Burnard, T. (2004) *Mastery, Tyranny, and Desire. Thomas Thistlewood and His Slaves in the Anglo-Jamaican World*, Chapel Hill and London, University of North Carolina Press.

Cannadine, D. (2001) *Ornamentalism. How the British saw their Empire*, London, Penguin.

Chafer, T. and Sackur, A. (2002) *Promoting the Colonial Idea. Propaganda and Visions of Empire in France*, Basingstoke, Palgrave.

Colley, L. (2003) *Captives: Britain, Empire and the World 1600–1850*, London, Pimlico.

Conklin, A. (2000) *A Mission to Civilize: The Republican Idea of Empire in France and West Africa, 1895–1930*, Stanford, Stanford University Press.

Dirks, N. (2006) *The Scandal of Empire. India and the Creation of Imperial Britain*, Cambridge, MA, Belknap Press of Harvard University Press.

Dubois, L. (2000) 'La République métissée: citizenship, colonialism, and the borders of French history', *Cultural Studies*, vol. 14, no. 1, pp. 15–34.

Ehlen, P. (2000) *Frantz Fanon. A Spiritual Biography*, New York, Crossroad Publishing.

Fanon, F. (1952) *Peau noire, masques blancs*, Paris, Éditions du Seuil.

Fanon, F. (1961) *Les Damnés de la terre*, Paris, François Maspero.

Garay, K.E. (1988) 'Empires of the mind? C.K. Ogden, Winston Churchill and Basic English', *Canadian Historical Association Historical Papers*, vol. 23, no. 1, pp. 280–91.

Howsam, L. (2005) 'Imperial publishers and the idea of colonial history, 1870–1916', *History of Intellectual Culture*, vol. 5, no. 1, pp. 1–15.

 Las Casas, Bartolomé de (1992 [1552]) *A Short Account of the Destruction of the Indies*, London, Penguin.

Loomba, A. (1998) *Colonialism/Postcolonialism*, London, Routledge.

Louis, W.R. (1999) 'Introduction' in Winks, L. (ed.) *The Oxford History of the British Empire*, vol. 5: *Historiography*, Oxford, Oxford University Press, pp. 1–42.

MacKenzie, J. (ed.) (1989) *Imperialism and Popular Culture*, Manchester, Manchester University Press, Studies in Imperialism.

Marshall, P. (1999) 'The first British empire' in Winks, L. (ed.) *The Oxford History of the British Empire*, vol. 5: *Historiography*, Oxford, Oxford University Press, pp. 43–53.

Mill, J.S. (1859) *On Liberty*, London, John W. Parker and Son.

Mill, J.S. (1861) *Considerations on Representative Government*, London.

Muthu, S. (2003) *Enlightenment against Empire*, Princeton and Oxford, Princeton University Press.

Naoroji, D. (1901) *Poverty and Un-British Rule in India*, London, Swan Sonnenschein.

Pagden, A. (1995) *Lords of All the World. Ideologies of Empire in Spain, Britain and France, c.1500–c.1800.* New Haven and London, Yale University Press.

Parker, G. (2001) *The World is Not Enough: The Imperial Vision of Philip II of Spain*, Waco, Markham Press.

Pitts, J. (2005) *A Turn to Empire. The Rise of Imperial Liberalism in Britain and France*, Princeton and Oxford, Princeton University Press.

 Porter, B. (2004) *The Absent-Minded Imperialists*, Oxford, Oxford University Press.

Potter, S.J. (2000) 'Empire, cultures and identities in nineteenth- and twentieth-century Britain', *History Compass*, vol. 4, pp. 1–21.

Said, E. (1979) *Orientalism*, New York, Vintage Books.

Schneider, W. (1982) *An Empire for the Masses: The French Popular Image of Africa, 1870–1900*, Westport, Greenwood Press.

Seeley, J.R. (1895) *The Expansion of England: Two Courses of Lectures*, London, Macmillan.

Slavin, D. (2001) *Colonial Cinema and Imperial France, 1919–1939*, Baltimore, Johns Hopkins University Press.

Smith, A. (1776) *An Inquiry into the Nature and Causes of The Wealth of Nations*, London, W. Strahan & T. Cadell.

Sullivan, E. (1983) 'Liberalism and imperialism: J. S. Mill's defense of the British empire', *Journal of the History of Ideas*, vol. 44, no. 4, pp. 599–617.

Thomas, N. and Eves, R. (1999) *Bad Colonists. The South Sea Letters of Vernon Lee Walker and Louis Becke*, Durham, NC, Duke University Press.

Thompson, A. (2005) *The Empire Strikes Back? The Impact of Imperialism on Britain from the Mid-Nineteenth Century*, Harlow, Pearson Longman.

Thornton, A.P. (1999) 'The shaping of imperial history' in Winks, R. (ed.) *The Oxford History of the British Empire*, vol. 5: *Historiography*, Oxford, Oxford University Press.

CONCLUSION TO BLOCK 1

Paul Lawrence

This first block of the course has sought to equip you for the rest of your study of A326 in a range of ways. The first unit provided you with a broad overview of the long-term development of empires. The second unit introduced you to some ways of thinking conceptually about and analysing empires and their component parts. The third unit demonstrated the importance of considering what we might call 'the idea of empire' – the various ways in which historical attitudes to and experiences of empires have influenced their development.

All the ideas you have encountered in this first block will be developed and referred to at various points throughout the course. Hence, you will probably find it useful to glance back at these introductory units from time to time – we certainly do not expect you to have memorised their contents the first time around. Unit 1 will be useful whenever you require clarification about the dates, geography and long-term processes of empire. Unit 2 will be helpful whenever you are asked to think conceptually about the component parts of empire and the way they function together. Unit 3 has tackled topics that will be developed at various points during the course, but particularly in Block 4. The main points to draw from this unit for later development are:

- empires have always been contentious (although at certain times much more so than at others)
- it is often hard to know how popular empires were at the metropole (or, indeed, whether this affected their running)
- some historians have argued that knowledge itself is a mechanism for imperial domination
- individuals experienced empires very differently; their overlapping trajectories and life stories reveal empires to be complex webs of interaction, rather than straightforward systems of domination.

BLOCK 2
HOW DO EMPIRES BEGIN?

Introduction to Block 2   **115**
Learning outcomes   115
The world in 1400   115
Motivations for imperialism   116
The topics of Block 2   118
Overall questions   119

Unit 4
The beginning of Atlantic empires: Spain in the New World   **120**
Aims   120
Introduction   120
Columbus   125
The 'Caribbean' phase of Hispanic conquest and settlement: 1492–1518   127
Bartolomé de Las Casas and the imperial Catholic conscience   129
Colonial institutions   131
Cortés and the conquest of Mexico 1519–22   135
The conquest of Peru 1532–35   145
Towards a silver-based empire   149
Conclusion   151
References   154

Unit 5
Pirates, pilgrims, plantations and pigs: the beginnings of the
British Atlantic empire 1497–1660   **156**
Aims   156
Introduction   156
Imperialism and ecology   159
Exploration and finance   164
The impact of privateering   170
Describing the New World   173
New England   180
Barbados   183
Conclusion   190
References   192

Unit 6
Empires of trade? The Portuguese and the Dutch in
east Asia 1580–1670   **194**
Aims   194

Introduction   194

The Indian Ocean context   195

The creation of the Portuguese empire in the east: the Estado da India   199

Japan, the Jesuits and the informal Portuguese empire   211

The Dutch challenge 1590–1620   214

Conclusion   224

References   225

Unit 7
The expansion of Russia 1500–1725   **227**

Aims   227

Introduction   227

The rise of Muscovy   228

The transition to empire   234

An imperial strategy   239

Drivers of empire   244

Conclusion   258

References   260

Conclusion to Block 2   **262**

INTRODUCTION TO BLOCK 2

Chris A. Williams

Learning outcomes

When you have completed your study of this block, you should:

- be able to understand some of the ways that broad explanations can be applied to the rise of major European global empires
- have gained knowledge and understanding of significant aspects of the origins of the Spanish, Portuguese, English, Dutch and Russian empires.

THE WORLD IN 1400

In the first block we have seen the amazing extent to which European states expanded their control over the globe in a process that culminated in the middle of the twentieth century. We have also learned about some of the ways that types of empire can be categorised, and how they have been justified. The next four units are intended to give you an idea of how empires begin.

For us, the story starts in about 1400. Asia remained the centre of the world, with India and China the centre of major civilisations. The Americas were entirely settled by a variety of groups, most of whom appear to have practised agriculture. By far the most densely populated area of the continent was the fertile Valley of Mexico, home to about a third of the continent's population. Africa was less densely populated. The north and east coasts were part of the Muslim world, but the interior was characterised by a very hostile disease environment. In this world, Europe was peripheral.

Nevertheless, Europe was connected with global networks. In the south, Venice had a strong position in the trade with Asia through the Mediterranean. In the century before Columbus, Europeans were trying to link themselves to the world economy in new ways. Although the Norse Greenland colonies died out some time around 1400, Bristol merchants developed a thriving trade with Iceland in the fifteenth century, following a long hiatus. To the south, the Italian trading city of Genoa sent expeditions into the Sahara to try to circumvent Venetian control of the trade in Niger Valley gold. Spaniards had colonised the Canary Islands (Canaries), and as well as taking Madeira, Portuguese navigators were systematically working their way down the African coast.

It was the sixteenth century, though, that saw the first great burst of successful European imperialism. Where did it spring from?

MOTIVATIONS FOR IMPERIALISM

One traditional way used to describe the motives for the first wave of imperial expansion was 'God, Gold and Glory'. Subsequent research has proved that we need to go beyond this attractive alliteration. I have a number of objections to this phrase, which fall under three broad headings: that these motives are too simplistic, that they are not the only ones that mattered, and that they are so general as to be meaningless.

The first problem is oversimplification. Within these brief one-word headings, there are a lot of different explanations that can been advanced, each one of which describes very different kinds of activity. Under the category of *God*: some imperialists went for the glory of god and to convert uncontacted heathen; others, to convert the heathen before their Christian rivals (Catholics or Protestants) did. Some went to kill heretics or infidels, while others were religious refugees (like the 'Pilgrim fathers') or groups whose commitment to the state religion was questioned (like Portuguese Christians of Jewish descent). Some travelled in attempts to make contact with the legendary Christian empire in the east, often called the kingdom of Prester John. Under *Gold*: some attempted to reach sources of profit that Europe already knew about, such as the furs of Siberia or the gold of West Africa; others, such as the conquistadores in America, stumbled on rich silver mines. Some were trying to set up profitable trading routes, notably to satisfy the hunger of European consumers for Asian products, while the objective of others was to discover new empires in the New World, and take their treasures. Under *Glory*: many early imperialists, from Columbus onwards, were motivated to win personal military renown and power by carving out new kingdoms. Others set off in the service of states (not always their own) to defeat rival European powers in their imperial holdings; this was sometimes, but not always, a result of war in Europe. So, overall, these three terms cover many contradictory ideas and actions.

The second problem is the many additional factors. Most of the overarching explanations that have been proffered for the beginnings of sustainable imperialism cannot be shoehorned into any one of the three categories above. These include:

- getting rid of beggars, lepers, criminals and the poor by shipping them overseas
- the greater chance for a career open to talent in overseas empires
- a thirst for knowledge about the world
- the impact of the adoption in Europe of new technologies – notably the **caravel** and the compass – on exploration
- microbiology; the contemporary study of which tells us that certain human populations in 1500 were very vulnerable to diseases carried by the rest of humanity

- ecology, another contemporary science, which shows that the New World had many empty niches that Europeans and their plants and animals could fill

- some chains of contingent events that are very hard to fit into any kind of overarching explanation.

The third problem is that the three terms are so general that they don't explain very much. Explanations are useful if they account for the events in question, but less useful if they also account for just about anything that was going on at the time. As far as God was concerned, this was a religious age, and most human activity in Europe was justified, sooner or later, in relation to Christianity. When we consider Gold, we have to recognise that almost all human activity, then as now, needs some kind of payback to cover its ongoing costs; very few enterprises are merely money sinks just for God or Glory, and this was especially the case in the early modern period when the amount of available surplus wealth and productive power was so much lower than it is today. People have to eat. As for Glory, see God, above: we are looking at a society obsessed with social position, chivalry and precedence, and it is unlikely that any events within it, including matters of life and death such as subsistence, war or medicine, can be explained without reference to the role played by the social structure.

'God, Gold and Glory' can only take us so far. But we have to do more than merely work up a longer list of all the reasons that encouraged the origin of empire at any time. Your job in Block 2 is to look at this variety of explanations for such a complex set of phenomena as 'empire', and begin to draw some general conclusions about the process. Bear in mind the following issues:

1   Unit 1 gave an overview of the way that the various world empires expanded. During Block 2, refer back to this unit to see how the case studies given here fit into larger patterns. Are they representative of the global picture, or exceptions to it?

2   In Unit 2 we have already given you some help in isolating different types of empire from the bewildering variety of examples. You can use these typologies to see if any correlate with different explanations – are the reasons for establishing trading posts different from those that led to colonies of settlement?

3   Bear in mind the chronology of the birth of empires: different reasons can be more important at different stages in a process. You will learn from Unit 4 that, although the conquistadores' lust for gold and glory impelled the initial conquest of New Spain, it was consolidated by state bureaucrats eager to advance the monarch's interests. The reasons that people stayed and prospered were often not the reasons that they went. Columbus wanted to find China and liberate Jerusalem, not found farms in Cuba; English people who settled in Virginia wanted to find gold, not become tobacco farmers – but that is what they ended up doing.

4   Often declared motives need to be looked at in context. If the only way to get an expedition financed was to announce that it would find lots of gold, is it any wonder that Walter Raleigh, a promoter of empire, wrote a lot (around 1600) about how he was about to find the wealthy kingdom of El Dorado in South America? Consider the various justifications for empire that were discussed in Unit 3: some of these were written as reasons to go in the first place, but most were *ex post facto* ('after the fact') apologias for ongoing activities.

THE TOPICS OF BLOCK 2

The four empires referred to in the first three units were all intimately related, and each served as an example for the others.

Unit 4 will consider the Spanish experience of empire, looking in detail at the background to Columbus's voyages, and the social systems that were established in the Spanish Caribbean. It will describe the exploits of the conqueror of Mexico, Hernando Cortés, and examine the extent to which we can rely on the often contradictory testimony of the conquistadores and their critics to understand the conquest. It will point out the importance of the plagues that the Europeans brought to the New World, and end on a number of general conclusions about the way that this empire began.

Unit 5 will look at the English in the Atlantic between 1500 and 1660 and show how, for nearly the whole of the sixteenth century, English enterprise was largely characterised by failure. Almost by accident, viable settlements were established, coalescing around slave plantation economies in the Caribbean and on Chesapeake Bay, which were provisioned by other colonies in New England. One theme that it will bring out is the way that – although governments became increasingly important – non-state organisations, and individuals, played a crucial role in the expansion of Britain overseas.

Unit 6 will shift the focus to the east, and introduce two mercantile empires: those of the Netherlands and Portugal. These did not (at this stage) gain wealth by settling or ruling large enclaves, but by using their maritime and financial power to support a network of lucrative trading enclaves. By adopting a comparative approach to the two empires, you can get some idea of whether or not there are necessary features common to all trading empires.

Unit 7, on Russia, presents a yet greater contrast. Here, we will be largely considering Russia's advance to the east, through Siberia, and to the south-east, towards Central Asia. Once Russia reached the Pacific, its imperial enterprise looked more like that of the western powers, but until then it was a very different kind of expansion – chiefly because it did not rely on sea power. One of the reasons that we included the example of the Russian empire is because it allows us to try to define the role that maritime power played in imperial expansion. But, like the other units, it will consider the motivations for expansion, and the practical, institutional and geographical limits on it.

As you will see, all these topics invite us to consider what we actually mean by 'begin'. What level of development does an empire have to attain before we can say that it has genuinely started? In Unit 4, on the subjection by Spain of central and south America, Bernard Waites sets as his end point, the emergence of a durable political structure, which was a very different process to the initial conquest. In Unit 5, I follow the story of English expansion from numerous false starts, through a crucial period between 1620 and 1640, to the achievement of a productive economy in the North Atlantic. In Unit 6, Ole Peter Grell examines how the Portuguese empire in the Indian ocean began in extreme violence, but reached a *modus vivendi* with local powers, while in Unit 7, Colin Chant describes how the expansion of Russia took centuries rather than decades, and also featured a process of accommodation whereby some 'sworn enemies became allies'.

OVERALL QUESTIONS

As you work through this block, there are some general questions that it is worth bearing in mind, and applying to all the units. They ought to give you a better idea of the general rules (if any!) that applied to the beginnings of empires, and also of the overall nature of imperialism that took shape.

- Can you identify examples of the different *forms* of empire and of imperial outposts that were identified in Unit 2?

- What features do the patterns of expansion have in *common*?

- What is *unique* about the different empires?

- Within each of the sample empires, is there any common *chronological* pattern: for example, an initial expansion followed by a contraction, then stability?

- What is the role of *geography*? For example, does Britain's position in the North Atlantic explain why the British ended up on the northern part of the American seaboard?

- What explains the *failures* and false starts of imperial expansion?

Do all this and, when you have completed Block 2, you ought to be a long way on the road to understanding how and why empires began.

UNIT 4
THE BEGINNING OF ATLANTIC EMPIRES: SPAIN IN THE NEW WORLD

Bernard Waites

AIMS

- To enable you to understand the origins of the Spanish American empire in the maritime expansion of the Iberian powers.
- To account for the devastating impact of European and African intruders on the native population of the Caribbean and mainland America.
- To specify the competitive advantages (technological, organisational, ideological) that enabled the conquistadores to overthrow 'advanced' civilisations in highland Mexico and Peru.
- To outline the institutional foundations of Spanish colonialism and, closely linked to that, the factors that secured the 'conquest after the conquest'.
- To indicate the long-term significance of the Spanish American empire for the integration of the world's continents and peoples.

INTRODUCTION

Adam Smith famously opined that 'The discovery of America and that of a passage to the East Indies by the Cape of Good Hope are the two greatest and most important events in the history of mankind' (Smith, 1910 [1776], vol. 2, p. 121). We might quibble about the world historic significance of the sea-route to India, which Vasco da Gama opened up in 1498, but as to Columbus's landing in the Antilles in 1492, Smith was surely right. It had unintended consequences that changed forever the trajectory of human history. How so? The short answer is by 'binding the continents'. Before the sixteenth century, the world's civilisations and cultures had evolved either relatively autonomously or, in the case of the Americas, in complete isolation. There were, of course, long-established trade routes that brought merchandise from Asia to Europe, just as there was a long history of the borrowing and adaptation by one culture of the techniques and ideas of another. But the discovery by Europeans of what they soon called the New World led to a sudden, step change in the flow of people, goods, resources, plants, animals and germs between the continents.

This unit explains the origins of the Spanish Indies in the 1490s and their dramatic expansion after 1518. In two decades, a few thousand Spaniards conquered the indigenous civilisations and established one of the most extensive and durable land empires ever created by Europeans overseas. It was the first great political instrument of intercontinental integration. Spain's dominions in the New World complemented a dynastic conglomeration of territories in Europe and, from the late 1570s, an Asian stronghold in the Philippines. From 1580 to 1640, Portugal was annexed to the Spanish crown, which consequently acquired territories in Portuguese Africa, India, the Far East and Brazil. This agglomeration of territories and titles was history's first truly global empire.

For reasons of space, I have given most attention to the conquest of Mexico or New Spain (1519–22) and said little about the equally dramatic conquest of Peru (1532–35). However, you will find the opening chapter of John Hemming's *The Conquest of the Incas* (2004 [1970]) on the course website (Secondary Source 4.1), as well as an extract from an Inca account of the conquest, which will give you some sense of how this cataclysmic event was experienced from the other side (Primary Source 4.7).

The origins and persistence of empires

In this block we are asking 'How do empires begin?' In other words, what were the necessary and sufficient conditions for their foundation? This unit should help you answer that question. But the historical explanation of empires cannot sever their origins from their persistence. Empires are structures of political domination that bind time as well as space: they impose life-long routines on subject populations and sustain long-term economic cycles of investment and exploitation. The Spaniards believed they had a duty to substitute their god and religious world-view for another. None of this could be accomplished by a single act of conquest, however spectacular. When the expeditionary force led by Hernando Cortés overthrew the Aztec empire in 1521, New Spain – the jewel of the Indies – still lay in the future. The permanency of Spanish rule was not predetermined; it depended to some degree on devastating epidemics that shattered and demoralised indigenous states and societies. The institutions that 'delivered' permanent Spanish rule had to be put in place and staffed by Spanish immigrants. Native collaborators had to be Christianised and Hispanicised. The great silver deposits that became the main driver of the colonial economy lay far to the north and were not discovered until the 1540s. Their exploitation required large-scale investment in fixed capital, technical skill and regular inputs of labour; none of these could be locally supplied. The indigenous **Chichimec** were, unlike the sedentary peoples of the Valley of Mexico, mobile hunter-gatherers who retreated before the Spanish advance. Until sedentary people could be persuaded to migrate for waged work, labour – some provided by black slaves – had to be drafted in. In brief, to comprehend the Spanish Indies as a durable political structure we must look beyond the dramatic early years to the 'conquest after the conquest' (Bakewell, 1995).

[handwritten margin note: Waites' view on what empires are]

[handwritten margin note: EMA]

The 'overwhelming' of an isolated hemisphere

Before the Iberians entered the western hemisphere, its societies, states and civilisations had evolved in isolation from the rest of humanity. The first immigrants probably arrived by a land bridge over what are now the Bering straits around 10,000 BC. Rising sea levels cut them off from the Eurasian landmass and contacts with the rest of the world were inconsequential before Columbus's landfall in the Caribbean. The only ones about which we can be certain arose from the Norse settlement in northeast America, which dated from around AD 1000. Why the Vinland colony – which lasted some three centuries – was not the origin of a Scandinavian Atlantic empire is an intriguing question that we cannot pursue here. It may simply have been in the wrong place, for it is generally believed that the colonists either died out or retreated to Greenland when climate change led to shorter summers and harsher winters, and so ended settled agriculture.

The simple fact of American isolation goes far to explain the overwhelming character of Iberian expansion in the New World. Its indigenous peoples lived in a great variety of political and social communities: some had evolved complex imperial civilisations, others were nomadic hunter-gatherers. Their one common characteristic was extreme vulnerability to the disease pathogens endemic in the Old World of Eurasia and Africa. As we now know, resistance to certain diseases can be acquired by experiencing them in childhood, when they often present in a comparatively mild form, or by inheriting a relative immunity as part of one's genetic make-up. Neither prophylactic was available to Native Americans, who were biologically defenceless against the germs introduced by Europeans and Africans. Whether they lived in the tropical lowlands or temperate highlands, Native Americans succumbed in huge numbers to 'virgin soil' epidemics. Figure 4.1 shows the distribution of Native Americans around 1500; Table 4.1 shows estimates for the population of the Americas at the same time.

Table 4.1   The population of the Americas at the time of European contact

Geographical area	Population in millions
North America	4.4
Mexico	21.4
Central America	5.65
Caribbean	5.85
Andes	11.5
Lowland South America	8.5
Total	**57.3**

(Source: Lockhart and Schwartz, 1983, p. 36)

Note: Estimating the pre-Columbian population of the Americas is fraught with problems. Reputable scholars have suggested totals for both continents ranging from 8.4 million to 112 million. The figures given here are not universally accepted, though all agree that Mexico and the Andes were the most densely populated regions. Nobody disputes that the native population declined precipitously in the century after contact; in Mexico, for example, there were only about 730,000 Amerindians in the 1620s (Bakewell, 1997, p. 152).

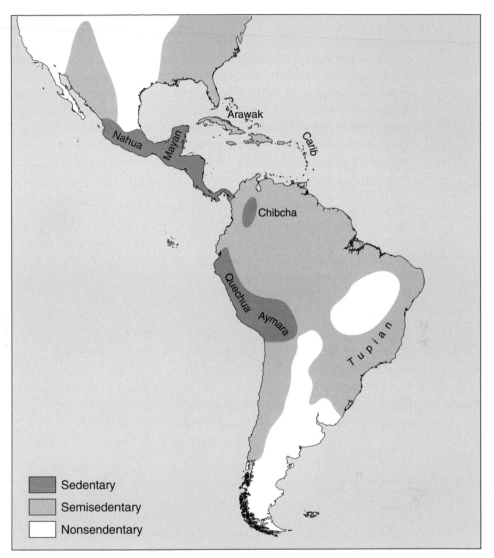

Figure 4.1 Approximate distribution of sedentary, semisedentary and nonsedentary peoples in South America at the time of European contact, adapted from Lockhart, J. and Schwartz, S.B. (1983) *Early Latin America: A History of Colonial Spanish America and Brazil*, Cambridge, Cambridge University Press, p. 35.

Additionally, the incoming Europeans had a clear 'competitive advantage' – to use the Darwinian terminology – in the technologies of violence and administration. Steel swords and helmets, crossbows, cavalry horses, war dogs and gunpowder meant tiny numbers of conquistadores could deploy 'shock and awe' tactics against the Native Americans, who were handicapped psychologically by their ritualised forms of combat, which aimed to wound and capture, not kill, and materially by inadequate weaponry, due to an ignorance of iron-smelting. In the clash of obsidian axe and steel sword, steel was far more lethal. Once the initial conquest was accomplished, the Spanish were so confident of their military superiority that they did not bother to fortify their towns in the most densely populated areas of New Spain and Peru. Serious concerted resistance to their rule came some decades after first contacts from peripheral and superficially 'backward' tribes, such as the **Auracanian** Indians of Chile. The 'advanced' state-civilisations of highland Mexico and Peru were, paradoxically, more friable: once decapitated, they lost the coherence that had been imposed on them by Aztec[14] and Inca conquerors and fragmented into local chieftaincies. The Spanish did not take over an indigenous ruling apparatus, perhaps because in their eyes there was none. They came from a political and legal culture where rulers ruled as much through the written word as by the sword; in the Indies, they conquered societies without alphabetic writing, still less print.[15] Amerindian societies had aristocracies and priests, and the more complex ones had officials who kept sophisticated pictorial records on paper. But there was no equivalent to the *letrados*, the university-educated bureaucrats who were the backbone of Spanish administration. In the 'conquest after the conquest', the Spanish crown brought to heel the first generation of free-booting conquistadores and imposed paper-based, bureaucratic government on the Indies. Through its support of **Dominican** and **Franciscan** missionary friars, the crown oversaw the conversion of its new subjects. Amerindian culture was not obliterated, for indigenous religion and myth survived beneath a Catholic carapace, but political and social hierarchies were overwhelmed by an irreversible defeat.

This overwhelming quality is also evident in the biological colonisation of the Americas by European livestock, which Chris Williams takes up later, in Unit 5. The Spaniards replicated their Mediterranean way of life by planting wheat, vines and olives wherever they would flourish. When mining developed in the dry, inhospitable highlands, inter-regional trade in grain, wine and oil quickly followed. All this represented a profound transformation in the techniques of agriculture and transport in the New World. Pre-Columbian Amerindians had few domestic or draught animals; they made no use of the wheel; and they cultivated the land with the digging stick. With no pack animals (apart from the Andean llama) inter-regional trade had been limited to luxuries. Many Amerindians continued to live half-apart from the colonial civilisation long after the conquest, but most sedentary communities adopted the plough, the mule, cattle, wheeled carts and wheaten bread.

---

[14] Or more appropriately 'Mexica', since 'Aztec' is an eighteenth-century invention.

[15] Pictographs were used in Aztec culture and the Incas used *quipu* (knotted strings) for mnemonic purposes, but only the Maya had developed writing, which had fallen into disuse long before the Spanish conquest.

The technological and 'moral' preconditions for Atlantic empire

The Norsemen had reached North America in stages, using open vessels without stern-post rudders and with minimal navigational aids. But whether their Dark Age maritime technology would have been good enough to conquer and sustain an Atlantic empire seems most unlikely. That required the evolution of more efficient sailing vessels and the adoption of the magnetic compass and **astrolabe**. The mastery of oceanic sailing gave the Spaniards another competitive advantage over the Amerindians, for exploratory contacts were quickly reinforced by permanent migrants. But the advantage was moral and psychological as well as technical. The Caribbean islands had been populated by skilled canoeists, able to travel considerable distances out of sight of land, but the 'advanced' highland civilisations were land-locked, physically and spiritually. Their rulers and priestly castes could not conceive of ordinary mortals arriving from great distances overseas and *may* – the evidence is dubious – have seen the conquistadores as the reincarnation of ancestral gods. Whatever the exact truth, there was clearly a radical mismatch in world-views: the Amerindians were fatalists for whom the divinely ordered world was a given; the conquerors saw the world as something to be encompassed and mastered by human effort. Literally so: the first global circumnavigation was completed in 1522. The role of maritime technology in consolidating and extending transoceanic empire was demonstrated when the Spaniards established a ship-building industry in Panama on the Pacific side of the isthmus. Vessels built in Panama began exploring the Pacific coast of South America in the 1520s. Fifty years later, a squadron built in New Spain crossed the Pacific and seized Manila, which was soon transformed into Europe's greatest stronghold in Asia. But technology alone did not determine such extraordinary feats of empire building; it had to be matched with an absolute confidence that political dominion would bring new subjects to the one true faith – and unshakeable cultural arrogance.

COLUMBUS

What prompted the Genoese mariner, Christopher Columbus (1451–1506) to set out across uncharted seas in August 1492 and sail for 32 days before reaching land? (You can follow his route in Figure 4.2.) What persuaded the Catholic monarchs of Castile and Aragon, Isabella and Ferdinand, to finance his expedition and grant this commoner extraordinary powers and titles? In the **Capitulations of Santa Fe** of April 1492, he was made admiral, viceroy, and governor general, under Castile, of any lands he might find in the west. One-tenth of any net profits from his explorations would go to him and he was to have commercial rights in any trade that might emerge from his discoveries. This strongly suggests that Columbus was motivated by the prospect of material gain and social honour but, while these were unquestionably important to him, he was also a man with a crusading mission. He began his journal of the first voyage by stating that his purpose was to reach 'Cathay' (China) and the 'Great Khan' (the emperor of China). The long-term

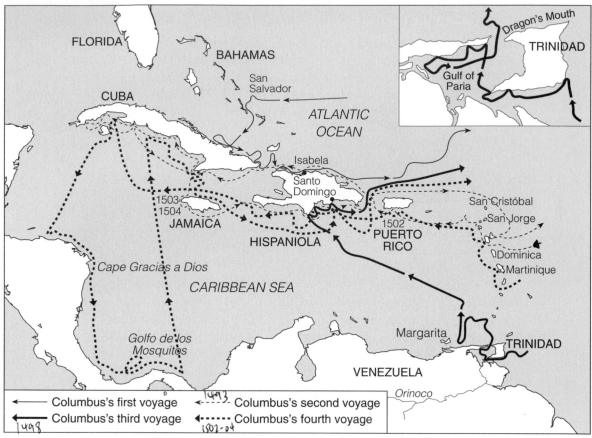

Figure 4.2   Columbus's Caribbean voyages, adapted from Thomas, H. (2003) *Rivers of Gold: The Rise of the Spanish Empire*, London, Phoenix, pp. 104, 149, 194 and 251.

goal – which he never relinquished – was to convert the khan to Christianity, enter an alliance with him against Islam, and re-conquer Jerusalem. Columbus considered himself an instrument of Divine Providence chosen to set in motion the events that would initiate the last age of the world's history – an epoch scheduled to be enacted before the Second Coming of Christ and the Last Judgement (Brading, 1991, p. 13). Columbus made three subsequent voyages (in 1493, 1498 and 1502–4), which led to the mapping of the major Caribbean islands and much of the South and Central American coast. Despite the mounting evidence that this was a hitherto unknown (and unimagined) quarter of the world, Columbus died believing he had discovered the insular fringes of Asia, or what Europeans called the 'Indies'. Hence the Caribbean islands were the 'West Indies', while all American natives were 'Indians'.

Columbus's crusading mission makes it easier to understand why the Spanish monarchs supported his expedition. Their forces had just completed the re-conquest of Spain by capturing Granada, the last Moorish kingdom in the peninsula, in 1492 – an event celebrated all over Christendom as a rare reversal of Muslim advance. The centuries-long **Reconquista** had profoundly influenced Spain's religious culture and political institutions: Spanish

"Inquisition"

Catholicism had acquired a militant edge not found elsewhere in western Europe and powerful monarchical states had emerged in Castile and Aragon. Through the personal union of Ferdinand and Isabella, Spain – hitherto a geographical expression – for the first time presented itself to the wider world as a formidable regional power. The Spanish monarchs hoped to carry the momentum from the fall of Granada into a broad-front onslaught on Islam. The evidence is sparse, but we may surmise that they saw Columbus's expedition as part of that onslaught. On his return, Pope Alexander VI granted the Catholic monarchs dominion over the isles and mainland of the ocean sea, while charging them with converting the inhabitants of these newly discovered lands. This papal donation of 1493 was to be the basis of Spanish legitimacy in the New World. The text cited the recent conquest of Granada as testimony of their sovereigns' eminent services to the church and so underlined the association between their nascent overseas empire and religious crusade.

THE 'CARIBBEAN' PHASE OF HISPANIC CONQUEST AND SETTLEMENT: 1492–1518

When Columbus's expeditions opened up what we now call the Caribbean there were two basic ways in which Europeans could exploit its natural and human resources. One was by setting up fortified trading posts and exchanging European goods for gold, dyestuffs, exotic foodstuffs, slaves and whatever else the natives had to offer. This was the Portuguese way of enterprise on the Guinea coast, where they established a string of *feitorias* (from which we derive 'factory', meaning trading depot) while continuing their search for the greater commercial prizes of the Indian Ocean and South China Sea. But the Spanish had evolved another, direct mode of exploitation in the course of the *Reconquista*, which involved the tributary subjection of frontier populations and their forcible conversion, and immigrant settlement. Columbus's second expedition of 1493 was decidedly 'Spanish' in character: it was the largest and most complete yet to leave Europe, and carried nearly everything needed to transplant a European way of life: men of different trades and social rank, seeds, plants and farm animals. The only absentees were European women, who were not admitted to Hispaniola, the initial site of Spanish settlement, until the early 1500s, when the first families began to arrive. The 1,500 or so male settlers of 1493 were expected to take native wives.

EMA

The colony's primary economic basis was gold extraction and what lured the settlers was the expectation of quick wealth. In the subsistence, barter economy of the native **Arawaks**,[16] gold had ornamental, not exchange, value. At first, they gave away what gold ornaments they had, along with food, without which the settlers would have starved. 'New' gold could not be acquired by trade – as gold dust was on the African coast – but had to be dug

---

[16] The Arawaks (or Aruaks) were one of the largest indigenous linguistic groups in pre-Columbian South America. The 'island Arawaks' of the Caribbean are sometimes referred to as **Tainos**.

out of the island's placer gold deposits. This required regular manual labour, which the Spanish were too proud to perform and Arawak society could not deliver without traumatic dislocation and disintegration. Although organised around chiefs (known as ***caciques***, which became the general term for Amerindian leaders throughout Spanish America), Arawak communities had no tradition of rendering tributary labour; indeed, the European concept of 'work' was alien to them. The settlers quickly repaid the Arawaks' hospitality and comparative docility by coercing the *caciques* into delivering labour drafts. When these no longer sufficed, they resorted to enserfment and slavery, for which they found legal justification in the Roman law doctrine that captives taken in a 'just war' could be enslaved: since the Arawaks could be construed as resisting the demands of their Christian conquerors, their enslavement was warranted. Moreover, educated Christians had learned from Aristotle – and there could be no higher intellectual authority – that slavery was the 'natural' condition of savages, who existed for the benefit of civilised men.

However, to comprehend the uninhibited sadism meted out to the Arawaks, we must look beyond routine arguments for slavery and grasp how the strangeness of this New World induced a loss of moral bearings. Europeans, who looked to the scriptures to explain the origin and dispersal of humanity, had chanced on people whose origins were obscure. Might they be a species of subhumans? Did they have rational souls? We know how some clerics answered these questions: some decades after the events I am describing a royal chaplain penned a diatribe in which the Amerindians were portrayed as '***homunculi*** in whom hardly a vestige of humanity remains'; they were 'like pigs with their eyes always fixed on the ground' (Juan Ginés de Sepúlveda, cited in Las Casas, 1992, p. xxviii). We can, I think, project back this uncomprehending contempt for the Amerindians onto Hispaniola's first colonists. The Columbus family, who were the island's nominal governors, were quite unable to restrain their obscene brutality. Within a decade, the native population was evidently in catastrophic decline. How much imported disease contributed to the mortality is difficult to determine. The first recorded smallpox epidemic came in late 1518 *after* the onset of demographic collapse, though it is very probable that many Amerindians had already succumbed to a virulent strain of influenza (Lovell, 1992, p. 428, citing the work of Francisco Guerra). Their diet deteriorated when pigs and other domestic animals introduced by the Spanish literally uprooted the gardens where they grew manioc and other staples. Women's fertility crashed, through physical exhaustion, poor diet and pervasive 'culture shock'. We can only speculate as to how many died in the holocaust. By 1530, the native population of the Greater Antilles was virtually wiped out.

One response to demographic decline on Hispaniola was to raid other islands, which had no gold deposits, for slaves; another was to import African slaves, initially from Iberia and the Atlantic islands. The first ***ladinos***, or Spanish-speaking blacks, reached Hispaniola in 1505. The first cargo to be shipped directly from West Africa to the Caribbean was probably landed in Puerto Rico in 1519. Ironically, Bartolomé de Las Casas had advocated their importation to relieve the Amerindians of forced labour; only in the 1540s did he recant his support of African slavery. African slaves exacerbated the vicious cycle of epidemics, because they originated in regions where **falciparum malaria** and yellow fever were endemic. They are not contagious or infectious, but transmitted by an intermediate vector, in this case the mosquito. Fairly early in the Atlantic slave trade, vectors must have 'jumped' the Atlantic because yellow fever and malaria became endemic in the Caribbean, which ironically made it increasingly inhospitable to European settlement. African slaves who had some immunity to these diseases had a better life expectation on the Caribbean plantations than their white masters.

BARTOLOMÉ DE LAS CASAS AND THE IMPERIAL CATHOLIC CONSCIENCE

In Unit 3, you were briefly introduced to Bartolomé de Las Casas (1484–1566), the Dominican friar who gained a European-wide reputation as 'Defender and Apostle of the Indians'. Now, I want you to undertake an exercise on extended passages from *A Short Account of the Destruction of the Indies* (Primary Source 4.1 on the course website). The chronology of Las Casas's life and times, accessible on the course website, enables you to set his writings in their biographical and historical context. The *Short Account*, which was addressed to Crown Prince Philip of Spain, was substantially completed in December 1542. The first printed version appeared in 1552. Figures 4.3 and 4.4 show illustrations from a Latin edition of Las Casas's tract published in Frankfurt, with engravings by Theodor de Bry.

EXERCISE

Now read the Preface and the chapter dealing with Hispaniola from *A Short Account of the Destruction of the Indies* (Primary Source 4.1 on the course website) and answer these questions:

1   How valuable is this testimony for our understanding of Spanish behaviour towards the Amerindians?

2   How would you summarise Las Casas's attitude towards the Amerindians?

3   Does he question the legitimacy of Spanish rule in the Americas?

SPECIMEN ANSWER

1   Las Casas tells us that he is speaking from first-hand experience, having been in the Caribbean from the early days of Spanish settlement (p. 3) and witnessed some of the atrocities he described (p. 5). For this reason, the testimony is uniquely valuable. Yet, it has limitations: Las Casas does not name any of the Spaniards who perpetrated the outrages (though he does identify some of their Arawak victims) so the conquistadores come across as undifferentiated and uniformly sadistic. Apart from a reference to their 'insatiable greed and overweening ambition' (p. 3) there is no attempt to understand their behaviour 'from the inside'. The catalogue of unremitting cruelty reads rather like a horror comic, with vivid vignettes but no psychological depth.

2   For Las Casas, the Amerindians were natural innocents and child-like in their simplicity and lack of guile. They were also 'the least robust of human beings', with 'delicate constitutions', which rendered them unfit for hard work and liable

Figures 4.3   Theodor de Bry after Winghe, 'Cruelties of the Conquerors', from Las Casas, B. de (1598) *Brevissima relación de la destruyción de las Indias* (*A Short Account of the Destruction of the Indies*), Frankfurt, T. de Bry & I. Saurii. British Library London, 980.e.25. By permission of the British Library.

to succumb to illness (p. 1). Las Casas clearly sensed their vulnerability to imported disease without understanding the aetiology of New World epidemics. His attitudes to the Amerindians were profoundly influenced by his religious convictions: they were naturally receptive to the Christian message and, although not explicitly asserted, their moral condition strongly resembled that of Adam and Eve before 'the fall' and the expulsion from the Garden of Eden. I think modern readers would regard Las Casas's response to these people as humane but paternalistic and unintentionally patronising.

3   Not in the least.

Las Casas has to be read against the broader political, religious and intellectual context in which Spaniards debated their rights and duties in the New World. At the Spanish court, he engaged in a public polemic with theologians and intellectuals who regarded the Amerindians as less than human, slavish by nature and fit only to be the chattels of their Spanish masters. One of the ironies of this debate was that Las Casas's principal intellectual opponent, Juan Ginés de Sepúlveda (cited above), was a distinguished humanist who defended Spanish rule over the Amerindians in

Figure 4.4 Theodor de Bry after Winghe, 'Cruelties of the Conquerors', from Las Casas, B. de (1598) *Brevissima relación de la destruycíon de las Indias* (*A Short Account of the Destruction of the Indies*), Frankfurt, T. de Bry & I. Saurii. British Library London, 980.e.25. By permission of the British Library.

thoroughly secular terms. Formally, at least, Las Casas won this argument: the Spanish monarchs were persuaded that they had a Christian duty to promote the spiritual and material welfare of their new subjects. The Americas had been 'granted and entrusted by God and His Church to the Spanish Crown so that they might be properly ruled ... and converted to the Faith' (Las Casas, 1992, p. 6). His advocacy played some part in the promulgation of the New Laws of 1542 prohibiting Amerindian slavery and severely restricting the colonists' access to Amerindian labour.

COLONIAL INSTITUTIONS

The focus of Spanish imperial expansion shifted decisively to the mainland around 1518 and the Spanish West Indies rapidly became an economic backwater. Nevertheless, the empire's 'Caribbean' phase was long enough to see the introduction of urban institutions and administrative practices that were eventually replicated throughout the Indies. The real founder of Hispaniola, and through it, of the Spanish Indies, was Fray Nicolás de Ovando, who in his eight years as governor (1501–9) laid the bases for economic survival and effective centralised control (Elliott, 1987, p. 16). Ovando ordered the rebuilding of Santo Domingo, after it had been destroyed by a hurricane in 1502, and the new stone-built capital was a model for all subsequent Spanish American cities. Their gridiron plan was very simple: a large square in the centre, a grid of perfectly straight streets extending from there in all directions, forming square or rectangular blocks. On one side of the square would be the principal church, on another the municipal council building, on another the residence of the governor or his representative; remaining properties facing the square, as well as those nearby, were the residences of the most important local citizens (Lockhart and Schwartz, 1983, pp. 66–7). Though Spain was overwhelmingly rural, even barely educated Spaniards identified 'civility', or a civilised way of life, with the city: it was the centre of law, religion and social hierarchy. The first high court or **audiencia** in the Indies was established in Santo Domingo in 1511; such courts were to be the basic building blocks of colonial administration. The city's great Gothic cathedral was built in 1527–40; it was, formally at least, endowed with a university in 1538. Wherever they settled in the Indies, the first act of the Spanish was to incorporate a city and **cabildo** (city council) on the lines of Santo Domingo.

By the end of Ovando's governorship, most of Santo Domingo's leading citizens (**vecinos**) were **encomenderos**, men granted by the governor the right to the labour of a group of Amerindians, usually the tribal following of a *cacique*. An *encomendero*'s Amerindians would spend part of their time working in his mines or on his **estancia**, normally a ranch specialising in European livestock, although the term could refer to any form of rural private property. Ovando instituted the **encomienda** in order to bring some order to the ruthless competition for Amerindian labour. Land was granted separately, usually by a city council, and could be sold or bequeathed as private property. As it happened, landowning and controlling Amerindian labour were intimately connected because the wealthiest citizens tended to become *encomenderos* and dominate the city councils, which made land grants. The following diagram (Figure 4.5) shows how *encomienda* labour, mines and agricultural supply activities complemented each other, to the ultimate benefit of the *encomendero* resident in the Spanish city.

With many regional variations and changes over time, the *encomienda* became a key institution in the early colonial economy. For the conquest generation on the mainland, to be granted an *encomienda* was the great prize in the scramble for riches, but its social consequences were less destructive than in the Caribbean. Cortés had learnt from the devastation and depopulation of Cuba that labour was the key to successful settlement. In New Spain, he distributed *encomiendas* to leading followers with the firm intention of preserving native sedentary life in a stable form. The institution represented an attempt to acquire Amerindian labour and produce through the use of traditional local

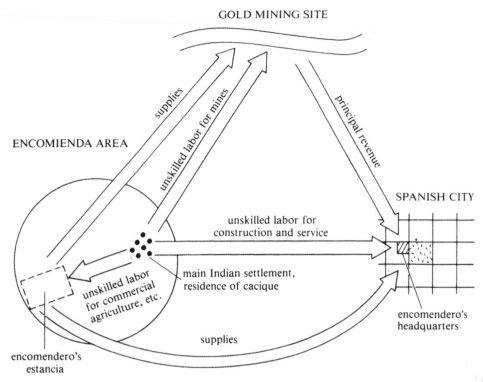

Figure 4.5 Schema of an *encomienda* on the Caribbean islands, from Lockhart, J. and Schwartz, S.B. (1983) *Early Latin America: A History of Colonial Spanish America and Brazil*, Cambridge, Cambridge University Press, p. 70.

indigenous authority, and on the basis of already existing socio-political units. Although the institution's basically secular character was never questioned, it was a key institution in the Christianisation of the Amerindians because the *encomendero* was responsible for his native dependants' religious welfare, which meant providing a resident or itinerant cleric.

Two further institutional developments during the Caribbean phase should be mentioned here, though their full significance became evident only later. One was the establishment in Seville of the **Casa de la Contratación,** or the House of Trade, in 1503. This royal agency administered economic relations between Spain and the Indies; it organised the passage of people, ships and merchandise across the Atlantic, while acting as a court in trade disputes. The volume of its business was small during the Caribbean phase: 212 ships left Seville for the Indies between 1506 and 1518, or roughly eighteen a year (Phillips, 1990). The recorded number of permanent emigrants before 1519 was fewer than 6,000. The conquest of Mexico in 1519–22 brought a dramatic increase in the number of ships leaving Seville for the Indies, which reached nearly 100 a year by the mid-1520s. The recorded number of permanent emigrants was 13,262 between 1520 and 1539, but this may well be an underestimate. Many more crossed the Atlantic temporarily (Boyd-Bowman, 1976). Under Castilian law, the crown was entitled to one-fifth of all 'treasure' extracted from the Indies, whether it was gold ornaments delivered by the

Amerindians or silver mined under the direction of Spanish entrepreneurs. This *quinto real* was levied by the Casa, along with other customs dues. Seville's merchant corporation or *consulado* had a monopoly on colonial trade, from which foreigners were legally excluded, but the city was a magnet for Genoese, Flemish, German and Portuguese merchants and bankers who participated in the nascent transatlantic economy through Spanish intermediaries.

The second development was the granting to the Castilian crown, by a **papal bull** of July 1508, of a monopoly on ecclesiastical appointments in the Indies: what was known as the universal *patronato*. This gave the Spanish monarchs enormous powers of patronage and an unprecedented degree of control over Spanish American Catholicism. They had the right to nominate candidates for church offices at all levels, to regulate the movement of clergy across the Atlantic, and to veto the sending of papal despatches to the Indies. 'In principle,' writes Bakewell, 'and broadly speaking in practice too, all this made the colonial church an arm of the state' (Bakewell, 1995, p. 301).

It was, of course, taken for granted that the conquistadores – acting in the name of the Catholic monarchs – were harbingers of Christianisation, but forcible conversion, such as Moors and Jews had undergone during the *Reconquista*, was not officially countenanced. In 1513, Spanish theologians laid down a formal procedure for conquest and theoretically voluntary conversion known as the *requerimiento*, or requirement. This was a proclamation, which had to be read out to the Amerindians, with or without interpreters, before they could be legally attacked. It began with a brief history of the world since the creation and proceeded to describe the donation of the Indies to Spain by Pope Alexander VI. The Amerindian audience was required to recognise the sovereignty of the Catholic Church, as exercised through the secular authority of the Spanish crown, and to permit the preaching of the faith. The Amerindians were then warned of the dire consequences if they refused to comply: the Spaniards would enter their lands by force and enslave their wives and children and do all the harm and damage they could. The *requerimiento* concluded:

> we protest that the deaths and losses which shall accrue from this are your fault and not that of Their Highnesses nor ours, nor of the knights who come with us.

> (cited in Cortés, 1986, p. 454)

Once the reading of the *requerimiento* had been witnessed by a notary, the way was morally clear for an assault. Astonishingly – to us – the conquistadores actually performed this legal charade in good faith.

Spanish emigration to the Indies

The total of Spanish emigrants in the sixteenth century is generally put at 200,000 to 250,000 (Elliott, 2006, p. 52). Eltis (2002, Table 1, p. 62) gives figures of 139,000 permanent migrants before 1580, and 188,000 between 1580 and 1640, which implies just over 200,000 before 1600. However, some estimates are considerably lower. Boyd-Bowman, who compiled emigration data from extant passenger lists, arrived at a total of 55,000 permanent Spanish emigrants to America before 1600 (Boyd-Bowman, 1976). He emphasised the many gaps in the records and the existence of illegal emigration, and warned against taking this total as definitive. Nevertheless, given the closely regulated character of Spanish transatlantic migration, it would seem unlikely that he 'captured' only one-quarter of emigrants.

CORTÉS AND THE CONQUEST OF MEXICO 1519–22

The Caribbean phase of Spanish expansion in the New World involved the infiltration and domination of stateless societies, which could not offer concerted resistance to the intruders. The exploration of the Yucatan peninsula in 1516–17, by two expeditions from Cuba, brought the Spanish up against the echo of a type of indigenous culture they had not previously encountered. The Yucatan had once been the site of an advanced civilisation – that of the **Maya**, who built magnificent stone temples, practised metalworking (though not iron making), used an elaborate astronomical calendar, and evolved a form of writing and mathematics. For reasons not properly understood, the classic Mayan civilisation decayed around AD 900, but material and cultural remnants survived in the shape of large towns with masonry buildings and religious practices more complex than anything the Spanish had yet seen in the New World. In the Maya Indians, they also encountered societies more effectively organised for violence than the Arawaks: in February 1517, the chronicler Bernal Díaz del Castillo (1492–1581) was in a reconnaissance party on the Yucatan coast that lost fifty men to Maya bowmen, armoured in padded cotton (Díaz del Castillo, 1963, p. 24).

The discoveries of 1517 prompted Diego Velázquez, the governor of Cuba, to despatch another expedition to survey western Yucatan and the Gulf of Mexico. This brought the Spanish within the political orbit of the 'Aztec empire', though whether that is an appropriate designation is a moot point. Suffice to note here that the Spanish learnt from the coastal people of a great political power, centred inland, that had cities, temples and a semi-divine ruler, and practised human sacrifice. From the finely decorated copper axes presented to the Spanish and the abundant use of gold ornaments, it was evidently a sophisticated and wealthy culture. When news reached Velázquez, he sent to Spain for permission to trade with this realm. But before authorisation arrived, Velázquez financed – either wholly or partly – an expedition of eleven ships,[17] for which he drew up strict instructions only to reconnoitre the coasts and not to proceed inland. This was a substantial force of 600 Spaniards (including

[17] Díaz says 'We had eleven ships in all' (Díaz del Castillo, 1963, p. 57), though modern scholars give different figures.

eight women), sixteen horses and fourteen small pieces of artillery under the command of Hernando Cortés, a *hidalgo* or minor nobleman from Extremadura in southwestern Spain. Cortés had some university education and legal training and, during his thirteen years in the Indies, had become an *encomendero* and Velázquez's secretary. Cortés may have invested his modest savings in the expedition or borrowed from Velázquez to do so – it is one of several points on which the chronicles conflict. The two, who had been friends as well as patron and client, fell out as the expedition was being prepared, and Velázquez tried to arrest Cortés before the flotilla set sail. The cause of their quarrel need not detain us, but to follow the tortuous narrative of the conquest of Mexico we must note that Cortés's most implacable enemy was Velázquez, in Cuba. It was soon evident that Cortés proposed defying the governor and venturing inland, with the aim of conquest and settlement. Despite this insubordination, the majority of the noblemen on the expedition elected him their 'captain' or *caudillo*. He was not the commander of a conventional military force and few of his men were professional soldiers. Like nearly all the expeditions that fanned out from the Greater Antilles, Cortés's force was a 'company' (*compaña*) of freebooters who went in search of plunder and status. Those who could invest more in the venture – by providing a horse for example – were promised a larger share of the spoils.

After landing at Tabasco, the expedition had a stiff skirmish with a party of Maya warriors and acquired a key native auxiliary in the form of a **Nahuatl**-and Maya-speaking noblewoman, named Doña Marina by the Spaniards. She became Cortés's mistress, bore one of his sons, and most importantly acted as the invaders' linguistic and cultural interpreter. Until she acquired some Spanish, translation from Nahuatl had to be through Maya. So how was that managed? Fortuitously, the expedition also stumbled across a Spanish priest, Gerónimo de Aguilar, who had been shipwrecked on the Yucatan coast in 1511, and had spent eight years in Maya captivity. Bear in mind when you read Cortés's account of what Montezuma[18] said that the latter's Nahuatl was mediated through Maya into Spanish. Even if Cortés had wanted to set down an unvarnished record of events, the potential for miscomprehension was almost limitless.

From Tabasco, the force sailed northward to a natural harbour on the Gulf coast, where it encamped and founded the town of Villa Rica de la Vera Cruz.[19] One reason for doing this was to create an authority – the town council – that was autonomous of the governor of Cuba and theoretically entitled to communicate directly with the crown; it covered Cortés's mutinous enterprise with the fig-leaf of legitimacy. Cortés spent four months at Vera Cruz, gathering

---

[18] The most accurate phonetic transcription, according to Pagden (Cortés, 1986, p. 460), is Motecuçoma. In his letters to Charles V of Spain, Cortés called him Mutezuma, which later Spanish authors rendered as Moctezuma, but to English readers he has always been Montezuma.

[19] The town, which was also called simply Vera Cruz, was later moved south to what is now Veracruz, as the new location had a better harbour. It was from the new location that Cortés began his journey to Tenochtitlan.

information about the Aztec state and its great lord Montezuma, and parleying with his emissaries, before setting out for the capital, Tenochtitlan, in mid-August 1519, leaving a garrison of 150 on the coast. His purpose was to take Montezuma alive in chains and make him subject to Charles V, ruler of Spain and, from June 1519, Holy Roman Emperor. Contrary to legend, he did not 'burn his boats', which were condemned as unseaworthy and beached. One ship had left for Spain in mid-July with two representatives of the new town (known as *procuradores*) whose task was to persuade the court of Charles V to acquiesce in the invasion of Mexico.

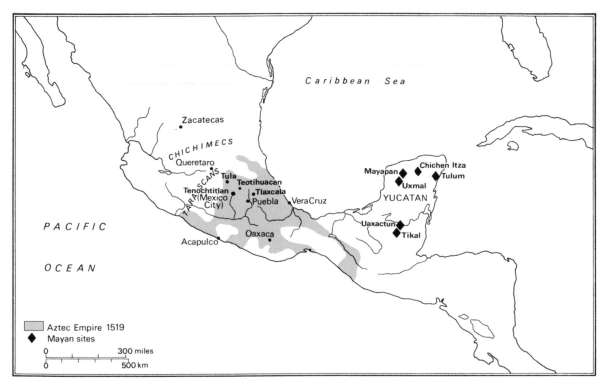

Figure 4.6   The Mexica empire in 1518, from Bethell, L. (ed.) (1984) *The Cambridge History of Latin America*, vol. 1, Cambridge, Cambridge University Press, p. 34.

The Aztec state was of quite recent origin. Figure 4.6 indicates its extent on the eve of the Spanish conquest. Rather than an 'empire', it is more accurately described as a confederation dominated by one tribe, the **Mexica**, who had founded their city state of Tenochtitlan on a large lake in the Valley of Mexico around 1330. (It was presumably sited for defensive purposes.) Over the following century, the Mexica were gradually militarised under warrior nobles led by an elected supreme leader (known as the 'great speaker king' or *uei tlatoani*). After allying with two neighbouring city states in about 1420, the Mexica began extending their power throughout the Valley of Mexico. The term 'Aztec' is properly applied to the culture of the whole valley, rather than the Mexica alone, but they appropriated this culture and gave it a remarkably bellicose and sanguinary edge. By 1500, many cities and communities beyond the valley had fallen under the tributary subjection of the Triple Alliance, which was itself dominated by Mexica warriors and their *tlatoani*. Subject populations had to furnish slaves, tribute and human sacrifices to Tenochtitlan, where the latter were ritually slaughtered to appease the Mexica's tribal god, **Huitzilopochtli** ('Southern Hummingbird'). According to their religious mythology, the working of the cosmos demanded that their god be fed with life itself, an essence found only in human blood. When the great pyramid of Huitzilopochtli was dedicated in 1487, probably 20,000 victims were sacrificed in a single day. Most were war captives, and only war could furnish victims on this scale (Bakewell, 1997, p. 25). 'Great speakers' were chosen on their promises of more conquests, which further accelerated the confederation's violent expansion. When Cortés landed, its territorial reach extended northeast of Tenochtitlan and south into what is now Guatemala; its total area was not far short of Spain's and its population was probably greater because central highland Mexico is exceptionally hospitable for human settlement. It lies within the tropics, but because of its altitude is neither hot nor humid while the soil is remarkably fertile and the summer rains usually support intensive agriculture. The indigenous population of Mexico – which was heavily concentrated in this central region – may have been as high as 21.4 million in 1519, when the combined population of Castile and Aragon was about 10 million. (Refer to Table 4.1 above. Scholarly estimates of the pre-conquest Mexican population have veered between 4 million and 25 million; see Thomas, 1993, pp. 609–14.)

In 1503, Montezuma II had become the ninth 'great speaker king' of the Mexica. He was both a successful warrior who greatly extended his dominions and a priest of Huitzilopochtli who augmented the power of the priesthood. He is credited with imposing rigidly centralised government, which almost certainly made it easier for alien conquerors to seize the state by capturing and deposing its supreme ruler. On their circuitous and protracted march to Tenochtitlan, the Spanish recruited Amerindian auxiliaries among the communities only recently incorporated into the Mexica empire, who had been forced to provide children as sacrificial tribute. According to Cortés's account, they asked for protection from Montezuma's tyranny and wished to become vassals of the king of Spain. The conquistadores' route also took them through the independent confederacy of Tlaxcala, which was engaged in a permanent, though ritualised, war with the Mexica. After overcoming fierce resistance by the Tlaxcalans, the Spaniards were joined by several thousand of these redoubtable warriors when it became clear that their goal was Tenochtitlan. Without these native allies, Cortés could not have overthrown the Mexica state. After the conquest, they were granted numerous privileges, including tax exemption, and often became administrators of petty principalities.

The massacre at Cholula

The most notorious incident on Cortés's march occurred at Cholula, a city that owed allegiance to Montezuma. You will find three accounts of what occurred on the course website: the first, in order of writing, is from Cortés's second letter to Charles V, dictated in late October 1520, relating what the expedition had accomplished since June 1519 (Primary Source 4.2); the second is from Las Casas's *Short Account of the Destruction of the Indies* (Primary Source 4.3); the third is from Bernal Díaz del Castillo's *True History of The Conquest of New Spain* (Primary Source 4.4). Díaz was a foot soldier in Cortés's army who wrote up his story when he was over seventy, partly to counter what he saw as the misrepresentations of Cortés's official biographer, Lopez de Gomara.

1   Read these accounts and write two or three paragraphs reconstructing the incident.

2   Is it possible to tell from these accounts what the real reasons for Cortés's behaviour were?

Look at Plate 2.1 in the Visual Sources Book and note how Cholula is located in relation to Tlaxcala and Tenochtitlan.

SPECIMEN ANSWER

1   Cortés's account is quite confusing, but these are the essential details. After spending twenty days in Tlaxcala, Montezuma's messengers asked him to go to Cholula. His Tlaxcalan allies warned him that Montezuma had prepared a trap in the city and surrounded it with 50,000 men. Cortés sent for the chiefs of the city to explain themselves, but they would not come, pleading sickness. He then sent a written command – witnessed by a notary – telling the chiefs of Cholula that their land now belonged to the king of Spain; if they were prepared to be his faithful vassals, well and good, but if they rebelled they would be punished according to the law. If such a document were sent, it would have been meaningless to its illiterate recipients; even if delivered by an interpreter, the message would have been barely comprehensible. However, according to Cortés, the chiefs of Cholula did then come to him and offer themselves as vassals of the king of Spain. This did not deter Cortés from going south to Cholula – that is, *away* from Tenochtitlan, his declared destination – accompanied by a large force of Tlaxcalans. After spending a night outside Cholula he was admitted the next morning by the leading citizens, and given quarters, though insufficient food. There were – he claimed – signs indicating a possible attack, which made the Spaniards more alert and cautious. On their third day in the city, Cortés learnt through Doña Marina that its people were in cahoots with Montezuma's men surrounding it, and planned to fall on the Spaniards and kill them all. So Cortés organised a pre-emptive strike: the chiefs were taken into custody and the many Amerindians outside the Spaniards' quarters were suddenly attacked, with the loss of over 3,000 lives. After the battle – in which the Spaniards were assisted by about 5,400 Amerindian auxiliaries – Cortés magnanimously freed the chiefs.

Las Casas – who was not there – gave a simpler version of events. Cortés is not named but, by implication, he organised 'a bloody massacre of the most public possible kind in order to terrorize these meek and gentle peoples' (p. 1). It was – Las Casas claimed – a cynical demonstration of ruthless savagery intended to overawe Montezuma and his subjects.

Díaz largely corroborates Cortés's version of events, but adds many circumstantial details, not all of which are entirely credible. How could he have known what the old cacique's wife said to Doña Marina? Did she have the linguistic competence to translate the complex speech reported on pp. 7–8 and *make it perfectly clear* to the Cholulan listeners? (Aguilar was not on the scene at that point.) Díaz blames Tlaxcalan allies for the worst excesses, which the compassionate Cortés tried to ?? restrain. According to Díaz, after the battle Cortés ordered the release of men and boys who were being fattened in cages for the sacrifice at which their flesh would be eaten. Díaz chided Las Casas for publishing untruths, and claimed that Franciscan friars who subsequently visited Cholula gathered testimony from its inhabitants that corroborated his version of events.

2   No, not without further evidence.

So who was telling the truth? Or which account is more credible? There is no record of Franciscan friars visiting Cholula in the early 1520s but there is further, largely unpublished, testimony given to the long enquiry into Cortés's conduct of affairs by royal officials after 1529. This learnt from one member of the expeditionary force, Vázquez de Tapia, that as many as 20,000 Cholulans were massacred in an unprovoked attack. Modern scholars generally favour the 'shock and awe' theory: Cortés's most plausible reason for going to Cholula was to terrorise its subjects and pave the way for unopposed entry into Tenochtitlan. Las Casas was basically right. Even historians who maintain that the Spaniards reacted to some sort of provocation, recoil from their astonishing ruthlessness.

Cortés and Montezuma

Some 400 Spaniards entered the Mexica capital of Tenochtitlan on 8 November. They approached it over a broad causeway from which – Díaz tells us – they could see 'great towns and **cues** [temples, step pyramids] and buildings rising from the water, all made of stone ... like an enchanted vision'. It was, he recalled, 'all so wonderful that I do not know how to describe this first glimpse of things never heard of, seen or dreamed of before' (Díaz del Castillo, p. 214). Plate 2.2 in the Visual Sources Book gives you an impression of the city's location and layout.

Cortés gave Charles V a vivid account of his meeting with Montezuma that I would like you to read (Primary Source 4.5 on the course website), along with Diaz's recollection of the event (Primary Source 4.6 on the course website). Summarise what happened. How credible do you find Montezuma's reported speech?

According to Cortés, Montezuma welcomed the Spaniard cordially, gave him treasures of gold, silver and feather work, then sat him down on a throne and made over the Mexica dominions to the king of Spain. The words put by Cortés into Montezuma's mouth surely beggar belief. Indeed, they seem so implausible that it is tempting to dismiss the incident as pure invention. As Díaz reports it, Montezuma simply said that he was not only at the Spaniards' service, but would share all he possessed with them. This is much more credible; it sounds like a gesture of extravagant courtesy. Yet, according to both Cortés and Díaz, Montezuma referred to the legend of ancestral return to justify the donation of his domain. There is a further point on which they *nearly* agree: according to Cortés, at the end of their meeting, Montezuma lifted his tunic and declared that he was mortal like any other man. According to Díaz, Montezuma did and said something virtually identical at a meeting on the following day (p. 223). If Díaz was following Cortés in fabricating the whole incident, then why did he displace this speech?

What *really* transpired between Cortés and Montezuma has been a matter of fascinating but inconclusive debate. Clendinnen (1991) and Brooks (1995) have argued that Cortés's second letter was an elaborate fiction, composed when the expedition's fortunes were at a low ebb and intended to persuade Charles V in Spain of the legitimacy of the enterprise. Thomas (1993), in the most detailed modern account of the conquest, argues that there is too much corroborative testimony for Cortés's account to be pure invention (p. 285). If you want to follow up this debate, the secondary sources can be accessed on the course website. One point worth adding is that Cortés was laying claim to two different legitimacies: the first derived from the late medieval Christian theory that a lawful ruler could voluntarily 'translate' his realm to a liege lord; the second from the Mexica's own belief that the descendants of an ancestral chief would return as conquerors. We have here the first hint that Montezuma identified Cortés with **Quetzalcoatl**, the plumed serpent in the Mexica pantheon, which became part of the conquest mythology in Nahuatl culture. Whether Montezuma in November 1519 actually made *this* 'mistake' seems unlikely; it is more probable that the Quetzalcoatl legend was used many years later to rationalise the cataclysm that overwhelmed the Mexica empire. But I cannot see why both Cortés and Díaz would fabricate the ancestral prophesy, which may well have psychologically disabled Montezuma and his court.

Six days after the first meeting, Cortés took Montezuma into custody, ostensibly while investigating the killing of four Spaniards in another city, which Montezuma had purportedly ordered. After two to three weeks, the chief who had killed the Spaniards arrived, with one of his sons and some followers. Cortés arrested and interrogated them, and then had them burned in a public square. Since they had implicated Montezuma, Cortés ordered him to be put in irons, though these were subsequently removed. In his own account, Cortés was now the power behind the throne, and able to extort from Montezuma considerable quantities of fine gold ornaments – which were melted down for their bullion value – and a public declaration of fealty to Charles V, made in front of the assembled Mexica nobility. The nobles then swore allegiance to Charles and promised to provide the tribute and service formerly paid to Montezuma. 'All of this', claimed Cortés, 'was said before a notary public, who set it down in a formal document ... attested by many Spaniards' (Cortés, 1986, p. 99).

Díaz and other witnesses confirm that the nobles made some kind of submission, though how *they* understood what they were doing is another matter. For Charles V and his advisers, the legalism of this purported transfer of power was immensely reassuring: it meant those Mexica who contested the donation could be treated as rebels; equally, those Spaniards who tried to subvert Charles's new subjects from their allegiance were traitors.

In April 1520, it appeared that Cortés had succeeded in seizing power in the Mexica empire by the consent of its supreme ruler. Over the winter, he had sent small groups of Spaniards to all corners of Charles V's new kingdom to survey its wealth. That they travelled unharmed over hundreds of miles indicates Montezuma's unquestioned authority and the regimented character of Nahuatl society. What fatally disrupted this seizure of power was the arrival at Vera Cruz of a second Spanish expedition, despatched from Cuba by Veláquez under the command of Pánfilo de Narváez. He had with him about 900 men and his orders were to hang Cortés and his chief lieutenants. Montezuma's agents made contact with Narváez before Cortés was aware of his presence and were soon attempting to enlist the newly arrived Spaniards in a bid to secure their emperor's freedom. When he learnt of Narváez's expedition, Cortés acted with great speed and daring: he left 150 men guarding Montezuma in Tenochtitlan and marched to the coast. There he bribed several of Narváez's captains into joining him and then seized Narváez in a surprise night attack. The next morning, he persuaded the great majority of Narváez's men to serve under him.

Meanwhile, his deputy in Tenochtitlan, Pedro de Alvarado, had derailed the strategy of peaceful take-over by massacring a gathering of young Mexica nobles at their most important religious ceremony. Alvarado claimed to be forestalling a coup, and may have been persuaded by his Tlaxcalan allies that one was afoot. Some sixty Spaniards hacked down the nobles as they danced trance-like in the city's main temple, and then turned on the spectators. Perhaps two to three thousand were butchered. At the same time, a group of courtiers cloistered with Montezuma were killed. This gratuitous violence destroyed Montezuma's charismatic authority over his people, who turned on him for welcoming the aliens into their midst. With so many nobles killed, the city's population was leaderless, unorganised and, initially, gripped by sullen mourning. When Cortés returned he found the city eerily quiet. The markets were shut and Alvarado's garrison was denied food and fresh water, while coming under sporadic attack. In an effort to restore imperial authority, Cortés permitted the release of Montezuma's brother, Cuitláhuac. This was a near fatal error of judgement, because the Mexica now had a warlord to organise the resistance. Urban guerrilla warfare soon engulfed the central precincts. Montezuma was stoned by insurgents as he had tried to act as peacemaker and died from his wounds. Sensing that his force was trapped, Cortés ordered a midnight retreat on 1 July across the shortest of the causeways. The Mexica were alerted and their canoe-borne warriors fell on the retreating column. About 600 Spaniards were killed or captured in the mayhem, along with several thousand Tlaxcalans. What became known as the ***noche triste*** – the tragic night – was all the more disastrous because most of the gold extorted from Montezuma had to be jettisoned.

How were the Spaniards able to recover from this appalling setback and, within thirteen months, reconquer Tenochtitlan and all its tributary dominions? Three factors stand out, though their relative significance is much debated. First, the on-going fragmentation of the Mexica empire brought the Spaniards new allies. While Cortés's force recouped in Tlaxcala, emissaries from other cities arrived and offered to become vassals of Charles V, a formula they cheerfully parroted in the belief they were enlisting a bunch of hardy mercenaries in their war of independence. With his Amerindian auxiliaries, Cortés probably had parity in numbers when he laid siege to Tenochtitlan. Second, the first great New World pandemic was sweeping through the Valley of Mexico. This was most probably smallpox, one of the commonest viral diseases in late medieval, early modern Europe, though in this instance

(handwritten margin note: societies)

(handwritten margin note: environmental disease)

allegedly introduced by an African slave (Crosby, 1967). Smallpox is highly infectious and normally communicated by breathing contaminated droplets, which enable the virus to enter a new host through the respiratory tract. Most Europeans who survived to adulthood acquired an immunity, which explains why the Spaniards were unaffected by the epidemic. Disease mortality among Amerindian communities was 30 per cent or more. Victims in Tenochtitlan included Cuitláhuac, Montezuma's successor, who had harried the Spaniards on their retreat to Tlaxcala. The sixty days during which the epidemic raged through the city afforded Cortés's force a much-needed respite. The dead were too numerous to bury, so suppurating bodies were tossed into the lake. Third, Cortés could draw on the superior technique of an oceanic civilisation to defeat a land-locked culture. Reinforcements arrived at Vera Cruz from the Caribbean with fresh horses, more cannon and gunpowder. But the most remarkable demonstration of technical superiority was the construction in Tlaxcala of a fleet of brigantines with which to blockade Tenochtitlan. These forty-foot flat-bottomed vessels were built in parts and then transported by about 8,000 Tlaxcalan bearers to the edge of the great lake. Each boat carried about thirty fighting men and had a small cannon mounted in the bow.

new technologies leading to war-like tendencies

Notwithstanding their native and biological allies, and their technical superiority, the Spaniards had to wage a grisly war of attrition to capture Tenochtitlan. The siege lasted seventy-five days; perhaps 100,000 Mexica were killed or died of starvation; and a masterpiece of urban design was comprehensively destroyed. In the aftermath, the Spaniards were pitiless in their search for loot: they had enlisted for personal profit and most were heavily indebted to their suppliers and the expedition's armourers and military surgeons. Surviving Mexica nobles were tortured in a vain attempt to locate the gold abandoned during the *noche triste*. In the event, the Spanish rank and file were outraged by their meagre share of the spoils; those who could write scrawled abuse on the walls of Cortés's residence. Had they known that he secretly despatched fabulous 'presents' to leading officials and churchmen in Spain, their rancour would have been boundless.[20]

Yet, despite their internecine quarrels, the Spaniards moved quickly from destruction to reconstruction. The rebuilding of Tenochtitlan as Mexico City was the largest enterprise of its kind in the world in the 1520s. The city's rebuilding depended on drafts of forced labour, made available by the widespread branding and enslavement of recalcitrant Amerindians both before and after the final victory. Some were distributed to native auxiliaries, others to Cortés's favoured captains or assigned to gold mining. According to a Franciscan chronicler who landed in New Spain in 1524, the forced labourers working on the city had to bring their own building materials and were not fed by their supervisors. Not infrequently, the latter were black slaves who were entrusted with intermediary positions between Spanish masters and native

---

[20] The 'presents' never reached their intended recipients because Cortés's treasure ships were captured by French privateers off the Azores.

helots. The new capital's topography faithfully replicated its predecessor's: the main plaza was on the same site, its great cathedral in the old temple compound, and the governor's palace was sited where Montezuma's had been (Lockhart and Schwartz, 1983, p. 89). Plate 2.3 in the Visual Sources Book offers a splendid panorama of Mexico City in the later seventeenth century. And just as Tenochtitlan had dominated the Mexica empire, so Mexico City dominated New Spain: it sucked labour and tribute from the surrounding countryside and attracted the bulk of Spanish immigrants; the grandest *encomenderos* lived there, as did the wealthiest merchants, once the extractive colonial economy began to function.

Amerindian society under Spanish rule[21]

For the Amerindians who survived their mistreatment, slavery was usually a transitory status. From the summer of 1522, Cortés embarked on a policy of depositing native communities with *encomenderos*, mostly his companions-in-arms, though they included a few native 'collaborators', who converted to Catholicism, adopted European dress and learnt Spanish. The crown heeded its Christian duty to its new subjects and prohibited all future enslavement on any pretext in 1530. Although compelled to rescind this prohibition four years later, Amerindian slavery was again outlawed under the 'New Laws' of 1542. In practice, the conquistadores preferred to impose a conscripted dependency on Amerindian workers, which ensured access to their labour without the obligation of life-long upkeep entailed by chattel slavery.

Had it not been for subsequent epidemics, native aristocrats would have played a significant role in the colonial hierarchy, for many quickly became literate in Spanish and Latin. Indeed, from the frequency with which the conquistadores took native noblewomen as wives and mistresses, one would have anticipated the emergence of a hybrid colonial ruling class: Cortés fathered at least two mixed-race children, one by a daughter of Montezuma. But the proximity of native aristocrats to the Spaniards left them exceptionally exposed to imported disease and by the later sixteenth century they had practically died out. What remained of Amerindian society was simultaneously fragmented into small units, each based on a ***pueblo***, or township, and homogenised. Amerindians were allowed a measure of self-government organised around the ***cabacera***, which might be loosely described as a 'county town' with satellite townships. The social distinctions that the Spanish originally tried to maintain between the 'natural lords' (***señores naturales***) and the common people were increasingly difficult to discern after 1550. The colonial ruling class, or ***criollos***, became racially exclusive and utterly dissociated from the indigenous population. (A *criollo* denoted an American-born Spaniard of pure European descent, usually fixated on ***limpieza de sangre***, or the 'purity of one's blood'.)

---

[21] This section draws on the work of Charles Gibson (1987).

Under the New Laws, jurisdiction over Amerindian communities was exercised by royal officials, known as **corregidores**, who were also responsible for exacting tribute and taxes, executing royal law, and maintaining order. Their record as guardians of the Amerindians was no better than that of the *encomenderos*; they became notorious for exacting money and goods illegally and demanding fees for functions they should have freely performed. By the later sixteenth century, the social spaces between the Amerindians and the *criollos* were being filled out by blacks and people of mixed descent: mestizos (white–Amerindian), mulattos (white–black) and **zambos** (black–Amerindian).

By 1600, just over 200,000 African slaves had been landed in the New World, over three-quarters of them in the Spanish American mainland. This was a mere trickle compared with eighteenth-century slave shipments, but roughly equal to permanent European transatlantic migration before 1600. Indeed, after 1550 or so, Africans outnumbered Europeans in the main colonial towns (Bakewell, 1997, p. 167).

THE CONQUEST OF PERU 1532–35

EXERCISE

Now read the chapter from John Hemming's history of the conquest of the Incas on the course website (Secondary Source 4.1) and make a note of those factors that weakened their resistance to the invaders. The chapter concludes with the seizure of the Inca emperor, Atahualpa, on 16 November 1532 – an extraordinary *coup de main*, given the disparity between Pizarro's 'company' and the Inca army at Atahualpa's command. After extorting a huge ransom from Atahualpa as the price of his release, Pizarro broke his word and had him executed in July 1533. The Spaniards then marched south to Cuzco, the Inca capital, where they installed Atahualpa's half-brother, Manco, as their client emperor in December. The conquest was far from over, yet Atahualpa's capture and death had clearly been pivotal events.

In what ways had the assault on the Inca empire up to this point resembled the conquest of New Spain? In what ways had it differed? (Use Figures 4.7 and 4.8 to help you.)

SPECIMEN ANSWER

Both conquests were launched from bases on the turbulent frontier, though in each case royal approval was sought for an inland expedition. From Panama, Pizarro had already undertaken two probing voyages before being authorised to discover and conquer Peru, so the 'preparatory' phase was longer than that preceding the invasion of Mexico. Like Cortés, Pizarro first learnt about a magnificent inland empire from coastal people. The two men met in Toledo in 1528 and the seizure of the Mexica empire was a 'brilliant inspiration' for Pizarro and his companions: the capture of the divine ruler, the exploitation of native political divisions, and exemplary use of terror all recalled Cortés's tactics. There were significant differences: Peru was more remote, the Inca empire was much more extensive, and the logistical problems confronting its invaders were more severe. Pizarro had the good fortune to enter the Inca realm when dynastic civil war had splintered its ruling hierarchy, and weakened its hold on subject peoples. He successfully manipulated factional conflict and, like Cortés before him, capitalised on the break-down of imperial authority over recently subjugated tribes. Fortuitously, too, Pizarro's

[handwritten margin notes:] maritime empire. landing on coasts required info. regarding a country's interior.

[handwritten margin notes, right side:] frontiers were coast-like land empires, frontiers were different.

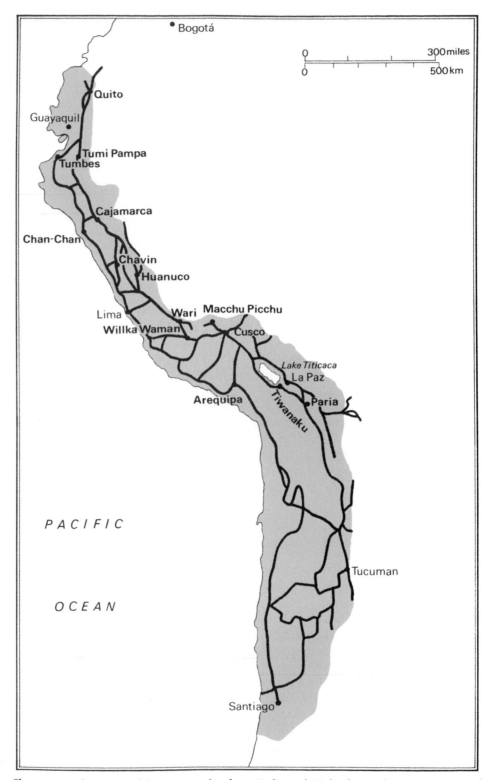

Figure 4.7   The extent of the Inca empire, from Hyslop, J. (1984) *Inka Road System: Survey and General Analysis*, New York, Academic Press.

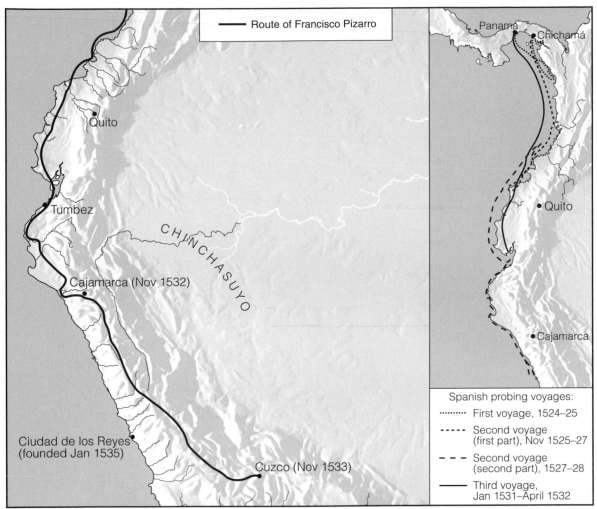

Figure 4.8   Francisco Pizarro's route from the coast to Cajamarca and on to Cuzco, September 1532 to November 1533, adapted from Hemming, J. (1970) *The Conquest of the Incas*, London, Macmillan, map 1 and 'The Conquest of Peru, 1531–1533', from Shepherd, W.R. (1923) *The Historical Atlas*, New York, Henry Holt and Company, p. 111, available from http://www.lib.utexas.edu (University of Texas Libraries). Note that Ciudad de los Reyes is modern-day Lima.

expedition had been preceded by a smallpox epidemic, which had swept south from Panama. There were similarities in the way Montezuma and Atahualpa responded to alien intruders: both were unsure whether to repel or welcome them; both seem to have been rendered psychologically vulnerable by their religious traditions.

The latter point should become clear when you read the extract from the account of the Spaniards' arrival, dictated by Titu Cusí Yupanqui for the benefit of Philip II of Spain in February 1570 (Primary Source 4.7). This remarkable source was rediscovered during the twentieth century: it provides an excellent historical summary of the Conquest through Inca eyes and is the only autobiographical memoir of a leading figure of *either* side. Titu Cusí (1530?–1571) was a son of Manco (d.1545), the client ruler who initially collaborated with the conquistadores in subduing the forces still loyal to the

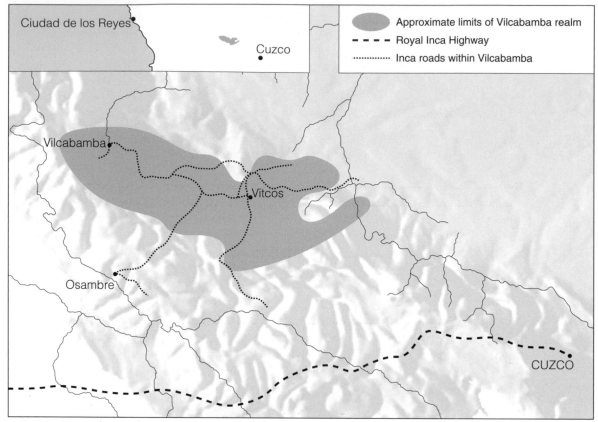

Figure 4.9   Neo-Inca state of Vilcabamba, adapted from Hemming, J. (1970) *The Conquest of the Incas*, London, Macmillan, map 4.

dead Atahualpa. But Manco soon found the Spaniards' greed, cruelty and contempt for indigenous religious practices intolerable, and in the autumn of 1535 led an uprising to expel them. Manco was eventually worsted in battle and retreated with substantial forces to the tropical jungles of Vitcos and Vilcabamba on the eastern slopes of the Andes, where they recreated a neo-Inca state that co-existed with the Hispanic world of the conquistadores for more than thirty years (see Figure 4.9). Titu Cusí succeeded to the throne after his father was murdered by Spanish fugitives, who had been outlawed during the Spaniards' own civil wars. Contacts with Vilcabamba were maintained mainly by missionaries, who converted the ruling circle to Catholicism and introduced the written word as an instrument of government. The state gradually became Hispanicised of its own accord and Titu Cusí acknowledged a vassal relationship with the Spanish crown. In terms of the typology in Unit 2, Vilcabamba was a 'protectorate', internally governed by a native elite, but externally subordinate to the Spanish authorities. Titu Cusí maintained a mestizo secretary, who transcribed the account you will read, which was dictated in **Quechua** to a resident missionary. It is obviously a hybrid document, composed long after the event, in which assertions and ideas have been mediated between languages and cultures. Nevertheless, the account represented Titu Cusí's attempt to make sense of the amazingly disruptive events of his own lifetime. He died in 1571, and in the following year a Spanish army invaded Vilcabamba and executed his successor, which ended the paternal line of the Inca dynasty.

EXERCISE

Read Primary Source 4.7 on the course website. What does it add to your reading of Hemming's chapter in Secondary Source 4.1?

SPECIMEN ANSWER

The factual details, for which Titu Cusí relied on oral tradition, are much less important than the insight we are given into how the Incas viewed the Spaniards from within their traditional cosmology. Also, Titu Cusí's pride in his legitimate ancestry and his disparagement of Atahualpa – the bastard child of a commoner mother 'who ruled the land as a tyrant ... and did not escape the punishment he deserved' (p. 5) – helps us appreciate the venomous disputes within the royal family, which Pizarro adroitly exploited.

TOWARDS A SILVER-BASED EMPIRE

Before 1518, probably fewer than 10 per cent of the native population of the Americas had had any contact with Europeans; by 1540, probably 80 per cent of the native population was under Spanish or Portuguese domination. Although exploration and conquest continued, their tempo slowed from this point because few Spaniards were attracted to the idea of settling a wilderness. Land without a sedentary indigenous population was of little value to them, for it was vassals rather than land they wanted. There was no land hunger in metropolitan Spain, nor were there any dissenting religious groups seeking to practise their faith beyond the control of the crown. Thus, the consolidation of the American empire depended not on 'push' factors in the metropolis but on 'pull' factors in the Indies. These changed dramatically in the mid-1540s with the near contemporaneous discovery of vast silver deposits in Potosí in Peru and Zacatecas in northern Mexico.

Large-scale silver production transformed the Spanish American economy and greatly increased the strategic value of the Indies to the Habsburgs: between 1521 and 1544, the output of the silver mines in their hereditary lands was nearly four times greater than the quantity produced by all the Americas; between 1545 and the later 1550s, this ratio was reversed. The Potosí ores were so abundant that for about twenty years Spanish entrepreneurs were content to employ Amerindian smelters to extract the silver by traditional methods. In northern Mexico, where there was no native metallurgical tradition, mining contractors had to invest in fixed capital to make their ventures pay. Their big breakthrough came in the 1550s with the introduction of mercury amalgamation, a process requiring water-driven mills to crush the ore, combine it with mercury and then wash the silver from the amalgam. There were evident economies of scale, and a mine-cum-amalgamation plant could remain profitable even when processing low-grade ore. Those in northern Mexico were among the largest industrial complexes of their day. The chance discovery of mercury deposits at Huancavelica in Peru prompted Spanish entrepreneurs to invest in the amalgamation process in Potosí. It led to spectacular increases in the production and export of silver. Total treasure imports into Seville, as recorded by the Casa de la Contratación, rose from 12 million **pesos** in 1551–55 to 17 million in 1576–80 and peaked at 35 million in 1591–95. An unknown quantity was smuggled into Spain and, as the colonial economy diversified, a considerable amount was retained in Spanish America. A mint was established in Mexico City in 1536 and another in Lima in 1565, which later transferred to Potosí.

The silver boom was registered in Potosí's extraordinary growth from a tiny Amerindian settlement 13,000 feet above sea level to a city of 100,000 by 1600, which made it one of the largest in the western world. An eighteenth-century print (Plate 2.4 in the Visual Sources Book) shows the streets and squares laid out in grid-iron fashion; to the left, the steep valleys are dammed to create the artificial lakes needed to power the amalgamation plant. Amerindian labour for the mines and mills was drafted in from hundreds of miles around by enforcing a tributary obligation on village communities that dated to Inca times. Known as **mita**, it kept costs down and profits up. Workers were paid, but generally less than the cost of their subsistence. They were selected by lot, served a fixed term and were supported by deliveries of food from their home communities. It was a paradigm case of colonial capitalism, which combined a coerced, pre-capitalist workforce with concentrated European capital and advanced technology.

The larger significance of American silver exports has been much debated and, though not properly germane to the 'beginning' of empire, can scarcely be altogether ignored. There can be no question that the Spanish crown enjoyed short-term advantages from the boost to its revenues that came from leasing out its subsoil rights to mining contractors and the taxation of silver output. Although only about 20 per cent of royal income in the late sixteenth century, the silver revenues came as cash and cost little to collect. They were readily accepted as collateral by the Genoese and Augsburg bankers whose loans kept the monarchy solvent. They helped pay for the Spanish armies in Flanders and other costly military enterprises. Without the liquidity of American silver, Spain's imperial policy in Europe would have been more constrained, the hegemony it exercised between about 1580 and 1640 more tenuous.

Yet, it is generally agreed that silver imports weakened the Spanish economy because they induced severe monetary inflation. Spain's traditional exports of raw wool and woollens were priced out of foreign markets and, though manufacturers enjoyed tariff protection, it could not prevent better-quality imports taking over the domestic market by the 1590s. By then Castilian industry was near the brink of bankruptcy (Lynch, 1991, p. 173). Not all the ills of the Spanish economy can be attributed to price inflation, from which certain groups – notably commercial farmers – benefited overall. Immigrant merchants at the hub of the transatlantic economy prospered mightily. But

Spanish manufacturing and commerce stagnated while the pace of economic development quickened in northwest Europe – a comparative economic decline largely, though not wholly, attributable to American silver.

The broader impact of American bullion imports on what we can loosely call the 'world economy' has been a matter of recurrent speculation since the emergence of economics as an intellectual discipline. The silver quickly diffused across western Europe, and some have argued it induced a secular price inflation that had a differential impact on those who owned productive assets (capitalists) and those who lived by selling their labour (wage earners). Capitalists passed on price rises to consumers, while real wages declined. Profit margins rose, so stimulating investment in commercial agriculture and manufacturing (Hamilton, 1929). If this thesis is correct, American silver acted like healthy tonic on early modern capitalism, though not at the metropolitan centre of the greatest of the Atlantic empires. Other commentators have been deeply sceptical about attributing profound change in the 'real' economy to the increasing supply of money; for them, rising population and increasing agricultural productivity were the dynamics of change. Whatever view we take of this debate, we must acknowledge that the export of silver from Spanish America, like the export of slaves from Africa, had the effect of 'binding the continents'. For over two centuries, the Mexican and Peruvian silver mines furnished about 80 per cent of the increment to the world's stock of monetary metal. American silver was used to settle transactions between Europe and Asia; without it, intercontinental trade could not have grown as quickly as it did because there was little demand in Asian economies for European manufactures.

CONCLUSION

The years between Cortés's march on the Mexica capital and Manco Inca's flight to Vilcabamba were the most momentous in the history of the western hemisphere. They saw the beginnings of a new type of transoceanic empire, sustained by the flow of trade, tribute and labour between *three* continents, and a new type of colonial society. To describe it as 'neo-European' is not entirely accurate, for this was a hybrid social form. *Criollos* were the dominant class, but the governors and administrators were Spanish bureaucrats. Catholicism was the official religion and civic institutions were European, but the labour force was Native American, mixed-race or black. Slavery, an increasingly marginal institution in Europe, became indispensable in this type of society wherever plantation labour was needed. In many ways the Spanish conquests were unrepeatable, 'unique' events, but from analysing them we can draw certain general theses that have a wider bearing on the history of empire.

- It is truism that the preconditions for conquests must include *power disparities* between conquerors and conquered, in both 'hard' military force and 'soft' ideological power, but how do they arise? What are their sources?

Superior technique is obviously one source: mounted warriors with steel weapons have a huge advantage over foot soldiers without them. But power disparities depend greatly on *context*: horses are useless throughout much of tropical Africa because of tsetse fly infestation; it is one part of the world that could not be conquered on horseback. Migration to *a radically different geographical and cultural environment* will often enhance power disparities because incomers bring techniques that give them a competitive advantage: literacy, for example, advantaged both Muslim and Christian invaders of pagan Africa, where writing was unknown, in much the same way as it advantaged the Spanish conquerors. It enhanced the 'soft' power of scriptural religions and also helped establish more stable and extensive systems of law and administration.

- Migration between disease environments brought *unintended germ warfare*: it was a major variable in imperial expansion up to the later nineteenth century, though in the tropics Europeans were normally the victims of disease. The disease barrier protected tropical Africa from invasion and settlement.

- Conquests irrupted from the *turbulent frontier*, not the metropolis. Before the invention of the telegraph, communication was far too slow for European governments to control events on the colonial periphery. They usually delegated state authority to private entrepreneurs hoping to profit by territorial expansion. A frontier environment was inherently unstable and prone to violence: incomers did not recognise native law and custom; their own laws were more difficult to enforce; and moral norms often broke down. Taking a concubine, which was sinful in Christian Europe, was the norm; rape of native women went unpunished.

- On the frontier, conquerors recruited *allies and auxiliaries*. Conquered states and societies have rarely been ethnically homogeneous: capitalising on the conflicts between dominant and subordinate ethnicities, persuading recently subjugated or enslaved peoples to rebel against their masters, have been common strategies of imperialist advance.

- Systematic exploitation of imperial conquests depended on *implanting institutions*: economic, legal and religious institutions (such as those shown in Figure 4.10), and social institutions such as the nuclear family. Obviously, institutions do not function without people, and settlers were needed to consolidate conquests, but in many parts of the Europeanised world they were surprisingly few in number before the mid-nineteenth century. Institutions secured the *'conquest after the conquest'*, to use Bakewell's (1995) phrase.

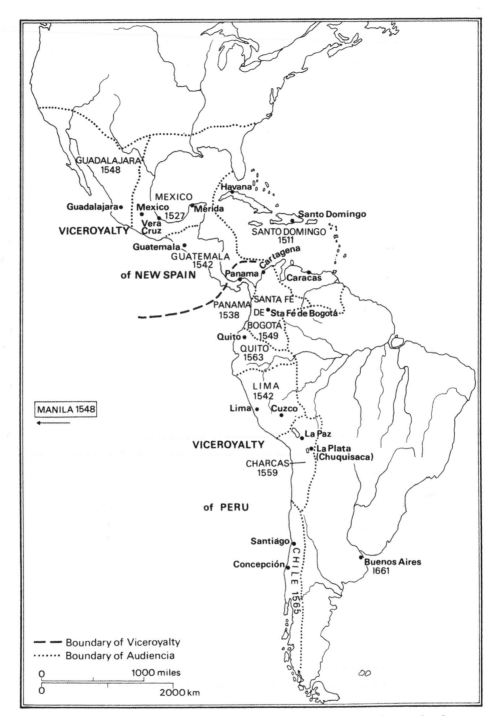

Figure 4.10   Viceroyalties and *audiencias* in the sixteenth and seventeenth centuries, from Padrón, F.M. (1975) *Historia general de América* (*General History of America*) (2nd edn), Madrid, Espasa-Calpe.

REFERENCES

Bakewell, P. (1995) 'Conquest after the conquest: the rise of Spanish domination in America', in Kagan, R.L. and Parker, G. (eds) *Spain, Europe and the Atlantic world*, Cambridge, Cambridge University Press.

Bakewell, P. (1997) *A History of Latin America*, Oxford, Blackwell.

Boyd-Bowman, P. (1976) 'Patterns of Spanish emigration to the Indies until 1600', *Hispanic American Historical Review*, vol. 56, no. 4, pp. 580–604.

Brading, D. (1991) *The First America: The Spanish Monarchy, Creole Patriots, and the Liberal State 1492–1867*, Cambridge, Cambridge University Press.

Brooks, F.J. (1995) 'Motecuzoma Xocoyotl, Hernan Cortes, and Bernal Diaz del Castillo: the construction of an arrest', *Hispanic American Historical Review*, vol. 75, no. 2, pp. 149–83.

Clendinnen, I. (1991) '"Fierce and unnatural cruelty": Cortés and the conquest of Mexico', *Representations*, vol. 33 (special issue: *The New World*), pp. 65–100.

Cortés, H. (1986) *Hernán Cortés: Letters from Mexico*, rev. edn (trans. and ed. A. Pagden; intro. J.H. Elliott), New Haven, Yale University Press (originally published by Grossman, 1971).

Crosby, A.W. (1967) '*Conquistador y pestilencia*: the first New World pandemic and the fall of the great Indian empires', *Hispanic American Historical Review*, vol. 47, no. 3, pp. 321–7.

Díaz del Castillo, B. (1963) *The Conquest of New Spain* (trans. and intro. J.M. Cohen), Harmondsworth, Penguin.

Elliott, J.H. (1987) 'The Spanish conquest', in Bethell, L. (ed.) *Colonial Spanish America*, Cambridge, Cambridge University Press.

Elliott, J.H. (1989) *Spain and its World 1500–1700: Selected Essays*, New Haven, Yale University Press.

Elliott, J.H. (2006) *Empires of the Atlantic World: Britain and Spain in America 1492–1830*, New Haven, Yale University Press.

Eltis, D. (2002) 'Free and coerced migration from the Old World to the New' in Eltis, D. (ed.) *Coerced and Free Migration: Global Perspectives*, Palo Alto, Stanford University Press.

Gibson, C. (1987) 'Indian societies under Spanish rule', in Bethell, L. (ed.) *Colonial Spanish America*, Cambridge, Cambridge University Press.

Hamilton, E.J. (1929) 'American treasure and the rise of capitalism', *Economica*, vol. 9, no. 27, pp. 338–57.

Hemming, J. (1970) *The Conquest of the Incas*, Basingstoke, Macmillan.

Las Casas, B. de (1992) *A Short Account of the Destruction of the Indies* (trans. and ed. N. Griffin; intro. A. Pagden), Harmondsworth, Penguin.

Lockhart, J. and Schwartz, S.B. (1983) *Early Latin America: A History of Colonial Spanish America and Brazil*, Cambridge, Cambridge University Press.

Lovell, W.G. (1992) '"Heavy shadows and black night": disease and depopulation in colonial Spanish America', *Annals of the Association of American Geographers*, vol. 82, no. 3, pp. 426–43.

Lynch, J. (1991) *Spain 1516–1598: From Nation State to World Empire*, Oxford, Blackwell.

Phillips, C.R. (1990) 'The growth and composition of trade in the Iberian empires, 1450–1750' in Tracy, J.D. (ed.) *The Rise of Merchant Empires: Long-distance Trade in the Early Modern World 1350–1750*, Cambridge, Cambridge University Press.

Smith, A. (1910 [1776]) *An Inquiry into the Nature and Causes of the Wealth of Nations*, 2 vols, London, Everyman.

Thomas, H. (1993) *The Conquest of Mexico*, London, Hutchinson.

Thomas, H. (2003) *Rivers of Gold: The Rise of the Spanish Empire*, London, Weidenfeld and Nicolson.

Titu Cusí Yupanqui (2005) *An Inca Account of the Conquest of Peru* (trans., intro. and annotated R. Bauer), Boulder, University Press of Colorado.

> **UNIT 5**
> **PIRATES, PILGRIMS, PLANTATIONS AND PIGS: THE BEGINNINGS OF THE**
> **BRITISH ATLANTIC EMPIRE 1497–1660**

Chris A. Williams

AIMS

- To help you structure your thinking about different explanations for the start of empire.

- To provide a brief chronological overview of the process of British expansion into the Atlantic world, and the most important features of that expansion.

- To present two brief case studies, on New England and Barbados, and describe how these fitted into an imperial system.

INTRODUCTION

The traditional answer to the question 'How did the British empire begin in the Atlantic world?' located its roots in the late fifteenth century, when King Henry VII commissioned a Venetian sailor, John Cabot, to sail across the Atlantic and look for a passage for the Indies. From this small beginning came the voyages of discovery and piratical exploits of the Elizabethan era. These led inexorably to the many rich colonies of the New World, which were economically successful by the middle of the seventeenth century, and under the control of the British crown – a situation that would endure until most of the American colonies broke off in 1783.

Like a lot of popular understanding of history, this is a misleading caricature of reality, mainly because it over-emphasises continuities in the process of imperial expansion. One of the main points that I will make in this unit is that, rather than being one single process, over the first 150 years, at least, British imperial expansion in the Atlantic is best understood as several very different kinds of activity, with very little in common save geographical area. People crossed the seas for many different reasons, and few of them thought that they were doing this to build an empire. So, when we employ hindsight to speak of 'expansion of empire', we are describing these processes in a very different way from how they were understood at the time.

The process began with Henry dispatching Cabot; it ended with the American colonies waging war on their king. These events, and the subsequent history of the 'second' British empire in the nineteenth century, create an impression that empire must always be willed and directed by the state. This is only partially true; in order to understand why, we need to understand the diffuse nature of the early modern state, and the methods that it habitually used to get things – not just overseas expeditions – done.

We also need to think closely about the economics of empire. Any movement of peoples needs an economic underpinning in order to be sustainable in the medium term, let alone to grow in the long run. Money normally made the difference between, on the one hand, a brief exploration or reconnaissance, and, on the other, an enduring presence in, or link to, an area outside Europe.

EMA

In the Far East, and with Iceland and Russia, enduring (if not especially profitable) trading links could be established with the indigenous societies. This process was much harder to establish in the New World, since, outside the Aztec and Inca empires, the economies of the native inhabitants had little to offer to Europe. The only exception to this rule was the trade in furs, but this resulted in dispersed trading posts rather than significant movements of people. All other commodities had to be extracted by European-controlled operations. The English colonies in the Atlantic world took off only once they had developed economically into a self-sustaining network, sustained largely by sales of two exceptionally profitable commodities – the cash crops tobacco and sugar – and the servicing of the plantation economies that produced them. Expansion was driven by a search for things to import back to Europe, not for markets for British exports.

essentially what an Empire was

Today, now that it is over, the actual process of British expansion in the Atlantic world is well known, as is the geography of North America. We know that there was no navigable northwest (Canada) or northeast (Russia) passage to the Far East, and no practical southwest (Cape Horn) route either. Furthermore, we know about a number of other determining factors: that there were only two large empires in the New World; that some cash crops would grow well in certain parts of the New World; where the silver and gold deposits existed. Sixteenth-century English people did not know these things; to understand their actions, we need to appreciate the massive extent of their ignorance, as well as their potential. We know that the Atlantic looks as it is displayed in Figure 5.1 – but this knowledge took centuries to accumulate; for the best guess in 1535, for example, look again at World map 2, which you were introduced to in Unit 1.

This ignorance was gradually overcome, partly by exploration, and partly by the work of geographer-propagandists such as John Dee (1527–1609), Richard Hakluyt (1552–1616) and Samuel Purchas (*c.*1575–1626), who devoted themselves to collating the results of the explorations, and advocating more of them. By the way, my use of 'British' and then 'English people' above is deliberate: the phenomenon that we are discussing was almost entirely an English enterprise until the second quarter of the sixteenth century, when its character became more British. Ireland also featured, both as a laboratory for imperial tactics such as colonisation, and as a potential alternative destination to America.

Exploring the way that English people moved over the Atlantic will also involve thinking about how we can construct explanations for long-term and complex historical processes – such as the beginnings of imperial expansion – from the surviving evidence that deals with the events of their beginnings. The

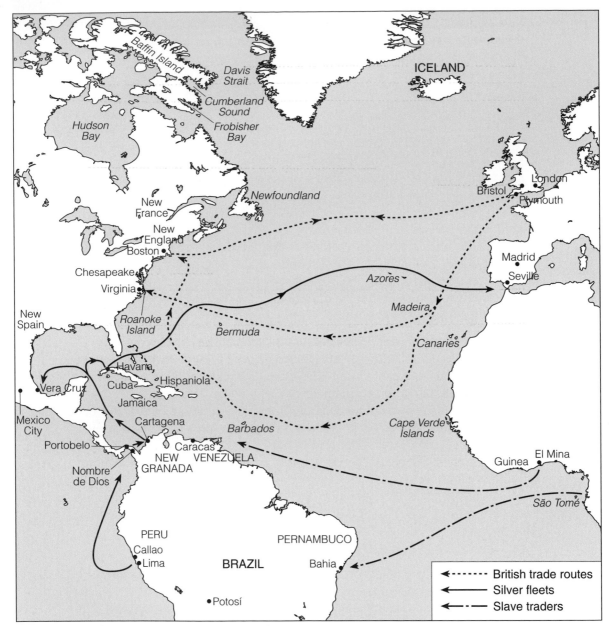

Figure 5.1   The early modern Atlantic world, adapted from Elliott, J.H. (2006) *Empires of the Atlantic World*, New Haven, Yale University Press, p. 50 and Steele, I.K. (1986) *The English Atlantic, 1675–1740*, New York, Oxford University Press, p. 82. This map shows the main sea trade routes used by the English and the Spanish, and gives an idea of the importance of the clockwise flow of currents.

unit will ask you to think clearly about the roles played by motives and explanations, and the questions that are involved when we talk about *contexts*, *determining factors* and when a process can be said to be *self-sustaining*. I would also like you to bear in mind the question of when an empire can be said to have 'begun'. Is it at the point of discovery, the establishment of a permanent dominant presence or the point at which the outpost becomes self-sufficient? The answer to this question must depend on the type of imperial activity (see the definitions in Unit 2) being measured: the establishment of a colony of settlement is very different from that of an enclave.

The first section of the unit will deal with underlying ecological and geographical factors in European settlement of the New World. The next will discuss the economics of maritime exploration, followed by an explanation for the limited role of the state in the process. Then we will look at the way that information made the journey from west to east, and how this was tied up with the process of propagandising for expansion. The unit concludes with two case studies, one looking at New England and the other at the West Indies: two very different societies, but both part of the English imperial system. The conclusion will return to the wider question of how empires begin.

IMPERIALISM AND ECOLOGY

In the era of sail, travel was highly dependent on geography. The routes between two points with the shortest travel times were rarely straight lines; instead, navigators deviated from direct courses to catch the most favourable winds and currents. Navigation was also seasonal: in the north to catch the spring easterly winds and escape the ice, in the south to avoid the hurricane season. Figure 5.1 shows how the trade routes of the early British empire were governed by the winds. Table 5.1 shows the time that travelling along its sea routes usually took in the seventeenth century.

Table 5.1   Approximate sailing times between England and America, *c.*1650

American port		Time in weeks
Boston	From England	5–7
	To England	4–5
Chesapeake	From England	9
	To England	6
Barbados	From England	9
	To England	8
Newfoundland	From England	5
	To England	3

(Source: Elliott, 2006, p. 50; Steele, 1986, p. 82)

England was well placed for its ships to ride the clockwise winds and currents to America and back.

Geography and ecology also played a key role on land. The British arrivals in North America received an enormous boost from the existing natural resources of the continent.

If you look carefully at Figure 5.2, you will see that the engraver has drawn three Amerindian villages, with fields of wheat surrounding them, as well as a fish trap just under the large island, and several canoes with Amerindians in

Figure 5.2   Theodor de Bry after White, 'The arrival of the Englishemen in Virginia', from de Bry, T. (1590) *A briefe and true report of the new found land of Virginia, of the commodities and of the nature and manners of the naturall inhabitants. Discouered by the English Colony there seated by Sir R. Greinuile ... In ... 1585 this fore booke is made in English by Thomas Hariot*, Frankfurt, Theodor de Bry, plate II. British Library, London, G.6837. By permission of the British Library. The map shows Roanoke Island, scene of some of the earliest English settlement in the New World. The 1590 edition of *A briefe and true report of the new found land of Virginia*, in which Thomas Harriot's text accompanied engravings of John White's images, was the first volume of de Bry's *America* (see 'Describing the New World' later in this unit).

'Interaction'
of superior
technology
with the
environment

them, fishing. The natives themselves had already changed the ecology of the continent, but the Europeans were to transform it in their quest for resources. Their superior technology allowed them to hunt food, take timber and (eventually) mine for ores, which had all hitherto been untapped because the native population had lacked the ability to do so on a large scale. This gave them a huge economic advantage: they were subsisting on the bounty of resources – fisheries, game to hunt, fertile soil and virgin forests – that had never been heavily exploited before.

Fish were an early import to Europe from the far side of the Atlantic – perhaps the earliest. Though it is difficult to be sure, it is possible that fishermen from Bristol (and other European Atlantic ports outside England) had already discovered the vast fisheries of the Grand Banks (off the coast of Newfoundland) when Columbus sailed to the Caribbean. This fishing industry was dominated by men from the West Country (Cornwall, Devon, Somerset and Dorset), who were also venturing to the coasts of Ireland and off Iceland (Kowaleski, 2000, p. 442). The English Atlantic fishing fleet grew throughout the sixteenth century, especially in the years after 1570, by which time it dominated the inshore fishing off Newfoundland. Each spring the fleet set out across the Atlantic, and the fishermen lived in shacks on the Newfoundland shoreline, where the cod were dried, before returning to England (Black 2004, p. 28). The southwestern ports, especially Plymouth and Dartmouth, were England's best jumping-off places for the Atlantic, since prevailing winds often halted westbound traffic from the Dover Straits for weeks at a time (Steele, 1986, 21–3). It was this geographical advantage that led to the pre-eminence of a closely linked group of Devon families – among them Grenville, Hawkins, Gilbert, Carew and Drake – in the English overseas enterprise.

Fish (including sea turtles and shellfish) were also of great use as food for the first waves of settlers. Game, which could be trapped or killed with firearms, also helped the newly arrived Europeans to subsist. It is likely that, despite a lack of consumer goods, the inhabitants of the American colonies in the seventeenth century had far easier access to meat than did the English who had stayed at home. Timber, in general, was too bulky to be profitably exported to Europe, but the vast forests of North America provided masts for export, and they also supplied cheap high-quality timber for the shipbuilding industries of New England. Again, the colonists were engaged in a one-off process of exploitation: this was especially the case for hardwood forests, which take hundreds of years to grow. Even so, despite the thousands of tonnes removed for export, by far the greatest impact on New England's forests was through clearing for agriculture, and such was their size that deforestation was not an issue in the seventeenth century. In Virginia, the pattern of tobacco cultivation relied on a system of slash and burn agriculture: cleared land would yield good crops for five to ten years, but then its fertility would be exhausted for many more. Since land was plentiful, the response of the planters was simply to clear more land. In the long run, this system of letting land lie fallow for long periods was sustainable, but it relied on access to large expanses of very cheap land.

This bounty provided the initial impetus for the profitable trade routes of the British Atlantic, summed up by an environmental historian, John Brooke, thus:

> Merchant trade networks operating around the Atlantic perimeter were the fundamental agents in the direct commodification of nature in the New World. Fishing fleets were financed, fur traders dispatched, and lumbering and ship-building camps set up, all through the efforts of partnerships of merchant capitalists, all the agents of a progressive erosion of the natural bounty of the New World.
>
> (Brooke, 2003, p. 51)

Thus, the resources the Europeans discovered in the New World gave them an edge, but their rapid expansion into it was also accelerated by the ecological impact of what they brought with them. As well as a movement of people, this process also saw a movement of associated bacteria, parasites, plants and animals. You will have learned from Unit 4 how the Spanish conquest of Central and South America was aided by the fact that the native populations had no immunity to European diseases. The fact that the Aztec and Inca civilisations were both ravaged and dislocated by smallpox and other diseases allowed very small bands of invading Spaniards to conquer empires of millions. Thus, to explain how this particular empire began, we need to know a little about **epidemiology** – the science of how and why diseases infect populations, and how immunity to them builds up, or fails to do so. In the last few decades, historians have also drawn heavily on another science – ecology – to explain the success of European invaders in the temperate regions of the New World. This explanation has been applied to Australia, New Zealand and the temperate regions of South America (mainly modern-day Argentina), as well as to North America. It involves an examination of how European settlement in these areas was so remarkably successful.

Ecological advantages held by European settlers

Perhaps the most influential work expressing this interpretation of how empires begin is *Ecological Imperialism: The Biological Expansion of Europe, 900–1900*, by Alfred Crosby (2004). Crosby is not merely looking at the Europeans, but at what he calls the 'portmanteau biota' – the bits of their ecosystem that they brought along with them. As well as diseases such as smallpox, this included plants and animals. Colonists and their descendants often remarked that European weeds took well to the New World, and many of these plants – such as wild oats – also helped the interloping animals. But perhaps the most significant direct impact came from the animals themselves, and it is one example of this that we will consider in detail here.

EXERCISE

Read the extract from *Ecological Imperialism* on the role of pigs in the New World on the course website (Secondary Source 5.1). The European explorers and colonisers are referred to here by Crosby as *marinheiros* – literally 'peoples of the sea'. The 'Neo-Europe' refers to North America, the southern part of South America, Australia and New Zealand. As you read, note the role of the settlers in this process. Are they consciously using their ecological advantages, and if so, how?

SPECIMEN ANSWER

The settlers do appear to have consciously played up some of their ecological advantages. Many of them deliberately released ('seeded') pigs into new-found territory, in order that they might multiply in the wild and provide a source of food in the long term. Some planted food crops for their swine, such as the orchards in Carolina and Virginia.

DISCUSSION

Despite these moments when settlers made conscious use of ecology – in this case pigs – it is worth remembering that they were also helped out by the plants and microbes that accompanied them, and they often remained in ignorance of the significance of these, especially the microbes. Livestock were an obvious focus for European ecological difference, but by no means the only one.

Why did the Europeans do so well? Crosby's overriding explanation for the situation in 1492 actually relies on the impact of the *first* human conquests of the New World. Most of the evidence suggests that when 'indigenes' (Amerindians, Maori, Aborigines, etc.) first arrived in virgin territory, they rapidly killed off most of the large animals they found there. Unlike the Old World species, which evolved along with humans, the New World 'megafauna' (large animals) were exceedingly vulnerable to human hunters, and succumbed in large numbers to these skilful predators. This process took place more than 40,000 years ago in Australia, and about 18,000 years ago in North America; the last of the huge flightless Moas of New Zealand appear to have been killed by the ancestors of the Maori at the same time that the first Europeans arrived in America. Because of this process, the New World had gaps in its ecosystems, which the domesticated and semi-domesticated animals from Europe were poised to fill. As Crosby puts it:

> The fields and forests of these impoverished lands and islands, when the *marinheiros* came, were more open to invading fauna than any other in the world. Had they been as thickly populated with herds of grazers and browsers and packs of carnivores as they had been when the very first humans arrived, or as, for instance, South Africa was when the Dutch settled there in the middle of the seventeenth century, the spread and triumph of European livestock, tame and feral, would have been slow and would have required considerably more human intervention than it did.
>
> (Crosby, 2004, p. 275)

It is worth noting here how Crosby is going about the task of explaining. He is comparing the experience of South Africa, where the megafauna had not been wiped out, with the New World ecosystems, where they had been. Thus the slowness of the South African experience is used to argue the point that it was the specific ecological conditions of the New World that facilitated the Europeans' expansion. Remember also how he mentioned causation in the longer extract you have just read: asserting (though at this point offering no evidence) that, without the changed environment the Europeans made, they would have almost certainly been unwilling, even if not actually unable, to settle. Crosby notes that this theory:

> places the Amerindians, Aborigines, and Maori, on the one hand, and the European invaders, on the other, in a fresh and intellectually provocative relationship: not simply as adversaries, with the indigenes passive, the whites active, but as two waves of invaders of the same species, the first acting as the shock troops, clearing the way for the second wave, with its more complicated economies and greater numbers.
>
> (Crosby, 2004, p. 280)

While Crosby stresses the long-term impact of the indigenes' presence, other historians such as Brooke have made the point that the particular circumstances of indigenous farming techniques and their demographic disaster gave the Europeans advantages in the short term. In 1600, the forests of New England and Virginia were not dense: they were kept open by the Ameridians, who used fire to clear fields for cultivation. With the deaths of most natives from European diseases, these fields were comparatively easy for the newcomers to take over and clear completely. This boon has been estimated as 'a capital endowment equivalent to a century of labour' (Brooke, 2003, pp. 57, 61).

As we shall see, the arrival of Europeans in numbers was a difficult and tortuous process, but it was rendered possible by a geographical and ecological situation that highly favoured the newcomers.

EXPLORATION AND FINANCE

In the late fifteenth century, in emulation of the Iberian monarchs, King Henry VII paid a Venetian sailor named John Cabot to explore the western shores of the North Atlantic. His voyages began in 1497. The main aim of this exploration was to find a northwest passage, through which the Spice Islands of east Asia could be reached directly from western Europe. This done, English merchants would be able to bypass the Portuguese stranglehold on the Indian Ocean (more of this in Unit 6), and thus could trade directly and lucratively with the spice islands of the Far East. It is easy to see how such a project could promise quick and definite returns, and thus attract support. Attempts to find such a shortcut continued for the rest of the century, without success. Cabot was the first to bring back the news of the existence of the North American continent, but this was the last contribution that England made to exploring the Atlantic in around fifty years.

By the middle of the sixteenth century, a pattern of how European states could profitably interact with the rest of the world had emerged. Spain had encountered two rich empires in the New World, plundered their gold, and additionally found silver mines. Portugal had established a lucrative new route to the trading networks of the east. So in reaction to this, in the sixteenth century, the vast majority of English 'imperial' effort in the Atlantic was in the service of three objectives.

1   To try to emulate the Portuguese, by reaching the east through the Northwest Passage (as the explorers Frobisher and Davis attempted) or the Northeast Passage (a more fruitful pursuit in that it led to the formation of the Muscovy Company).

2   To try to emulate the Spanish, by finding another rich indigenous civilisation to plunder (such as Raleigh's quest for El Dorado). This type of enterprise was informed by knowledge of Cortes's exploits, after his account of the conquest of Mexico was published in English in 1578 (Elliott, 2006, p. 6).

3   To get gold from the Spanish. This was largely achieved by raids, related to the Anglo-Spanish wars in Europe, but also involved attempts to trade with them (such as Hawkins's attempts to profit from shipping African slaves to the Spanish).

Attempts at colonisation before 1620 were subsidiary to these three main goals. But El Dorado was not found, and nor were the passages to the east. Raiding was profitable if the income of all the raiders is counted against all their costs, but it was very risky for each individual enterprise. There were far more individual losers than winners, but the winners did very well indeed. Raiding never succeeded in diverting the main flow of treasure away from Spain.

Most of the explorers whose voyages were chronicled by Richard Hakluyt sailed under an English flag, but they were not employees of the English crown. Many of them were not even English: during the first half of the sixteenth century, in particular, the skills needed for deep-sea navigation were largely confined to Iberian and Italian sailors, although their willingness to hire themselves out to other countries helped to spread their techniques. Attempts to find a shortcut to the lucrative spice trade were partially successful. No route to the Far East was found (though many men died trying to find it) but English explorers who rounded the North Cape (the northernmost point of present-day Norway) found a way to trade directly and profitably with Russia. The Muscovy Company, a syndicate of merchants formed to monopolise this trade, was incorporated in 1555, and its individual members took a leading role in exploring the North Atlantic. But aside from this, nearly all English efforts to open up trade in undiscovered land in the sixteenth century were what the historian J. R. Andrews called 'a long and painful series of failures and disasters' (Andrews, 1984, p. 1).

One example of these can be found in the expeditions to discover the Northwest Passage, to the north of present-day Canada. The experience that British mariners already had, in trading with Iceland and fishing off Newfoundland, is one explanation of the desire to explore these particular hostile waters. Martin Frobisher made three voyages, in 1576, 1577 and 1578. The first discovered Baffin Island (see Figure 5.1 above), and 'Frobisher Strait', which he saw as the start of a passage to China; most sixteenth-century explorers returned with a convincing tale of near success. Alas, today we know Frobisher Strait as 'Frobisher Bay'. Frobisher also claimed to have found gold-bearing ore on Baffin Island, and despite doubt from almost all metallurgists, this helped him to outfit his two subsequent expeditions, including miners, before the ore was found to be worthless. The third voyage also took with it a number of men who were to found a base at the entrance to the 'passage', in order to dominate any trade through it, although this enterprise was abandoned. Six years later, the exploration of the 'passage' was taken up by a Devon navigator, John Davis, who also mounted three expeditions. He explored and mapped the strait (now 'Davis Strait') between Canada and Greenland, and charted (though did not enter) the entrance to Hudson's Bay (modern-day Hudson Bay), which he too reported as the probable entrance to the Northwest Passage. Davis's voyages were highly successful in terms of the new land he discovered – look at Plate 2.5 in the Visual Sources Book to see (to the north of present-day Canada) the strait named after him reproduced on a seventeenth-century map.

But geographical success did not mean financial reward. Davis's optimism that he had found the beginning of the passage was not justified, and his backers did not get their money back (Andrews, 1984, pp. 171–82).

Much of the history of these expeditions is lost to us, but some detailed records survive, from which we can gain useful insights into the process of Elizabethan exploration. Reproduced below in Table 5.2 are some of Frobisher's estimates of costs incurred in the run-up to his second attempt to discover the Northwest Passage ('voyage for Cathai'). Pamphlets and prospectuses were often quite unreliable guides to the process of exploration: fragmentary financial accounts like this one, which survived because it was presented to the government, are among the most useful primary sources that we have. Note here that 'IIJ' is 'three', '*li.*' means pounds sterling; 'Ma[tie]' is an abbreviation of 'Majesty', 'IJ' means 'two', 'venturars' is being used not in the modern sense of 'adventurers' but to describe investors in the enterprise; 'ordonans/ordenans' refers to weapons (**ordnance**); and 'vyttelles' refers to food and drink (**victuals**).

Table 5.2   A BRYEF NOTE OF THE COSTE AND CHARGE OF THE IIJ SHIPPS AND FURNYTURE FOR THE SECOND VOYAGE FOR CATHAI, ETC.

	li.		
For the shyp Ayde, to the Quenes Ma[tie]	750	0	0
For the ij barkes Gabriel and Michael, wth almaner furnyture and ordonans	400	0	0
For new buyldinge and translating the same ships and for new tackelyng and implementes	650	0	0
For ordenans and munytion new bought	550	0	0
For vyttelles	950	0	0
For wagys of men	650	0	0
For necessaryes, for the mynes and workmen	150	0	0
For marchandyse, for traffyke, and provision	300	0	0
Sum of all	4400	0	0

This account is but gessed very nere the trewthe for that thaccounttes are not yett brought in parfectlye.

And the whole stock of the venturars sett downe in certayntye as yet dothe amonte but	3000		
Whereof is yet received but	2500		
And so thear lachethe in stock of the venturars to supplye this whole charge	1400	0	0

Ffor the w[ch] summe of *li.*1400, the venturars are to take order presentlye to dyscharge the debt owinge to dyvers men for thinges had for the furnyture of the said shyps and voyage, whiche is most humbly besched by Michael Lok, who hathe gyven his promesse to them for the payment therof by order of the Commyssyoners.

(Source: Collinson, n.d., p. 103)

Look at Table 5.2 above and answer the following questions:

1   What conclusions can you draw from it about Frobisher's priorities on this voyage?
2   What difficulties does it demonstrate that he faced?

1   The total projected cost of the expedition was £4,400. Of this, only £300 was trade goods and £150 the cost of the miners. Most of the cost went on the ships themselves. From the small amount spent on trade goods, we can deduce that the backers did not seriously expect the expedition to reach 'Cathai' (China), and it would not have turned a profit even if it had.

2   All three ships needed very large sums spent on them to modify and refit them for the voyage; this implies that early modern ships were made of materials that steadily deteriorated, making them 'wasting assets' which required a lot of maintenance each year if they were to be kept useable. When we consider the investments in the voyage, we can see that Frobisher was in financial trouble. Although the Queen had provided a ship (here valued at £750) as her share, subscribers were not coming up with the full amount of the rest of the cost: of the £3,000 pledged, only £2,500 (which included the Queen's ship) had been delivered, and this was well short of the £4,400 estimated cost. The gap was going to be filled by Michael Lok.

The troubles of Frobisher and Lok (his main backer) on this voyage were similar to those that afflicted most sixteenth-century voyages of discovery. Capital was hard to come by for such risky ventures. The Queen was willing to lend a large warship (which she already owned, of course) but would not part with cash, and it was the expedition's job to refit this ship. Sixteenth-century ships were not permanent things: they needed regular refitting, often involving the complete replacement of their (expensive) rigging. At this time, the annual revenue of the English state was between £200,000 and £300,000 per year: £4,400 was a considerable sum of money. Even if Frobisher had made it to China, it is unlikely that the backers of this voyage would have turned a profit – although had they genuinely struck gold on Baffin Island, they might have done. Lok, a merchant, lost about £20,000 backing Frobisher's voyages of exploration.

Explorers and the state

In the early modern period, much state enterprise was farmed out to private contractors, hence the divide between state and private is not as straightforward as we might now think (Williams, 1979). Often, joint-stock enterprises were arranged by royal decree. Sometimes these had royal investment in them as well; at other times the crown's involvement was limited to political approval. Royal officials also took part, but it is sometimes hard to label their involvement as necessarily 'public', since they were expected to treat their office as a source of private profit. For example, the 1558 expedition to Guinea (West Africa), authorised by Queen Mary I, involved four ships. Two of them were royal vessels and the other two private ships. The finance for the voyage came from a London syndicate, aided by the lord high admiral, but he was working in a private capacity, and his share of the profits was destined for his private purse. In 1564, Elizabeth 'ventured' a 300-ton warship (a large vessel for that time), which was equipped and armed, on a similar voyage. The merchants behind the voyage had to find the crew, their food, their wages, and £5,000 worth of trade goods. The Queen's share of the gross profit was to be one-sixth – but this was to be delivered to the Navy Board, not the Exchequer (central fund). In essence, Elizabeth was renting out part of the Royal Navy, so that it could help pay for its keep (Andrews, 1984, p. 104).

The English state was not wealthy enough to be able to waste money. There were also other major drains on the country's resources, notably the ongoing efforts to suppress Irish independence, and 'colonisation' (then called 'plantation' because it involved the 'planting' of communities) as a political and state tactic was tested out first in Ireland. Before the Munster rebellion of 1579–83, the crown allowed wealthy and loyal English proprietors to colonise as part of the strategy to subdue Ireland. After this, the process got active crown backing as a facet of the Anglo-Irish struggle. This educated a generation of military/political entrepreneurs in the mechanics of the process of settlement – and gave some, like the promoter of colonisation Humphrey Gilbert, experience of war tactics that approached genocide (Andrews, 1984, p. 184). It also sucked up an enormous amount of resources. By means of a royal invitation, which was essentially a command, the City of London spent much of the first two decades of the seventeenth century putting capital into founding and improving the city of Londonderry in the north of Ireland. Capital spent in Ireland could not be spent in America (Canny, 1998, p. 165). On balance, the English intervention in Ireland probably slowed down English expansion to America.

[handwritten margin note: prior settlements]

When Tudor and Stuart governments wanted something done, they usually issued a commission to one of their subjects to do it. Since they generally lacked the money to pay these people wages, they instead offered a large proportion of the expected profits from the task – once the royal court's share had been extracted. Such commissions were a way for subjects to make money, and hence often could be offered for sale as a lucrative source of crown income. Like commissions, royal charters and licenses also often conferred monopoly powers on the recipient (which might be an individual, a partnership, or a joint-stock company). These were mainly used to regulate economic activity at home, but they soon became the preferred way to manage exploration and settlement, and favoured courtiers such as Walter Raleigh were in a good position to extract them from the queen. Other courtiers who wished to hazard some of their money on the scheme might join in, for a share in the proceeds. The name of the process, 'venturing', is a clue that it was a gamble. Though a few merchants backed speculative voyages, most were keen to stick to more secure investments; finance for exploration generally came from gentlemen. Sometimes the financial backers sailed with the expedition, and (unless the backers themselves were experienced men such as Drake and Hawkins) the result was nearly always dissention, idleness and disaster. This was especially the case on colonising voyages, since gentlemen tended to have very little experience of (or desire to perform) the kind of unremitting skilled labour needed to plant a colony.

EXERCISE

Read the first two paragraphs of John Janes's report of the 1585 voyage of John Davis on the course website (Primary Source 5.1). Where did the money come from to back Davis's expedition?

SPECIMEN ANSWER

As listed in the preamble, the backing was from a variety of individuals from the court and outside it, and from unnamed merchants in London and the West Country. The main backer 'the greatest adventurer with his purse' was the London merchant William Sanderson.

DISCUSSION

This pattern of backers appears to have been representative. London was where most merchants were concentrated, while the West Country provided a disproportionate number of the seafarers of the sixteenth century. Sanderson appears to have played a similar role to Michael Lok, Frobisher's backer in the 1560s and 70s, as the main financial promoter of the enterprise, who would stand to gain a fortune if it came off, but would lose one if it failed.

It was courtiers and landed gentry who tended to favour colonisation in the sixteenth century: after 1600, when it began to look like a more realistic proposition, more merchants joined them. Monarchs thought like courtiers, rather than like far-sighted promoters of expansion for its own sake. Both Elizabeth and her successor James only supported imperial enterprise when it promised a quick return. Pious proclamations might have insisted that the monarch was aiding expansion in order to serve the interests of the country as a whole, but this was usually less important than the needs of the moment. The crown was more interested in expeditions to find treasure than trade routes.

Both groups were disappointed. The efforts of the sixteenth-century explorers bore very little fruit. The enormous sums of cash, and the hundreds of lives, invested in them were largely lost, and aside from the Muscovy trade through northern Russia and some contact with West Africa, the grandiose schemes for making money out of the new-found lands came to nothing. Perhaps their greatest long-term significance was that they were later woven into a nationalistic tale of maritime expansion, chiefly by Richard Hakluyt and Samuel Purchas. Overseas exploration became conflated with the rose-tinted image of Elizabeth's England: daring, new, staunchly Protestant and highly hostile to Spain. The failures could be forgotten about as the few triumphs – such as Drake's voyage round the world – were celebrated. Figure 5.3 shows a modern-day replica of the *Golden Hind*, the ship in which Drake sailed round the world in 1577–80.

This was a rare example of a successful voyage of discovery and plunder, and even involved trade for cloves in the Far East. When Queen Elizabeth knighted Drake on the deck of the *Golden Hind* in April 1581, she created a powerful image of the link between royal power and the piratical and ultra-Protestant Drake. Yet she had waited to gauge the Spanish reaction to Drake's piracy before deciding to honour him, and at the same time she initiated proceedings that led to some of the plunder being restored. Elizabeth's backing was also governed by broader political considerations, and it is to these that we now turn.

Figure 5.3   Modern-day working replica of the square-rigger sailing ship, *Golden Hind*, used by Sir Francis Drake in the sixteenth century. Photographed by Joel W. Rogers. Photo: © Joel W. Rogers/CORBIS. The replica shows how English vessels – which were relatively small and heavily armed with canon firing through gunports in their sides – were built for fighting rather than bulk trade.

THE IMPACT OF PRIVATEERING

Even during times of relative peace, the English legal doctrine about who possessed the New World was consistent. Protestant England did not recognise the blanket Spanish (or Portuguese) claims to all the newly discovered lands, which had been recognised by the papacy in the Treaty of Tordesillas. Instead, Elizabeth and James proclaimed a doctrine of 'effective occupation': English mariners would only be restrained by the English crown if they were trespassing on land that was under *effective* Iberian occupation and control. This left vast tracts of land open to English settlement.

Another legal institution that fuelled conflict in peacetime was the practice of issuing **letters of reprisal**. This was granted by the English crown to sailors (or their representatives) who had suffered harm in Spain or in Spanish-controlled territory, authorising them to capture, by force if necessary, Spanish property equal to the loss suffered. The activities of the Spanish Inquisition, which sometimes targeted foreign heretics, provided a pretext for the issue of letters of reprisal, which themselves offered a pretext, as can be imagined, for depredation beyond their authorised scope. Such letters were not, though, issued without regard to their consequences, and when the English court was keen to preserve peace with Spain, they were less likely to be issued.

A third important legal factor was the concept of privateering. A **privateer** was a private citizen who (usually in time of war) had been given **letters of marque** by the government, entitling him to make war upon the crown's enemies, normally with a view to profiting from the plunder involved. Privateering, relying as it did on private citizens to wage war, was another illustration of the comparative weakness of the early modern state.

The English crown was interested in relations between states: not in empire as an end in itself. Some of its prominent servants were consistent supporters of exploration. Sir Francis Walsingham, for example, was one of the queen's chief advisors between 1573 and 1590, and advocated an aggressive policy towards Spain. He was son-in-law of a Muscovy merchant, and gave political and financial support to many expeditions. However, reasons of state could also block moves to the New World. In 1574, with relations with Spain relatively stable, Elizabeth vetoed Grenville's plan to raid the South Atlantic and Pacific; but, in 1577, when they were frostier, she gave Drake leave to do just that.

During the last quarter of the sixteenth century, first a 'cold' war and then a declared one between Spain and England led to an explosion in the number of ships on privateering missions. Many of these headed to pick up prizes near Spain, but some crossed the Atlantic to raid the Caribbean and the 'Spanish Main' – the mainland of Central and South America. The Caribbean, with its numerous anchorages and beaches, was already relatively hospitable territory for privateers and pirates, but it was the low degree of instituted authority that made it especially attractive for them. By 1550, many Spanish settlers had largely moved on to the greater wealth of the mainland. Thus, although Spain claimed the whole area, it was in practice 'impoverished and consequently indifferently governed and inadequately defended' (Scammell, 1989, p. 29).

There was one exception to this state of affairs: the flota, the annual treasure fleet from Mexico and Peru (which later also transported merchandise from the handful of galleons that crossed the Pacific from the Philippines). This was the chief conduit whereby the American silver (which you learned about in Unit 4) reached Spain. The flota, and the ports that it called at, were all heavily defended. Pirates and privateers might dream of capturing it – and its presence probably attracted many to the region – but it was a tough nut to crack. In 1573, Francis Drake managed to capture some of the silver from Peru as it was being carried over the mountains of the Panamanian isthmus; in this enterprise he was given decisive aid by the communities of Cimmerans – escaped African slaves living in Panama. For a while, English raiders hoped that the Cimmerans might be strong enough to become a permanent ally against Spain, but the escapees soon reached an accommodation with their former masters: in return for non-interference, they would stop helping other fugitives and remain loyal to Spain. The British offered the escaped slaves of Cockpit County in Jamaica a similar peace settlement in 1740. Both episodes point to the fact that, without a state to protect them, the communities of escapees and refugees remained far more vulnerable than even a weak indigenous state. The flota was captured just once in the seventeenth century, by the Dutch fleet under Admiral Piet Heyn in 1628: significantly, this was the result of state, rather than piratical, action.

When peace arrived in 1604, some privateers turned to outright piracy, but others were available for a series of efforts to explore and exploit the New World. One outcome of the war had been to train large numbers of sailors in deep-sea navigation, a skill that had previously been rare in England. By now, the gradual expansion of English long-distance trade had also led to the development, largely in London, of a significant group of men engaged in extra-European trade: to Russia, North Africa, the Levant (Middle East) and the Mediterranean. Some of these were willing to put their money behind further exploration and colonisation efforts to the west. Privateering also created a number of wealthy backers, the majority of whom were from London and the West Country ports. One problem was that they were used to quick returns, and this preoccupation did not help attempts at colonisation. For example, at the first enduring settlement in Virginia, at Jamestown, the colonists wasted time looking for gold when they ought to have been planting their crops.

Changing technology assisted the process of expansion. By 1630, the average English merchant ship was handy (easy to sail) and heavily armed, suitable for defending high-value cargo in disturbed environments. *Golden Hind* (see Figure 5.3 above) is one early example of this type. But their large crews made them comparatively short-ranged, and expensive to operate, compared with the usual Dutch merchant ships of the era, the *fluyt* (not to be confused with the much larger and rarer Dutch East Indiamen), which had higher capacity and smaller crews. The English ships were suited to warfare and chaos. John Hawkins's pioneering slaving voyages of the 1560s have become infamous. His heavily armed ships allowed him to raid for slaves in West Africa, and also to sell them at gunpoint to (probably genuinely unwilling) Spaniards in the West Indies. But violence was necessary at each end because he lacked any institutional involvement in the trade. His Portuguese competitors, on the other hand, dealt with willing partners at both ends; thus they did not need to pay for an expensive military operation like Hawkins's and could use more cost-effective ships and thus undercut him: the English did not re-enter the slave trade for half a century (Andrews, 1984, p. 128).

Throughout the period of 'heroic failure', the price was paid by the common sailors who died in their droves. By the standards of the times, Drake was a brilliant sailor, but although he left with 160 men in his fleet in 1577, only 100 returned. Because of the high levels of uncertainty, disease and danger from uncharted shores, seamen were apt to threaten to mutiny rather than sail into unknown waters. Ashore, the successful planting of colonies or outposts introduced new problems of discipline for the proprietors. Thus, from the very beginning, empire involved elements of coercion to extract labour from those who had no immediate incentive to provide it. Especially in the relatively hospitable Caribbean, coercion created runaways like the Cimmerans: **buccaneers**, logwood cutters, **Maroons**, escaped slaves and servants, who could enter the service of other states, live semi-wild off the land, or in some cases even 'go native'. The expanding frontier provided a standing invitation to lower-class Europeans who wished to escape oppressive discipline (Linebaugh and Rediker, 2000, p. 34). It is difficult to ascertain how many indentured servants saw their condition as a reasonable payment for an otherwise unaffordable passage and a stake in a rapidly growing colony, but a significant number saw their situation as oppressive. In 1629, indentured servants, who made up most of the militia called up to defend the English island colony of St Kitts from a Spanish attack, refused to fight. Many of them even deserted to the enemy, some shouting 'Liberty, joyful liberty!' as they did so. This overspill from a system of coercion reminds us that the English expansion into the Atlantic world was steeped in violence, which was directed both outwards at foreigners, and inwards against sailors, indentured servants and slaves.

DESCRIBING THE NEW WORLD

Information was essential to make imperial expansion work. Any scheme of conquest, commercial system or wave of colonisation needed to have some kind of publicity associated with it – even if this was confined to a small group such as a royal court or religious minority. The imperial expansion of Britain was conducted by semi-official joint-stock enterprises, and it was motivated by a mixture of religious enthusiasm, desire on the part of individuals for wealth, and political motives. This form of expansion therefore needed a degree of public support, in order to attract volunteers and backers, as well as elicit approval (or at least acquiescence) from the court. This section of the unit will illustrate some of the ways that information about the New World was communicated to the Old, and the ways that this communication took place in practice, with reference to the paintings of the English settler and artist John White.

John White and Theodor de Bry

White may have accompanied the English sailor Martin Frobisher on his fruitless attempt to discover the Northwest Passage (in what is now northern Canada) in 1576. Almost the first definite record of him is as a member of the 1585 expedition to North America. This was led by Richard Grenville, as part of the colonisation movement that was sponsored in London by Sir Walter Raleigh. It followed a far smaller expedition of the previous year, which had mapped the coast of 'Virginia' (present-day North Carolina) and identified a number of possible sites for a permanent settlement. Grenville's expedition was to occupy a site on Roanoke Island, fortify it and attempt to trade with the local inhabitants. The programme of expeditions needed more wealthy backers, political support from the court and parliament to deliver favourable laws and trade monopolies, and enthusiastic and able-bodied volunteers. Thus Raleigh and Grenville had made plans for the expedition to include a writer (Thomas Harriot) and an artist (White), whose job it was to record the details of the land the expedition explored, in order to facilitate future exploration and to create a public account that could be published to garner more support.

White's paintings mainly derive from a relatively short stay (less than a month) in North America in 1585 (Sloan, 2007). Harriot's text began with a long list of the various commodities and resources available in North America – an extended list of what potential colonists would find there, and could perhaps begin to ship back for profit. Much of Harriot's list dealt with foodstuffs, and White painted details of new edible species said to abound in the West Indies and North America, such as sea turtles and grouper fish. Another potential commodity, with high value and low transport costs (remember the eastern spice trade), was raw materials for medicine; White painted and described plants that the Amerindians used for medicinal purposes. Most famously, he also painted around twenty pictures of the Amerindians themselves – Algonquians living near the shores of 'Virginia'.

Grenville's expedition had intended to buy food from the natives. When the supply dried up, they shifted towards raiding for food, with predictable consequences: by 1586, they felt themselves to be so threatened that they abandoned the settlement and returned to England in the ships of Francis Drake when he called there that year. The next expedition was led by John White himself, and the 100 or so putative colonists included his daughter and son-in-law. The colony did badly, and White returned to England to get help, but the national mobilisation against the Spanish Armada of 1588 ended transatlantic communication for a year.

Raleigh's efforts to mount a relief expedition thus demanded access to men and ships at a time when these were devoted to the war. This was the context for the first mass exposure of White's pictures. Along with Harriot's text, they formed the basis of a significant project by the Flemish publisher Theodor de Bry, published in 1590 as the first volume of his series *America*. De Bry engraved (or paid others to engrave) copies of the paintings. Unlike watercolours, engravings can be printed in quantity. They did not allow colour to be reproduced (although they can be laboriously hand-coloured one at a time after they have been printed), so knowledge of the bright and vibrant colours of White's originals remained the preserve of a few.

De Bry's engravings added details that were not present in White's originals – they must have been made up by the engravers. For example, while White only gave one view of the Algonquians in their traditional costume (see Plate 2.6, White's watercolour of a 'werowance' – the Algonquian term for a chief – in the Visual Sources Book), de Bry gave front and back views of the 'same' individual (Figure 5.4). De Bry also altered some of the images to change their content. In a watercolour of an Algonquian **charnel house**, White included a small idol, in the shape of a squatting man, to one side of the bodies of the dead (see Plate 2.7). De Bry's work (Figure 5.5) gave the idol a hut of its own,

Figure 5.4 Theodor de Bry after White, 'A weroan or great Lorde of Virginia', from de Bry, T. (1590) *A briefe and true report of the new found land of Virginia, of the commodities and of the nature and manners of the naturall inhabitants. Discouered by the English Colony there seated by Sir R. Greinuile ... In ... 1585 this fore booke is made in English by Thomas Hariot*, Frankfurt, Theodor de Bry, plate III. British Library, London, C36.i.18. By permission of the British Library.

and made it significantly bigger. Compare also Figure 5.6 with Plate 2.8 and note how de Bry's version substantially alters the figures' poses.

The uses of White's work

Significantly, and to our minds strangely, an appendix to de Bry's work also included a number of White's paintings 'of the Picts which in the olde tyme dyd habite [inhabit] one part of the great Bretainne'. These five pictures showed male and female warriors, labelled as 'Picts' or 'ancient Britons' – names for the people who lived in Great Britain at the time the Romans arrived. They were shown largely naked, covered in paint and tattoos, all (including the women) carrying weapons. One carries the severed head of a man whose beard is cut in the sixteenth-century fashion.

EXERCISE

Look through Primary Source 5.2 on the course website, paying attention to the first image (which is headed 'Some pictures of the Pictes'), and note down a brief answer to this question: What possible message could de Bry be sending out by the inclusion of these antiquarian pictures in the same volume as pictures of Virginia?

Figure 5.5   Theodor de Bry after White, 'Ther Idol Kiwasa', from de Bry, T. (1590) *A briefe and true report of the new found land of Virginia, of the commodities and of the nature and manners of the naturall inhabitants. Discouered by the English Colony there seated by Sir R. Greinuile ... In ... 1585 this fore booke is made in English by Thomas Hariot*, Frankfurt, Theodor de Bry, plate XXI. British Library, London, C36.i.18. By permission of the British Library.

SPECIMEN ANSWER

De Bry shows the Algonquians as primitive, but the text of the book makes the explicit point that they are not savages like the Picts. In fact, at the start of the appendix, de Bry writes that he has included these pictures 'for to showe how that the Inhabitants of the great Bretannie have bin in times past as sauvage as those of Virginia'.

DISCUSSION

The point that White and Harriot were keen to make, and de Bry was prepared to disseminate, was that the inhabitants of the New World were not subhuman or irredeemably savage, but capable of rising up to a civilised existence; for, after all, the Britons had managed this (Canny, 1998, p. 152).

Thus White's own work was used to advertise the colonising effort in the New World, and to assert that success in the venture was possible. But it was also later re-used in other ways.

More than forty years after they were originated, de Bry's engravings of White's images were also drawn upon by the engraver Robert Vaughan, when he illustrated Captain John Smith's 1624 account of his time in Virginia: *The General History of Virginia, New England, and the Summer Isles*.

Figure 5.6   Theodor de Bry after White, 'A cheiff Ladye of Pomeiooc', from de Bry, T. (1590) *A briefe and true report of the new found land of Virginia, of the commodities and of the nature and manners of the naturall inhabitants. Discouered by the English Colony there seated by Sir R. Greinuile ... In ... 1585 this fore booke is made in English by Thomas Hariot,* Frankfurt, Theodor de Bry, plate VIII. British Library, London, C36.i.18. By permission of the British Library.

EXERCISE

Vaughan's main illustration for Smith's account is reprinted in the Visual Sources Book as Plate 2.9. Look at it, and compare it with the de Bry illustrations (especially Figures 5.7 and 5.8) and the original White paintings (Plate 2.10, John White's watercolour of an Algonquian dance, and Plate 2.11, John White's watercolour of an Algonquian fire ceremony, both in the Visual Sources Book). You could also look back at the other White and de Bry illustrations reproduced in this chapter and in the Visual Sources Book.

1   What elements of White's paintings have survived, and what has been changed?

2   Why might this be the case?

SPECIMEN ANSWER

1   Although the main elements of White's paintings are present, they have all been altered to some degree. Most of the pictures are given new captions that suggest they are episodes in the story of Smith's adventures with the Amerindians. Smith himself has been added to the pictures, which have become illustrations of action rather than attempts to record the activity of the native population. Vaughan has obviously based his interior picture on the charnel house, but this is now represented as a place for potential human sacrifice. The dance, which had taken place in a circle around three girls, now centres on a captive Englishman.

Figure 5.7   Theodor de Bry after White, 'Their danses which they use att their hyghe feastes', from de Bry, T. (1590) *A briefe and true report of the new found land of Virginia, of the commodities and of the nature and manners of the naturall inhabitants. Discouered by the English Colony there seated by Sir R. Greinuile ... In ... 1585 this fore booke is made in English by Thomas Hariot,* Frankfurt, Theodor de Bry, plate XVIII. British Library, London, C36.i.18. By permission of the British Library.

2   White's pictures were drawn in an era when the newly arrived English relied on the local inhabitants' tolerance, and were keen to stress that they were not total savages. By 1624, relations between the two groups in Virginia were much more violent.

DISCUSSION

If you look through the whole edition of de Bry's volume available on the primary source database on the course website, you will see that almost every element of Vaughan's engraving was taken from de Bry, but used as a prop in a visual story that pits English settlers against Amerindians. By the 1620s, it was clear to the English that relations with the Amerindians would not be smooth: the settlers were competing with them for land, and interaction was characterised by friction, massacre and counter-massacre. De Bry's woodcuts were thus reworked by Vaughan to give verisimilitude to an account of conflict.

Figure 5.8   Theodor de Bry after White, 'Their manner of prainge with Rattels abowt te fyer', from de Bry, T. (1590) *A briefe and true report of the new found land of Virginia, of the commodities and of the nature and manners of the naturall inhabitants. Discouered by the English Colony there seated by Sir R. Greinuile ... In ... 1585 this fore booke is made in English by Thomas Hariot*, Frankfurt, Theodor de Bry, plate XVII. British Library, London, C36.i.18. By permission of the British Library.

[handwritten margin notes: propaganda ↓ how societies were depicted to "support" efforts to colonise. Britain had no money, was fighting a war against Spain]

This is all very interesting, but what does it have to do with how empires begin? The answer is that White's pictures were drawn (and Harriot's account was written) for a reason – to provide information about the New World that would support the colonising project. They were not the product of a neutral and objective observer. The context became even more important after de Bry's version was produced in large numbers. With Vaughan's use of the images, their import had changed completely, but the underlying motivation – to serve the interests of the colonisers – was the same. Messages from over the seas, and their accompanying images, were edited and manipulated, usually in the service of attempts to make the imperial enterprise look attractive. These feedback mechanisms played an important role in maintaining and increasing support for the enterprise.

NEW ENGLAND

We will now move on to examine one place where, eventually, colonisation worked. New England is one of the classic examples of what Fieldhouse would describe as a 'settler colony' (see Unit 2). The colonies of New England (what is now the northeastern seaboard of the United States, in the states of Massachusetts, Rhode Island, Connecticut, Vermont and New Hampshire) were fundamentally different from the attempts that had pre-dated them. In New England, settlement was not a necessary precondition for another aim involving the generation of profit and its channelling back to the metropolis, but an end in itself. The point was to create self-sustaining groups. The settlers' motivation was to escape what they saw as intolerable restrictions on their practice of religion: notably the limitations on the extent to which their congregations could have power to rule themselves in all matters.

When the 'Pilgrim Fathers' sailed in the *Mayflower* to what is now Plymouth, Massachusetts, in 1620, they were not attempting anything that was entirely new. There had been earlier proposals for religious minorities to leave Britain. Some – such as the short-lived Anglo-French Huguenot settlement on the coast of Florida of 1565 – involved religious minorities, but had been motivated by the desire to raid the Spanish. For others, settlement was an end in itself. In the 1580s, English Catholics had considered an organised migration to North America in order to escape the newly instituted penal laws passed by Elizabeth. In the 1590s, it was the Brownists, radical Protestants, who considered emigration. Both Catholics and Brownists had, like the Pilgrims after them, professed their loyalty to the monarch, and argued that, given the government's policy of religious uniformity in Britain, the *only* way they could express that loyalty was to form a separate loyal community overseas.

New England itself was a reasonably well-charted place. The Italian explorer Giovanni da Verrazano, who sailed in the service of France, had first mapped its coasts in 1524, and waxed lyrical in his accounts about the potential of Narragansett Bay (in present-day Rhode Island). Bristol and West Country men dominated an attempt in 1607 to plant a New England colony in Maine. This failed, but associated fishing and fur trading worked. There was another model for New England: Ireland. In Ireland, settlement (called 'plantation') was at root inspired by political considerations, as a tactic to control the country, rather than as the end of the exercise. 'Godly' imperialists like Humphrey Gilbert, who was prominent in the attempts to settle Virginia, had been prominent in Elizabeth's long grinding war to subdue and control Ireland. The 'plantation' of settlers in Munster and then Ulster provided a model for settlement in New England, especially by militant Protestants. The model of a 'plantation' was of a culturally distinct and self-sufficient community, but, as was the case in nearly every European encounter with the wider world, 'natives' were important. This can be seen in an extract from Bradford's history of the Plymouth colonists.

EXERCISE

Read the extract from Bradford's history of the Plymouth colonists on the course website (Primary Source 5.3), and pay attention to the various roles played by Amerindians in the encounter.

DISCUSSION

It is obvious from this extract that the barrier between indigene and newcomer – which we had already seen a few Europeans cross to 'go native' (see p. 173 above) – was permeable in the other direction as well. The reason in this case seems obvious: demographic disaster meant that Squanto was the last survivor of his tribe.

EXERCISE

Now, I would like you to read a long extract from 'New England in the Seventeenth Century' by Virginia DeJohn Anderson, which is from the *Oxford History of the British Empire* (Secondary Source 5.2 on the course website). Make a note of the chief factors that led to the success of the colonial enterprise in this region.

SPECIMEN ANSWER

The main factors are the following:

- Nearly all of the Amerindians died off because of European diseases, leaving clearings and food.
- The original colonists had a shared religion and often (initially) close-knit communities committed to mutual aid, often described as 'corporatist'. They wrote of the strength of religious obligations – 'covenants' – that they shared.
- They had access to capital in London.
- They quickly reached agreement on government, which prevented dangerous divisions. The Massachusetts Company took this a step further and moved to America: thus their development was not hampered by remote control from London.
- Cheap land and redistribution enabled all to have the chance to support themselves.
- They successfully fought off Amerindian attacks, especially in 1637 and 1675–77.
- Their economy relied on resource transfer with immigrants until 1640, then on various local resources – fish, trade, shipbuilding.
- Equal sex ratios led to a swift population expansion.

[handwritten margin note: societies × environments]

DISCUSSION

A list like this can suggest that the success of New England was 'over-determined': that all events and factors worked in its favour. We must bear in mind that each of these advantages helped to overcome a severe problem which could otherwise have crippled the colony.

Table 5.3 shows, among other things, the numbers of Britons who moved to North America. It gives a good indication of the relative prominence of English colonists compared with other newcomers, and when they arrived.

Table 5.3   European-directed transatlantic migration 1500–1760, by European nation and continent of origin (in thousands)

	Africans arriving in American regions claimed by each nation	Africans leaving Africa on ships of each nation	Europeans leaving each nation for the Americas (net)
Before 1580			
Spain	45	10	139
Portugal	13	63	93
France	0	0	0
Netherlands	0	0	0
Britain	0	1	0
Total	**58**	**74**	**232**
1580–1640			
Spain	289	100	188
Portugal	204	590	110
France	2	0	4
Netherlands	8	20	2
Britain	4	4	126
Total	**507**	**714**	**430**
1640–1700			
Spain	141	10	158
Portugal	180	226	50
France	75	50	45
Netherlands	49	160	13
Britain	277	371	248
Total	**722**	**817**	**514**
1700–1760			
Spain	271	0	193
Portugal	730	812	270
France	388	456	51
Netherlands	123	221	5
Britain	971	1,286	372
Total	**2,483**	**2,775**	**891**

Notes: Spain and Portugal are treated as separate countries despite the crowns of the two countries being united between 1580 and 1640. The grand total for the Netherlands includes Dutch Brazil. The British total for the eighteenth century includes migrants from Germany and Africans carried on British American vessels.
(Source: reproduced and slightly abridged from Eltis, 2000, p. 9)

The vast majority of the English who migrated before 1640 did so in the 1630s, a decade that saw the first mass migration out of the British Isles. While more of the emigrants ended up in the Chesapeake and the West Indies than in New England, the latter's social structure meant that its immigrants formed stable and productive family units far more easily, and population grew through natural increase accordingly. By around 1660, New England was one of the three key parts of the British Atlantic empire, along with Virginia and Barbados. Note how, in Figure 5.10 (the title page of the book whose cover forms Figure 5.9), these three places are prominent in the frontispiece to this general history. It is to the West Indies that we will now turn, for a second case study of one of these key points: the island of Barbados.

BARBADOS

We are looking for beginnings of empire, and one thing that this unit has shown so far is that we cannot find much in the sorry tale of the first century of British Atlantic enterprise. We need to find a state of affairs that we can credibly call the 'end of the beginning' – an enduring and successful set of institutions and economic relationships – and examine how this came about. One of the first places where we can see such a pattern is on the island of Barbados, the easternmost island of the West Indies.

Barbados was the motor of the British Atlantic economy: in the 1640s and 1650s it took off as a sugar-exporting island, and regularly produced a profit of hundreds and thousands of pounds. It was undoubtedly the single most economically successful element of the 'first' British empire. As you saw in Figure 5.1, Barbados was very easy to reach from Britain. Ships could sail south from the mouth of the Channel until they picked up the prevailing southeasterly winds off Spain, then run to the latitude of Barbados by way of Maderia. The return journey continued the clockwise journey round the Atlantic, with the prevailing winds.

The first British settlers arrived in Barbados in 1627. Initially it was intended as a colony of settlement, and the farms on the island were mainly smallholdings growing subsistence crops, cotton or tobacco. The great migrations of the 1630s affected the West Indies as well as the American seaboard, and the population of Barbados rapidly grew. This was despite the fact that the island had two rival proprietors, both of whom had been granted the right to control (and hence tax) settlement by the king, and their followers frequently clashed. The making of Barbados's economy was sugar. This had been cultivated in southern Europe before 1450, then on the Canaries and Azores, and then in Brazil by the Portuguese. Each of these places, and Barbados, hosted one episode of the 'sugar revolution', which has been defined by economic historians in the following terms:

> The six central elements of the sugar revolution are commonly regarded as a swift shift from diversified agriculture to sugar monoculture, from production on small farms to large plantations,

Figure 5.9 Emblematic engraving of America, from Gorges, F. (1659) *America Painted to the Life: the true history of the Spaniards proceedings in the conquests of the Indians*, London, printed for Nath. Brook at the Angel in Cornhill. Photo: Cambridge University Library.

from free to slave labour, from sparse to dense settlement, from white to black populations, and from low to high value per caput output. More broadly, it is claimed that the sugar revolution had five effects: it generated a massive boost to the Atlantic slave trade, provided the engine for a variety of triangular trades, altered European nutrition

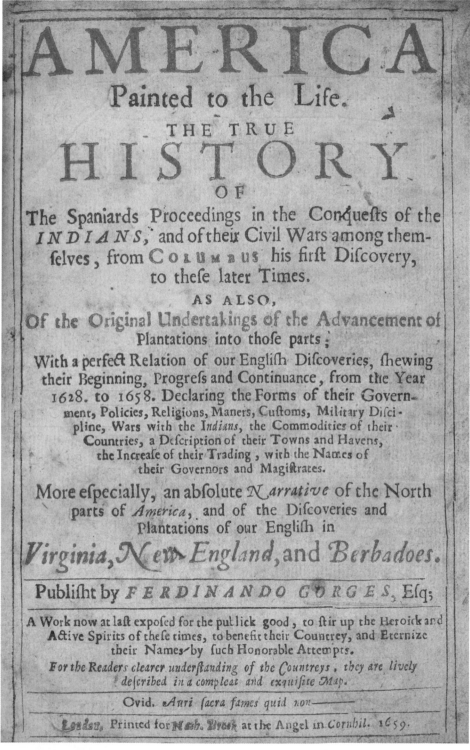

Figure 5.10   Title page from Gorges, F. (1659) *America Painted to the Life: the true history of the Spaniards proceedings in the conquests of the Indians*, London, printed for Nath. Brook at the Angel in Cornhill. British Library, London, E.969.(1-4). By permission of the British Library. This book was intended to present a comprehensive picture of the colonisation of America; the list of subjects covered is a clear indication of what the publisher thought would sell.

and consumption, increased European interest in tropical colonies, and, more contentiously, contributed vitally to the industrial revolution.

(Higman, 2000, p. 213)

Sugar, then, was one of the most important tradable commodities of the early modern period.

The sugar revolution

It is easy to trace this 'sugar revolution' in the primary source accounts of the island's history.

EXERCISE

During the 1650s, Richard Ligon, who had worked on a plantation in Barbados, wrote a long account of the island's history. I would like you read the extract from it that is on the course website (Primary Source 5.4). This extract, which begins at the point of initial settlement, sums up the shift in its economy during the 1630s.

Can you identify the three different phases in the agriculture of Barbados that had already occurred at the time of Ligon's visit?

SPECIMEN ANSWER

On arrival, the settlers began by planting subsistence crops, including potatoes, maize and plantains. After this, they experimented with varying success with the cultivation of cash crops for export; tobacco, indigo, cotton and fustick wood (a wood from which valuable dye could be extracted). But once they had discovered its potential, they moved towards one cash crop: sugar.

DISCUSSION

Note also the role played by meat from semi-wild pigs, which had earlier been introduced to the island.

Sugar arrived in 1637, brought by a Dutchman from the sugar-producing area of Pernambuco in South America. (The Dutch captured Pernambuco from the Portuguese and governed it for a few years until it was recaptured; this is another example of the way that the various European colonial empires interacted.)

Barbados had, in Fieldhouse's terms (see Unit 2), been a colony of *settlement*, with an economy largely characterised by subsistence faming. With the development of sugar refining, it was transformed into a *plantation* colony, where the economy and society were devoted to the production of one commodity for export. Land prices on Barbados increased by up to 30 times between the mid-1630s and *c*.1650, when the techniques of sugar refinery had been mastered. The landholding pattern changed, to one better suited to plantation economy, with larger plantations that could be worked more efficiently. Sugar planting was highly capital intensive: as well as the expense of the refinery, planters had to wait two years between planting and the sale of sugar. So, the sugar industry, though highly profitable, was very expensive to enter.

Sugar refining was a complex process of several stages. Look at Figures 5.11a and 5.11b, taken from Ligon's account; these show a schematic plan of a sugar refinery and an index to the plan. They give us some idea of the number of different processes needed in sugar production. Canes were crushed, and the extracted juice boiled, potted, set, then re-boiled. White sugar could sell for 20 pence a pound in London, but the growing and processing of the crop required a great deal of hard and unpleasant physical labour.

Sugar created a massive demand for labour on Barbados. Although slaves had been there from the start, most of the labour was initially performed by English indentured servants, who were bound to a master for seven or so years as a way of paying for their passage across the Atlantic. The civil wars in the British Isles of the 1640s and early 1650s also led to a large number of prisoners of war (perhaps in excess of 10,000), many from Ireland, being sent there as semi-permanent labourers. But once this supply dried up, the planters turned to African slaves for labour. Barbados was the first significant slave economy in the British empire. Between 1650 and 1680, more than 30,000 white people left Barbados for other colonies in the West Indies (mainly Jamaica) or for North America. They were replaced by a comparable number of black slaves.

EXERCISE

Refer back to Table 5.3 'European-directed transatlantic migration 1500–1760', and answer the following questions:

1 What is the most obvious feature of the period between 1640 and 1700 in the columns that refer to slavery, and what does this say about the alteration in Britain's role?

2 What part could Barbados have played in this?

SPECIMEN ANSWER

1 The table shows how, after 1640, the market for slaves in the Americas drew many more British merchants into the slave trade, which previously had largely been directed towards the Iberian colonies, and carried out by the Spanish and Portuguese.

2 Barbados's need for slaves to work on sugar plantations was probably one important cause of this change.

DISCUSSION

Before the demand produced by the profitable cultivation of sugar, almost entirely on Barbados, British involvement in slavery was insignificant; afterwards it was substantial. This trade led to the creation and strengthening of enclaves (defined in Unit 2) on the West African coast, such as Cape Coast Castle, which served as depots where slaves were brought, held and traded. The European population of these enclaves was never large, but they were a significant part of the British Atlantic system.

The wealth of Barbados was one of the major reasons why, in 1655, the British government launched the 'Western Design', whereby a large military and naval force was sent against the chief Spanish island in the Caribbean – St Domingue. This was the first significant *state-controlled* attempt by the English to take and hold Spanish territory in America. It failed, although one spin-off was the capture of Jamaica, at the time undeveloped, but later to become a sugar-producing island. Aside from Jamaica, at this stage the only other significant departure from the model of the joint-stock company was in

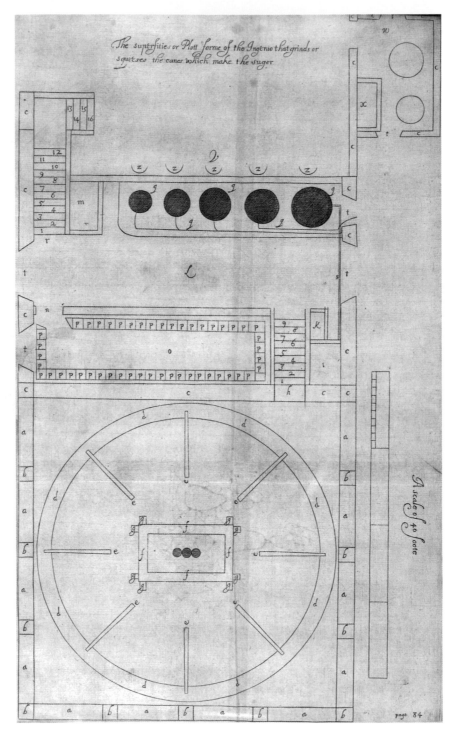

Figure 5.11a   'The superfities or Plott forme of the Ingenio that grinds or squeeses the canes which make the suger' ('A superficial or diagram view of the engine that grinds or squeezes the canes which make the sugar'), from Ligon, R. (1673) *A True & Exact History of the Island of Barbadoes*, London, Peter Parker ... and Thomas Guy. British Library, London, 796.ff.20. By permission of the British Library. The detail of this drawing and the key in Figure 5.11b show how Ligon's account of the history of Barbados was intended to provide a great deal of technical information about how sugar was refined.

An Index to the Platforme or Superficies of an Ingenio, that grinds or squeezes the Sugar.

A. THe ground-plat , upon which the Posts or Pillars stand , that bear up the house, or the Intercolumniation between those Pillars.

B The Pillars or Posts themselves.

C The wall between the Mill-house and Boyling-house.

D The Circle or Circumference, where the Horses and Cattle go, which draw the Rollers about.

E The Sweeps, to which the Horses and Cattle are fastned , that draw about the Rollers.

F The Frame of the *Ingenio.*

G The Brackets or Butteresses , that support that Frame.

H The Dore, that goes down stairs to the Boyling-house.

I The Cistern, into which the Liquor runs from the Ingenio, immediately after it is ground, and is carried in a Pipe under ground to this Cistern, where it remains not above a day at most.

K The Cistern that holds the Temper, which is a Liquor made with ashes, steept in water, and is no other than the Lye we wash withall in *England.* This temper , we straw in the three last Coppers , as the Sugar boyles, without which, it would never Corn, or be any thing but a Syrope; but the salt and tartarousness of this Temper, causes it to turn, as Milk does, when any soure or sharp liquor is put into it; and a very small quantity does the work.

L The Boyling-house.

The five black Rounds are the Coppers, in which the Sugar is boyled , of which the largest is called the clarifying Copper, and the least, the Tatch.

M The cooling Cistern, which the Sugar is put into, presently after it is taken off the fire, and there kept till it be Milk-warm ; and then it is to be put into Pots made of boards, sixteen inches square above, and so grow taper to a point downward; the Pot is commonly about thirty inches long , and will hold thirty or thirty five pounds of Sugar.

N The Dore of the Filling-room.

O The Room it self, into which the Pots are set, being fill'd, till the Sugar grow cold and hard, which willbe in two dayes & two nights,& then they are carried away to the Cureing house.

P The tops of the Pots, of sixteen inches square, and stand between two stantions of timber , which are girded together in several places ,

with wood or Iron , and are thirteen or fourteen inches assunder; so that the tops of the Pots being sixteen inches, cannot slip between, but are held up four foot from the ground.

Q The Frame where the Coppers stand, which is raised above the flowre or level of the room, about a foot and a half, and is made of Dutch Bricks , which they call Klinkers, and plaister of *Paris.* And besides the Coppers, there are made small Gutters, which convey the skimmings of the three lesser Coppers , down to the Still-house, whereof the strong Spirit is made, which they call *kill-devil,* and the skimmings of the two greate. Coppers are conveyed another way, as worthless and good for nothing.

R The Dore that goes down the stairs to the fire-room , where the Furnaces are , which cause the Coppers to boyl; and though they cannot be exprest here, by reason they are under the Coppers ; yet, I have made small semi-circles , to let you see where they are , behind the partition-wall, which divides the fire-room from the boyling-house ; which wall goes to the top of the house , and is mark'd with the Letter (*c*) as the other walls are.

S A little Gutter made in the wall , from the Cistern that holds the first Liquor, to the clarifying Copper, and from thence is conveyed to the other Coppers , with Ladles that hold a gallon a piece, by the hands of Negres that attend that work day and night , shifting both Negres and Cattle every four hours, who also convey the skimmings of the three lesser Coppers down to the Stillhouse, there to be twice distill'd; the first time it comes over the helme, it is but small , and is called Low-wines; but the second time, it comes off the strongest Spirit or Liquor that is potable.

T All Windowes.

U The Fire-room, where the Furnaces are , that make the Coppers boyl.

W The Still-house.

X The Cistern that holds the skimmings, till it begin to be soure, 'till when, it will not come over the helme.

Y The two Stills in the Still-house.

Z The Semi-circles, that shew where about the Furnaces stand.

Place this after Folio 84.

Figure 5.11b 'An Index to the Platforme or Superficies of an Ingenio, that grinds or squeezes the Sugar', from Ligon, R. (1673) *A True & Exact History of the Island of Barbadoes*, London, Peter Parker … and Thomas Guy. British Library, London, 796.ff.20. By permission of the British Library.

Virginia: the Virginia Company had collapsed in 1624, when it became clear that the developing tobacco boom of the settlement would not be enough to pay the accumulated debts incurred setting it up. The crown took it over, but this was an exception to the rule that (before 1660 at least) most English colonies were ruled with a light touch from London. In an echo of Cortes's use of the legal authority of the (at the time) largely fictitious city council of Vera Cruz to gain his independence from Cuba, in 1632 the Massachusetts Company took advantage of the fact that their charter did not specify a site for their headquarters, and took it over the Atlantic to Boston. It would be tempting to see this as the first shot in the American War of Independence – but the concerns of the colonists in their seventeenth-century footholds cannot be compared to those of the later prosperous multitudes who would try to break free entirely from London.

In 1651, the English government passed the first of the Navigation Acts. These were mercantilist measures designed to integrate shipping with the empire. They prohibited colonies from trading directly with any country except for England – although they were allowed to trade with one another. All colonial trade was funnelled through England, and was to be undertaken by English ships. This had the effect of freezing the Dutch (whose shipping remained the cheapest) out of the trade; their response was to fight an unsuccessful war in an attempt to overturn the Acts. For nearly 200 years, the Acts (insofar as they could be enforced) 'created a self-contained commercial system' (Zahedieh, 1999, p. 144). Within this protection, English (and, after 1707, Scottish) traders engaged in a free market; the Atlantic trade was largely free from interference by monopolistic chartered trading companies. Over the next century, it grew into a self-sustaining and profitable enterprise, supporting the meteoric expansion of the American colonies.

CONCLUSION

How did the British empire begin?

One of the historian's jobs is to explain why things happened as they did. The answers to any question beginning 'why?' can easily suffer from one of two failings. The first is to be too specific, the second too general. The first problem involves 'explanations' that degenerate into an undifferentiated list of factors and events. They are merely descriptions of the way that the world was before and during the process in question, and they often commit the fallacy know as *post hoc prompter hoc* – the mistaken belief that just because event A happened before event B, it must therefore have caused it. The second problem goes to the opposite extreme, and involves the selection of one factor and the reduction of the explanation to just this: it over-simplifies. Our job, when we are making general statements, is to try to avoid both these problems: our explanations must be just complex enough to work, but not so complex that they become meaningless.

To say 'why', we have to understand 'how', and here are a number of key concepts that we have to bear in mind as we try to explain this process:

- Structural factors – the geography and ecology of the Atlantic world.
- Failures – when didn't imperial ventures work?
- Interaction – what was the role of other imperial enterprises in this process?
- Stages – nothing happens all at once, and successful institutions always take time to establish themselves.

EXERCISE Skim the unit and list one example of each of the above concepts, as it affected the expansion of the British Atlantic empire.

SPECIMEN ANSWER Possible examples include those listed in Table 5.4.

Table 5.4   Key concepts in the expansion of the British Atlantic empire

1 Structural factors	Pigs; disease; position of England in relation to trade winds *natives*
2 Failures	Roanoke; Northwest Passage
3 Interactions	Lure of Spanish gold; Dutch sugar-refining expertise
4 Stages	Barbados; New England

DISCUSSION You might have noted that the four concepts concern different kinds of things. The first refers to common and structural factors, the second and third to particular categories of events, and the fourth to a process that was the same for several separate long-term developments.

One way that we can understand complex situations is to look at failure as well as success. A question that we can consider is 'What factors did successful settlements have in common that failures lacked?' An obvious answer to this question is that the successes were part of a plantation economy, exporting highly profitable commodities. New England's success was due to supplying this economy. This neatly dates success to the early years of the seventeenth century – but these years also saw the great extension of long-range sailing expertise following the privateering years, and a far better idea of how to settle a new land, derived painfully from so many false starts. So perhaps the commodities were the effect of a new professionalism, rather than a cause.

One aspect that you may have expected the unit to spend more time dealing with is motives. Why did people want to start an empire? Partly this gap is because the issue has been touched on already in Unit 3, but mostly it is because my study of this area has convinced me that motives were not enough, and other, usually material, factors – whether they were economic or ecological – had by far the greater influence. *and*

But we must be aware of the ways that the perceptions of the present influence the way that explanations are offered. In the nineteenth century and before, the most common explanation for the eventual success of Britain's expansion was that it was a sign of God's good will. The story went that they won because they were blessed. This was replaced by an explanation, popular during the later Industrial Revolution and the period of technical advance in the early twentieth century, that stressed the extent to which the triumph of the Europeans was derived from their superior technology and social systems. The story was that they won because they were better. Alongside decolonisation during the late twentieth century, more voices pointed to the great extent that imperialism depended on violence. By now, the story was that they were nastier. By the end of the twentieth century, with the work of historians like Crosby, a new 'meta-explanation' had arrived, which looked to ecological factors that were out of control of Europeans and natives alike. Finally, they were luckier. Yet even if we accept ecology as one of the big ideas that must be present in every explanation, we should by now realise that a lot of other factors also need to be considered – related to society, context and circumstance.

REFERENCES

Andrews, J.R. (1984) *Trade, Plunder and Settlement: Maritime Enterprise and the Genesis of the British Empire, 1480–1630*, Cambridge, Cambridge University Press.

Black, J. (2004) *The British Seaborne Empire*, New Haven, Yale University Press.

Brooke, J. (2003) 'Ecology' in Vickers, D. (ed.) *A Companion to Colonial America*, Oxford, Blackwell, pp. 44–75.

Canny, N. (1998) 'England's New World and the Old, 1480s–1640s' in Canny, N. (ed.) *The Origins of Empire: British Overseas Enterprise to the Close of the Seventeenth Century*, Oxford, Oxford University Press, pp. 148–69.

Collinson, R. (ed.) (n.d.) *The Three Voyages of Martin Frobisher*, New York, Franklin.

Crosby, A. (2004) *Ecological Imperialism: The Biological Expansion of Europe, 900–1900*, Cambridge, Cambridge University Press.

Elliott, J.H. (2006) *Empires of the Atlantic World: Britain and Spain in America, 1492–1830*, New Haven, Yale University Press.

Eltis, D. (2000) *The Rise of African Slavery in the Americas*, Cambridge, Cambridge University Press.

Higman, B.W. (2000) 'The sugar revolution', *Economic History Review*, vol. 53, no. 2, pp. 213–36.

Kowaleski, M. (2000) 'The expansion of the south-western fisheries in late medieval England', *Economic History Review*, vol. 53, no. 3, pp. 429–54.

Linebaugh, P. and Rediker, M. (2000) *The Many-headed Hydra: Sailors, Slaves, Commoners and the Hidden History of the Revolutionary Atlantic*, London, Verso.

Scammell, G.V. (1989) *The First Imperial Age*, London, Routledge.

Sloan, K. (2007) *A New World: England's First View of America*, London, British Museum Press.

Steele, I.K. (1986) *The English Atlantic, 1675–1740: An Exploration of Communication and Community*, Oxford, Oxford University Press.

Williams, P. (1979) *The Tudor Regime*, Oxford, Clarendon Press.

Zahedieh, N. (1999) 'Making mercantilism work: London merchants and Atlantic trade in the seventeenth century', *Transactions of the Royal Historical Society*, Series 6, vol. 9, pp. 143–58.

Ole Peter Grell

AIMS

- To enable you to understand why trading empires came into existence.
- To offer some suggestions as to what made them possible.
- To describe the nature of, and similarities and differences between, the Portuguese and Dutch trading empires.

INTRODUCTION

In this unit you will encounter the beginning of what historians have portrayed as the first two major European maritime trading empires of the sixteenth and seventeenth centuries, both preceding the British empire. Before you start, you should return to Unit 1, especially the section on mapping empires 1500–1680, to remind yourself of the scale and duration of the Portuguese empire in particular. You would also be well advised to have another look at the section on typologies of colonies in Unit 2, where the discussion of the category of enclaves is particularly pertinent.

It has baffled historians how two small and relatively unimportant European territorial states, one poor and a backwater (Portugal), the other wealthy, but small in terms of land and population (the Dutch Republic), managed to build large trading empires in east Asia, in particular, during this period. When you have finished this unit, you should have a clearer idea about whether or not they are adequately understood as trading empires only, and to what extent they differed from each other.

Portugal

Around 1500, Portugal had a population of less than 1 million people. It was a poor country with almost no natural resources. Trade was therefore important, not just as the only avenue for individual success, but also as the only way of achieving funds and status for the crown. Portugal had not yet developed any of the institutions associated with the early modern state, but it possessed one major asset: the harbour city of Lisbon, situated where the two great maritime economies of Europe met – the Atlantic, reaching north into the Baltic, and the Mediterranean. It remained a feudal society ruled personally by the king. Most of the country, including the towns, was controlled by the nobility, the **military orders** and the church. Military forces were raised by the leading feudal lords who relied on the sons of the gentry (*fidalgos*), who had sought employment within their households, to run their private armies. Likewise it was the *fidalgos* who constituted the knights of the four military orders (Santiago, Avis, Christ and Hospital) and provided many of the personnel for the royal armies and frontier and costal fortresses. Military service was the only avenue to success open to this often ambitious group. They were later to provide the Portuguese crown with a pool of military expertise that could be used in the **Estado da India** (the Portuguese empire in India). Since the conquest of the Moroccan coastal town of Ceuta in 1415, these military orders had been committed to crusade or *Reconquista* while seeking material rewards in the process.

Traditionally, the Portuguese empire has been seen as primarily a feudal trading system that sought to control the trade in the Indian Ocean through a system of tributes and customs duties. In other words, it wanted to skim off profits from regional trading systems that it attempted to dominate, but never sought to change. Ideologically, this enterprise was driven by the crusading ambition of bringing Catholic Christianity to the 'heathen'. At the back of this religious agenda lurked **apocalyptic beliefs** and hopes centred on the ambition to make contact with the mythical Christian community supposedly established in Asia by the legendary medieval king Prester John. The Portuguese trading system, according to most historians, eventually proved no match for the Dutch capitalist system represented by the Dutch East India Company (VOC), which appeared a century later. The VOC was not particularly interested in proselytising (i.e. spreading their type of Christianity, namely Calvinism). It is presumed to have been driven purely by profit. Accordingly, the VOC is supposed to have changed the regional trading system fundamentally in order to maximise its profits.

In dealing with these issues, this unit will start with an examination of the Indian Ocean context that the Portuguese encountered on their arrival and the nature and rationale of the first Portuguese voyages to India. It will then discuss the Portuguese empire in the east – both the official empire, the so-called Estado da India, and the unofficial empire, especially in the Far East and Japan. Finally, it will examine how and why the VOC managed to challenge Portuguese supremacy in the east.

THE INDIAN OCEAN CONTEXT

Historians agree that the Portuguese arrived at a most opportune moment in the Indian Ocean. By the beginning of the sixteenth century, the great land-based powers in the east were concerned primarily with their land borders, while warfare in the Middle East and the eastern Mediterranean had closed the traditional overland spice routes by the end of the fifteenth century. For a European naval nation like Portugal to be looking for an alternative route was therefore understandable at this precise time. As you have seen in Unit 4, the beginning of the Atlantic empires, which took place at the same time, was also rooted in the ambition to find an alternative route for the spice trade: that is, a new route to Asia. Furthermore, when the Portuguese arrived in the Indian Ocean, their potential threat to the local, eastern powers appears to have come low down the agenda for most, if not all, of the major Asian powers of the day, who were preoccupied with defending or expanding their territories and showed little interest in maritime power.

Muslim influence over trade in the Indian Ocean and beyond was significant long before the arrival of the Portuguese. Initially, Indian Ocean long-distance trade, through the Bay of Bengal and into the South China Sea, was dominated by Persian merchants, but by the fourteenth century the rise first of the Fatimid and later the Mamluk dynasties of Egypt had served to move the routing of long-distance trade away from Bagdad and Damascus and on to Aden and Cairo (Fustat). Simultaneously, in India, the Turkish sultanate of Delhi conquered Gujarat in 1303–04, thereby bringing its wealthy coastal towns within the reach of Islam, while around the same time the ports and coastal kingdoms of the Indonesian archipelago began converting to Islam.

Thus, until 1400, Muslim merchants dominated trade to and from the east, while growing numbers of people in the east converted to Islam. Arab shippers and traders were more or less in control of the sea routes in the east, not only to Gujarat in India, but also to southeast Asia and Guangzhou (Canton) in China. It was no coincidence that some Muslim, Middle Eastern cities, such as Cairo and Alexandria, were considerably larger and wealthier than any European cities at this time – Cairo having a population of no less than 600,000 people. However, after 1400, a decline began to set in. The Mamluk empire suffered badly from the Mongol invasions at the beginning of the century, and saw several of its prominent cities plundered and destroyed. This disruption of trade occurred at a time when the Middle East was not only witnessing a severe population decline as a consequence of the Black Death (1347), but also encountering a shortage of gold, which further harmed commerce. Even so, the Islamic states of the Middle East remained important players in the long-distance and maritime trade in the East Indies. Proof of this can be seen in the foundation and Islamisation of the new entrepôt state of Malacca, which converted to Islam around 1425, and the subsequent rapid spread of Islam within the maritime zone of southeast Asia.

However, despite the continued significance of Arab Islamic merchants and strong Islamic states such as the Ottoman empire, it was the Chinese empire, recently resurrected to its former glory by the Ming dynasty (1368–1644), which became the dominant force in maritime trade in the east by the beginning of the fifteenth century. This is hardly surprising, bearing in mind China's vast human and economic resources. Between 1404 and 1433 a series of large, Chinese naval expeditions were organised. The first, consisting of 62 ships and carrying 28,000 men, reached Calicut on the Malabar coast, while the fourth expedition travelled as far as Hormuz and Aden. Some might even have reached the coast of east Africa. These were also the years when Chinese merchants regularly arrived in the harbour cities of India, Ceylon and even in Hormuz. But the Ming dynasty abandoned the expensive fleets after the last one in 1433, in order to concentrate on threats to its northern borders. Thereafter, subsequent Ming emperors closed China's port cities to foreigners and forbade Chinese merchants to travel overseas (Chaudhuri, 1985, pp. 58–61).

This marked a decline in long-distance trade in Asia until the arrival of the Portuguese. Instead, three semi-autonomous trading zones – the western Indian Ocean, the Bay of Bengal and the South China Sea – emerged. This turned the ports of Calicut and Malacca, which had until then served as reprovision points for the long-distance trade, into 'terminal emporia points', where goods from the different zones were transported and exchanged (Prakash, 1999, pp. 175–81).

Furthermore, the Asian powers had mainly left their port cities to manage their own affairs. Asian governments did little to support or control trade and, more often than not, merchants from outside dominated trade in the port cities. The phenomenon of armed trading – Mediterranean style – was unknown in Asia before the arrival of the Portuguese in 1498. In contrast to Asian governments, by the sixteenth century most European states appear to have developed an economic/trade policy that benefited their own burghers and sought to create the best framework for trade. Simultaneously, the political influence of the European merchant class had become considerable and, unlike their Asian counterparts, they were able to influence government policy directly (Pearson, 1991, p. 76).

The first Portuguese voyages to India

The Portuguese put the building blocks in place for their empire nearly a century before the Dutch. Rapid progress was made in the two decades after Vasco da Gama's return from his voyage of discovery to India in 1499 (see Figure 6.1). The fleets the Portuguese crown sent to the east intended to open up commercial contacts between Portugal and the pepper-trading states of India. The first, consisting of thirteen ships under the command of Pedro Alvares Cabral, a minor nobleman like da Gama, set out in March 1500 with the task of establishing a factory in the major Indian pepper-trading port city of Calicut. At this stage, the Portuguese crown had no intention of trying to establish a monopoly or trading empire. It is noteworthy that at least one of the ships in the royal fleet was privately owned and chartered by a **syndicate of merchants**, some of whom were Italian. In fact, a second, smaller fleet, which left Lisbon before Cabral had returned, may well have been fully funded by a syndicate of merchants, again with considerable Italian input. Even from the outset, the rulers of Portugal found it difficult to fully finance the first steps towards a trading empire.

The first Portuguese fleet to India may have been a success in terms of the geographical and navigational information it brought back, but financially it was close to a disaster. Cabral had lost five ships and many men, while the cargo he had brought back did not even cover the cost of the expedition. More seriously, however, not only had he failed to establish a factory in Calicut, but he had also fallen out with the Muslim merchants who controlled the city.

Despite this disappointment, the royal council decided to send another fleet to the east in March 1502. This time, however, Cabral was replaced by

Figure 6.1   Gregorio Lopes, *Vasco da Gama*, *c.*1524. National Museum of Ancient Art, Lisbon. Photo: Bridgeman Art Library. Da Gama (born 1460) discovered the sea route to India and died in Cochin in 1524.

Vasco da Gama, who promised the king that he could make the fleet pay for itself. This voyage was characterised by a mixture of piracy and trade in order to maximise profit. Da Gama's fleet was supported by another fleet that left Lisbon the following year under the command of Alfonso de Albuquerque. Together the two fleets succeeded in establishing a number of trading posts, or factories, in Cochin and Cannanur in India, supported by warships and a system of alliances. Da Gama himself returned a seriously rich man, having amassed around 40,000 ducats, according to contemporaries. Using a mixture of plunder, piracy and trade, Vasco da Gama had proved that the Portuguese crown could make this enterprise profitable while individuals from commanders downwards could acquire personal wealth beyond their dreams.

It was upon the return of Vasco da Gama from his voyage of discovery to India in 1499 that the **Casa da India** grew into a major government department, taking responsibility for supplying and paying for the fleets while also taking over the valuation and sale of cargoes. It was supported by another rapidly expanding department of state, the armoury, which had traditionally kept stocks of arms and armour for royal forces but now expanded into ship building because of the growth of the maritime empire. Its naval dockyards quickly became some of the largest in Europe, producing the great **carracks** (or *naus*) that sailed on the route to India, supplying them with some of the finest cannons produced in its own foundry. Technologically, however, the Portuguese added nothing new – they simply took over a medieval type of vessel developed by the well-established Italian trading cities of Venice, Genoa and Pisa.

THE CREATION OF THE PORTUGUESE EMPIRE IN THE EAST: THE ESTADO DA INDIA

From the outset, the Portuguese king, Dom Manuel I, realised that he needed access to private finance to bankroll this enterprise, and syndicates of Genoese and Florentine merchant bankers played a prominent part early on. Within a few years, the original plan for the *carreira da India* proved untenable. The idea had been that each year a fleet sponsored by the crown would sail to India and return with a cargo, and that part of the profit made would finance the following year's fleet. Instead, permanent factories had to be established and protected by soldiers, while the need for the permanent presence of some warships became recognised. But such a naval presence raised new issues of supply and maintenance.

[handwritten margin note: Impossible to finance a fleet each year.]

In 1505, Dom Manuel and his advisors decided that a viceroy had to be sent to India to take charge of the crown's interests and rule the new empire, which became known as the Estado da India. This was clearly a different undertaking from the creation of a pepper-trading empire and amounted to the creation of a new Portuguese state in the Indian Ocean, with its own government and armed forces. The first viceroy, Francisco de Almeida, left with a fleet of twenty-two ships. His instructions ordered everyone to 'comply with all his requirements and commands ... as though we [the King] in person had spoken and commanded it', adding:

> In all cases both civil and criminal and even in the death penalty he shall have entire say and his judgements and commands shall be carried out and no appeal shall be made against them ... Furthermore we bestow upon him our full power over all the affairs of our revenues, whether it be in buying or selling of our merchandise to

> load the *naus* or in any other thing concerning our revenues ... We
> bestow upon him the power to remove and dismiss the captains of the
> fortresses and the *naus* when such would seem desirable for the good
> of our service ... and to remove the factors of the factories or of
> the *naus*.

The viceroy was also to be given:

> full power to contract for us and in our name treaties of peace and
> friendship with all the kings and lords of India for the welfare of our
> service ...

> Furthermore we confer upon him our full powers to wage war and to
> order it to be waged by sea or by land against any of the kings and
> lords of India whenever he may deem fit.

(cited in Newitt, 2005, pp. 73–4)

[handwritten: All this to protect the crown's interests in India]

As you can see, these were close to full royal powers that were granted to the viceroy. He was meant to act for the king in the east with full political control over foreign policy, from treaties to making war or peace. Like the king in Portugal, he was the ultimate judge of all things civil and criminal. Internally, the viceroy could hire and fire at will within the administration of the Estado da India, from the captains of the fortresses down to those who commanded individual ships. Likewise, he had full jurisdiction over all financial and mercantile decisions.

The primary purpose of this 'new state' was to try to secure the control of the pepper trade from the Malabar coast in India. The intention was that factors should be appointed by the crown in the main pepper-trading ports, where they then purchased pepper at prices negotiated with local rulers. This, in turn, was paid for by silver and copper shipped out from Europe and gold from east Africa. Like trade in pepper, the gold trade was declared a royal monopoly, as was the import of horses into India, to which was later added the trade to Europe in cloves and cinnamon. Every ship in the Indian Ocean had to buy a pass (*cartaz*) from the Portuguese, declaring their cargo and passengers, and to pay customs duties. To enforce the regulations, the Portuguese established a string of fortified factories or fortresses on the Indian west coast (Malabar) and in the gold-trading areas of east Africa, especially Mozambique, and, of course, maintained a substantial naval presence.

Francisco de Almeida followed in the footsteps of da Gama and set the tone for future viceroys, when he used all the means available to him in the east to enrich himself and his family, while meticulously setting aside a fifth for the crown and a share for the Catholic Church. The policy of plunder and extortion can be seen as a necessary complement to the policy of monopoly. Those communities and states who failed to accept Portuguese claims to monopoly of the spice trade were attacked, and the subsequent plunder served to supply the Portuguese fleet and keep its military and naval personnel happy. Warfare, plunder and trade had become intimately linked.

[handwritten: ability to wage war common to land, maritime, or trading empires.]

From the outset, a major motivating factor in the Portuguese crown's creation of the Estado da India and a monopoly over the pepper trade had been the prospect of dealing a serious blow to Muslim power in the Middle East. It would do this by undermining the traditional trade routes through the Red Sea, which were controlled by the sultan of Egypt.

Almeida was succeeded by Alfonso de Albuquerque (see Figure 6.2), an experienced soldier with extensive service in the east who, back in 1506, had established a temporary Portuguese foothold in the Arabian stronghold of Hormuz. Albuquerque, however, proved a controversial character, who pursued well-defined political and military objectives that did not always correspond to those of his royal master in Lisbon, Dom Manuel. To achieve the crown's aim of establishing a monopoly of the gold and spice trades, Albuquerque unilaterally decided that Portugal needed well-defended territorial strongholds, or enclaves, and direct control of the shipping routes between Europe and the east. Thus, he took the opportunity offered by the death of the sultan of Bijapur in central India to conquer the main port city of Goa in 1510, *personal decisions, however,* without having obtained royal authority. The city, after all, had no significance for the pepper trade, even if it was the principal port for the importation of horses into India from Arabia. Albuquerque, however, saw the strategic opportunity, and wanted to turn Goa into a sovereign Portuguese territory, *not those of the state.* offering a base for future naval and military operations. It proved an important decision, and Goa remained the centre of the Portuguese trading empire of the east for more than a century. The following year, Albuquerque used the pretext of an attack on the Portuguese trading fleet that had visited the busy trading port of Malacca on the Malay peninsula, which controlled trade with the Far East, China, Japan and Indonesia, to conquer that city.

Albuquerque quickly realised that action was needed to secure the commercial position of Goa and generate capital that would produce revenue for the crown, which in turn could justify the conquest of the city. He proceeded to create civil and civic institutions that regulated life and trade in Goa, and encouraged Portuguese sailors and soldiers to settle there and marry local Indian women, uniting the Christian and Hindu populations against their Muslim enemy.

It was the five-year governorship of Albuquerque that laid foundations of a Portuguese trading empire which, even if it fell short of dominance, played a significant part in trade between the east and Europe for more than a century. Shortly before his death in 1515, Albuquerque also conquered another thriving trading centre, Hormuz (Figure 6.3), which made the Portuguese a major power in the Persian Gulf. Within this short period, Portugal had taken on the responsibilities of a great power, which eventually proved beyond its resources to maintain.

Among Albuquerque's many achievements was his success in convincing Dom Manuel, whose main political objective remained the destruction of Muslim power in northern Africa, that his actions in the Far East constituted an important part of that objective. In this he was helped by his predecessor Francisco de Almeida's decisive victory over an alliance of the major Muslim

AFOMGODAL
BVQERQVEGOVE
RNADOR

Figure 6.2   Unknown artist, *Alfonso d'Albuquerque*, *c.*1558, watercolour, from the *Livro de Lizuarte de Abreu* (1558–65), a manuscript depicting Portuguese viceroys and governors in India. The Pierpont Morgan Library, New York, MS M.525, f. 5. Photo: © 2007 Pierpont Morgan Library/Art Resource/Scala, Florence. Albuquerque was Portuguese viceroy of the East Indies from 1509 to 1515.

powers in the region (the sultanate of Gujarat, Calicut, which was dominated by Arab Muslim merchants, and the Egyptian Mamluks) off Diu in northern India in 1509 just before he took over the position of viceroy. This victory

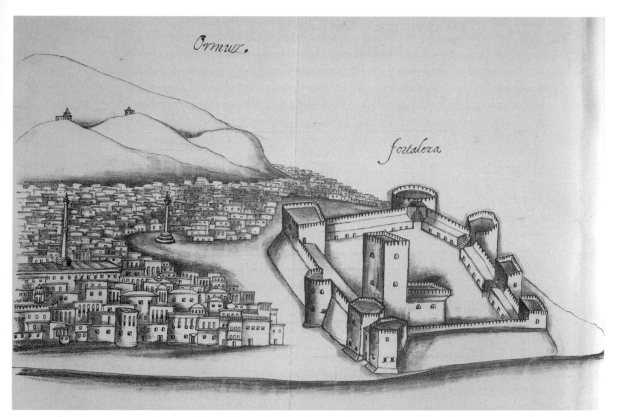

Figure 6.3 View of Ormuz (Hormuz) from the sea in the nineteenth century, engraving, from Correa, G. (1858–64) *Lendas da India*, Lisbon. British Library, London, 9056.i.15, opp. p. 439. By permission of the British Library. Notice the size of the fortress (*fortaleza*) built by the Portuguese and still dominating the city more than 300 years later.

more importantly also saw off the greatest military threat to the emerging Portuguese empire.

After the conquest of Goa, the city became the headquarters not only of the Portuguese viceroy, but also of the missionary branch of the Portuguese Catholic Church, especially the Jesuits, who quickly recognised the potential in the east for conversions.

Towards the end of the sixteenth century, the Dutch traveller and merchant Jan Huygen van Linschoten (see Figure 6.4) published his famous *Itinerario* (1595). This had a considerable impact on merchants and governments throughout northern Europe, and in particular on the dynamic merchant communities in the Netherlands and in England, where it was translated soon after its appearance in Dutch. Linschoten was originally apprenticed to a Spanish merchant in Seville (Spain) and had set out for India as an employee of the Fugger merchant house in Augsburg; he spent years in the east and resided in Goa in the mid-1580s. In his book he provided extensive information about the Portuguese trading empire, not to mention detailed navigational and geographical information necessary for those who sought to undertake a trading voyage to the east.

Figure 6.4   L. Cornely, *Jan Huygen van Linschoten, aged 32*, 1595, engraving. Photo: Mary Evans Picture Library. Note the corner details showing a view of Goa and a map of Mozambique at the top, and two views of St Helena at the bottom, indicating Linschoten's prestige as an experienced explorer.

Linschoten also provided a description of the Portuguese viceroy and his administration in Goa.

EXERCISE

Read the extract from Chapter 32 of Jan van Linschoten's account of his voyage to the East Indies on the course website (Primary Source 6.1) and answer the following questions:

1   How does Linschoten's description of the power and role of the viceroy compare with the instructions given to the first viceroy, Francisco de Almeida?

2   What is Linschoten's opinion of the way the Portuguese Estado da India is administered by the viceroy and his captains?

SPECIMEN ANSWER

1   In many ways it seems similar, emphasising the near absolute power of the viceroy and the support he receives from a number of advisory councils similar to those that served the king back in Lisbon. However, the viceroy has lost the right to make the final decision in civil legal cases, which can be sent back to Portugal in case of appeal. Similarly, by the 1580s, the viceroy was no longer allowed to judge criminal cases that involved 'gentlemen', presumably meaning anyone from minor noblemen (*fidalgos*) upwards. In other words, the viceroy's legal powers have been limited in some instances, whereas his political and economic powers appear undiminished.

2   Jan van Linschoten did not consider this system beneficial, except for the viceroys and the captains who served under them. He specifically mentions how the viceroys use their last year in post to inspect the outlying forts around Goa, not only for administrative reasons, but to fill their own pockets. Linschoten then goes on to describe how the viceroys generally use their position to enrich themselves and their families. Recently they had even managed to lay their hands on gifts that had traditionally been passed onto the Jesuits. Linschoten concludes that none of the viceroys are interested primarily in furthering the king's or commonwealth's interest because of their short tenure of office. Instead, their priority is to enrich themselves as much as possible in the short time available to them. In this they are imitated by their immediate subordinates: the captains of the fortresses.

Historians differ in their explanation of how the Portuguese managed to establish their trading empire (look back at Figures 2.6a and 2.6b in Unit 2), even if the majority lean towards the views of Carlo Cipolla, who considered Portugal's colonial achievement to have been based on the large, ocean-going warship with its heavy artillery (Newitt, 2005, p. 97). But was Portuguese power in the East Indies simply dependent on military or naval might alone? Some historians, such as G. V. Scammell, think that this was far from being the case.

EXERCISE

Read the article 'Indigenous assistance in the establishment of Portuguese power in Asia in the sixteenth century' by G. V. Scammell (Secondary Source 6.1 on the course website). How does Scammell explain the success of the Portuguese?

SPECIMEN ANSWER

Scammell argues that Portuguese success in the east depended on the ability to exploit local conflicts and divisions while securing the necessary indigenous assistance. He points out that technological superiority was far from being a guarantee of military success, and that Portuguese achievements in the east did not consist of one long line of military triumphs, but involved a fair number of failures and defeats. Furthermore, the indigenous people they encountered in India and beyond were quick to learn and copy both their vessels and use of guns and cannons. The Portuguese, on the other hand, soon realised that the local hostility between Muslims and Hindus could play into their hands and they often relied on large numbers of local Hindu troops fighting for them under their own commanders, and in some cases they even used Muslim troops. Scammell underlines the fact that Portugal had only insignificant military forces in the east, and estimates that there were less than 10,000 Europeans at any given time in the east before 1600, of whom only a minority belonged to any organised military force. Collaboration with and assistance from indigenous people was a necessity, and without Malabar seamen and Hindu mercenaries the Portuguese would not have been able to expand overseas into a populous and wealthy Asia.

DISCUSSION

Scammell's arguments certainly serve as a warning not to make too much of Portuguese technological and military advantages, while pointing to the problem of the Portuguese shortage of manpower in the east. Undoubtedly local mercenaries played a huge part in the Portuguese expansion, as did the growing **Luso-Asian** (Portuguese-Asian) population sponsored by a succession of viceroys, but was Portugal's military advantage really of so little consequence? It is worth remembering that Portuguese military tactics in the east were based primarily on **amphibious operations** – they were able to move large forces undisturbed by sea, thereby being able to concentrate their forces when and where needed. Similarly, their well-built and well-armed fortresses could be easily supplied and reinforced by sea, while the heavy guns on their carracks could quickly be moved into position to provide cover and support for their land-based operations, which were, after all, primarily in coastal areas.

Overseas expansion needs more than military power and political ambition – it needs people, and Portugal benefited from a steady population growth from the late fifteenth century until the early sixteenth century. It has been calculated that 80,000 Portuguese, nearly all males, left for the east during the first twenty-seven years of the sixteenth century and that this rate of emigration to the east was maintained, if not exceeded, over the next fifty years, while the annual average may have declined somewhat over the next forty years to somewhere between 2,000 and 3,000. Obviously, some of these people returned, and it has been suggested that as many as 50 per cent eventually made their way back. Though it has to be borne in mind that mortality rates in the east remained high among European settlers (Newitt, 2005, pp. 217–18).

For the common soldier and sailor, or those who failed to make a fortune in the east, the cost of a return journey could, however, be prohibitive, as can be seen from the information provided by Jan van Linschoten.

EXERCISE

Read the extract from Chapter 93 of Jan van Linschoten's account of his voyage to the East Indies on the course website (Primary Source 6.2) and answer the following questions:

1 Why did soldiers and lower ranks find it so difficult to return to Portugal?
2 How does Linschoten's information on the numbers returning to Portugal compare with what you have read above?

1   In order to return, the soldiers and sailors needed passports from the viceroy, without which they would not receive what they were owed from their services. Even after years of service, that often proved inadequate, in which case the soldiers were forced to remain in India and marry local women. Soldiers who had completed their contracted period of service were given free passage, but they still had to raise substantial sums for their food and drink during the passage; most of those who made it back to Portugal depended on their commanding officers or captains to help them out. Furthermore, the customs charged on what the returnees brought back with them had become increasingly severe, according to Linschoten, with the result that only relatively few made it back to Portugal.

2   Of the more than 1,500 soldiers that Linschoten estimated were sent out to India from Portugal every year, less than 100 returned. The rest were either killed in action or by disease, or were unable to raise the money needed to return. Linschoten's numbers for the annual intake from Portugal is substantially lower than those given above. This may well be due to the fact that he only referred to soldiers; that so few soldiers, in his opinion, were able to return, on the other hand, may well mean that the estimated figure in the text above for those who returned is too high. It is also noteworthy that, according to Linschoten, those Portuguese who remained in India and married locally did so out of necessity rather than choice.

Historians have tended to see the Portuguese Estado da India as an empire of trade rather than as an empire of settlement – a type which is seen to have been characteristic for the Spanish Atlantic empire. Recently, however, the historian Malyn Newitt has argued that the empire in the east was as much an empire of settlement – though within relatively small enclaves – as that of the Atlantic (Newitt, 2005). The fact that large numbers of Portuguese merchants and soldiers settled in the cities conquered by the Portuguese from where the Estado da India controlled tens of thousands of square miles makes the trading empire of the east look very similar to the empire of settlement in Brazil. Also, in both places the Portuguese had sexual relations with the local population, creating a growing mixed-race population closely linked to the Portuguese empire.

The Portuguese trading empire in the east reached its peak between 1550 and 1580. The administrative structure of this empire – the Estado da India – had at its pinnacle the king in Lisbon, but was in reality controlled and run by his representative, the viceroy, resident in Goa. The viceroy controlled around fifty fortresses, stretching from east Africa to the Far East, which were under the command of captains. These fortresses protected the Portuguese trading factories and coastal trading cities. The captains were responsible for the collection of customs duties for the crown, which gradually came to constitute the crown's most important source of revenue from the trading empire in the east. The captains also issued shipping passes (*cartaz*) to foreign merchants – another source of revenue for the crown – many of whom chose to sail under the protective umbrella of the royal Portuguese convoys. By 1571, the

Portuguese eastern empire had become too large to be administered directly by the viceroy in Goa; consequently it was split into three governorships centred on Mozambique, Goa and Malacca.

The Estado da India followed a well-regulated pattern. Every year, five or six large carracks, each around 700 tons, left Lisbon for the east, loaded with silver, and carrying artillery, arms and military provisions for the fortresses. Travelling on the ships were new soldiers and their officers, the latter recruited among the Portuguese lower nobility (*fidalgos*), who all hoped to make a fortune in the east. The fleet returned to Lisbon packed with spices, pepper, cotton, silk, jewels and other luxury items. The trade in spices, gold and ivory was a crown monopoly controlled by royal factors who bought and sold these items on behalf of the crown. They were eventually among the first part of the Estado da India to be privatised when the crown was short of cash.

The Estado da India stretched from east Africa to Malacca on the Malay Peninsula. This, however, did not mean that the Portuguese crown controlled all trade in these territories, but only that it had a controlling influence. Below the official empire existed another unofficial or informal empire. This informal empire dominated trade to the east of Malacca, which was largely outside the crown's control – only one fortress existed here, namely Ternate, which had a controlling influence in the spice trade on the Molucca Islands. The most important settlement of the informal empire was the city of Macao, from where Portuguese merchants bought Chinese silk, which they exported to Japan in exchange for silver. Together with the Jesuits, they had a strong hand in the lucrative trade between China and Japan, centred on Nagasaki. The only exception to this type of trade was the arrival of one royal Portuguese ship in Nagasaki every year.

Linschoten was not the only keen observer and chronicler of the Portuguese empire in east Asia towards the end of the sixteenth century. Another was the Florentine merchant and voyager Francesco Carletti. He was far from atypical, since a fair number of Italian merchants operated within the Portuguese trading empire of east India in the sixteenth century. Born in Florence in 1573, Francesco had, like Linschoten, been sent to Seville when eighteen to learn the ropes of the international maritime trade. He set out from Spain in 1594, a decade after Linschoten, on what was originally intended to be a brief slave-trading voyage, but which turned into an eight-year odyssey that took him to Japan, China and India; he finally returned to Europe in 1602. He would have returned a wealthy man had not the Portuguese ship on which he travelled been conquered by the Dutch off the island of St Helena. Subsequently he served the grand dukes of Tuscany Ferdinando de Medici and Cosimo II as a courtier, during which period he wrote down his chronicles – an account of his eight-year journey to east India. It is important to note that Carletti was first and foremost a merchant in pursuit of profit, even he comes across as a keen and realistic observer.

In the spring of 1599, Carletti left the island of Macao in China on one of two Portuguese ships heading for Goa in India. Three weeks later he arrived in Malacca, which had been under Portuguese rule since Albuquerque had conquered it in 1511.

EXERCISE

Read Carletti's description of Malacca (Primary Source 6.3 on the course website). How important is Malacca for Portuguese control over the spice trade, according to Carletti?

SPECIMEN ANSWER

Carletti has no doubt that Malacca is the cornerstone of the Portuguese spice trade. Apart from a detailed description of which spices come from where, he emphasises how all of them are available and traded in Malacca to such an extent that the houses and streets of the city smell of 'aromatic things which offends the brain of anyone not inured to it, to whom it is very bothersome'. Carletti then informs his readers of the fortunes made by the Portuguese captain-governor of Malacca through his monopoly (on behalf of the crown) on trade in these spices (nutmeg, cloves and mace). He alone can trade with the Indian and Javanese merchants who bring the spices to Malacca and immediately proceeds to sell these goods to resident or visiting Portuguese merchants at a considerably higher price, often taking the cotton cloths they have imported from India in exchange, which he can then use in his trade with the Javanese merchants. According to Carletti, the captain-governor's profit for this simple transaction amounted to between 70 and 80 per cent or, as Carletti himself put it: 'So that without any capital and without any risk whatever, but with the merchandise of others, by buying at sea and selling on land, he makes the abovementioned profit all at once, putting into this dealing nothing but words.' Within their three-year term of office the captain-governors become extremely rich and can return to Portugal to live off their wealth, if it is not stolen from them by corsairs, by which Carletti clearly means the Dutch to whom he lost a fortune when on the return journey on a Portuguese ship.

All ships travelling to and from China, Japan and the Molucca Islands were, according to Carletti, obliged to stop in Malacca and pay customs duties at the rate of 7 per cent to the king of Spain in his capacity as king of Portugal, irrespective of whether they unloaded any merchandise (Carletti, 1965, p.196).

On his arrival in Goa (see Figures 6.5 and 6.6), the centre of the Portuguese East India empire, Carletti was forced to stay on for 20 months awaiting the arrival of the second Portuguese ship on which he had stored many of his goods.

EXERCISE

Read Carletti's description of Goa (Primary Source 6.4 on the course website).
1   How does Carletti describe life among the Portuguese in Goa?
2   How well were the Portuguese culturally and racially integrated?

SPECIMEN ANSWER

1   The Portuguese lived in large and beautiful houses and had a number of fine churches, the best belonging to the Jesuits, who were such an essential part of the Portuguese empire. Their houses were furnished with the finest objects, including porcelain and furniture from China. Here they tended to spend most of the day because of the considerable heat. They only went out in the morning

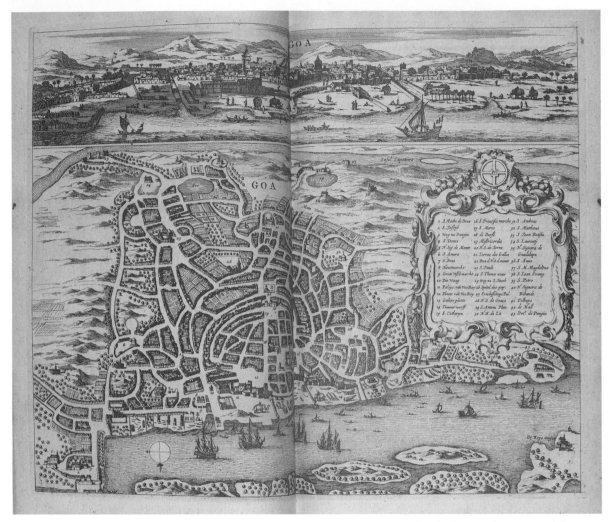

Figure 6.5   Sea view and plan of Goa, engraving, from Baldaeus, P. (1672) *Naauwkeurige beschryvinge van Malabar en Choromandel* (Accurate description of the Malabar and Choromandel), Amsterdam, J. Janssonius van Waasberge & J. van Someren. British Library, London, 147.h.9. By permission of the British Library.

or late afternoon, and mostly travelled on Arab horses. They were always escorted by troupes of slaves who acted as footmen and pages. Both women and men were carried in covered litters called **palanquins**. Clearly, on Carletti's evidence, the Portuguese residents in Goa lived a luxurious existence.

Most of the Portuguese men resident in Goa were married to Luso-Asian women by the late sixteenth century, indicating that the Portuguese had intermarried with the local populations for decades. Considering that this is supposed to have been a deeply Catholic community, to a large extent supervised by the Jesuits, the rather loose sexual mores described by Carletti strike one as surprising and clearly of considerable interest to his Tuscan audience. In terms of food, the Portuguese in Goa had adopted many dishes and methods of cooking that were unknown in Europe.

Figure 6.6   City of Goa, from van Linschoten, J.H. (1599) *Navigatio ac itinerarium J. H. Linscotani in Orientalem sive Lusitanorum Indiam* (Navigation and travel of J.H. Linschoten in the Orient or Portuguese India), The Hague, A. Henrici. British Library, London, 569.g.10. (1) opp. p. 44. By permission of the British Library. The drawing shows Goa's famous market: note the mixture of European and Indian traders and customers.

JAPAN, THE JESUITS AND THE INFORMAL PORTUGUESE EMPIRE

As you have seen, bringing Catholic Christianity to the 'heathen', especially Muslims, was of paramount importance for the Portuguese crown. This deep religious commitment to convert or expel Muslims, in particular, was exploited by Alfonso de Albuquerque in his attempts to secure royal backing for his expanding undertakings in the east. In fact, it could be argued that the creation of a Portuguese trading empire in the east was closely linked to the crown's religious commitment – part crusade, part enterprise. From the outset it rested on a series of papal bulls granting the Portuguese crown sovereignty and ecclesiastical rights over the newly acquired areas in the east. Two bulls in particular, *Romanus Pontifex* (1455) and *Inter Caetera* (1456), came to form the foundation for the crown's claim not only to all land conquered in Africa and the east from the heathen, but also ecclesiastical patronage and jurisdiction in these territories – the so-called ***padroado real***.

A century later, shortly after the establishment of the Inquisition in Portugal, the newly created **Counter-Reformation** order called the Society of Jesus (Jesuits) quickly formed close contacts with the Portuguese crown, from which it received exceptional favours and patronage. With the Jesuits' commitment to missionary activities, they rapidly became hugely influential within the Estado da India. Well educated and often recruited from the cultured and aristocratic classes, the Jesuits were able to fill an administrative void in the Estado da India. As already mentioned, the Estado da India was an ambitious enterprise for a small, relatively poor country like Portugal, with its elaborate set of commercial monopolies, an administrative bureaucracy, and a military set-up on the other side of the world. There was a shortage of qualified and trained people to take on the necessary roles in these organisations, which were instead filled by Jesuits, while others were sent on embassies and missions for the crown. By the late sixteenth century, the fortunes of the Portuguese crown in the east and the Jesuits were inextricably fused together.

The Jesuit mission to the east benefited from the presence of one of the order's founders, Francis Xavier, who travelled out in 1542 and remained there until his death off the coast of China ten years later. Xavier insisted that Jesuits should learn the local languages before attempting to convert people. Writing about Japan in 1549 he argued: 'If we knew the Japanese language we should long ere have been at work in this large uncultivated field' (cited in Newitt, 2005, p. 132). From the outset, the Jesuits pursued their missionary activities beyond the limits of the official Portuguese empire, in contrast to the Inquisition and the Dominicans, who focused their activities on Goa. The Jesuits' endeavour brought together the official empire and the more sprawling unofficial empire further east.

They proved particularly successful in Japan, where Xavier had led the first mission. While Portuguese trade with Japan was growing, the Jesuits were able to act as brokers in the bullion trade (Japanese silver) and with papal permission entered the silk trade too. This, in turn, proved a way of gaining influence with a number of Japanese feudal lords (**daimyos**), some of whom, together with their followers, converted to Christianity. The Jesuits happily mixed trade with religion. By the time Xavier left Japan, a Christian community of close to a thousand had come into existence. By 1560, the Jesuits had established a mission in the capital, Kyoto, where they had managed to ingratiate themselves with Oda Nobunaga, who was the dominant political figure in Japan from 1568 to 1582. In 1571, they were able to secure Nagasaki as a free port for the import of silk into Japan. Here they took on the role of customs officers collecting port dues, part of which was handed over to the local *daimyo*, while the rest was used to sponsor their missionary activities. It has been estimated (Newitt, 2005, p. 159) that, by that date, there were 30,000 Christians in Japan, and within the next decade their number increased rapidly to 150,000, mainly due to the Jesuits' success in making converts among the ruling elite along with their retainers. More than 200 churches had been built and more than eighty-five Jesuit priests were active.

Portuguese cultural influence proved paramount in these years when firearms and horses were adopted by the Japanese elite, but because of a tacit agreement between the Jesuits and the Japanese there was to be no presence of the Estado da India in Japan. As in China, there was no room for the official Portuguese empire. The only influence the Portuguese crown held in this part of the east was through its control over Portuguese shipping. From the time Macao was founded in 1556, an annual royal ship under the command of a captain-major was sent to Japan. The highly lucrative captaincy of the Great Ship, as it became known because of its vast size, was sold to a nobleman (*fidalgo*) who generally fronted a consortium of wealthy merchants and bankers. This ship had a monopoly on the trade from Malacca to Macao, and from there the sole right to export silk from China, mainly obtained in Guangzhou (Canton), to Japan. Buying the Japan–China voyage was a colossal investment and an extremely risky enterprise – ships were lost to pirates and typhoons – but it offered its investors the greatest potential of vast and immediate wealth out of all the possible investments in the Estado da India.

The Florentine merchant Francesco Carletti arrived in the port city of Nagasaki in June 1597, only six months after a mass execution of Christians had taken place outside the city. Upon embarkation, he and some of his fellow travellers 'went immediately to see the spectacle of those poor (as regards this world) six monks of Saint Francis of the discalced Spanish order [Spanish Franciscans], who had been crucified with twenty other Japanese Christians – among them three who had donned the habit of the Jesuits' (Carletti, 1965, p. 105).

EXERCISE

Read Carletti's description of the events in Japan that had resulted in this persecution of Christians (Primary Source 6.5). Who, according to Carletti, had caused the persecution?

SPECIMEN ANSWER

Carletti is in no doubt that the Spanish Franciscans, who had arrived four years earlier from the Philippines, had caused this persecution. Initially the Franciscans had managed to ingratiate themselves with the Japanese ruler. They were granted a house at his court in Kyoto, where they proved very aggressive in their missionary activities and clearly upset the Jesuits, who until then had held a monopoly on the Christian mission to Japan. It was, however, the Franciscans' intervention some years later on behalf of the owners of a richly loaded Spanish merchant ship, which had become stranded on the Japanese coast, that did the damage. According to Japanese law, the stranded ship and its goods belonged to the Japanese king. Confident in their influence at court, however, the Spanish Franciscans tried to intervene to have the ship returned to its Spanish owners, adding pressure by pretending that a large part of the rich merchandise on board belonged to their brethren in Manila. The attempted intervention backfired and caused the Japanese king to spot the inconsistency in the Franciscans' position – on one hand claiming poverty and, on the other, ownership in the treasure on board this ship. The king then decided to take action against what he perceived to be deceitful and dangerous Christians and started the persecution that forced Christians underground even in Nagasaki.

Thus, it was not the Portuguese crown that undermined the Jesuits and the unofficial Portuguese presence in Japan, but Spanish Franciscans coming from Manila in the Philippines who had been trying to take their mission to Japan since the 1580s. Still, the persecution proved short-lived and petered out when the Japanese ruler, Hideyoshi, died the following year. Christianity appears to have flourished in Japan for the next decade, at least. However, the arrival of Dutch and English merchants in the early seventeenth century, and the expansion of direct trade between China and Japan, made the Portuguese Jesuits and their associated Portuguese merchants less important to the Japanese rulers, while their influence was further undermined by the continuous clashes and competition with Spanish Franciscans. In February 1614, Hideyoshi's successor announced the expulsion of all missionaries from Japan, and over the next couple of decades Christianity was systematically eradicated there.

Carletti finished his report on Japan by stating that:

> Japan is one of the most beautiful and best and most suitable regions in the world for making profit by voyaging from one place to another. But one should go there in our sort of vessels and with sailors from our regions [Italy]. And in that way one would very quickly make incredible wealth, and that because of their need of every sort of manufacture and their abundance of silver as of the provisions for living.

(Carletti, 1965, p. 132)

[handwritten margin note: desire to get rich. OMA]

THE DUTCH CHALLENGE 1590–1620

As you have seen, the Dutch merchant Jan van Linschoten and the Florentine merchant Francesco Carletti, both of whom witnessed the Estado da India in action during the last couple of decades of the sixteenth century, agree that the Portuguese trading empire, with its ambition to establish a monopoly in the spice trade, was suffering from serious shortcomings, not least because of the many short-term interests that drove and controlled it. At the same time, the Portuguese were for the first time faced with serious competition from other European naval powers and trading nations who wanted part of the action, namely the Dutch and, to a lesser extent, the English. By then the Portuguese crown, being short of cash, had already sold off much of its 'monopoly on trade' in the east to consortia of bankers and merchants. This, however, like so much else, was done on short-term contracts, which only served further to enhance the short-termism that characterised the Estado da India.

[handwritten margin note: privateers – merchants & bankers vs English pirates.]

The Dutch Republic

The Dutch Republic – also known as the United Provinces – came into existence in 1572 when a number of the northern provinces of the Netherlands took up arms against Spanish hegemony. The revolt proved a long one and only towards the end of the 1580s did the young republic manage to consolidate itself. It gradually came to be dominated by the wealthy burghers and merchants of the major cities, such as Amsterdam, Rotterdam and Middelburg. Despite being officially Calvinist, the republic provided a tolerant environment for other Christian denominations and for Jews. It attracted enterprising refugees from across Europe and quickly established itself as a leading mercantile, cultural and intellectual centre. Undoubtedly the republic's

innovations in technology – caravel ↓ carrack ↓ galleon

attraction was linked to its pre-eminence in trade, shipping and finance, not to mention technology and agriculture. During the first half of the seventeenth century, the republic established itself as one the leading military powers in Europe, with the most powerful navy of the day, despite having a relatively small population, which by the middle of the seventeenth century did not exceed two million. Apart from the size of the country and its population, the Dutch Republic could not have been more different from Portugal.

By 1590, at the latest, the Dutch Republic was well positioned to challenge the Portuguese dominance in the east. It held one of the largest and most modern stock of ships of any European power. In contrast to the Portuguese, who had failed to keep up with innovation in shipbuilding technology, the Dutch relied on the **galleon** rather than on the carrack (*naus*). The Portuguese had held onto the carracks, making them ever larger and eventually producing huge 2,000-ton specimens. The carrack was basically a large barge with castles built fore and aft for purely military purposes. They were slow and difficult to operate, but they offered space for enormous quantities of goods. Unchallenged they had proved their worth, but faced with the much faster, lighter and better-armed galleons of the Dutch they stood no chance. The galleons were multidecked structures with space for many more guns. Despite being significantly smaller – maximum 500 tons – they were a better financial proposition as they were faster, easier to sail and in need of far fewer crew.

Furthermore, the Dutch Republic had seen a recent influx of capital and wealthy merchants after the fall of Antwerp in 1585, which until then had controlled the trade in spices, pepper and sugar in northern Europe. This now switched to the Dutch Republic, and in particular to Amsterdam, coinciding with the onset of Dutch dominance of the so-called '**rich trades**', which included spices. This was helped by Philip II of Spain lifting the trade embargo against the Dutch in 1590.

Knowledge and interest in the east was also growing within the Dutch Republic during these decades, through travel descriptions such as Jan van Linschoten's. This focus on the east was further enhanced by the newly exiled Portuguese crypto-Jewish community – so-called **New Christians** – who had arrived in Amsterdam in these years, and who possessed detailed knowledge of the spice trade and much important navigational and geographical information about the east.

Moreover, the last decade of the sixteenth century proved an opportune time to get directly involved in the sea-borne spice trade. Much of the trade that had continued to depend on overland routes across the Levant was more or less halted from 1590 for the next forty years – a far more serious blockage than that which had encouraged the Portuguese to become involved a century earlier (Wallerstein, 1982). The opportunity was obviously great and the Dutch took it. They may have been further encouraged by the fact that their old enemy, Spain, had been united with Portugal in 1580 in a dynastic alliance, and that accordingly the Spanish Habsburgs controlled Lisbon – the European port of entry for spices.

The superior maritime technology of the Dutch meant that they could shift the principal shipping lanes of the Indian Ocean from the northern half (from the Red Sea via the Persian Gulf) to the southern half (the so-called Cape route). In the words of the economic historian J. H. Parry: 'the square sail triumphed over the lateen, the trade wind over the monsoon' (cited in Wallerstein, 1982, p. 103). As a result, journeys by Dutch ships to the east and back became much faster and more regular.

[handwritten margin note: overcoming the environment. At a time when two societies – Spain + Portugal – were united.]

A look at the statistics (Newitt, 2005, pp. 193–4) of the number of ships and their tonnage leaving Lisbon for the east would indicate that the first two decades of the seventeenth century were superb for Portuguese trade, with more and larger ships leaving the city than in the previous two decades. Considering that this is the exact time when the Dutch challenge to Portuguese domination in the east is supposed to have begun to hurt, this is somewhat baffling. However, it was shipping losses that were to cause the Portuguese serious problems. Between 1580 and 1590, only 8 per cent of outward-bound Portuguese ships had been lost; in the subsequent decade it accelerated to no less than 18 per cent; settling at a considerable 12 per cent over the next two decades. Losses on the homeward journey proved even more damaging and grew from a problematic 16 per cent between 1580 and 1590 to an unacceptable 45 per cent in the next decade. Some were clearly captured by the Dutch while others were far too heavily loaded and sank as a consequence. The figures appear to confirm that Francesco Carletti's experience was far from unique.

When Carletti travelled back in 1601, on one of the regular Portuguese carracks leaving Goa for Portugal in December, reaching the island of St Helena in March 1602, he saw the threat the Dutch presented at first hand. Normally the Portuguese ships travelled in a convoy of four, but that year there were only two. Despite the advice of the passengers, most of whom were undoubtedly merchants and concerned for the safety of their cargo, and worried about the possible presence of hostile English and Dutch ships, the captain anchored off St Helena. Here they encountered two Dutch ships which attacked them.

EXERCISE

Read Carletti's account of Portuguese worries about the Dutch threat to their trade (Primary Source 6.6 on the course website), then read his description of the battle between the Portuguese and the Dutch off St Helena on his return journey (Primary Source 6.7 on the course website). Then answer the following two questions:

1   How serious a threat did the Portuguese consider the Dutch to be, according to Carletti?

2   What was Carletti's opinion of the Portuguese in battle?

SPECIMEN ANSWER

1   At the time Carletti wrote his account– probably during the first or second decade of the seventeenth century – the Portuguese had already lost the trade

in spices from the Molucca Islands to the Dutch and their trade in China had been ruined. Carletti emphasises how strong the Dutch presence had become in the Indian Ocean and how trade on Mozambique and Hormuz had been affected. But it is noteworthy that by then the Dutch had only managed to make an impact in what constituted the informal Portuguese empire.

2   Carletti finds the Portuguese disorganised by comparison with their ruthless Dutch opponents. He describes their disarray and lack of organisation and the non-existent leadership among their officers. Shortly after the start of the battle, the Dutch managed to kill the Portuguese bombardier – who was from Genoa and the only person with reasonable expertise in gunnery on board – with the result that the Portuguese ship was left more or less defenceless. Carletti blames this on the Portuguese practice of selling such jobs to the highest bidder without checking their qualifications.

If the Dutch were as ruthless in their commercial undertakings as Carletti found them in this naval engagement, it would seem that they, and especially the Dutch East India Company (VOC) founded in 1602, represented a new type of commercial capitalism that was superior to the tributary, crown-controlled system of the Portuguese.

The first attempt to establish a Dutch trading empire in the Far East was the creation of the Long-Distance Company in Amsterdam in March 1594. It was a consortium of nine prominent merchants, two of whom played major roles in civic government. The capital raised – 290,000 guilders – paid for a fleet of four ships, with a crew of 249 men, armed with 100 canons supplied by the States of Holland, which also exempted the company from customs duties on the prospective imports from the East Indies (Israel, 1995, pp. 318–19). The fleet set sail the following year and three of the ships returned safely two years later, but with only eighty-nine of the crew still alive. Like its Portuguese forerunners nearly a century earlier, the profits from this first voyage proved disappointing. Despite that, willing investors were not in short supply and the original consortium doubled its number of investors and trebled the capital. Together with another two fleets it set out for Asia in 1598 and returned with four richly loaded ships fourteen months later. The vast profit it generated – 400 per cent after deduction of costs and losses – excited the Amsterdam business community.

This success story, combined with the Spanish embargo of 1598 on all Dutch shipping, goods and merchants in Spain and Portugal, caused Dutch merchants to put a lot of energy into building a trading empire in the east. The Spanish/Portuguese embargo threatened the Dutch domination of the 'rich trades' within Europe by preventing them from buying these goods when they arrived in Lisbon. The Dutch merchants realised that they needed to set this trade up on a grand scale in order to import enough pepper and spices to service their considerable distribution network across Europe. The following year, no less than eight companies were involved in trade in the East Indies. Two years later, fourteen Dutch fleets, totalling sixty-five ships, had set sail for the East Indies.

However, too much competition proved a problem, and in 1601 spice prices and profits began to fall steeply. The Dutch merchants realised that this approach was unsustainable and asked the **States of Holland and Zeeland** to intervene to create some order in the long-distance trade to Asia. Under the watchful eye of the **advocate of Holland**, Johan van Oldenbarnevelt, merchants and politicians devised a totally new commercial organisation: the chartered joint stock company, which held a monopoly and was backed by the state. It was divided into regional chambers and kept its capital and commercial operations separate under the control of a federal board of directors. Of the seventeen directors, eight were elected by Amsterdam, four were elected by merchants based in Zeeland, while the rest were distributed across the republic. Finally, after lengthy negotiations, the VOC received its charter from the **States General**, the supreme political body of the republic. It was given rights to maintain its own troops, set up garrisons, deploy warships, impose governors on Asian populations, conduct negotiations with Asian princes, sign treaties and create alliances. The VOC intended from the start to carve out a principal position in the trade in the East Indies and all its fleets were heavily armed.

By 1605 it had captured the Indonesian Spice Islands (Ternate, Tidore and Amboyna) from the Portuguese (see Plate 2.12 in the Visual Sources Book), but it was another four years before the directors decided to appoint a governor-general and a council to look after its factories and conquests. The first appointee, Pieter Both, resided in Bantam, at the western tip of Java, and even if he is often referred to in the sources as a viceroy, his powers could not have been further from those of the Portuguese viceroy. He did not directly represent a crowned head of state, and neither he nor his successors were noblemen: they were merchants who needed the consent of their council before they could act.

The alliance of military power with the pursuit of profit ran like a guiding thread through the actions of the VOC, as can be seen from the often quoted extract from a letter written by Jan Pieterszoon Coen (see Plate 2.13) to the VOC's board of directors five years before he became the company's fourth governor-general in 1619:

> From experience, your lordships ought to know very well that in India trade is driven and maintained under the protection and favour of your own weapons, just as the weapons are furnished from the profits of trade, in such wise that trade cannot be maintained without war, nor war without trade.

> (cited in Tracy, 1991, p. 1)

However, profit was the principal driving force behind the activities of the VOC, and the cost of military and naval operations that were not clearly geared to this end had to be avoided. Three years later, the directors of the VOC told Coen to pursue a less-aggressive policy in the Banda islands, reminding him that the reason for the VOC's presence out there was profitable trade not armed conquest and suggesting that the number of factories and fortified places be reduced to lower costs (Steensgaard, 1982, p. 255).

The directors had good reason to be worried. From the foundation of the VOC, the running costs of military and naval aspects of its operations had grown from a hefty 50 per cent to an alarming 70 per cent. The cost of building fortifications on the principal islands of the Moluccas from 1605 to 1612 amounted to around one-third of the VOC's initial capital (Parker, 1991, p. 179).

militarism uses up profits!

EMA

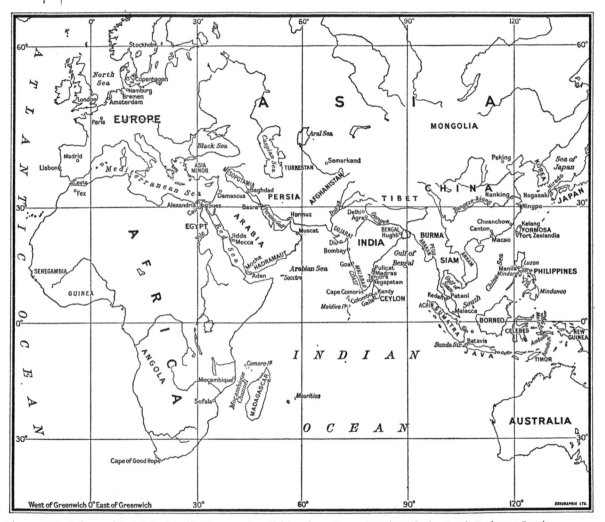

Figure 6.7   Sphere of Dutch East India Company's activities, from Boxer, C.R. (1973) *The Dutch Seaborne Empire 1600–1800*, London, Penguin Books (by arrangement with Hutchinson), map 2.

The VOC clearly offered something very different from the Portuguese Estado da India in terms of both investment and organisation, but in some respects its *modus operandi* did not differ that much from the Portuguese set-up (see Figure 6.7 for a general view of the VOC's sphere of influence at this time). When, in the late 1670s, the Huguenot traveller and merchant

Figure 6.8a   Johann Hainzelman, *Jean-Baptiste Tavernier, Baron d'Aubonne*, engraving, 24.2 × 17.5 cm, from Tavernier, J-B. (1676–77; 1679) *Les six voyages de Jean-Baptiste Tavernier en Turquie, en Perse, et aux Indes, pendant l'espace de quarante ans* (*The six voyages of Jean-Baptiste Tavernier in Turkey, Perisa, and the Indies, over forty years*), Paris, G. Clouzier. Châteaux de Versailles et de Trianon, Versailles. Photo: © RMN/Gérard Blot. This portrait shows Tavernier as a highly respected European man, as evidenced by his title and crest. Compare this view of Tavernier to the one in Figure 6.8b.

Figure 6.8b Johann Hainzelman, *Jean-Baptiste Tavernier, Baron d'Aubonne*, 1679, engraving, 21.5 × 14.6 cm. Châteaux de Versailles et de Trianon, Versailles. Photo: © RMN/Gérard Blot. This portrait – in contrast to Figure 6.8a – shows Tavernier in elegant and costly indigenous attire, indicating his standing in India, where he was widely travelled.

Jean-Baptiste Tavernier (Figures 6.8a and 6.8b) published the story of his travels in India, his report of his visit to Batavia (Figure 6.9) in 1648, which had then become the headquarters of the VOC's governor-general and council, provided great insight into how the VOC's officials operated.

EXERCISE

Read the extract from *Travels in India* by Jean-Baptiste Tavernier on the course website (Primary Source 6.8).

1   What is Tavernier's opinion of the honesty and adherence to company policy of prominent employees of the VOC?

2   To what extent do you think what he relates corresponds with what you have already read about Portuguese officials in the Estado da India?

SPECIMEN ANSWER

1   As a diamond trader, Tavernier was evidently well acquainted with officials of the VOC, who had regularly invested large sums through him. He had no doubt that commanders and officers of the VOC regularly made in excess of £20,000 through illegal personal trade and fees. He claimed that more or less all top officials were involved in this practice and that the VOC lost around £120,000 annually because of such malpractice. Only if and when a case became notorious would the governor-general take action. Even then the chance of having someone brought to court and convicted were not great, since the corrupt majority generally conspired against informers and witnesses. It is noteworthy that the prospect of a criminal case against M. Constant, with whom Tavernier had had dealings, was eventually abandoned by the authorities in Batavia because of fear that Tavernier might divulge embarrassing information about similar dealings by some of the VOC's leading officers in Batavia and back in the Netherlands.

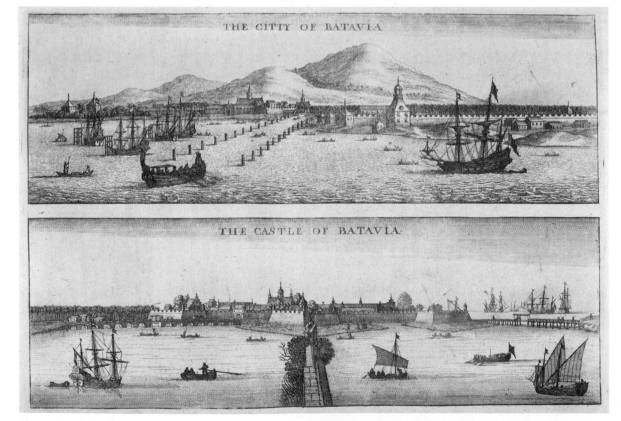

Figure 6.9   'The Citty of Batavia' and 'The Castle of Batavia', engravings, from Nieuhof, J. (1669) *An Embassy from the East-India Company of the United Provinces to the Grand Tartar Cham, Emperour of China*, London, printed by John Macock for the author. British Library, London, X 1202. By permission of the British Library.

2   Tavernier's report bears many similarities to the reports by Jan van Linschoten and Francesco Carletti about the Portuguese and the way they administered the Estado da India. In both cases, the personal interests and greed of high officials would appear to have been damaging to the interest of the trading organisation, be it the Portuguese crown or the VOC.

In other respects, the Dutch trading empire differed significantly from the Portuguese. For instance, it developed no informal empire in parallel with its semi-official empire, the VOC. Similarly, not many of the people employed by the VOC remained overseas when their contracted period came to an end. The VOC mainly employed men, as did the Portuguese Estado da India, and it proved difficult to get respectable Dutch women to emigrate. In 1612, the VOC's first governor-general, Pieter Both, advised the directors back in the Netherlands not to allow more 'light women', as he put it, to emigrate, since too many such scandalous women of dubious morals were already present in the east, causing great offence. Instead, he suggested, as did many of his successors, that the VOC encouraged its employees to marry indigenous women, as long as they were not Muslims. This happened at a time when the VOC began to permit married men whose service had come to an end to settle in the east and to trade in certain limited commodities that did not undermine the VOC's monopoly on spices. Five years later, the VOC specified that those who stayed on – the free burghers – could only marry Asian or **Eurasian** women (the latter primarily of Luso-Asian origin) if they were Christians. Those Dutchmen who settled in the east appear to have done so out of necessity rather than from any ambition to make their lives out there. These time-expired merchants, clerks, sailors and soldiers were, as the governor-general put it in 1615, 'the scum of our land', who go on to marry 'the scum of the East Indies' (Boxer, 1965, p. 244). Later attempts to encourage married Dutch couples to settle in the east failed. The long journey, the climate, deadly diseases and the trading restrictions imposed by the VOC prevented the development of prosperous Dutch enclaves or settlements. The early Dutch trading empire did not generate any sizeable mixed Dutch-Asian population on a par with the Luso-Asian population. Most Dutchmen who stayed on appear to have married Luso-Asian women, but rather than adopting Dutch mores and the Calvinist religion of their husbands, these women and their families seem to have hung on to their Catholic Luso-Asian culture (Boxer, 1965, pp. 241–72).

Despite such shortcomings, by the middle of the seventeenth century the VOC had managed to displace not only the maritime enterprise of the Estado da India but also the traditional overland caravans between the Indian Ocean and the Mediterranean, which had dominated the spice trade in the sixteenth century, while dramatically changing the intercontinental trade routes to the east. What exactly made this possible has preoccupied historians for some time, who have debated whether or not new techniques or institutional innovations can explain this change.

EXERCISE

Read the extract from the article 'Indigenous assistance in the establishment of Portuguese power in Asia in the sixteenth century' by N. Steensgaard on the course website (Secondary Source 6.2). What, according to Steensgaard, were the main reasons for the VOC's success?

SPECIMEN ANSWER

Steensgaard is convinced that the VOC was a novelty because it was a business venture. It was created to make money for its investors, but it neatly integrated the functions of a sovereign power with that of a business partnership, not least due to the fact that many of the leading investors represented the political elite of the day. This meant that the expenses for naval/military actions were added to company costs or overheads. This gave a transparency that made it possible to debate and question the desirability of these costs, as can be seen from the objections raised in 1610 and 1612. Likewise the marketing policy pursued by the VOC was one of planned rationality, creating price stability in the pursuit of profit over the longer term, rather than trying to maximise profit in the short term with the risk of destabilising markets. The VOC also benefited from an excellent communications network, well ahead of anything seen at the time, and was able to conduct operations efficiently from its eastern centre at Batavia.

Dutch

Portuguese

In turn, this 'rational' business depended on the novel creation of a permanent capital (2.9 million florins), even if its creation was more due to accident than intent. The VOC's charter of 1602 had only intended the original subscription to last for a decade. That this did not happen was, according to Steensgaard, because the power within the VOC came to rest with its managers (*bewindhebbers*) and not its participants or investors, even if the investors managed to circumscribe the managers' rights when the VOC's charter was renewed in 1623 and 1647. In the end, however, the investors accepted the permanence of their investment, despite rather meagre dividends during the first decades of the VOC's existence, when most of the profit was ploughed back into the company. This undoubtedly was made possible by another unforeseen aspect to the VOC, namely the possibility for investors to sell their individual shares.

CONCLUSION

So how did these empires begin and are we justified in describing both the Portuguese Estado da India and the Dutch VOC as trading empires? With regard to the Portuguese, most modern historians, such as Niels Steensgaard, M. N. Pearson and, recently, John Darwin, agree that Portuguese maritime expansion in the east was, to a large extent, undertaken as a crusading drive against Islamic adversaries. Likewise, King Manuel of Portugal, his royal council and the most prominent *fidalgos* were motivated by a totally different economic ideology from that of contemporary merchants, who were interested in developing and controlling long-distance trade. Instead, they saw the expansion in the east as a legitimate way of extracting financial and political levies through military means. This was done by creating a system for extorting protection money and customs duties from the seaborne trade in the Indian Ocean, Persian Gulf and Red Sea – that is, the Estado da India. For these historians, the Estado da India was therefore neither a trading empire nor, for that matter, an empire of settlement or enclave (Steensgaard, 1972, pp. 81–103; Pearson, 1976, pp. 52–6; Darwin, 2007 p. 53).

Those historians, such as K.N. Chaudhuri and M. Newitt, who disagree with this interpretation, have emphasised the significance of the part played by Portuguese officials, and merchants resident in the east, in Indian Ocean commerce; that is, the importance of the informal empire versus the official empire run and controlled by the Estado (Chaudhuri, 1985, pp. 69–71; Newitt, 2005, *passim*). They point to the fact that a substantial number of Portuguese merchants settled in a variety of coastal cities in India, from Goa to Cambray and Gujarat, to mention a few, where they became prominent in local as well as long-distance trade, thereby seriously questioning the prevalent view that the Portuguese were primarily concerned with creating a tributary system in the east. They see the Portuguese enterprise in the east as a trading empire, and, in the case of Newitt, even as something akin to an empire of settlement or enclave.

[handwritten marginal note: based on royal patronage.]

Concerning the Dutch, historians have little or no doubt that the VOC constituted a trading empire, and that the company's rationale for establishing itself was based purely on commercial considerations. However, they do not agree about the nature and novelty of that empire. Did the VOC really represent such an innovation, as claimed by Niels Steensgaard and others (i.e. a new type of trading company – a capitalist institution purely geared to maximise profits), or are the similarities between Portuguese and Dutch practices referred to in the unit characteristic of a more complex approach that was basically similar to that of the Portuguese? That is the view of some historians; for example, J. C. van Leur argues that the VOC 'showed no characteristics of any new capitalist development', even if he has to admit that, from an organisational and bureaucratic point of view, the VOC represented a more advanced form of organisation than the medieval/feudal type of government that characterised the Estado da India (Leur, 1955, pp. 227, 235).

REFERENCES

Boxer, C.R. (1965) *The Dutch Seaborne Empire 1600–1800*, London, Hutchinson.

Carletti, F. (1965) *My Voyage Around the World* (trans. H. Weinstock), London, Methuen.

Chaudhuri, K.N. (1985) *Trade and Civilisation in the Indian Ocean. An Economic History from the Rise of Islam to 1750*, Cambridge, Cambridge University Press.

Darwin, J. (2007) *After Tamerlane: The Global History of Empire*, London, Allen Lane.

Israel, J.I. (1995) *The Dutch Republic. Its Rise, Greatness, and Fall 1477–1806*, Oxford, Oxford University Press.

Leur, J.C. van (1955) 'Dutch and Asian bureaucracy' in *Indonesian Trade and Society. Essays in Asian Social and Economic History*, The Hague, W. van Hoeve, pp. 221–45.

Newitt, M. (2005) *A History of Portuguese Overseas Expansion, 1400–1668*, London, Routledge.

Parker, G. (1991) 'Europe and the wider world, 1500–1700: the military balance' in Tracy, J.D. (ed.) *The Political Economy of Merchant Empires. State Power and World Trade 1350–1750*, Cambridge, Cambridge University Press, pp. 161–95.

Pearson, M.N. (1976) *Merchants and Rulers in Gujarat: The Response to the Portuguese in the Sixteenth Century*, Los Angeles, University of California Press.

Pearson, M.N. (1991) 'Merchants and states' in Tracy, J.D. (ed.) *The Political Economy of Merchant Empires. State Power and World Trade 1350–1750*, Cambridge, Cambridge University Press, pp. 41–116.

Prakash, O. (1999) 'The Portuguese and the Dutch in Asian maritime trade: a comparative analysis' in Chaudhury, S. and Morineau, M. (eds) *Merchants, Companies and Trade. Europe and Asia in the Early Modern Era*, Cambridge, Cambridge University Press.

Scammell, G.V. (1980) 'Indigenous assistance in the establishment of Portuguese power in Asia in the sixteenth century', *Modern Asian Studies*, vol. 14, pp. 1–11.

Steensgaard, N. (1972) *Carracks, Caravans, and Companies: The Structural Crisis in the European-Asian Trade in the Early 17th Century*, Copenhagen, Scandinavian Institute of Asian Studies monograph series, no. 17.

Steensgaard, N. (1982) 'The Dutch East India Company as an institutional innovation' in Aymard, M. (ed.) *Dutch Capitalism and World Capitalism*, Cambridge, Cambridge University Press, pp. 235–57.

Tracy, J.D. (ed.) (1991) *The Political Economy of Merchant Empires. State Power and World Trade 1350–1750*, Cambridge, Cambridge University Press, pp. 1–21.

Wallerstein, I. (1982) 'Dutch hegemony in the seventeenth-century world-economy' in Aymard, M. (ed.) *Dutch Capitalism and World Capitalism*, Cambridge, Cambridge University Press, pp. 93–145.

UNIT 7
THE EXPANSION OF RUSSIA 1500–1725

Colin Chant

AIMS

- To give an account of the chronological and spatial development of the early Russian empire, and the emergence of an imperial system.

- To assess the contribution of various possible drivers of early Russian imperial expansion.

- To compare and contrast the Russian territorial empire with the maritime empires dealt with in this block.

- To use and interpret primary sources as evidence for both the material and the cultural conditions of the early Russian empire.

- To engage critically with secondary-source interpretations of Russian imperialism.

INTRODUCTION

In 1639, a small band of Russian **Cossacks** led by Ivan Moskvitin reached the Sea of Okhotsk on the northern Pacific coast of Asia and made a winter camp. This seemingly inauspicious event can be seen in retrospect as the culmination of a quite remarkable expansion of Russian territory from its landlocked heartland. It was remarkable both in space and time – the Pacific coast is a good 7,000 kilometres in a direct line from the capital Moscow, and the intervening land was conquered in less than a century. But was the Russian expansion quite as extraordinary as my opening fanfare suggests? Were the massive extent and terrestrial integrity of the Russian empire simply functions of the geography of the Eurasian land mass? Or were there some specific features of the original Muscovite state from which the Russian empire sprang that explain its role reversal from conquered to conqueror?

In order to tackle these questions, this chapter will begin with two chronological sections, the first charting the rise of the state of Muscovy in European Russia, and the second surveying the first two centuries of its great territorial expansion. Thereafter the structure is thematic. After a section on the development of an imperial system and strategy, you will examine a range of possible drivers of the Russian empire. Among these are the unique Eurasian natural environment, and the various ways Russians attempted to turn it to their practical advantage. Geography, economics and the military will be dealt with in turn. You will finally consider how and to what extent Russia's imperial history was influenced by cultural and intellectual developments. How important was the mission of the Russian church to uphold the Orthodox faith against the threat of heretical Latin Christianity and Islam? Russia's relationship with the rest of Europe was ambivalent from the outset and the subject of unending internal debate over the centuries. How influential was this ambivalence on the course of Russian imperial history?

It is undoubtedly artificial to separate out strands that are interwoven in the historical fabric; this process of analysis should, however, help you to arrive at an overall view of the how and why of early Russian colonisation. At the end you should be in a position to ponder Russia's essential differences from the west European maritime empires. First, however, you need some sense of the pattern of events, and of the means by which Russia acquired its territory. In a block dealing with the origins of empire, there is only scope to consider the initial process of expansion, and establishment of an apparatus and strategy of imperialism. This will take us to a historical crux – the reign of Peter the Great, the first self-proclaimed 'emperor' of all the Russias. Now the momentum of Russian expansionism shifted decisively from the east towards the south and west. Having learned about land empire from its Asiatic Mongol conquerors, and built one to match the contemporary domains of the Ottoman Turks, Safavid Persia and Manchu China, the Russian leadership now aspired to make Russia an international imperial power to rival those that you have already studied in the block.

THE RISE OF MUSCOVY

The core of the Russian empire was the territory occupied by the principality of Moscow, at the heart of the vast, relatively unobstructed Eurasian land mass stretching from central Europe to Siberia. The delicate position of Moscow's territory made it both the object and the subject of imperial ambitions on its western, southern and eastern sides. Indeed, Muscovy had barely emerged from imperial vassalage at the start date of the course. Its experience as a subject people was profoundly influential, and so a glance back before 1500 is needed to understand better the developments that rapidly unfolded thereafter.

The eventual transcontinental dominance of the Moscow region would have been unimaginable during the first few centuries of Russian history. By tradition, the first recognisable Russian state emerged in the ninth century when East Slavic farmers accepted the rule of Viking (Varangian) merchant warriors (the 'Rus') intent on establishing a north–south trade route from the Baltic Sea to Byzantium. The new principality centred on the city of Kiev, situated far to the south of Moscow on the river Dnieper in modern Ukraine (see Figure 7.1).

At its zenith, the authority of 'Kievan Rus' extended from the Black Sea to the Baltic, though this authority weakened as the trade route diminished in importance. Moreover, the principality's core location on the southern steppes exposed it to raids from Turkic nomads, who periodically despoiled the Slavic farmers' land and took captives to be sold in the slave markets of Arabia and Persia. These depredations, and the underlying conflict between nomadic herdsman and settled agriculturalist on the steppes, would persist throughout the main period covered in this chapter.

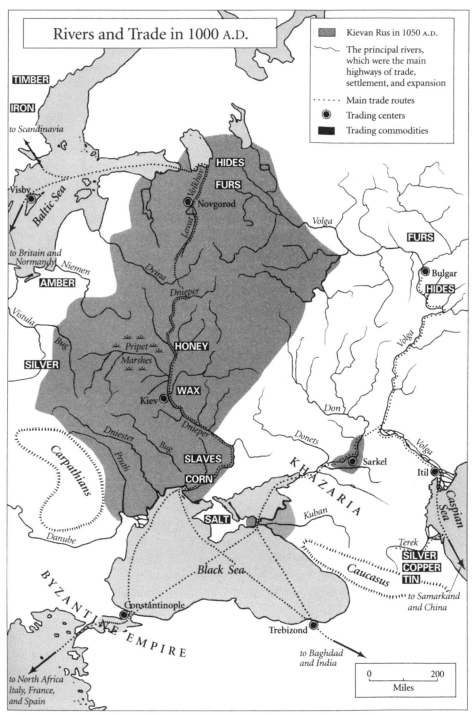

Figure 7.1   'Rivers and Trade in 1000 A.D.', from Hosking, G. (2002) *Russia and the Russians: From Earliest Times to 2001*, London, Penguin Books Ltd. Reproduced by permission of Penguin Books Ltd. Reprinted by permission of the publisher from *Russia and the Russians: A History*, by Geoffrey Hosking, Cambridge, MA, The Belknap Press of Harvard University Press. Copyright © 2001 by Geoffrey Hosking.

The menace of the southern nomads probably contributed to a migration of East Slavs to the forested northeast of Russia in the region of the Upper Volga and Oka rivers. There the soil only supported subsistence agriculture, but the area was well stocked with timber, furs, bees and fish. It was on this economic basis that the principality of Moscow would eventually emerge. However, it was the republican city state of Novgorod to Moscow's north which, having won its independence from Kiev in the twelfth century, took on the southern city's mantle as the main Russian trading centre. Novgorod was oriented by river to the Baltic Sea (see Figure 7.2) and became a member of the Hanseatic League of trading cities that monopolised both the Baltic and the North Sea.

Novgorod's chief export to northern Europe was furs, the quest for which would continue as the main propeller of Russian eastward expansion throughout the early imperial period (Fisher, 1943). By the middle of the twelfth century, Novgorod's sphere of influence and entrepreneurial activity extended as far east as the Ural mountains (the main physical boundary between Asia and Europe), and possibly even beyond them to the Ob, the first of the great northern Asiatic river basins that Russia would eventually colonise. It included the direct rule of tribes that spoke different (Finno-Ugric) languages and had different (animistic) religious beliefs and practices, though they were not organised into any kind of state.

EXERCISE

Novgorod has been labelled a 'fur empire'. In the brief account given above, can you find a reason to doubt whether it really was an empire? You should quickly remind yourself of Motyl's discussion of cores and peripheries in Unit 2.

SPECIMEN ANSWER

The main objection to using the term 'empire' here is the lack of political structure of the non-Russian peoples: there was no organisation of Novgorod's territory into 'culturally distinct administrative units' (Secondary Source 2.1, p. 2, on the course website)'. We should therefore hesitate to apply the term to this juncture of Russian history.

DISCUSSION

In order to make a positive case for Novgorod as an imperial core, you would need more information on the nature of its relationship with the land over which it held sway – to what extent was the hegemony political as well as economic? But the main point of this question is that, for Motyl, the lack of a well-defined periphery would be enough to rule out empire in this case.

For all its economic success, the Novgorod city state was vulnerable. Though ideally placed to trade furs with its Baltic neighbours, it was deficient in land suitable for food production and consequently lacked population. Its territory was therefore open to attacks on its supply chains, both of furs and of food. Emergent principalities in the Upper Volga heartland began to covet Novgorod's northeastern possessions. However, the cavalry literally came to Novgorod's rescue, as the nomadic heirs of the Mongol warrior Genghis Khan poured across the steppes and through the 'Ural Gates', the great gap between the Urals and the Caspian Sea. By 1240, the Mongols (or Tatars as the Russians called them) had assimilated most of the Russian states to

The Republic of Novgorod obtained self-government from Kievan Russia in 997, and complete independence in 1136. The Republic styled itself "Lord Novgorod the Great" and was governed by a grand prince and an assembly of citizens. Novgorod was for over three hundred years a flourishing trading and cultural center, and successfully fought off attacks by the Teutonic Knights, the Swedes, the Lithuanians, and the Mongols. In 1478 it was finally crushed into complete submission by Ivan the Terrible and annexed to Moscow. The town itself was largely destroyed by fire in 1695.

The Republic of Novgorod, 1136–1478

Territory of the Republic of Novgorod, 1136–1478

Province of Pskov, gaining its independence from Novgorod in 1348

Principal military attacks on the Republic by the Swedes, the Teutonic Knights, the Lithuanians, and the Mongols; with dates

0   100
Miles

Figure 7.2   'The Republic of Novgorod, 1136–1478', from Hosking, G. (2002) *Russia and the Russians: From Earliest Times to 2001*, London, Penguin Books Ltd. Reproduced by permission of Penguin Books Ltd. Reprinted by permission of the publisher from *Russia and the Russians: A History*, by Geoffrey Hosking, Cambridge, MA, The Belknap Press of Harvard University Press. Copyright © 2001 by Geoffrey Hosking. In the top left-hand box, for 'Ivan the Terrible' read 'Ivan the Great'.

Novgorod's south into the Golden Horde, one of the successor states of Genghis Khan's vast Mongol empire.

The 'Mongol yoke' is usually seen as a defining schism in Russian history: it brought to an abrupt halt the ambitions of the Upper Volga princes to establish a state centred on a largely riverine trade highway from the Baltic to the Caspian Sea. Impoverished by the payment of regular tributes to the Golden Horde, the defeated Russian states duly suffered encroachments on their western lands by Lithuania and the militantly Catholic Teutonic Knights. Although the Mongol yoke lasted for more than two centuries, it loosened somewhat under a regime with no interest in settling the territory of the Eastern Slavs. This loosening allowed the resurgence of principalities in the Upper Volga region that would again challenge Novgorod's north Russian hegemony. Of these states, Moscow emerged the strongest, partly through the adroitness of its dealings with the Golden Horde. For most of the fourteenth and fifteenth centuries, Moscow and Novgorod were almost constantly engaged in diplomatic jockeying for position, raids, skirmishes and outright warfare.

It was during the reign of Ivan III (the Great) (1462–1505), grand prince of Moscow, that the three-century struggle between Novgorod and the Upper Volga principalities came to an end. When Orthodox Novgorod concluded a defensive alliance with the Lithuanian Prince Casimir, Ivan made it a pretext for a 'crusade' against such treachery to faith and fatherland. By 1478, Novgorod and its colonies had been subjugated to Moscow. Moscow now felt its strength. No more tributes were paid to the disintegrating Golden Horde after 1480, when Ivan successfully faced down the remnants of its army. With the help of the northern bishopric of Perm, which had Christianised the pagan Finno-Ugric tribes on the European side of the Urals, Russian influence was extended across the mountains into what would be called Siberia. Ivan also succeeded in reclaiming much of the land of the old Kievan Rus that had been seized by the recently amalgamated Polish-Lithuanian state in the wake of the Tatar invasion (see Figure 7.3).

Ivan the Great had started an expansionary drive from the landlocked principality of Moscow that would continue over the next four centuries. He was the first Russian ruler (albeit informally) to take the title of 'tsar of all the Russias', and the ambiguity of the term corresponds nicely with the ambiguities that attach to the concept of a Eurasian empire. The reference of the word 'tsar' (caesar) to the Roman empire is obvious enough. The leaders of the Russian Orthodox Church urged its adoption more specifically to establish Russia as the true inheritor of fallen Byzantine empire: they even traced the descent of the princes of Rus back to the Roman emperor Augustus through his brother Prus (Hosking, 2002, p. 107). However, the Russians originally applied the term 'tsar' to the Tatar khans as well as to the Byzantine emperors. Its adoption by a Russian prince in part indicates some indebtedness to Tatar imperial practice. But did Ivan the Great's forcibly conjoined Russian domains add up to an empire? Again, this is doubtful: although all the

The Rise of Moscow, 1261–1533

0   200
Miles

- The principality of Moscow by 1462
- The further expansion of Moscow by 1533

The Princes of Moscow

Ivan I	1325–1341
Simeon	1341–1353
Ivan II	1353–1359
Dmitrii	1359–1389
Vasilii I	1389–1425
Vasilii II	1425–1462
Ivan III	1462–1505
Vasilii III	1505–1533

THE SWEDISH EMPIRE

White Sea

REPUBLIC OF NOVGOROD

Gulf of Finland

Ivangorod
Novgorod
Riga
PSKOV

PERM

VIATKA

Vologda
Kostroma

Suzdal   Nizhnii
Moscow   Novgorod
Kaluga

Kazan

KAZAN KHANATE

Vilna
Smolensk
Minsk

L I T H U A N I A

RIAZAN

Kulikovo

THE NOGAI HORDE

Pinsk
Chernigov
Kiev

Sarai

ASTRAKHAN KHANATE

CRIMEAN KHANATE

Azov

Astrakhan

Caspian Sea

Black Sea

Constantinople

THE OTTOMAN EMPIRE

The town of Moscow was first prominent in 1147. Between 1261 and 1533 the principalities of Rus fell increasingly under its control. In 1322 Moscow became the See of the Orthodox Church. In 1380 Dmitrii defeated the Golden Horde at Kulikovo, and by 1480 Mongol dominance was thrown off. Novgorod was conquered in 1487, Viatka in 1489, Pskov in 1510, and Riazan in 1521. The first victory over the Lithuanians and the reconquest of Smolensk took place in 1514.

Figure 7.3 'The Rise of Moscow, 1261–1533', from Hosking, G. (2002) *Russia and the Russians: From Earliest Times to 2001*, London, Penguin Books Ltd. Reproduced by permission of Penguin Books Ltd. Reprinted by permission of the publisher from *Russia and the Russians: A History*, by Geoffrey Hosking, Cambridge, MA, The Belknap Press of Harvard University Press. Copyright © 2001 by Geoffrey Hosking.

component states were multi-ethnic, the majority of the population in each case were Russians subscribing to the same Russian Orthodox religion.

THE TRANSITION TO EMPIRE

Ivan the Terrible

An unarguable transition from state to empire took place during the reign of the paranoid religious zealot Ivan IV (the Terrible) (1547–84), grandson of Ivan the Great and Russia's first official tsar (Madariaga, 2005). Ivan the Terrible had ambitions to expand his realm both to the west and the east (see Figure 7.4).

He took advantage of the waning powers of the Teutonic Knights in Livonia to make major gains on the Baltic coastline, including the new fortified port of Ivangorod, but all were lost as the established powers of Poland-Lithuania, Denmark and Sweden reacted to the upstart Russian's pretensions. He had more lasting success in Asia. In response to a traumatising raid on Moscow itself in 1571 by the khanate of Crimea, a protectorate of the mighty Ottoman Turkish empire on the Black Sea, he ordered the construction of a defensive line of forts and fortifications from the Dnieper in the west to the Volga in the east. Ivan went on the offensive against the Tatar khanate of Kazan which, along with the Crimeans, had plagued the Muscovite principality since its foundation in the fifteenth century. After a series of traditional attempts to install a khan who was friendly to Moscow, Ivan lost patience. In 1552, the Russians successfully laid siege to the fortified city of Kazan, and by 1558 the entire territory had been brought to heel. This was the first time that the Russians had conquered a state with its own ruling class, language and (Islamic) religion.

The khanate of Kazan

Kazan was one of the succession states established during the disintegration of the Tatar Golden Horde from the end of the fifteenth century. These have been described as 'rudimentary city-states with a peculiar combination of sedentary and nomadic lifestyles' (Khodarkovsky, 2002, p. 11). The khanate of Kazan was favourably located in the Middle Volga region, where a number of trade routes connected up, and where forest and arable land fruitfully conjoined. It was accordingly unlike the fully nomadic Tatar polities and groupings of the open, treeless steppes. The socioeconomic structure of the Kazan polity consisted mainly of a Tatar ruling aristocracy; a Tatar middle class of merchants, officials and clerics; and Finnish- and Turkic-speaking farmers, fisherman, hunters and forest bee-keepers. The Tatar ruling class retained its nomadic way of life, deriving its income from taxes on agriculture and trade. After the Russian conquest, the Tatars continued to elect a khan, through whom the Russians exerted influence, as well as the exaction of tribute. The khanates therefore functioned as client states, or protectorates, of the Russian empire.

Figure 7.4   'Muscovy, 1533–1598', from Hosking, G. (2002) *Russia and the Russians: From Earliest Times to 2001*, London, Penguin Books Ltd. Reproduced by permission of Penguin Books Ltd. Reprinted by permission of the publisher from *Russia and the Russians: A History*, by Geoffrey Hosking, Cambridge, MA, The Belknap Press of Harvard University Press. Copyright © 2001 by Geoffrey Hosking. Note that the box in the key denoting 'Muscovite conquests by 1598' should be shaded dark grey.

A further imperial step was rapidly taken. In 1554, Ivan sent a force to the mouth of the Volga to subdue the relatively recently founded khanate of Astrakhan, which had challenged Moscow's advance through alliances with Nogai Tatar tribes and the aggressive Crimean khanate on the Black Sea. In taking Astrakhan, Ivan completely wrested from the Tatars the vital trade highway along the River Volga to the Caspian Sea. Thus the Muscovite project of connecting the Baltic and the Caspian Sea was completed. The khanates were clearly imperial conquests, though of a distinctive character: they were the remnants of another multi-ethnic imperial regime, rather than independent peoples or states of long standing. The capture of the Volga served Moscow's interests by dividing the steppe into two distinct zones. On the right bank, the Russian stance was defensive, as Moscow sought to repel the incursions of strong states, notably Poland-Lithuania to the west and the khanate of Crimea to the south. But from the left bank of the Volga, the way was now clearer for the Russians. The steppe, however, was still a zone in which the sedentary Russians were outperformed by the skilled Tatar cavalry with their powerful 'compound bows' of wood, horn and sinew (Lieven, 2000, p. 207). This was a military disparity that persisted until the middle of the eighteenth century.

By far the most fruitful zones of expansion were the northern belts of forested **taiga** and frozen or swampy **tundra**, partly because these were the natural habitat of the Russians, but also because their muskets gave them a decisive military advantage over the spears and arrows of the hunter-gatherer tribes that sparsely populated these regions. Frequently the movement was led by the unrulier elements of Russian society, notably the Cossacks, the Russian frontiersmen, discussed at greater length below. A piratical Cossack force commanded by Ermak crossed the Urals in the early 1580s and succeeded in taking Isker, the capital of the only real political obstacle to Russian ambition in northern Asia – the khanate of Western Siberia, another remnant of the Mongol empire. Ermak himself was killed shortly after, but in 1587 the surviving Cossacks founded Tobolsk, which would be Russia's administrative centre in Western Siberia throughout the seventeenth and eighteenth centuries. However, the Cossacks were not strong enough to hold on to the territory; it would take concerted state action to establish Russian power in Asia.

Boris Godunov and the first Romanov tsars

The next empire builder of note after Ivan the Terrible was Boris Godunov. Boris was an influential adviser to Ivan who, after a period as regent, was himself elected tsar (1598–1605). In his time, there was activity on all Russia's fronts. Some of the Baltic land lost by Ivan to Sweden was reclaimed. The northern port of Archangel was built at the mouth of the Northern Dvina, opening trade with northern Europe by way of the Arctic Ocean, at any rate during the ice-free months of the year. A new defensive string of fortified towns to the south of Ivan's defensive line of 1571 was built in the 1580s and 1590s, from Smolensk on the Dnieper in the west across to Ufa in the eastern Volga basin. Further east, Boris's forts were instrumental in a concerted attacking move to reclaim the temporary gains of Ermak in Western Siberia – a more literal instance of 'conquest after the conquest' (Bakewell, 1995) than those you have already met in this block. This time a more measured troop-led strategy established control of the Ob basin, the first of the great river systems running up to the Arctic Ocean on the Asian side of the Urals.

The momentum of Boris Godunov's imperial strategy slackened during the early years of the seventeenth century. This was a period commonly termed the 'Time of Troubles', when Moscow was wracked by acute political instability in the absence of a legitimate hereditary claimant to the throne. Nevertheless, Russia's 'sub-imperialists' – local officials, adventurers, traders and hunters – were still hungry for tribute and new supplies of fur, and they kept the eastward drive going to the next great river basin, the Enisei and its tributaries. A firm grip on the Enisei system was only achieved when Russia stabilised under the Romanovs, a dynasty of tsars that would rule from 1613 until the Russian Revolutions of 1917. The new fort of Eniseisk (1619) acted as the basis for the fortification and later settlement of the Enisei basin during the 1620s. The lust for furs led inexorably to the third great northern river system, the Lena, stretching almost the entire north–south axis of Siberia from its source in the mountains by the massive Lake Baikal. Again, traders led the way, with the state not far behind in search of its cut of the bounty. The highlight of this private, unruly and violent campaign were the exploits of Peter Beketov, who with a small force of Cossacks succeeded in 1632 in subjugating the Iakut people who had dominated the region. We now return to the starting point of this unit: the arrival in 1639 of Moskvitin's band of Cossacks at the Sea of Okhotsk (see Figure 7.5).

Russia's first foothold on the Pacific coast of Asia was symbolic, but it was not until 1648 that the port of Okhotsk was founded. In the far east as a whole, it again took some years of state-led action before the hunter-gatherer indigenes were quelled. Throughout the process of eastern colonisation, Russian rule was initially established through a thin layer of fortified outposts, which initially relied on provisions from the more settled parts to the west. It was some time before migrant agriculturalists could provide food for the new settlements. Control of the Lena led not only to the Pacific coast but eventually, in the second half of the eighteenth century, across the Bering Strait to Alaska, as once again the prime fur of a conquered region was exhausted. The upper Lena also drew the Russian adventurers south to the Amur, the fourth and last great northern Asiatic river system. This copious waterway flowed not north into the Arctic Ocean but east into the Pacific. Russian traders and officials were hopeful for another bonanza, now including gold and silver, but the riches failed to materialise. Moreover, the Russian advance came up against a much stronger force than the tribesmen of Siberia. The Manchu dynasty of China was a match for the Russians militarily, and being nearer home could muster a far larger army. In the end, they forced the Russians to retreat from the Amur basin, and, through the Treaty of Nerchinsk, to agree a border with China that would last for nearly two centuries.

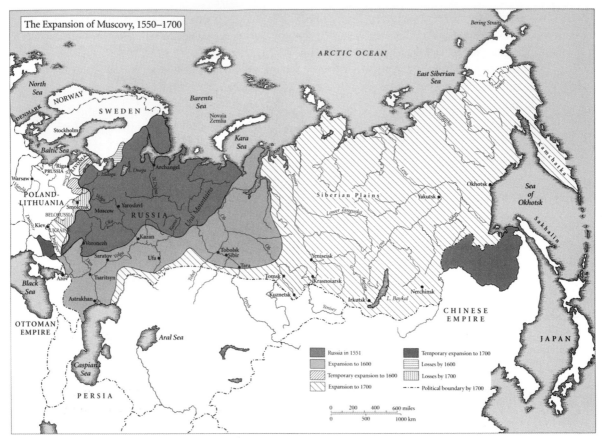

The Expansion of Muscovy, 1550–1700

Figure 7.5   'The Expansion of Muscovy, 1550–1700', from Hosking, G. (2002) *Russia and the Russians: From Earliest Times to 2001*, London, Penguin Books Ltd. Reproduced by permission of Penguin Books Ltd. Reprinted by permission of the publisher from *Russia and the Russians: A History*, by Geoffrey Hosking, Cambridge, MA, The Belknap Press of Harvard University Press. Copyright © 2001 by Geoffrey Hosking.

Peter the Great

The confrontation with China was not the end of the Russian advance in Asia, which had been largely confined to the forested north – a century of hard-won colonisation of the steppes to the south would follow. The Treaty of Nerchinsk nevertheless marked a change of tempo and emphasis. It coincided with the start of the reign of Peter the Great (1682–1725), the great westernising tsar of Russian history (Hughes, 1998; see Plate 2.14).

Peter's father, Tsar Aleksei, had been receptive to western ideas, science, technology and administration, and in a long campaign against Russia's inveterate enemy Poland had also succeeded in bringing half of the prized grain-producing region of the Ukraine under Russian rule. But Aleksei's western orientation pales alongside his son's driving sense of mission. Peter's passion for the west had been nurtured by the time he spent as a child in the 'German quarter', an enclave of foreign merchants in Moscow, and was further reinforced during his epochal Grand Tour of northern Europe of 1697–98. He was the first tsar to aspire to remodel his domain along European lines. After a protracted war against Sweden, concluded by the Treaty of Nystadt in 1721, he made permanent gains on the Baltic, including the valuable granary of Estland. As early as 1703, he had a secure enough hold on the Gulf of Finland to build a symbolically Europe-facing new capital, St Petersburg. The south remained a hard nut to crack. Peter's capture of land on the northern Black Sea coast was temporary, but the die was cast, as the Ottoman empire passed its zenith after the failed siege of Vienna in 1683. Peter's successors in the eighteenth and early nineteenth century would establish Russia on the Black Sea, and go so far as to assimilate much of Poland, including Warsaw. The Russian emperors were now truly international players.

EXERCISE	Using Fieldhouse's typology (Unit 2), how would you classify Russia's colonisation of northern Russia?
SPECIMEN ANSWER	Siberia appears to have begun as an occupation colony based on a network of fortified outposts. Later, after Russian agriculturalists moved into the region, it became a settlement colony.
DISCUSSION	According to Fieldhouse himself, Siberia was 'a settler colony resembling Australia, created by a similar process of penal and voluntary emigration' (1982, p. 334). However, this is a retrospective judgement in a brief section on the later history of Russia's Asian conquests.

Look on the course website at the date chart for this unit. This will give you a reminder of the chronology of the early Russian empire before you move on to the remaining thematic sections.

AN IMPERIAL STRATEGY

Before any analysis of the possible reasons *why* the Russian land empire emerged and developed as it did, it might be helpful to ask *how* it did so. By what means did the Russians acquire and consolidate their vastly growing territory? It will be clear enough to you from the narrative above that military strategy and technology were essential both to the initial acquisition of the empire and to the 'conquest after the conquest': they will be dealt with in more detail in a later section. But, as Paul Lawrence argued in Unit 3, empires are systems of interaction as well as of domination: this is a point stressed in a number of recent studies of the Russian empire (Kappeler, 2001; Khodarkovsky, 2002; Witzenrath, 2007). As well as bloody conflict and double-dealing at the southern and eastern fronts, there was often rational negotiation, as each set of actors weighed their interests – Motyl's notion of 'significant interactions' is relevant here (Unit 2). Deals were struck on the level of tribute, gold and silver changed hands, sworn enemies became allies, and hostilities between tribes were exploited: the Muscovites were especially adept at 'divide and rule'. The dealings with the khanates were particularly complex and ambiguous: what were oaths of allegiance and imperial gifts for the tsars could be regarded as peace treaties and taxes by the khans, and interpreters often had an important role to play in bridging the two understandings (Khodarkovsky, 2002). The Russian imperial project was founded on a geopolitical awareness sharpened in their dealings with their Slavic neighbours and their west European rivals in the context of the Mongol **suzerainty**. They had also shared their European territory for centuries with semi-settled or nomadic peoples. For this reason, among others, the engagement between colonisers and colonised during the early history of the Russian empire – violent and ruthless though it often was – was some way removed from the culture shock and radical change that Karl Hack associated with the building of the transoceanic empires in Unit 2.

The germs of a consistent policy of colonisation can be seen in the first conquest of the khanate of Kazan from the 1550s. At the outset, military force was applied ruthlessly: all Tatar opposition was crushed, and a ban placed on the carrying of arms. A system of fortresses was built to maintain order, and Russian merchants were settled in the towns: 'the towns of the khanate became Russian enclaves in a non-Russian environment' (Kappeler, 2001, p. 39). But in the longer term, a policy of relative restraint was urged from the centre. Cooperation was cultivated with non-Russian elites, who could be admitted to the Russian nobility. Native traditions, institutions and religious practices were tolerated.

The government took a similar stance with regard to the much less culturally advanced Siberian peoples, who were frequently provoked to rebellion by the lawlessness and rapaciousness of the advance guard of Russian mercenaries. Such outrages were followed by the often arbitrary and venal administration of the local military commander (*voevoda*), the Russian counterpart of the Spanish *corregidor* and the Portuguese captain-governor (Units 4 and 6). 'The Siberian colony ... never knew any administration except that of the voevodas' (Lantzeff, 1943, p. 33): the *voevoda* and his staff of *sluzhilye liudi* ('serving people') were located in the new fortified settlements and acted as the 'metropolitan representatives' at the periphery (Unit 2) in the system of direct rule of the Siberian colony. Quite how representative they were at such distances was, however, often in doubt. The central government looked more to the longer-term levying of tribute, and so preached respect for the traditional customs and beliefs of the subject peoples. The problem for the government was that local officials and traders were often cruel and selfish, and so undermined the policy and put the continued collection of revenue at risk. There were limits even to the government's attempts to co-opt the tribal chieftains into the business of maintaining the empire. Unlike the Tatar elite, the chieftains were considered unworthy of the rank of the Russian nobility.

EXERCISE

Which basic feature of imperial rule identified by Finley (section on 'Definitions of empire' in Unit 2) can you discern in the Russians' treatment of their subject peoples?

SPECIMEN ANSWER

There is a clear hierarchy, as Finley requires. This hierarchy is quite complex, and includes the notion of a hierarchy of subject peoples themselves – the Tatar nobles ranking higher than the tribal chieftains.

Was the Russian policy of toleration and cooperation an expression of its culture, or the only viable one at such distances, with the limited resources at the government's disposal?

With this question in mind, read the instructions and despatches sent from central government and the tsar to various *voevody* during the period 1644–1670 (Primary Sources 7.1–7.3 on the course website).

It is a matter of interpretation, but the urgent need to maximise state revenues can be read between the soft lines about 'consideration', 'peace and quiet' and 'gentleness and kindness' (Primary Source 7.1).

The documents reveal a deal of nervousness within the metropole in the middle decades of the seventeenth century about the potential loss of state revenues, whether the loss of tribute through harsh treatment of the subject peoples or unauthorised private trading, or else of tax revenues through the inadequate measurement of agricultural land, or the flight of peasants from European Russia to Siberia. The documents also give you a detailed picture of the process of colonisation from the colonisers' viewpoint. They convey the tension between the long-term fiscal interest of the metropole and the shorter-term greed and opportunism of the *voevody* and other metropolitan representatives at the periphery. Note also the evident economic impetus to settle the newly conquered territory; the taking of hostages as one of the means to ensure the cooperation of the tributary peoples; and the benefits to be gained from voluntary baptism – all part of the developing imperial strategy.

The imperial strategy of military action, colonisation and pacification was part of the march of empire, but its consolidation required the development of a system of administration and an infrastructure that could be effective over the rapidly increasing distances between the centre and the periphery. The Russian mode of empire building depended on heavy taxation of its own peoples and tribute (*iasak*) from those assimilated into the empire. An imperial bureaucracy grew piecemeal from the royal household. However, for the period covered in this chapter, it was very small in relation to the extent of the empire and in comparison with west European states. The real growth of an imperial bureaucracy awaited the development of suitable educational institutions during the eighteenth century, as Peter the Great's successors continued his project to build a modern European absolutist state.

The administration of ever-lengthening chains of command presupposed effective methods of transport and communication. The question arises whether a great land empire was easier or harder than far-flung maritime empires to acquire, defend and administer. As you know from Block 1, west European maritime empires consisted of widely dispersed colonies accessible to the dominant state only by ship. This arrangement made sense given the relatively limited land mass of western Europe and the technological parameters of the pre-railway era. Before the comprehensive mechanisation of transport undertaken during the nineteenth century, moving people and goods over water was much more efficient than by land. This disparity helps explain the rise of the ancient Athenian and Roman empires in and around the Mediterranean basin. As you have learned from Units 4, 5 and 6, developments in ship technology enabled the early modern west European successors of Athens and Rome to traverse oceans just as the ancients had sailed the Mediterranean. As a consequence, a system of overseas colonies could, in effect, be closer to the imperial core, and therefore more under its control, than the peripheral regions of continuous land masses. On the other hand, it can be argued that the Russian system of inland transport was easier to defend than ships on the open sea (Lieven, 2000, p. 225) – Ole Grell described in Unit 6 the severe losses sustained by the Portuguese merchant fleet. How did Russia deal with the great distances of its territorial empire (see the box on transport and communications)?

Transport and communications

In the technological conditions of the pre-industrial era, the rapid establishment of Russian economic and political control across the vast Eurasian forest zone would have been inconceivable without its abundant natural endowment of river systems (see Figure 7.7 later in this unit and Plate 2.15 in the Visual Sources Book). The Russians were able to exploit the geographical contingency that the tributaries of each of the great northern river systems – the Ob, the Enisei and the Lena – were quite close to each other. The process of colonisation could therefore take place mainly by boat, with relatively short land portages between the rivers. The standard vessels were flat-bottomed river boats (*doshchaniki*) up to 15 metres long, equipped with oars and sails as great distances had to be travelled upstream.

Peter the Great looked to western hydraulic engineering to enhance Russia's natural waterways. He was closely involved in the construction of the Vishny Volochek canal system, which somewhat improved the difficult passage of goods between the Upper Volga and the Baltic. The essential contribution of Russian waterways has led some historians to liken the great northern river basins to the oceans crossed by the west European maritime powers (Lensen, 1964, p. 3). This might be an imaginative leap too far; nevertheless, the distinction between land and maritime empires, while real, needs to be qualified: water transport held the key for both types of empire until the advent of the railways.

The primacy of water transport notwithstanding, overland transport had an essential supporting role in the logistics of a terrestrial empire. The Russians had the precedent of the Mongol empire for a system of land communications, and it was in imitation of this that Ivan the Great managed his extended Muscovite domains with a relatively efficient system of inns and postal stations (*iamy*) using horse-drawn coaches and sledges in the winter. During the frozen winter months, land transport in the north came into its own: communication and the movement of light goods were actually quicker by sledge across snow and ice.

The imperial strategy was a composite of decisive military action, fortification, enforced colonisation by Russians, and an appeasing policy towards non-Russians. But it is important to recognise that the strategy presupposed at a more fundamental level an entire socioeconomic system geared to the imperial project. Empire, autocracy and **serfdom** seemed to go hand in hand. The welding of Russia as a militant, military state capable of accumulating a vast Eurasian empire required the subordination of its formerly fractious elements into a whole that could act in concert against all its enemies. Starting with Ivan the Great, the tsars achieved this aim by breaking the regional power of the **boyars**, and then tying their noble successors to state military service through gifts of land with peasant labour attached. This was the beginnings of a hierarchical society with the tsar-autocrat at the top, a nobility tied to state service immediately below, a dependent class of merchants and townspeople in Russia's relatively meagre urban network, and a vast, largely enserfed peasant majority at the bottom.

The Cossacks

A distinctive role in the Russian imperial strategy was played by a group that stood outside the hierarchy serving Russia's imperial project: the Cossacks (*kazaki*) (Witzenrath, 2007). The use of renegades in the forging of empire was not unique to Russia: you have the example of the Cimmerans and runaways in the early history of the British empire (Unit 5). But there was no comparable group with such a long and complex history; and one that became so established that they have been numbered among the 'client societies' cultivated as part of Russia's imperial strategy (LeDonne, 2004).

There is a difficulty in pinning down the Cossack identity that goes to the ambiguous heart of the Russian empire. The term is of uncertain and debated origin: one view is that it derives from a Turkic word meaning 'free man' (Hosking, 2002, p. 115). It may originally have referred to a lower rank of Tatar warrior, and was then transferred to Tatars in the Russian service. By the sixteenth century it connoted Russian frontiersmen, who originally filled empty spaces on the southern steppes left by the break up of the Golden Horde; as befitted the territory, they adopted the Tatars' nomadic way of life, including the plunder of settlers. As the frontier diversified, the term came to cover both low-born regulars in the Russian army, and self-governing groups of often predatory outsiders on the Russian imperial fringe, including runaway serfs, criminals and well-born adventurers. These groups (called *voiska* – 'hosts') may also have given refuge to Russians escaping from the slavery into which so many were sold by raiding Crimean and Nogai Tatars. The Cossacks alternated piratical acts with a distinctive role as mercenaries further abetting the expansion of the Russian land empire, not only in the east but south into the Caucasus region. From the reign of Ivan the Terrible, the renegade Cossacks struck a bargain with the Russian state, to which they were loosely attached by their sense of a Russian identity and profession of Orthodoxy. In return for a much greater measure of freedom and independence than that enjoyed by their enserfed compatriots, and for certain land rights, grain and armaments, they were available for dirty work on the fringes of empire.

DRIVERS OF EMPIRE

We now turn to the possible reasons underlying the Russian expansion.

Geographical necessity?

An issue that we need to address in this section is **geographical determinism**. Past generations of Russian historians have certainly flirted with the proposition that the unique geography of Russia might be sufficient to explain the unique character of its transcontinental land empire:

> The fundamental urge which directed the Russian people eastward lies deep in history ... It was not 'imperialism' nor was it the consequence of the petty political ambitions of Russian statesmen. It was in the last analysis, perhaps, simply the inevitable logic of geography which lies at the basis of all history.
>
> (Vernadsky, 1969, p. 8)

Let us first weigh the positive case for the influence of Russian geography on the nature of its polity.

EXERCISE

Read the introductory geographical note to Nicholas Riasanovsky's history of Russia on the course website (Secondary Source 7.1). What features of Russia's imperial history and structure can be linked to its geography?

SPECIMEN ANSWER

Features of Russia's imperial history and structure that can be linked to its geography include:

- uniquely extensive plain presenting few natural obstacles to expansion
- essentially landlocked nature of Russian territory giving rise to an expansionary interest in the Baltic, the Black Sea and the 'Straits' (the Bering Strait to the east, the Baltic Sound in the northwest, and the Bosporus and Dardanelles in the southwest)
- relatively easy eastward movement on the natural communication network of the great rivers and their tributaries
- severe climate, distinctive zones of vegetation and scarcity of agricultural land, as a result of which the population in the east was sparse and scarcely able to stem the Russian advance
- distinctive steppe ecology underlying the prolonged conflict between nomad and settler and consequent militarisation of Russian society.

Riasanovsky emphasises the historical importance of Russia's location in both Europe and Asia. This accident is surely a seminal ambiguity in Russian history, even though the geographical border between the two continents is the most notional of all the continental divides. Gibson (2002) laments the neglect of Russia in a number of surveys of European imperialism, and attributes this oversight to the failure of many historians to recognise that Russia is, culturally, 'essentially European'. He concedes, however, that there is a geographical ambivalence:

> Russia is Asian as well as European, being located on the easternmost edge of Europe and the northernmost margin of Asia. Its 'Asianness' is strengthened by its large size, minor relief, and climatic continentality, all of which stand in stark contrast to the generally small size, major relief, and climatic maritimity of its European neighbours to the west.

> (Gibson, 2002, p. 182)

It is surely fundamental to any comparison of the Russian land empire with, say, the British maritime empire that Russia has one linear mile of coast per 800 square miles of territory, whereas in the British Isles the ratio is 1:12 (Gibson, 2002, p. 188).

Geographical contingency needs to be included among necessary conditions for the unfolding of the Russian land empire, but is it sufficient? You will consider more fully in a later section whether territorial vulnerability on the Great Russian Plain can be considered the main source of the Russian imperial drive. The Muscovite heartland was indeed vulnerable on terrain that historically had offered Asiatic horsemen a virtually clear run into Europe, but there were also positive advantages. In relation to the other medieval Russian states, Muscovy was strategically well situated between the fertile 'black-earth' region to the south and the exportable raw materials of northern forests and woodland. Its own thick woodland setting gave it military advantages over its southern neighbours.

The point has already been made that rivers of Russia were crucial in facilitating Muscovy's conquest of the vast Eurasian land mass. Transport on the Dnieper, Don and Volga in European Russia was fundamental to the trading system that resourced the imperial drive, and it was the abundance of rivers further east that made possible the administration and exploitation of annexed Siberia. As you read in the Riasanovsky extract (Secondary Source 7.1), one massive advantage of the Muscovite heartland was the globally unique contingency that the sources of several major rivers leading to the Baltic in the north and the Black Sea and Caspian Sea in the south lay quite close to one another in flat habitable land. The point has also been made that the northern location of Russia's colonies largely freed them from the endemic diseases of hotter climes. This is not to say that the indigenes of Siberia were immune to pathogens brought by Russian settlers: at various times, epidemics of smallpox and venereal disease periodically wrought havoc, though without quite the genocidal devastation visited on the indigenes of the transoceanic 'neo-Europes' (Unit 4; Crosby, 1986, pp. 37–39; Lieven, 2000, p. 225).

EXERCISE

This section started with a quotation from Vernadsky placing geography at the very foundation of history. You then read in the Riasanovsky extract (Secondary Source 7.1) that various other historians of Russia have loaded similar explanatory weight on its geography – he even discerns a 'rigid determinism' in some interpretations. Now read the brief extract from Dominic Lieven's fine comparative study of the Russian empire on the course website (Secondary Source 7.2). On what grounds does he dismiss 'geographical determinism'?

SPECIMEN ANSWER

Lieven argues that the Russian dialogue with the west and tsarist politics have been more influential on Russia's imperial trajectory than its geography. He concedes that the influence of geography on its culture and politics 'cannot be discounted' (p. 3), but geography is insufficient to explain Russia's political traditions and cultural choices – not least the Orthodox religion.

In rejecting geographical determinism, we should take care not to throw the baby out with the bathwater. Historical geography offers fruitful ways of interpreting Russian imperial history. In his own magisterial history of Russia, Geoffrey Hosking emphasises not just Russia's physical geography, but its position in relation to certain geographically based cultural '**ecumenes**' and geopolitical 'heartlands' – he is explicit about the influence here of Sir Halford Mackinder, introduced to you by Robin Mackie in Unit 1. Russia's three diversely influential cultural ecumenes were Asian imperial practices, the Catholic and Protestant culture of Europe, and Byzantine religion. Its geopolitical heartland was 'Inner Eurasia', defined as the territory of the Soviet Union plus Mongolia and Xinjiang in China. This was a heartland defined not only by natural features but also its boundaries with other variously important heartlands: China, Persia, Turkey, Poland and Scandinavia. Within Inner Eurasia, Russia's strategic position in the northwest favoured its eventual domination. However, because of the region's huge expanse and resource imbalances, continuing domination required a massive investment in military power, which stunted the growth of civil society (Hosking, 2002, pp. 1–6).

What, in the final analysis, needs to be disentangled, I suggest, is the political in 'geopolitical'. On its own, Russian geography facilitated a huge eastward movement at relatively little cost, whereas powerful imperial interests as well as (sometimes) geographical obstacles blocked an equally desirable expansion to the west and south. As Gibson (2002) argues, one of the main reasons for the vastness of the Russian empire is that there was a vast amount of land to the east of Russia in which no other imperial power was interested.

Economic gain?

To what extent were trade and the quest for material resources an impetus to Russian expansionism? You have seen that trade and trading companies led the way in the development of the Portuguese, Dutch, French and British transoceanic, mercantilist empires. You also learned in Block 1 that Asian empires were characterised more by state control than by private initiative. What role did Russian private enterprise play in the expansion of Russia? Across the entire period of the course, it looks weak compared with the dynamic mercantilist and capitalist cultures of western Europe. The Russian economy was overwhelmingly agrarian, and from the seventeenth century until the emancipation of the serfs in 1861, agriculture was dominated by the institution of forced labour, or serfdom. Beyond the 'black-earth' region of the southern steppes, agriculture was relatively unprofitable, and Russian noble landowners took little interest in it. One of Peter the Great's most radical reforms was the meritocratic Table of Ranks of 1722, which made the achievement of noble status dependent on state service. This measure reinforced the tendency for landowners to look for advancement to St Petersburg or Moscow, very often well away from their estates. Military service was the major route to the higher noble ranks, though state service also embraced the church and the imperial bureaucracy. Within this overall economic and social system, the Russian middle class was chronically weak and subservient to the nobility, with trade and industry mostly state directed and politically driven. Imperial expansion, it might seem, drove the economy, rather than economic initiative leading the empire.

It would be a mistake, however, to project this well-founded view of post-Petrine Russia back onto the period of early imperial expansion. You have seen that Kievan Rus and Novgorod were polities dedicated to trading. Muscovy's rise rested partly on its favourable location near the intersection of two important trading routes. Much of the subsequent settlement of the land to Muscovy's east and south went ahead of the state, partly as peasants sought land that they could cultivate without the obligations of serfdom or the burden of taxation. The main motive force of the pre-Petrine Russian advance to the Pacific by way of the Ob, Enisei and Lena river basins was the material interest of private fur traders, such as the Stroganov family (see the box on the Stroganovs). The nets and traps of the European hunters were far more effective than indigenous bows and arrows, and as one region was exhausted of its prized sable pelts, a fur rush to the next great river system took place: 'no search for any single commodity has ever resulted in the acquisition of so huge an area as the one acquired by Russia in this quest' (Lantzeff and Pierce, 1973, p. 17).

The Stroganovs

An outstanding example of the mercantile thrust of Russian eastward expansion was the activity of the Stroganov family of merchants, a business dynasty with possible origins in Novgorod. Much of their wealth came from the northern fur trade, though their peculiarly important role in the growth of empire was connected above all with the manufacture of salt in the northerly Perm region on the European side of the Urals. For this purpose, Ivan the Terrible granted them tax exemptions and special powers to build forts and villages, and to fill them with Russian agricultural settlers. The merchants and settlers were faced with continual harassment by the indigenous hunter-gathering population, who were encouraged from the other side of the Urals by the khan of Western Siberia. The Russian government was consequently only too happy to equip the Stroganovs to take military action against the Tatars as they turned their enterprise to the quest for mineral sources. It may well have been the Stroganovs who financed Ermak's trans-Ural adventures. Although the analogy could be stretched too far, there are surely parallels here with the powers granted by western states to British and Dutch entrepreneurs (Units 5 and 6).

Private material gain continued to play a part in the further expansion of Russian territory: the Russian-America Company, chartered by Tsar Paul in 1799 was responsible for some of the colonisation of Russian America (Alaska) in pursuit of further gains from the fur trade. The fur trade was extremely important in the early history of the Russian empire, not only as a lure to exploration, but as a source of revenue for the state (see Figure 7.6). It has been estimated that the proportion of state income from the fur trade was as much as 10 per cent for most of the seventeenth century, though it shrank to little more than 2 per cent by the time of Peter the Great, under whom expenditure doubled (Fisher, 1943, pp. 118, 120). But the emphasis should not be wholly on the northern fur trade. The Volga yielded fisheries and access to the markets of Persia; the Urals were a source of raw materials – its iron deposits in conjunction with an abundance of timber fuel enabled Russia to become the world's leading producer in the eighteenth century; and the steppe frontier offered arable land that was much more fertile than other soils in the Russian domain.

EXERCISE

The material incentives for the Russian expansion were nowhere more evident than in the activities of private hunters and traders in the north of Russia. Read the extract from Fisher's classic study of the Russian fur trade on the course website, which gives us a clear summary of economic and political activity in Siberia (Secondary Source 7.3). How does Fisher distinguish the economic from the political in the colonisation of Siberia?

SPECIMEN ANSWER

Scarcely at all. The lure of personal gain is vividly depicted, but the passage as a whole underlines the point that private gain is hard to disentangle from the imperial interest.

Even where personal profit was the initial driver, the state was never far behind, seeking to extract its own share of the bounty. At the very least, material gain was part of the imperial strategy. This is apparent in what might seem the most disinterested of activities. In the eighteenth century, another dimension of empire was opened up by the Academy of Sciences, the brainchild of Peter the Great but finally opened by his widow in 1726. The Academy sponsored various expeditions throughout the empire that added a scientific and technological rationale to the expansion of the eighteenth and nineteenth centuries. There was often, however, an economic as well as a political motive for state sponsorship of exploratory expeditions. For example, it appears that the underlying motive for the famous maritime expeditions of the Dane Vitus Bering in Russia's far east was to revitalise the flagging Siberian fur trade.

Figure 7.6   Fur tribute (*iasak*) paid at a Siberian fort (*ostrog*), from Kerner, R.J. (1946) *The Urge to the Sea:The Course of Russian History: The Role of Rivers, Portages, Ostrogs, Monasteries, and Furs*, Berkeley and Los Angeles, University of California Press, p. 85.

In weighing the contribution of economic motivation in the expansion of the Russian empire, it first needs to be stressed that it is only in the eastern theatre that it plays a leading role. Material gain can be assumed to be the main goal of the private traders, but even in their case the state was heavily involved, using them as agents of conquest and collectors of tribute. The state was not slow to turn the rich pickings of the fur trade to the support of its developing imperial strategy.

Attack is the best form of defence?

Private economic enterprise seems to be a relatively weak driver of Russian imperial expansion as a whole, and even in the east is hard to untangle from a state-led military strategy. How important was military power and strategy in explaining the early expansion of Russia on all its fronts? A military strategy was clearly necessary to conquer such a vast terrain – a strategy, moreover, that had to adapt to the changing circumstances of a rapidly moving open frontier. The dilemma for the tsars as their territory grew was the tension between material or strategic gain and increased risk of external aggression. The acquisition of agricultural land and sources of raw materials was essential to resource a growing army, but in the east the remarkable movement of the frontier came at the price of an ever-lengthening southern border with powerful states (Hosking, 2002, p. 85).

How were troops raised? At the start of the drive there was no regular standing army. The tsar relied on his warrior princes and nobles (boyars) and their men. A prominent role was played by junior members of boyar clans, or boyar sons (**deti boiarskie**), the counterparts of the Portuguese *fidalgos* (Unit 6). Further developments in the organisation of the army were essential if the expansionist drive were to continue. The acquisition of Novgorod enabled Ivan the Great to establish a contract between the tsar and the various princes and boyar clans. They were granted landholdings (**pomestia**) from newly conquered territory on the understanding that, when required, they would levy troops from the peasants who worked these lands. This principle was extended by Ivan the Terrible in a decree of 1556: all landholding, whether the traditionally hereditary sort (**votchiny**) or the new *pomestia* would now be contingent on the fulfilment of state service. In this way Russia became increasingly a military state – a 'Eurasian Sparta' (Darwin, 2007, p. 72) in which the process of conquest became self-propelling. In order to conquer more land, more military power was needed; and more land was needed to generate the military power.

How was the army equipped? To start with, the mounted noble warriors had armour, swords, spears and bows and arrows. To these Ivan the Terrible added several thousand musketeers (**streltsy**), drawn tellingly not from the agriculturalist noble ranks but from the common townspeople accustomed to a certain measure of urban industry. It was the deployment of muskets and cannon, as well as the intervention of the Volga Cossacks, that enabled Ivan to gain the upper hand in the war on Kazan. Firearms continued to play a vital colonising role: as in the American Wild West, it was the colonisers' muskets and pistols that conferred a huge technological advantage over the bows and arrows of the indigenes, and helped explain how such small numbers could subdue whole tribes – another instance of the 'weapons gap' mentioned in Unit 1. It was mostly down to sheer material superiority, but the perceived magic of the weapons also contributed. During the campaign in the Enisei basin against the Buriat tribes, one of the more resistant of the Asiatic peoples, the natives managed to overcome a fort and massacre the *streltsy* within. Uncomprehending of the Russian weapons, they made a fire of the guns, bullets and gunpowder, with the result that some of them were killed by the dead soldiers' stray bullets. This freak accident only added to the colonialists' mystique, and the Buriats were easily dispersed by Russian reinforcements (Lantzeff and Pierce, 1973, p. 147). It should be stressed that the subjugation of the Siberian tribes was no simple matter of ethnic Russians imposing themselves on other peoples. The Russians were no less willing to co-opt 'auxiliary' troops than the other imperial powers dealt with in this block. For example, an expeditionary force of some 1,500 men sent from Tobolsk to erect another fort in the Ob basin included Polish and Lithuanian prisoners of war, and a number of Cossacks – but by far the largest ethnic component was Tatars, whether directly employed in Russian service or else paying tribute (Lantzeff and Pierce, 1973, p. 114).

Russian firepower was sufficient to make rapid headway in the east, but means were also required to consolidate gains and defend territory, both existing and new. The building of forts and the fortification of existing towns and villages was essential both to the defence of the imperial core and the expansion of the periphery. They facilitated the capture and subsequent discipline of territory peopled by nomadic tribes. They enabled a constant watch to be kept for large-scale movements, and also offered protection from nomadic arrows. They were also vital in the defence of Muscovy against the persistent depredations of the khanate of Crimea, which led to Ivan the Terrible's defensive line of fortifications of 1571. These and subsequent lines (*cherty*) were more than a sequence of forts: they included ditches and ramparts on the steppes, with stationary guards and mobile patrols (Kerner, 1942, p. 66). Other defensive measures included the blocking of Tatar trails with felled trees, and of fords with sharp stakes, while nomadic grazing lands were scorched. Warnings of impending raids were conveyed by horse riders and smoke signals.

The building of forts and fortified towns continued throughout the imperial period to be a fundamental aspect of the Russian colonial strategy, both to police the region and to make trading links. A brief account of activity during the regency and reign of Boris Godunov should clinch the point. In the western theatre during the late 1590s, the much-contested city of Smolensk was heavily fortified to counter the threat from the Polish-Lithuanian state. To the south, in the region of the Upper Don and below Ivan's line of fortifications of 1571, Livny and Voronezh were constructed in the 1580s, and the old town of Kursk fortified – the greater depth of defence was a sign that the tide was turning on the steppes. The process of fortification and town building extended eastward, and the purpose shifted from defence to offence, if subtly at first. To start with, the main trails of the nomadic Crimeans and their Nogai allies were blocked. The subsequent building of Tsaritsyn, Saratov and Samara on the eastern side of the Volga was ostensibly to defend the Volga trading highway. These new forts were correctly perceived by the Nogais as a direct threat, despite the Russians' assurance that they would offer them protection from Cossack river pirates. In Siberia, the survivors among Ermak's Cossacks had founded Tiumen in 1586 on a tributary of the Ob, helping to link the northern colony with Kazan to the southwest. The following year, on another Ob tributary, they built the new fort of Tobolsk, which would serve as the centre of a network (*razriad*) of subsidiary forts cementing the Russian grip on the Western Siberian region (see Plate 2.15 and Figure 7.7).

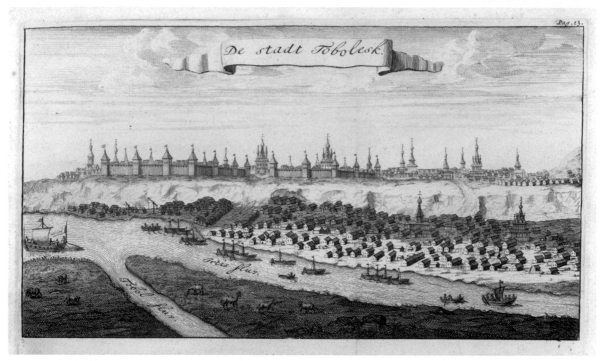

Figure 7.7   'De stadt Tobolesk' (City of Tobolsk), engraving, from Ides, E.Y. (1706) *Three Years Travels from Moscow Over-land to China, thro' Great Ustiga, Siriania, Permia, Sibiria, Daour, Great Tartary, etc. to Peking*, London. Photo: Mary Evans Picture Library/Grosvenor Prints. The engraving shows the location of the city on the confluence of the Tobol and Irtysh rivers.

The later foundation of Tara (1596) and Tomsk (1604) on southern tributaries of the Ob presaged both the further eastward drive into Siberia and also a later expansion down the overland trade routes to Central Asia.

You have primary-source evidence for the importance of fortification as a tool of Russian eastward imperial expansion in the document you read earlier: 'Instructions to the voevody of the Lena, February 10, 1644' (Primary Source 7.1). The forts' permanence and relative strength were symbolic of the economic and cultural gulf that existed between the Russians and the nomadic and semi-settled tribes that were swept aside by the advance. In the south, the forts served to divide the grazing lands of the nomads, a strategy that hindered concerted action between the Tatar khanates, and also drastically limited the transhumance that underpinned the nomadic way of life. This was literally a case of divide and rule, and ensured the eventual triumph of the agriculturalist settler over the pastoralist nomad on the Eurasian plain.

Was the imperial drive a consequence of a positive desire for territorial domination, or was it at heart a defensive strategy? This conundrum has long been the subject of debate among historians of Russia. We see a mix of motives in Boris's fortification programme, and the tension between opportunity and threat runs throughout Russian history. Many historians, and also many apologists of the Russian empire (and the Soviet Union), have taken the view that an expansionist policy was necessary and justified because of

Russia's vulnerability or 'encirclement'. John LeDonne (2004) has argued against this consensus that the imperial drive from about 1650 was the result of the Russian rulers' self-conscious 'Grand Strategy' to control the Eurasian heartland in opposition to western Christianity and Islam. LeDonne insists that this strategy was in no way defensively motivated, but a genuinely expansionist view of Russia's historical destiny. The self-confessed problem with this hypothesis is that the strategy is nowhere articulated by the actors involved, but inferred from consistent practice: the building of a military–industrial complex, the creation of a network of client states, and the implementation of a consistent military strategy.

Another conventional view of later Russian expansion – one you have already encountered in the Riasanovsky extract (Secondary Source 7.1) – emphasises the ambition to transcend the landlocked nature of the heartland. The epitome is Peter the Great's aspiration to gain access to the Black Sea, which was encircled by the Ottoman Turks, and the Baltic, dominated by Poland and Sweden. At the economic level, trade would thereby be released from the fetters of Russia's restriction of the northern port of Archangel, which was ice-bound for much of the year. At the level of politics and diplomacy, Russia would become a big player in the European international arena. The greatest physical legacy of Peter's reign and a monument to his maritime orientation was the founding of St Petersburg, the new capital on the Baltic shore (see Plate 2.16 in the Visual Sources Book). Access to the sea was surely an important imperial driver for Peter the Great, the nautical obsessive who learned personally how to build a frigate in the wharves of the Dutch East India Company in Amsterdam. But did the quest for warm-water ports drive the Russian expansion through the centuries, not only to the south and west, but also to the east, where the Russians reached the Pacific coast well before their entry into the west European naval theatre?

EXERCISE

This view was advanced by Robert J. Kerner during the Second World War (Kerner, 1942), but after the war was over it was dismissed by certain analysts, including John A. Morrison (1952). This debate is long gone, but there are historical lessons to be learned from revisiting it. Read the (much edited) extracts from Kerner (Secondary Source 7.4) and Morrison (Secondary Source 7.5) on the course website. How convincing do you find the selected passages from Morrison's rebuttal, and how important is the context in which it was made?

SPECIMEN ANSWER

Kerner's derivation of an 'urge to the sea' all the way from the Valdai Hills and the very inception of the Muscovite state is surely an easy target, but perhaps Morrison unduly minimises the strategic importance for Russia of ports on the Baltic and Black Sea. There still seems to be a tenable position between the two extremes, whereby an urge to the sea becomes an important aspect of post-Petrine imperial policy. States with naval power came to dominate the international stage in the period of European imperialism dealt with in the course. The question remains whether an important driver of Russia's later expansionism was the ambition to transcend its own massively terrestrial character, and become a naval power to rival

Spain, Portugal, the Netherlands and Great Britain. Morrison's own hostility to the notion of a Russian 'urge to the sea' is expressed in a Cold War context, when sympathy for Soviet access to warm-water ports could be seen as dangerous.

Spreading the faith?

Historical interpretations of the Russian empire, it would seem, have an ideological context. Can the same be said of the historical origins and development of the empire itself? A full explanation of Russian expansion surely needs to include the development of an imperial belief system. The purposes of such a system would be (i) to reconcile the heartland to the high costs the imperial strategy laid upon it; and (ii) to justify to the peripheries their subordinate relationship to the imperial core. The two ends were not always achievable by the same set of beliefs.

Attending to ideologies in this section counterbalances my preoccupation up to this point with the various ecological and geopolitical drivers of Russian expansionism. This is no easy task: the ideological history of the Russian empire is notably complex, reflecting the ambiguities of its peculiar geopolitical position straddling Europe and Asia. Geography, the choice of the Orthodox religion and the Mongol yoke combined to isolate Russia from the great changes of early modern European culture: the Renaissance, the Reformation, the rise of capitalism and the scientific revolution. Some saw this as a mark of Russia's special, untainted destiny, while others – not least Peter the Great – regarded it as a cultural deficit, one that needed to be made good if Russia were to be taken seriously as a great imperial power.

How important was religion in the expansion of Russia? Religion was undoubtedly fundamental in the construction of a Russian identity. In 988, Vladimir, grand prince of Kiev, effectively inaugurated the Russian Orthodox tradition. He accepted the recommendation of his envoys that Russia should adopt the Orthodox version of Christianity practised in the Greek-speaking Byzantine relic of the Roman empire. According to the Russian chronicles, it was the beauty of the Greek Orthodox liturgy that captivated the envoys. You may recall from the Lieven extract (Secondary Source 7.2) his argument that there was nothing in Russia's geographical position that predetermined its choice of religion. It needs to be recognised, however, that at the time there were important trading links between Kievan Rus and the Byzantine empire that made the choice of the Orthodox religion more pragmatic than the chroniclers' story suggests (Hosking, 2002, p. 38). The Byzantines, however, had weakened economically, politically and ideologically by the time of Ivan the Great: the Russians saw the fall of Constantinople to the Ottomans in 1453 as divine punishment for the eastern church's latter-day compromise with the western variant. The Russian Orthodox Church became increasingly independent of Constantinople, gaining its own patriarch in 1589, during the regency of Boris Godunov.

The full ideological justification of empire goes back to Ivan the Great, during whose reign Russia embarked self-consciously upon imperial expansion. It is tempting to look for an ideological underpinning for the early expansion in the ecclesiastical doctrine of 'Moscow – the third Rome'.

EXERCISE

Now read the classic statement of the doctrine by the monk Filofei in a letter to Tsar Vasilii III, son of Ivan the Great and father of Ivan the Terrible, on the course website (Primary Source 7.4). What does the document imply about the relationship between the church and the tsar?

SPECIMEN ANSWER

On the face of it, the author is unequivocal about to the power of the tsar over the Orthodox Church. But he is also insisting on the essentially Christian nature of the Russian realm and the essentially Christian mission of the tsar – a mission that the church was clearly seeking to define.

DISCUSSION

You will see that an exclusively Christian definition of the Russian realm was not best fitted to its subsequent imperial expansion.

According to this doctrine, after the fall of the first Rome to the barbarians, the torch of the true Orthodox faith passed to Constantinople. But following the capture of Constantinople by the Ottoman Turks in 1453, the Russian church regarded Moscow as the new custodian of the Christian faith, against western heresies as well as Islam. In the early years of the reign of Ivan the Terrible, the Russian Orthodox Church was aggressively anti-Islamic. When Kazan was taken in 1552, its mosques were razed to the ground, and churches built in their place; and those of the Tatar nobility who refused to be baptised were put to death by drowning. It is significant, however, that the state insisted on a relaxation of this aggressive policy as soon as 1555. Historians are by no means agreed on the significance of the doctrine of 'Moscow – the third Rome' for the expansionary drive that followed its articulation (Kappeler, 2001, p. 26). Even at this early stage, it is likely that the tsar saw the difficulties in administering a growing multi-ethnic empire – especially one with a large Islamic minority – through a policy of enforced conversion.

With certain exceptions – notably the traditionalist 'old believers' who rejected seventeenth-century reforms of the Orthodox Church, and the westward-leaning version of Orthodoxy practised in the Ukraine – the Russian administration was generally tolerant of the religions practised within its imperial borders. In this respect Russia was following the example set by its Mongol tutors in empire. The policy could be seen as enlightened self-interest – the best means of securing the consent of a wide variety of peoples in the attempt to administer a far-flung empire with stretched resources and pre-industrial technology. But this policy may also flow from the internal nature of Russian Orthodoxy, which was a notably liturgically oriented faith, with a strong other-worldly, ascetic (**hesychast**) tendency. It was much less predisposed than the western varieties of Christianity either to theology or to proselytising. Its hostility to the west was usually a defensive, reactive stance; there seems to be little evidence of a countervailing drive to convert others, including the subject peoples of the empire, to the true path. It was only during the latter half of the nineteenth century that a Great Russian nationalism bore heavily on the religious beliefs and practices of other peoples of the empire.

There were numerous local deviations from the central policy of religious toleration and respect for native traditions. In the 1650s, the exceptionally harsh treatment meted out by Ivan Pobakhov, a notorious *voevoda* in Transbaikalia, provoked an uprising of the local Tungu tribespeople. His regime had included submerging them in cold water through a hole in the ice, a notably cruel form of baptism. Pobakhov's motivation, however, was not to save their souls: only baptised natives could be turned into slaves (Lantzeff and Pierce, 1973, p. 152). Despite the cynicism of this *voevoda*, we need to keep in mind the ever-present religious context of imperial activity, even if context may not amount to active cause. For example, religion was a visible aspect of the Cossack campaign led by Ermak in the sixteenth century: each company had colours with an image of Christ, the Virgin Mary or one of the saints; and their preparations for battle included fasting in order to gain the grace of the Lord. But it would be hard to draw a convincing parallel between the fur-led drive across Siberia and the religious motivation of the Spanish and Portuguese oceanic voyages (Units 4 and 6).

Evidence of missionary work in the pre-imperial history of Muscovite expansion and the early history of the empire is not entirely lacking. The monasteries played an important role in the colonisation of the forest lands of northern and eastern parts of European Russia during the thirteenth to fifteenth centuries. This was often unwitting, as the attraction of the forests to the ascetic monks was their quietness and solitude, and almost despite itself the monastery would little by little act as a node of settlement. One of the best-known examples of active missionary work by an Orthodox cleric is the conversion of the Permian region at the foothills of the Urals by Stephen, bishop of Perm (*c.*1340–96) and his successors. Stephen was born in the northern frontier town of Ustiug, which by then had switched its allegiance from its Novgorodian founders to the grand princes of Moscow. He established churches and monasteries in the region, and these acted as nuclei for settlers and merchants. Whether intentionally or not, Stephen's missionary work 'was important in taming the wilderness in preparation for later conquest by Moscow' (Lantzeff and Pierce, 1973, p. 38). Kappeler puts the episode into perspective: 'It was the first example of missionary activity helping the cause of Russian expansion' though its 'enlightened methods were to remain the exception' (Kappeler, 2001, p. 16).

Hostility and suspicion towards the west characterised the theocratic period of Russian imperial rule. A more relenting view of the west was taken by the first Romanov tsars, who were happy to include western technical and military experts among their advisers. But their somewhat arms-length approach to the west was nothing next to the bear hug of Peter the Great. This avid young westerniser returned from his European Grand Tour to launch an astonishing assault on traditional Muscovite beliefs, attitudes and dress. He abolished the patriarchate, and ruthlessly converted the Russian Orthodox Church into an arm of the expansionist, westernising bureaucracy intended to remake Russia as a rival to the west European powers.

EXERCISE

Read the statute of the Holy Synod of 25 January 1721 on the course website (Primary Source 7.5). What evidence does this document provide on the changing relations between church and state?

SPECIMEN ANSWER

The threat to the temporal autocrat of a single spiritual leader is made quite explicit; this is unacceptable, as the power of the autocrat derives from God, whereas the authority of the patriarch evidently does not. Such is the ascendancy of the temporal over the spiritual that it is apparently immune to all the arguments against vesting power in one individual.

Ironically, along with this assertion of the supremacy of temporal over spiritual authority, Peter revoked the tolerance of his predecessors, and ordered the enforced baptism of certain other religious groupings in his realm, such as the Siberian shamanist tribes. It is difficult, though, to see this policy as a mark of the tsar's religious devotion; it seems more like the aspiration to build a tightly controlled modern absolutist state. All the more so, as Peter's policy towards the Baltic states of Estonia and Livonia, acquired from Sweden in 1710, was tolerant, allowing the practice of the Lutheran religion and the use of German as the language of administration. Perhaps this was an expression of Peter's own westernism and Lutheran leanings, though it also made political sense to appease the Baltic Germans and use their high level of education and administrative expertise in the service of the Russian empire.

Peter's actions may have had more to do with the legitimation of autocracy than with his own rather lukewarm feelings about the national religion. The ideological justification of empire seems in general to weaken after the theocratic phase of Russian state building. Could it be that the Russian empire is a case in which military and political considerations really are decisive? According to Gibson (2002), there was little explicit theological or evangelical justification of empire after the early phase of expansion. Indeed, the expansion of Russian territory may not even have been seen as colonisation by educated Russians – at least until the second half of the nineteenth century, when Russia looked to join in the competitive European scramble for colonies, and popular imperialism was promoted through the press (Rieber, 1994).

The attitude of the Russian ruling class and it apologists oscillated throughout the tsarist period between xenophobia and enthusiasm for the west. Russia was both the controversial recipient of western European culture, science and technology, and in its own turn a conduit of European culture among its assimilated Asian peoples. Some westernising tsars, notably Peter the Great, were motivated by the desire to make good a perceived deficit. Others saw salvation in Russia's escape from the heresies of the west, whether religious or political. Crucially, the anxiety of the Russian Orthodox Church to maintain ideological purity in the face of heretical western ideas ran counter to the tsars' pragmatic dependence on western techniques to equip their expansionist drive. In the end, the need to maintain the empire was stronger than the need to maintain the faith.

CONCLUSION

The Russian polity expanded remarkably from the mid-sixteenth century to the mid-nineteenth, to the point where the tsar-emperors ruled over nearly one-sixth of the world's land mass. By that time only the combined colonies of the widely dispersed maritime empire of Great Britain occupied a greater area, and only the Mongol empire that preceded the Russian had ever occupied a greater continuous land mass. As a vast continuous land empire in the tradition of Rome, China and the Mongol empire, imperial Russia makes on the face of it a striking contrast with the other cases you have studied in this block. The process of acquisition was the inverse of the colonisation undertaken by the west European maritime powers: instead of crossing vast oceans in the quest for far-flung colonies, the Russians cut swathes of imperial conquest across a vast terrain towards distant coastlines. Only when its traders began to settle Alaska at the end of the eighteenth century did the Russian empire resemble in any way the distributed maritime or overseas variety – and then only until 1867, when it sold its one and only transoceanic colony to the United States.

But was the Russian land empire so different from the maritime empires dealt with earlier in this block? Some historians (perhaps, like Geoffrey Hosking, influenced by Sir Halford Mackinder's geopolitical views) have emphasised Russia's unique destiny within the natural confines of the great Eurasian plain. This is a destiny seen as quite distinct from those of the states on the west European coastland (LeDonne, 2004). But others (including Lieven in Secondary Source 7.2) have seen the Russian drive into Asia as the eastern terrestrial (or riverine) equivalent of the maritime adventures of the west European peripheral states: Russia was 'one of the frontier states that played a vanguard role in Europe's expansion' (Darwin, 2007, p. 21). More specifically, the Russian eastward and American westward drives to the Pacific coast have been seen as part of a 'European tide that inundated Asia and America in the Age of Exploration', both propelled by the 'lust for fur' (Lensen, 1964, pp. 1, 3). Siberia has been likened to a 'Wild East' comparable to American Wild West, with lawless brigands not only battling indigenous peoples but fighting with each other. Kappeler considers the parallel with the United States, though argues that Canada, where French and British traders competed for beaver furs, was a better match with the Russian case (Kappeler, 2001, pp. 38, 55; Innis, 1962; Eccles, 1983). I want to leave you with the bigger question of whether Russian imperialism should be seen as the eastern arm of the globalisation of European culture; or whether it is better seen as the culmination of the long contest for domination of the Eurasian plain. Perhaps the remainder of this course will help you to a conclusion!

Let's finally return to the more confined issue of the origins of the Russian empire. You have now considered how and why the Russian state began its imperial drive. It seems incontrovertible that the geographical setting, including the distribution of natural resources, was massively influential on the shape, type and direction of growth of the empire. But the geographical setting is itself passive: it scarcely supplies the motive for empire building. A limited case can be made for the economic motivation of empire and a much stronger one for the military, though whether it is defensive or offensive in origin remains a historical conundrum. It seems that less of a historical case can be made for the spiritual destiny of Russia as a driver of empire. But is military action within the context of chronic geopolitical uncertainty sufficient to explain the remarkable rise of the Great Russians in Eurasia? Where does the drive come from? This could lead us into an infinite regress of questions, but it is worth highlighting the importance of individual human agency, especially when the object of analysis is an autocracy that confers on an individual with the appropriate qualities an unusual scope for personal intervention in the course of history. It is no accident that certain individuals – Ivan the Great, Ivan the Terrible, Boris Godunov and Peter the Great – have loomed large in this unit.

It is important to recognise that, for most of the period of the course, Russia was less advanced economically than many of its neighbours, and that this had a big influence on the direction and pace of its imperial growth. Once the challenge of the Tatar khanates had been stifled, the tsars met relatively little resistance to the east as Russian settlers and adventurers led the push across the forests, marshes and tundra up to the farthest shorelines, the most inhospitable deserts and highest mountain ranges. There was more resistance to the south and west, from cultures that were more advanced than that of the Russians. That conquest was eventually achieved perhaps tells as much about the weakening of the Mongol empire, the Ottoman empire and the Polish-Lithuanian state, as it does about the waxing of the Russian empire.

It is tempting to generalise the Russian imperial trajectory as a transition from the traditional ambition to emulate the Asiatic empires that held sway over its vast lands, to the modern aspiration to become a west European maritime power. After the eastward drive of the sixteenth and seventeenth centuries, the clear objective of the Russian rulers from Peter the Great was renewed access to prized European trading routes. During the eighteenth century, footholds were established on the Baltic and Black Sea coasts; the Baltic provinces were annexed from Sweden; the mountain warriors of the Caucasus were subdued with great difficulty; and much of dismembered Poland was absorbed. Russia could now meet the higher redefinition of 'imperial' proposed by Lieven and Osterhammel (Unit 2), and assert itself as an imperial power on the international stage.

REFERENCES

Bakewell, P. (1995)'Conquest after the conquest: the rise of Spanish domination in America' in Kagan, R.L. and Parker, G. (eds) *Spain, Europe and the Atlantic world*, Cambridge, Cambridge University Press.

Crosby, A.W. (1986) *Ecological Imperialism: The Biological Expansion of Europe, 900–1900*, Cambridge, Cambridge University Press.

Darwin, J. (2007) *After Tamerlane: The Global History of Empire*, London, Allen Lane.

Eccles, W.J. (1983) *The Canadian Frontier 1534–1760*, rev. edn, Albuquerque, University of New Mexico Press.

Fieldhouse, D.K. (1982) *The Colonial Empires: A Comparative Study from the Eighteenth Century*, 2nd edn, Basingstoke, Macmillan.

Fisher, R. (1943) *The Russian Fur Trade*, 1550–1700, Berkeley, University of California Press.

Gibson, J. (2002) 'Russian imperial expansion by context and contrast', *Journal of Historical Geography*, vol. 28, no. 2, pp. 181–202.

Hosking, G. (2002) *Russia and the Russians: From Earliest Times to 2001*, London, Penguin.

Hughes, L. (1998) *Russia in the Age of Peter the Great*, New Haven, Yale University Press.

Innis, H.A. (1962) *The Fur Trade in Canada: An Introduction to Canadian Economic History*, rev. edn (prepared by S.D. Clark and W.T. Easterbrook), New Haven, Yale University Press.

Kappeler, A. (2001) *The Russian Empire: A Multiethnic History* (trans. A. Clayton), Harlow, Longman.

Kerner, R.J. (1942) *The Urge to the Sea: The Course of Russian History. The Role of Rivers, Portages, Ostrogs, Monasteries and Furs,* Berkeley, University of California Press.

Khodarkovsky, M. (2002) *Russia's Steppe Frontier: The Making of a Colonial Empire*, Bloomington, Indiana University Press.

Lantzeff, G.V. (1943) *Siberia in the Seventeenth Century: A Study of the Colonial Administration*, Berkeley, University of California Press.

Lantzeff, G.V. and Pierce, R.A. (1973) *Eastward to Empire: Exploration and Conquest on the Russian Open Frontier to 1750*, Montreal, McGill-Queen's University Press.

LeDonne, J.P. (2004) *The Grand Strategy of the Russian Empire, 1650–1831*, Oxford, Oxford University Press.

Lensen, G.A. (ed.) (1964) *Russia's Eastward Expansion*, Englewood Cliffs, Prentice-Hall.

Lieven, D.C.B. (2000) *Empire: The Russian Empire and its Rivals*, London, John Murray.

Madariaga, I. de (2005) *Ivan the Terrible: The first Russian Tsar*, New Haven, Yale University Press.

Morrison, J.A. (1952) 'Russia and warm water: a fallacious generalization and its consequences', *US Naval Institute Proceedings*, vol. 78, pp. 169–79.

Rieber, A.J. (1994) 'Russian imperialism: popular, emblematic, ambiguous', *Russian Review*, vol. 54, no. 3, pp. 331–5.

Vernadsky, G. (1969) *A History of Russia*, 6th rev. edn, New Haven, Yale University Press.

Witzenrath, C. (2007) *Cossacks and the Russian Empire, 1598–1725: Manipulation, Rebellion and Expansion into Siberia*, London, Routledge.

CONCLUSION TO BLOCK 2

Chris A. Williams

In the Introduction to this block, we asked you to consider a number of overarching questions about how empires begin. Now, you can probably answer most of them.

We have seen that, by the end of the initial period of expansion, almost all of the different forms of colony identified by Fieldhouse (see Unit 2) were present in some form. But was there a common progression between forms? The Portuguese and Dutch empires began as a series of enclaves, but the Spanish empire took off as a looting expedition followed by an occupation colony whose elite was sustained by exploitative bullion mining and plantation agriculture. New England was a settler society from the start, but Barbados quickly evolved from a settler to a plantation model.

The block has made it clear that geography sets limits on the extent to which general rules can ever operate. One reason that the Portuguese got to the Indian Ocean and its staging posts first is the location of Portugal in Europe. The fact that the rivers of Siberia run as they do provided the Russians with a head start in their move east: Russia's was also to a great extent a water-borne empire. In addition, ecology and epidemics had a massive general impact on the speed of large-scale European expansion.

One common conclusion of all the units is that, although the nature of the imperialist states was important, the nature of what they encountered when they arrived was perhaps more so. The indigenous environment – geographical, human or ecological – had an enormous impact on how (and whether) empires began.

GLOSSARY

advocate of Holland: the political leader of the State of Holland.

amphibious operations: troops carried by boat.

apocalyptic belief: belief that the last days of the world and Christ's second coming are imminent.

Arawak: an indigenous ethnic group inhabiting the pre-Columbian Caribbean and much of mainland South America.

astrolabe: instrument used at sea for estimating latitude (north or south of the Equator).

audiencia: Spanish high court of justice.

Auracanian: indigenous ethnic group inhabiting what is now Chile and southern Argentina.

boyar: highest rank of Russian aristocracy before the reforms of Peter the Great.

buccaneer: sixteenth-century term for men, largely of European origin, living on islands in the Caribbean, living off the land, and from selling the skins of wild cattle.

cabacera: Spanish term for an Amerindian township and seat of Amerindian administration.

cabildo: Spanish term for a city council.

cacique: 'chief', originally an Amerindian word, but naturalised into Spanish.

Capitulations of Santa Fe: name for the titles and privileges conferred on Columbus by Ferdinand and Isabella before his first transatlantic voyage.

caravel: a relatively small two- or three-masted ship, used by Spanish and Portuguese sailors for voyages of exploration in the fifteenth and sixteenth centuries. Their triangular sails allowed them to sail close to the wind, although they could also be rigged with square sails for greater speed. Two of Columbus's ships in 1492, *Nina* and *Pinta*, were caravels.

carrack (*nau*): large cargo ship that could also be fitted for fighting with large platforms fore and aft.

carreira da India: The annual India voyage controlled and sponsored by the Portuguese crown.

cartaz: a shipping pass that ships trading in the Indian ocean had to buy from the Portuguese.

Casa da India: body responsible for the administration of the *carreira da India*.

Casa de la Contratación: 'House of Trade', established in 1503 to control trade and migration between Spain and the American Indies.

caudillo: leader or commander of a Spanish expedition.

charnel house: building used to store the bones of the dead.

cherta (pl. *cherty*): Russian term for a line of fortification.

Chichimec: indigenous ethnic group inhabiting what is now northern Mexico.

compaña: 'company' – name given to the Spanish expeditions which set out from the Caribbean to explore and conquer the mainland of South America.

compass roses and rhumb lines: compass roses are circles on a map with marks for degrees; rhumb lines are lines linking these points. Together they provided a geometric grid that was used both to construct late-medieval Mediterranean maps and to navigate by them. Pilots could use them to work out the required bearing to reach their destination. Although maps such as the Piri Reis and the Cantino ones (Plates 1.1 and 1.3) were never intended to be used for navigation, the same grid system was used in drawing them. This can most easily be seen in the complete Cantino map.

consulado: Spanish term for a merchant guild.

core: the institutions and territory in which imperial power is situated. A core dominates two or more peripheries or colonies.

corregidor: Spanish official responsible for Amerindian administration in the New World.

Cossacks: Russian frontiersmen of mixed origins, who acted at some times as marauders and at others as agents of imperial expansion.

Counter-Reformation: the reform movement within the Catholic Church, also known as the Catholic Reformation, which among other things resulted in the Council of Trent.

creole: local-born descendants of settlers in a colony, as distinguished both from those born in the mother country and from the native inhabitants. *See also criollo.*

criollo: American-born Spaniard of pure European descent. *See also* creole.

cue: Nahuatl term for a stone-built temple or step pyramid.

daimyo: Japanese feudal lord.

Declaration of the Rights of Man: one of the fundamental documents of the French Revolution, defining a set of individual rights and a set of collective rights that applied all citizens. The First Article stated that 'Men are born and remain free and equal in rights. Social distinctions can be founded only on the common utility'. The declaration was the first step on the road to the French constitution. It did not, however, address the rights of women. *See also* natural rights.

deti boiarskie: *see* **syn boiarskii**.

direct rule: rule involving the direct control of finances, security and other aspects of administration, including appointing lower-level officials. *See also* indirect rule.

Dominican: religious order (founded in 1215) that supplied many missionaries to the American Indies.

doshchanik (pl. *doshchaniki*): Russian flat-bottomed river boat.

ecumene: geographical term for an area that is continuously inhabited.

effective occupation, doctrine of: the English crown in the sixteenth and seventeenth centuries consistently refused to recognise claims by other states to lands outside Europe, where these were not backed up by 'effective occupation'. This was most significant in relation to the claims of the Spanish and Portuguese monarchies to the entirety of the New World, by virtue of papal grant. The English therefore considered that they had a right to settle unoccupied (by Europeans) areas of the Americas, and thus to defend themselves against all comers, but that they had no right, in times of peace, to displace existing Iberian (and other) settlements. Policy, especially during periods of 'cold war' with Spain in the late sixteenth century, was sometimes less restrained than the doctrine demanded.

enclave: a small area of a larger country or territory (often a town or even part of a town or city) that falls under the dominance or rule of an imperial power.

encomendero: a conquistador who was granted *encomiendas* in the Spanish New World.

encomienda: the grant of Amerindian labour services to Spanish settlers in the New World.

entrepôt: a trading centre at which goods are imported and then exported. It acts as a nodal point for the redirection of goods.

epidemiology: a branch of medical science that explains how disease affects people in large numbers. It deals with the way that diseases are transmitted, become more or less virulent, and have an impact on large populations.

Estado da India: the state of India; the Portuguese empire east of the Cape of Good Hope subject to the viceroy of Goa.

estancia: Spanish term for any rural property in Spanish-America, though usually a ranch specialising in European livestock.

Eurasian: of mixed European and Asian descent.

extraterritorial privileges: rights, either for all within a designated area or for a specified group or groups, to be administered and tried under foreign laws.

factory: a trading place in a foreign land; literally somewhere a factor (a trader in goods) stays and stores goods in between visits of ships.

falciparum malaria: the most lethal form of malaria, endemic in coastal West Africa.

feitoria: Portuguese word meaning 'fortified trading station', from which the term factory is derived. *See also* factory.

fidalgo: Portuguese gentleman or minor noble.

formal rule: rule made formal by conquest or treaty that gives *de jure* (legal) rights and duties over a territory. *See also* informal rule.

Franciscan: religious order (founded in 1209) which supplied many missionaries to the American Indies.

galleon: a ship used by the Dutch that was lighter, faster and better armed, though smaller, than the carrack.

geographical determinism: belief that geographical setting is the most powerful or fundamental influence on the course of human history and the nature of human societies.

hegemony: dominance exercised through ideas or economic or political preponderance, rather than through the use of force or the threat of force.

hesychasm (adj. **hesychast**): Russian Orthodox tradition of retiring from the world in order to experience God through stillness and prayer.

heuristic: term describing a model used for teaching and explanatory purposes that is accepted as falling short of a complete explanation.

hidalgo: Spanish term for a minor nobleman.

homunculi: Latin word meaning 'little men'.

Huitzilopochtli: 'Southern Hummingbird', one of the Mexica's gods.

iam (pl. *iamy*): Mongol inn and postal station, imitated by Muscovites.

iasak: material tribute required from subject peoples of Mongol and Russian empires.

indirect rule: rule effected through subordinate local rulers who control detailed finances, appointments, and may enjoy significant autonomy in decisions. *See also* direct rule.

informal rule: rule without formal conquest or treaty, and so without *de jure* (legal) rights and duties over a territory. This involves sustained influence supported by economic, military or other power. *See also* formal rule.

khanate: a district or territory ruled by a khan. The title 'khan' was for centuries commonly used for military or sovereign rulers throughout much of central Asia, and beyond. They could vary from petty tribal leaders to major empire builders.

ladino: a Spanish-speaking black slave in the New World.

letrado: a university-educated official in the Spanish royal service.

letter of marque: legal instrument, issued by a state, allowing its holder to wage war as a 'privateer' on that state's enemies. Letters of marque were issued from the late medieval period up to the end of the nineteenth century.

letter of reprisal: legal instrument, more limited than a 'letter of marque', issued to someone who had suffered a loss at the hands of a foreign power, or one of its subjects, authorising them to take goods or money up to a certain value from that foreign power, as compensation for their loss, by force if necessary.

limpieza de sangre: Spanish term meaning 'purity of blood'.

Luso-Asian: of mixed Portuguese and Asian descent.

mandates: territories governed by the Allied powers after the First World War with the authority conferred on them by the League of Nations. After the First World War, it was decided that the former German colonies and some of the Arab territories of the Ottoman empire were to be governed by the Allied powers, but that these should be answerable to the League of Nations. The territories were held in trust and were to be prepared for self-government, although this was seen as a long-term goal.

Maroons: escaped slaves and their descendants, living in their own autonomous communities, usually in or around the Caribbean.

Maya: an 'advanced' civilisation located on the Yucatan peninsula, which flourished around AD 250–900.

mercantilism: an economic philosophy based on maximising the immediate income of the state practising it. It usually took the form of duties on imported commodities (tariffs), and regulations which demanded that all or part of the trade with colonies had to pass through the metropole, and in ships from the metropole or its colonies.

mestizo: Spanish term applied to descendants of unions between Europeans and people indigenous to an area of imperial domination, such as Spanish–Filipino and Spanish–Amerindian offspring.

metropole: the home territory and institutions of an imperial power.

Mexica: the dominant ethnic group in the Aztec Confederation.

military orders: Portuguese Christian military organisations established to defend the frontier areas against Muslim incursion – loyal to the crown.

mita: Quechua term for a form of coerced labour in Spanish Peru. *See also* Quechua.

mulatto: descendants of unions between Europeans and Africans. Some now avoid the term because of its negative associations (with slavery, and from its origin in Latin and Spanish words meaning mule), favouring less-specific terms such as biracial or multiracial.

Nahuatl: principal indigenous language of central Mexico.

natural rights: universal rights inherent in the nature of people and not contingent on human actions or beliefs. This concept was developed during the Enlightenment, in opposition to the idea of the divine right of kings. By contrast to legal rights – rights created by a government or a society – a natural right exists above and beyond man-made rights. *See also* Declaration of the Rights of Man.

nau: *see* carrack.

nawab: a governor of a province in the Mughal empire.

neo-colony (**neo-colonial**, **neo-colonialism**): a notionally independent country, whose political or economic sovereignty is in reality impinged upon in a sustained way by another country, perhaps especially by the former colonial power.

neo-Europe: an area to which European people, animals and crops are successfully transferred, establishing a kind of 'Europe abroad'.

New Christians: recently converted Jews who often remained crypto-Jewish, having been forced into conversion.

noche triste: 'tragic night', refers to the occasion when Hernando Cortés and his 'company' were attacked while attempting to leave Tenochtitlan.

ordnance: (archaic spelling 'ordonans/ordenans') a general term for guns, especially cannons, and ammunition.

padroado real: patronage of the king of Portugal over the church.

palanquin: covered litter carried by two to four people.

papal bull: an edict of the pope with his seal affixed.

patronato: the privilege of making all ecclesiastical appointments in the American Indies granted by the pope to the Spanish monarchs.

periphery: a fringe or outlying area. In imperial terms, a colony or territory under the control of a foreign power.

peso: Spanish monetary unit.

pomestie (pl. *pomestia*): land granted by the tsar in return for military service.

privateer: an individual (though sometimes used to refer to a ship) who was authorised by a state to make war on its enemies, and to keep any plunder or other profit obtained in the process.

procurador: representative of a Spanish town council (especially in dealing with the royal government).

projection: a geometrical or cartographic method of representing on a flat surface all or part of the earth's surface. Since the earth is a sphere, any representation on a two-dimensional map will involve distortion.

protectorate: a state or territory placed or taken under the protection of a stronger power. Protectorates were often declared by colonial powers over territories where they did not wish to create extensive new systems of government. Existing authorities were allowed to continue, but were now subordinated to the colonial authorities. In practice, of course, colonial rule meant that power relations were irrevocably changed.

pueblo: Amerindian township in Spanish America.

Quechua: principal indigenous language of the Peruvian Andes.

Quetzalcoatl: 'Plumed Serpent' – one of the Mexicas' gods.

quinto real: 'royal fifth' – a levy on precious metal and other goods imported into Spain from the American Indies.

quipu: Quechua term for knotted strings used for mnemonic purposes in the Andes. *See also* Quechua.

razriad: hierarchy of towns and forts in Siberia.

Reconquista: the 'reconquest' of Muslim Spain by Christian forces over a period of 750 years.

requerimiento: 'requirement' – a legal declaration that had to be read out before Spaniards attacked Amerindians in the New World.

responsible government: government in which the executive, including ministers and a first minister if there is one, are 'responsible' for their actions to a representative body.

rhumb lines: *see* compass roses and rhumb lines.

rich trades: high-value trade in goods such as spices, as opposed to bulk trade of lower value.

señores naturales: 'natural lords' – Spanish term for native nobles in the American Indies.

sepoy: Indian infantry (from *sipâhi*, the Persian word for 'soldier').

serfdom: institution tying people to a particular landed estate and obliging them to give certain services to the landowner, who effectively owned them.

States General: joint political body of all the seventeen states or provinces of the Netherlands.

States of Holland and Zeeland: two of the major states or provinces of the Netherlands who broke away to form the Dutch Republic, also known as the United Provinces.

strelets (pl. *streltsy*): Russian infantryman or musketeer.

suzerainty: imperial relationship in accordance with which a dominant nation or state allows a tributary people a limited amount of self-rule.

syn boiarskii (pl. *deti boiarskie*): 'boyar-son' – originally meant a junior member of the boyar clan; later more generally applied to lesser nobility; the Russian counterparts of the Portuguese *fidalgos*.

syndicate of merchants: merchants who have formed a company with a board to run it.

taiga: forested belt of northern Russia.

Tainos: a branch of the Arawak ethnic group inhabiting the pre-Columbian Caribbean.

terra nullius: Latin for 'empty land'. The term is used to describe the doctrine advanced by John Locke and later British thinkers that unsettled land was empty and therefore belonged to no one. It formed the basis to the legal claim of much territory in neo-Europes, including South Island of New Zealand.

transcolonial: affecting two or more colonies.

transoceanic: extending across the ocean. A transoceanic empire is one that stretches across the ocean.

tundra: northernmost Russian belt of frozen or swampy land.

uei tlatoani: Nahuatl term meaning 'great speaker'; title of the Mexica's emperor.

vecino: Spanish term for a townsman or citizen in the original sense of privileged inhabitants of a city.

viceroy: a governor acting in the name of the sovereign (king).

victuals: (archaic spelling 'vytelles') a general term for food and drink.

voevoda (pl. *voevody*): local governor and military commander in Siberian administrative hierarchy; the Russian counterpart of the Spanish *corregidor*, and the Portuguese captain-governor.

votchina (pl. *votchiny*): land estate that could be inherited.

zambo: a person of mixed African and Amerindian descent.

ACKNOWLEDGEMENTS

Grateful acknowledgement is made to the following sources for permission to reproduce material in this book.

Text

p. 163: Crosby, A.W. 'Explanations', *Ecological Imperialism: The Biological Expansion of Europe, 900–1900*. 2004 © Cambridge University Press, reproduced with permission.

Figures

Figure 2.8: Motyl, A.J. (2001) 'The structure of empire', *Imperial Ends: The Decay, Collapse and Revival of Empires*, New York, Columbia University Press. Copyright © 2001, Columbia University Press.

Figure 2.9: Motyl, A.J. (2001) 'Types of empire', *Imperial Ends: The Decay, Collapse and Revival of Empires*, New York, Columbia University Press. Copyright © 2001, Columbia University Press.

Tables

Table 4.1: Adapted from Denevan, W.M. (ed.) (1976) *The Native Population of the Americas in 1492*, Madison, University of Wisconsin Press, p. 291.

Table 5.3: Adapted from Eltis, D. (2000) 'European-directed transatlantic migration 1500–1760, by European nation and continent of origin (in thousands)', *The Rise of African Slavery in the Americas*, New York, Cambridge University Press. Copyright © David Eltis, 2000, Cambridge University Press. Data in columns 1 and 2 is from Curtin, P.D. (1969) *The Atlantic Slave Trade: A Census*, Madison, University of Wisconsin Press, p. 116.

Every effort has been made to contact copyright holders. If any have been inadvertently overlooked the publishers will be pleased to make the necessary arrangements at the first opportunity.

INDEX

Abernathy, D. 44, 45–6, 52–3

adventure stories, and popular perceptions of the British empire 91–3

Africa
    in 1400 115
    Angola 23, 35, 36, 59
    British empire in 31
    decolonisation 35
    expedition to Guinea (1558) 167
    French empire in 30, 31
    historical overview of empire 24, 29, 31, 32
    Imperial British East Africa Company 48
    Mozambique 36, 59, 200, 208
    Nigeria 61–2
    nineteenth-century 'scramble for' 31, 64, 65, 106
    on the Piri Reis map 12, 13
    Portuguese empire in 22, 23, 58
    sea route around 14, 20, 21, 22
    slave trade 25, 187

Africans, and transatlantic migration 182

agriculture
    in Barbados 183–9
    in Russia 247, 248
    in Spanish America 124
    in Virginia 161

Aguilar, Gerónimo de 136

Alaska 29, 237, 258

Albuquerque, Alfonso de 198, 201–2, 211

Aleksei, tsar of Russia 238

Alexander the Great 14

Alexander VI, Pope 127, 134

Alexandria 196

Algeria 28, 30, 31, 60, 67, 89

Algonquians, White's paintings of 174–80

Almeida, Francisco de 199–201, 201–3, 205

Alvarado, Pedro de 142

Amboyna massacre 6–9, 10–11

American War of Independence 27, 28, 43, 82, 190

Americas
    in 1400 115
    European discovery of 20–1, 37

first immigrants 121–2
history of empires 20–1, 24, 27
and the Piri Reis map 13
population at time of European contact 122
see also British Atlantic empire; Spanish America; United States

Amerindians
    and the ecology of North America 159–60, 164, 181
    in New England 181
    Spanish America 121, 122–3, 124, 125, 127–8
    Arawaks 127–8, 129, 135
    Auracanians 124
    Chichimec 121
    Christianisation of 132–3
    cruelty to 86, 87, 88, 129–31
    and European diseases 122, 128, 129, 142–3, 162, 181
    Inca 22, 124, 145–9
    Maya 135
    and Spanish rule 144–5
    in White's paintings/de Bry's engravings 174–9

amphibious operations, and the Portuguese empire 206

analytical approaches to empire 76

ancient Greece and Rome 43–4, 242

Anderson, Virginia Dejohn, 'New England in the Seventeenth Century' 181

Andrews, J.R. 165, 166, 168, 172

Anglo-Dutch war (1673) 10

Angola 23, 35, 36, 59

animals, and European ecological difference 162–3

Arawaks 127–8, 129, 135

Archangel, Russian port 236, 253

Aristotle 44

armed forces
    Dutch Marechausee 73
    and international power systems 71–2
    military power and strategy in Russia 249–54

the arts, and French perceptions of empire 95

Asia
in 1400 115
discovery of new routes to 21, 164
and Indian ocean trade 195–7
Russian imperial expansion in 237, 244–5, 258

astrolabe, Spanish America and maritime technology 125

Atahualpa, Inca emperor 145, 148, 149

Athenian League 43, 44

Atlantic Ocean, and the Piri Reis map 12, 13–14, 15

Atlantic slave trade 23

audiencias, in Spanish America 132, 153

Auracanian Indians of Chile 124

Australia
and definitions of empire 46
land colonisation 44
perceptions of aboriginal inhabitants 91–2

Austria-Hungary 32

Austrian empire 28

the Azores 13, 21, 58

Aztec Mexico 22, 124, 135–45

Babur, Muhammad 23, 37

Baffin Island 165, 167

Balfour, Arthur 98–9

Baltic Sea, and Russian imperial expansion 228, 230, 232, 242, 244, 245, 253, 259

Baltic states, and Russia 257

Banks, Joseph 17

Barbados 183–90
sailing times from England to 159

'Basic English', Churchill's speech on 79

Bay of Bengal 196, 197

Bayly, Christopher 27

Beketov, Peter 237

Berlin Conference 65

Berlin, Congress of (1878) 29

Black Sea, and Russian imperial expansion 239, 244, 245, 253, 259

Both, Pieter 218, 223

boyars, in Russia 243, 250

Bradford, William, *Of Plymouth Plantation* 181

Brazil 20, 21, 22, 23, 28, 59

British Atlantic empire 118, 156–92
American colonies 52, 62, 82, 84, 156, 190
New England 180–3, 191
Virginia 52, 159–61, 174–80, 183
Barbados 159, 183–90
describing the New World 173–80
and ecology 102, 159–64
economics of 157, 187, 190
exploration and finance 164–9
explorers and the state 52, 156, 167–9
and Franco-British wars 25–6
and the geography of North America 157, 158, 164
historical overview 156–7
key concepts in the expansion of 181
and the Navigation Acts 190
and privateering 170–3
and Russia 245, 258
sailing times between England and America 159
and the state 156
and transatlantic migration 182–3

British empire
and the Amboyna massacre 8–9, 10
beginnings 190–2
and Cook's first map of New Zealand 17–18
debates on 80–5
dominions 46
'first empire' (seventeenth century) 82, 183–90
forms of government 20
historical overview 25–7, 27–8, 29–30, 31
imperial system 67
India 26, 29, 35, 70, 98, 106, 107
mercantilist system of trade 64, 73, 190
naval bases 72
and 'new imperialism' 73–4, 106
and popular culture 90, 91–4
and power projection 72
protectorates 50
trading outposts 9, 187
see also East India Company (EIC)

Brooke, John 161, 163

Brotton, J. 14

Brownists (radical Protestants) 180

Bry, Theodor de, engravings of the New World 129–31, 160, 174–9

buccaneers 173

Byzantine empire 24, 228, 254

cabacera, in Spanish America 144

Cabot, John 21, 37, 156, 164

Cabral, Pedro Alvares 21, 197

caciques, in Spanish America 128

Cairo 196

Calicut 21, 196, 197, 202

Canada 24, 46, 258
    and the Northwest Passage 165–6, 173
    Quebec 25, 26, 50

Canary Islands 13, 22, 69, 115, 183

Cannadine, David 105

Cantino Planisphere map 15, 22

Canton see Guangzhou

Cape of Good Hope 20, 21, 120

Cape Horn 157

Cape Verde Islands 13, 21, 58

capitalism
    and empires as systems 64–5
    silver production in Spanish America 150–1

Capitulations of Santa Fe 125

caravel 116

Caribbean islands
    Barbados 159, 183–90
    Columbus's voyages to 126
    decolonisation 36
    Hispanic conquest and settlement 127–9, 131–2, 133
    historical overview 22, 24, 25, 28
    Jamaica 101–4, 171, 187
    on the Piri Reis map 13
    St Domingue 27, 187
    St Kitts 173
    slave plantation colonies 118

Carletti, Francesco 208–10, 213, 214, 216–17, 223

carracks (naus), and the Estado da India 199, 200, 208, 214, 216–17

carreira da India 199

Casa da India, Portugal 199

Casimir, Lithuanian Prince 232

Catholic Christianity
    English Catholics and the New World 18
    and the Portuguese empire 195, 203
        in Japan 203, 208, 209, 211–14
    in Spanish America 121, 124, 126–7, 132–3, 134, 151

caudillos, in Spanish America 136

Chafer, Tony 94–5

Chancey, K. 8

Charles V, Holy Roman Emperor 137, 138–9, 140, 141, 142

charnel house, Algonquian 174, 177

chartered companies 51–2

Chaudhuri, K.N. 225

Chichimec people 121

China 37
    in 1400 115
    and Columbus's voyages 125–6
    defensive modernisation 32
    extraterritorial privileges 48
    and Frobisher's voyages 166–7
    Guangzhou (Canton) tradehouses 68
    Macao 47, 52, 208, 209, 213
    Manchu Qing emperors 70
    maritime fleets to southeast Asia 53, 196
    Ming Dynasty 23, 25, 55, 196
    Mongol emperors 70
    and the Portuguese empire 23
    Qing Dynasty 25, 26, 29, 55, 56
    and Russia 237, 246, 258
    settler colonies 55
    Shanghai 48–9
    sixteenth-century 20, 21, 23
    wars with Japan 32

Cholula, massacre at 138–40

Christianity
    in the Dutch Republic 214–15
    and individual experiences of empire 105
    Lutheranism in the Baltic states 257
    as a motivation for imperialism 116, 117
    Russian Orthodox Church 227, 232, 243, 254–8

and settler colonies in New England 180, 181
and Spanish rule in the New World 121, 124, 126–7
see also Catholic Christianity

Churchill, Winston, speech on empires and 'Basic English' 79

cinema, and French perceptions of empire 95

Cipolla, Carlo 205

citizenship, and empire in France 95

class
and individual experiences of empire 104–5
in the Russian empire 243, 247

Coen, Jan Pieterszoon 10, 218

Cold War, and Russia 254

Colley, Linda 101

colonies
empires as systems for controlling 62–70
types of rule in 60–2
typology of 46–60

Columbus, Christopher 116, 117, 118, 122, 160
and the Piri Reis map 13–14, 15, 17, 21
voyages to America 20, 21, 37, 125–7

communications
and conquest 152
and imperial expansion in Russia 241–2, 244
and the 'new imperialism' 65
in North Atlantic 158–9

compaña 136

compass roses, on the Piri Reis map 13

Conklin, Alice 95

Constantinople 14, 23, 27, 254, 255

consulado (Seville) 134

Cook, Captain James, first map of New Zealand 15–18

Cook's Straits 17

core/periphery relationships 76–7
and definition of empire 44–5, 46
and empires as systems 63, 67, 69–70
and imperial systems of power 74–5
and Russian imperial expansion 241

corregidores, in Spanish America 145

Cortés, Hernando 22, 118, 132, 134, 136–7, 138, 151, 164, 190
and the massacre at Cholula 138–40
and Montezuma 140–4

Cossacks 227, 236, 243, 251, 256

Counter Reformation, and the Jesuits 211

Coupland, Reginald 90

creoles
in Latin America 28
and rule in colonies 59, 62

Crimean khanate 234, 236

criollos, in Spanish America 144, 151

Crosby, Alfred 162–4, 192
Ecological Imperialism 49, 162–4

Cuba 132, 136, 137, 190

cues, in Tenochtitlan 140

cultural ecumenes in Russia 246

cultural empires 42–3, 45

cultural turn 98

culture, empires as systems of 98–9

Curtis, Lionel 90

daimyos (Japanese feudal lords) 212

Darwin, John 224

Davis, John 164, 165–6, 169

Declaration of the Rights of Man 94

decolonisation 35–6

Dee, John 157

defensive modernisation 31–2

Denmark 24

deti boiarskie in Russia 250

Dias, Bartolomeu 20

Díaz del Castillo, Bernal 135
True History of the Conquest of New Spain 139–40, 141

Diderot, Denis 86–8

direct rule 60–2, 75

diseases
and conquest 152
epidemiology 162
and native populations
New England 181
Siberia 245

Spanish America 122, 128, 129, 142–3, 162

Dominican missionary friars, in Spanish America 124

doshchaniki (Russian river boats) 242

Drake, Sir Francis 168, 169, 171, 172, 174

Dryden, John 10

Dutch East India Company (VOC) 25, 217, 218–24, 225
    and the Amboyna massacre 6–11
    charter 218, 224
    gold ducat 84
    marketing policy 224
    marriages of employees 223
    and the Portuguese empire 195
    settlements 51, 52

Dutch Republic 27, 35, 59, 118, 214–25
    and the Dutch East India Company (VOC) 52
    and the Estado da India 214, 216–17, 222, 223
    Long-Distance Company, Amsterdam 217
    seventeenth-century 24, 25
    and the Spanish/Portuguese embargo 217
    spice trade 215, 215–16

eastern Mediterranean, sixteenth-century 20, 195

East India Company (EIC) 25, 26, 51, 85
    and the Amboyna massacre 6, 7–8, 9
    sepoys 71–2
    settlements 52

ecology
    and the British Atlantic empire 159–64, 192
    ecological imperialism 49
    European ecological difference 162–4
    and sustainable imperialism 117

economics of empire 42–3, 64–7
    British Atlantic empire 157, 190
    Russia 246–9

ecumenes, in Russia 246

Edney, Matthew 19

effective occupation 65, 170

Egypt 33
    and Indian Ocean trade 196, 202
    and the Ottoman empire 14

Elcano, Juan Sebastián de 21

El Dorado, quest for 118, 164, 165

elites
    and colonial rule 62
    and empires as systems 63, 70
    and neo-colonialism 56–7

Elizabethan exploration 164–9
    financing 166–7
    and privateering 170–1
    and the state 167–9

Elizabeth I, Queen of England 167–8, 169, 180, 181

Empire Marketing Board 94

empires
    beginning of 37
    debating empire 80–90
    definitions of 41, 42–6, 71
    end of 37–8
    experience of 38–9
    individual experiences of 100–8
    and popular culture 90–100
    survival and renewal of 37
    as systems 62–76
        for controlling colonies 62–70
        international power systems 71–6

enclaves 47–9, 53, 54, 58, 59, 118, 169
    and the slave trade 187

encomenderos, in Spanish America 132, 133, 144

encomienda, in Spanish America 132–3

Endeavour, and Cook's first map of New Zealand 15–17

English civil wars (1640s) 187

English language, 'Basic English' 79

the Enlightenment, and debates about empire 83, 86–8

entrepôts 47

epidemiology 162

equal rights, and empires 43

Ermak, Cossack commander 236, 237, 248, 251, 256

Estado da India 195, 199–210, 224–5
    administration 205, 207–8
    and the Dutch Republic 214, 216–17, 219, 222, 223

governorships 208
and the Jesuits in Japan 203, 208, 209, 211–14
Luso-Asian population 206, 210
marriages and sexual mores 210
mortality rates 206
power and role of the viceroy 205
soldiers and sailors 206–7

Estonia 257

Eurasian landmass
pivot area 34, 35
and Russia 246, 259

Eurasian women, and Dutch East India Company employees 223

extraterritorial privileges in China 48

falciparum malaria 129

Fanon, Frantz 96–7
Black Skin, White Mask 96, 97
The Wretched of the Earth 96, 97

Ferguson, Niall 34, 72

fidalgos 194–5, 205, 224

Fieldhouse, D.K., typology of colonies 47–55, 180, 186, 239

financial accounts, and Elizabethan exploration 166–7

Finlay, M.I. 43, 240

First World War 27, 29, 32, 65

fishing industry, and the British Atlantic empire 160–1, 181

flota 171–2

forests, and the ecology of North America 161, 163–4

formal empires 72, 74, 75, 76, 90

Franciscan monks
in Japan 213–14
missionary friars in Spanish America 124

freedom, J.S. Mill on 84–5

French empire 24, 28, 30–1
Algeria 28, 30, 31, 60, 67, 89
concept of 41
conflicts with Britain 25–6
debates about 86–90
Indochina 30, 49
perceptions of in France 94–7

protectorates 30, 50
and transatlantic migration 182

French Revolution (1789) 27, 28, 43, 88, 94, 95

Frobisher, Martin 164, 165, 166–7

frontiers, and empires 19

fur trade 25, 181
Russia 230, 237, 247, 248–9, 258

Gallagher, J. 74, 91

galleons, and the Dutch Republic 215

Gama, Vasco da 14, 21, 22, 37, 197, 198–9, 200

Gandhi, Mahatma 106

gender, and individual experiences of empire 105

Genghis Khan 230, 232

Genoa 115

geography
of North America, and the British Atlantic empire 157, 158, 164
and Russian imperial expansion 244–6, 259

geopolitics, and US policy 35

German empire 32, 37
Third Reich 70

Ghana 35

Gibson, J. 244–5, 246, 257

Gilbert, Humphrey 168, 181

Ginés de Sepúlveda, Juan 130–1

globalisation
and enclaves 48
and maritime empires 67–8

glory, as a motivation for imperialism 116, 117

Goa 201, 203, 204, 207, 208
Carletti's description of 209–10

Godfrey, R.B., engravings of New Zealand 16

Godunov, Boris 236–7, 242, 251, 254, 259

gold
and Anglo-Spanish wars/raids 164
and the Estado da India 200, 201
as a motivation for imperialism 116, 117–18

Golden Hind 169, 170, 172

the Golden Horde 232, 234, 243

Greece 28

Green, Charles 17

Greenland 20, 115, 122, 165

Grenville, Richard 171, 173–4

Guangzhou 48, 68, 196, 213

Guinea, expedition to (1558) 167

Habsburg empire 55, 67

Hakluyt, Richard 157, 165, 169

Hall, Stuart 97

Hancock, Sir Keith 41

Harley, J.B. 13

harm principle 85

Harriot, Thomas 174, 176, 180

Hawkins, Sir John 164, 168, 172

hegemony
    and imperial systems of power 75
    rise of American 34

Hemming, John, *The Conquest of the Incas* 121

Henry VII, King of England 156, 164

hesychast tradition, in the Russian Orthodox church 255

heuristic models of empire 41, 55

Heyn, Admiral Piet 172

hidalgos 136

Hideyoshi, Japanese ruler 213

Higman, B.W. 186

Hispaniola, Spanish colonisation of 86, 87, 127–8, 132

history of empires (overview) 18–36
    1500–1680 20–5
    1680–1830 25–9
    1830–1914 29–32
    1914–2000 32–6

Hitler, Adolf 49

Hobson, J.A., *Imperialism* 64, 65

Holland *see* Dutch Republic

Hong Kong 47, 48

Hormuz 14, 196, 201

Hosking, Geoffrey 246, 258

Huitzilopochtli, Mexica tribal god 138

iamy (Russian postal stations) 242

iasak (tribute), and Russian imperial expansion 241

Iceland 115, 157, 161

ideology, and imperial rule 79

Imperial British East Africa Company 48

imperial federalism, and settler colonies 81

imperialism, definition of 71

imperial power systems 71–6

Inca empire 22, 124, 145–9

indentured servants, and the British Atlantic empire 172–3, 187

independence
    of former empires 35–6, 38
    and neo-colonialism 57

India
    in 1400 115
    British empire in 26, 29, 35
    British rule in 26, 29, 35, 70, 98, 106, 107
    European idea of 19
    Franco-British conflict in 25, 26
    Islam in 196
    Mughal empire 24, 26, 28, 37
    Mutiny Rebellion (1857) 31
    Portuguese first voyages to 197–9
    Queen Victoria as empress of 41, 42
    sixteenth-century 20
    voyages to 21
    see also Estado da India; Goa

Indian Ocean
    and China 23
    Portuguese empire 20, 22, 58, 164, 195–9
    seventeenth-century empires 24

indigenous peoples
    and the Amboyna massacre 10
    and Cook's first map of New Zealand 17
    and the economics of empire 157
    in the Estado da India 205–6
    Maoris 17, 18, 44

popular perceptions of 91–3
and settler colonies 49, 50, 54
see also Amerindians

indirect rule 60–2, 75

individual experiences of empire 100–8
Dadabhai Naoroji 106, 107
Joseph Pitts 100–1, 103, 104
Thomas Thistlewood 101–4, 105
Vernon Lee Walker 105–6, 107–8

individual rights, and empires 43, 44

Indochina 30, 49

Indonesia 35, 73, 218
Amboyna massacre 6–11

industrialisation, and the 'new imperialism' 65

informal empires 72–3, 74, 75, 76, 91

the Inquisition, and the Portuguese empire 211, 212

institutions, and conquest 152

interaction, empires as systems of 108

international power systems, empires as 71–6

Iraq 33, 45

Ireland
and the British Atlantic empire 157, 168
'planting' of 82, 168, 181

Islam
British slaves and conversion to 101, 104
and the Estado da India 201–3, 205–6, 211
and French Algeria 60
in India 196
and Indian Ocean trade 196, 197
Muslim-ruled empires 23–4
and Orientalism 98
and the Ottoman Empire 27
and the Piri Reis map 14, 15
and the Russian Orthodox Church 255
and the Spanish *Reconquista* 127

Ivan III (the Great) of Russia 232–4, 242, 243, 255, 259

Ivan IV (the Terrible) of Russia 234–6, 243, 250, 251, 255, 259

Jamaica 101–4, 171, 187

James I and VI, King of Scotland and England 8, 169

Janes, John 169

Japan 32, 41
defensive modernisation 32
the Jesuits and the Portuguese empire 23, 208, 211–14

Jesuits (Society of Jesus), in Japan 203, 208, 209, 211–14

joint-stock companies 9, 168, 187–90

Kalakaua, King of Hawaii 105

Kappeler, A. 258

Kazan, khanate of 234, 240

Kerner, Robert J. 253–4

khanates 25, 46, 234, 236, 239–40, 251, 252, 259

Kievan Rus 228, 232, 247, 254

labourers
indentured servants as 172–3, 187
and settler colonies 49, 50

ladinos in the Caribbean 128–9

land empires
and Fieldhouse's typology of colonies 55
and maritime empires 68, 69
peripheries 69–70

Las Casas, Bartolomé de, *A Short Account of the Destruction of the Indies* 86, 87, 129–31, 139, 140

Latin America 28

League of Nations, mandated territories 54

LeDonne, John 253

Lenin, V.I., *Imperialism: The Highest Stage of Capitalism* 64–5

letrados in Spanish America 124

letters of marque 171

letters of reprisal 170–1

Leur, J.C. van 225

liberation ideology, and nineteenth-century empires 28

Lieven, Dominic 69–70, 71, 72, 246, 254, 258, 259

Ligon, Richard 186–9

limpieza de sangre, in Spanish America 144

Linschoten, Jan Huygen van 203–5, 206–7, 214, 223

literature, and French perceptions of empire 95

Livonia 257

Locke, John 44, 82

Londonderry 168

Loti, Pierre, *Le Roman d'un spahi* 95

Lugard, Lord 61

Luso-Asian population, in the Estado da India 206

Macao 47, 52, 208, 209, 213

MacCartney, Lord 56

MacKenzie, John 91, 92, 93

Mackinder, Sir Halford 35, 246, 258

Madagascar 88

Madeira 12, 13, 58, 69, 115, 183

Magellan, Ferdinand 17, 21

Malacca 59, 196, 197, 201, 208, 213
    Carletti's description of 209

Malay Durbar (Kuala Lumpur) 61

Manco Inca 147–8, 151

mandated territories 54

Manuel, Dom, king of Portugal 199–200, 201, 224

Maoris 17, 18, 44

maps 12–18
    Cantino Planisphere 15, 22
    Cook's first map of New Zealand 15–18
    Piri Reis 12–15, 18, 19, 21, 27
    Waldseemüller 14
    see also world maps of empires

Marco Polo 21

maritime technology
    and the British Atlantic empire 172, 191, 192
    and the Portuguese empire 199, 200, 208, 212–13, 215
    and Spanish America 125
    see also ships

Maroons 173

Mary I, Queen of England 167

Massachusetts Company 181, 190

Mayan civilisation 135

mercantile empires 64, 73, 118

mesitzos 50

metropole (mother country)
    and colony 36
    and the early British empire 9
    English perceptions of empire in 180
    and French perceptions of empire 97
    and Russian imperial expansion 241

metropolitan culture, role of empire in shaping 95–6, 99

Mexica empire 137–44

Mexico
    conquest of 20, 121, 133, 135–45, 164
    flota from 171
    silver production 149–50, 151
    Valley of 115, 121, 137

Mexico City 143–4

microbiology, and sustainable imperialism 116

Middle East, and Indian Ocean trade 195, 196

military orders in Portugal 194

military power and strategy, in Russia 249–54

Mill, John Stuart
    Considerations on Representative Government 85
    On Liberty 84–5

mita, and silver production 150

mixed colonies 47, 53, 54, 58–9

Molucca Islands 208, 209, 219

Mongol empire 23, 196, 230–2, 240, 242, 254, 259
    see also Tatars (Mongols)

monopoly capitalism 64–5

Montezuma, king of the Mexica 136, 137, 138, 139, 140–4, 144

Morocco 30, 50, 100–1

Moskvitin, Ivan 227, 237

Motyl, Alexander 76, 239
    definition of empire 44–5
    model of imperial systems 62–4, 66–7, 69, 70

Mozambique 36, 59, 200, 208

Mughal empire 24, 26

mulattos 50

Muscovy 227, 228–34, 245, 251

Muscovy Company 164, 165

Muthu, Sankar 82

Nahuatl language 136

Naoroji, Dadabhai 106, 107

Napoleonic Wars 28, 29, 30

nationalism, and the Ottoman Empire 27

nation states, and empires 43, 69

naus (carracks), and the Estado da India 199, 200, 208, 215

naval bases 47, 72

navigation, and the British Atlantic empire 159, 172

Navigation Acts 190

nawab of Bengal, EIC defeat of 26

neo-colonialism 57

neo-colonies 36, 56, 57–8, 70

neo-Europes 49, 65, 68–9, 162

neo-Mediterraneans 49

neo-metropoles 49

Nerchinsk, Treaty of 237, 238

Netherlands *see* Dutch Republic

New Christians, in the Dutch Republic 215

New England 180–3, 191

Newfoundland 21, 160, 161, 165

Newitt, Malyn 200, 207, 225

New Spain *see* Mexico

New Zealand 44, 47
    Cook's first map of 15–18

Nigeria 61–2

Nobunaga, Oda 212

noche triste, and the Spanish conquest of Mexico 142, 143

Norse Greenland colonies 20, 115, 122, 125

North America
    Franco-British wars in 25, 26
    geography of, and the British Atlantic empire 157, 158, 164
    land colonisation 44
    and transatlantic migration 182–3

North Borneo Chartered Company 50

Northwest Passage, attempts to discover 164, 165–6, 173

Novgorod Republic 230–2, 247

Nystadt, Treaty of (1721) 239

occupation colonies 47, 49–50, 52, 53, 54, 59

Okhotsk, Russian port 237

ordnance, and Elizabethan exploration 166

Orientalism 98–9

Osterhammel, J. 71

Ottoman empire
    capitulations 48
    corsairs 101
    defensive modernisation 32
    historical overview 23–4, 26–7, 28, 29, 37
    janissaries 72
    and local elites 70
    and the Piri Reis map 14
    and Russia 253, 254, 255, 259

Ovando, Fray Nicolás de 132

Pacific coast, and Russian territorial expansion 237, 253, 258

Pacific islands 36

padroado real 211

Pagden, A. 84

Pakistan 35

palanquins in Goa 210

Pánfilo de Narváez 141–2

papal bulls
    on ecclesiastical appointments in Spanish America 134
    and the Portuguese empire 211

Paris, Treaty of (1763) 25

Park, Mungo 17

Parry, J.H. 216

patronato, in Spanish America 134

Paul, Tsar of Russia 248

Pearson, M.N. 224

pepper trade, and the Estado da India 199, 200, 201

peripheries
    and definition of empire 44–5, 46
    and empires as systems 63, 65, 69, 70
    enclaves 47–9
    and Russian imperial expansion 241

Pernambuco 186

Persian Gulf 21

Persia (now Iran)
    Safavid empire 23, 24, 26
    sixteenth-century 20, 23

Peru
    conquest of 121, 124, 145–9
    flota from 171
    silver production 149, 150, 151

Peter the Great, Tsar of Russia 228, 238–9, 241, 242, 247, 248, 259
    and military power and strategy 253, 254
    and the Russian Orthodox Church 256–7

Philip II, King of Spain 86, 147, 215

the Philippines 21, 24, 29, 52, 120, 171
    and Spanish Franciscans 213
    and the USA 56–7

Picts (ancient Britons), in White's paintings of the New World 175–6

pigs, and ecology in the New World 162

Pilgrim Fathers 180

Piri Reis map 12–15, 18, 19, 21, 27

Pitts, Jennifer 82, 85, 88

Pitts, Joseph, *Account* 100–1, 103, 104

Pizarro, Francisco 20, 22, 145–7

plantation colonies 47, 53, 54, 58–9, 190, 191
    Barbados 186–90
    and the British 'first empire' 82, 118

Plymouth, Massachusetts 180–1
    colony 9

Pobakhov, Ivan 256

Poland, and ecological imperialism 49

pomestia, in Russia 250

popular culture and empires 90–100

Porter, Bernard 80
    Absent Minded Imperialists 93

Portugal 194–5
    Casa da India 199
    discovery of sea route round Africa 14

fidalgos 194–5, 205
    military orders 194
    population growth 206
    seventeenth-century conflict 24
    syndicate of merchants 197
    and transatlantic migration 182
    unification with Spain 215–16

Portuguese empire 118, 119, 120–1, 194–214
    in Africa 22, 23, 58, 59
    Atlantic islands 12, 13, 58
    Brazil 20, 21, 22, 23, 28, 59
    and Catholic Christianity 195
    first voyages to India 197–9
    historical overview 20, 21, 22–3, 35, 37, 38
    Indian Ocean 20, 22–3, 164, 195–9
    Macao 47
    trading outposts 52
    typology of colonies 57–9
    see also Estado da India

postcolonial studies 99, 100

Potosí silver production, Peru 149, 150

Potter, Simon 90

Poverty Bay, New Zealand 16, 17

power relations
    and definitions of empire 45–6
    international power systems 71–6
    in Spanish America 151–2

Prester John, mythical kingdom of 116, 195

privateering, and the British Atlantic empire 170–3, 191

privateers 171

procuradores 137

projection, on world maps 19

propaganda, and imperial rule 79

property rights, and land colonisation 44

protectorates 30, 50, 52, 54, 55

Protestants, and settlement in New England 180, 181

Prussia 24

pueblos, in Spanish America 144

Purchas, Samuel 157, 169

Quebec 25, 26, 50

Quechua 148

Quetzalcoatl 141

quinto real 134

race
  in the Dutch East Indies 223
  in the Estado da India 206, 210
  and French perceptions of empire 96–7
  and individual experiences of empire 105
  in Spanish America 145

Raleigh, Walter 118, 164, 173–4

Raynal, Abbé, *History of the East and West Indies* 88, 89

razriad (subsidiary forts), in Russia 251

Reconquista of Spain 126–7

religion *see* Christianity; Islam

requerimiento, and Catholicism in Spanish America 134

rhumb lines, on the Piri Reis map 13

Riasanovsky, Nicholas 244, 245–6, 253

rich trades, and the Dutch Republic 215

Robinson, R. 74, 91

Round Table movement 90

Russia 227–59
  Academy of Sciences 248
  and Alaska 29, 237, 258
  and China 237, 246, 258
  Cossacks 227, 236, 243, 251, 256
  English trading links with 157
  fortified towns 236–7, 240, 251–2
  fur trade 230, 237, 247, 248–9, 258
  geography 244–6
  historical overview of empire 28, 29, 32, 33
  imperial strategy 239–43
  and the khanates 25, 46, 234, 236, 239–40, 251, 252, 259
  Kievan Rus 228, 232, 247, 254
  military power and strategy 249–54
  military service 243, 247
  Mongol yoke 230–2, 254
  Muscovy 227, 228–34, 245, 251
  Novgorod Republic 230–2, 247
  protectorates 55
  river systems 230, 237, 242, 245, 247, 248
  Romanov dynasty 237
  St Petersburg 253

Stroganov family of merchants 247–8
  territorial expansion 24, 25, 26, 118, 227–39, 258
  trade and economic gain 246–9
  'urge to the sea' 253–4
  wars with Japan 32

Russian-America Company 248

Russian Orthodox Church 227, 232, 243, 254–8
  and the Russian state 256–8

Sackur, Amanda 94–5

Safavid empire 23, 24, 26

Said, Edward, *Orientalism* 98–9

sailors
  and the British Atlantic empire 172
  and the Estado da India 206–7

St Domingue 27, 187

Salmond, Anne 17

Sanderson, William 169

Santo Domingo 132

Scammell, G.V., 'Indigenous assistance in the establishment of Portuguese power in Asia in the sixteenth century' 205–6

Second World War 30, 34
  and racism in France 97

Seeley, Sir John, *Expansion of England* 80–1, 85, 89

Selim I, Ottoman Sultan 14

Senegal 31

señores naturales, in Spanish America 144

sepoys, British East India Company 71–2

serfdom in Russia 243, 247

settler colonies 9, 47, 49, 52, 53, 54, 55
  Barbados 186
  and the British Atlantic empire 159
  ecological advantages held by European settlers 162–4
  and imperial federalism 81
  New England 180–3
  Siberia 239

Seven Years War 25

Seville
  Casa de la Contratación 133–4, 150
  consulado 134

ships
    and the British Atlantic empire
        changing technology 172, 191, 192
        costing Elizabethan exploration
        166–7
        the *Golden Hind* 169, 170
        navigation skills 159, 172
        sailing times 159
    Dutch Republic 215
        flota 171–2
    the *Mayflower* 180
    and the Portuguese empire
        carracks (*naus*) 199, 200, 208, 215,
        216–17
        the Great Ship to Japan 212–13
    transport and empire building 242

Siberia, Russian imperial expansion in 25,
236, 237, 239, 240, 245, 250–2

silver production, in Spanish America 134,
149–41, 171

Singapore 47

slaves 23
    and the British Atlantic empire 172
    British slaves in North Africa 101
    diaries of slave overseer in Jamaica
    101–4
    and settler colonies 49
    in Spanish America 121, 128–9, 131,
    143–4, 145, 151

slave trade 23, 25, 28, 73
    and the British Atlantic empire 164, 172
    and the sugar industry in Barbados
    184–6

smallpox epidemics
    in Siberia 245
    in Spanish America 142–3, 147

small tide-water trading settlements 47

Smith, Adam 82–4, 120
    The Wealth of Nations 82

Smith, Captain John, account of Virginia
176–7

Solander, Daniel 17

soldiers
    and the Estado da India 206–7
    in the Estado da India 206–7

South Africa 28

south Asia, history of empires 20, 21, 24

Soviet Union 33

and the American policy of containment
34–5
    break up 36

Spain
    Anglo Spanish wars/raids 164, 170–1
    debates about empire 86
    and the Philippines 21, 24, 29, 52
    Reconquista 126–7, 134
    seventeenth-century conflict 24
    silver production and the Spanish
    economy 150–1
    and transatlantic migration 182
    transoceanic empire 22
    unification with Portugal 215–16

Spanish America 52, 62, 119, 120–53
    biological colonisation of 124
    colonial institutions 131–5
    conquest of Mexico/New Spain 20, 121,
    133, 135–45
    conquest of Peru 121, 124, 145–9
    Hispaniola 127–8
    historical overview 20, 22, 24, 28
    initial conquest 123–4
    motivations for empire 117, 118
    silver production 134, 149–41
    Spanish emigration to the Indies
    134–5
    'treasure' from 133–4
    vulnerability of Caribbean 171
    see also Amerindians

Spanish-American War (1898) 32

Spanish Franciscan monks, in Japan 213–14

Spanish monarchy, and the conquest of the
New World 125, 126–7

Speult, Herman van 8

Spice Islands 164

spice trade 21, 25, 67, 164
    Dutch 215, 215–16, 216–17, 223
    Portuguese 195, 200, 201, 209, 214

Sri Lanka 59

the state, and the British Atlantic empire
52, 156, 167–9

States General, and the Dutch East India
Company (VOC) 218

States General (Holland), and the Dutch
East India Company (VOC) 52

States of Holland and Zeeland, and the
Dutch trading empire 217, 218

Steensgaard, N., 'Indigenous assistance in the establishment of Portuguese power in Asia in the sixteenth century' 224, 225

Stirring Tales of Colonial Adventure 91–2

streltsy, in Russia 250

Stroganov family of merchants 247–8

sub-imperialist transnational actors, and European imperialism 52–3

Suez Canal 73

sugar production in Barbados 183–90

suzerainty, Mongol 240

Sweden 24

syndicate of merchants, and the Portuguese royal fleet 197

Syria 33

taiga, and Russian territorial expansion 236

Tatars (Mongols) 25, 230–2, 234, 236, 240
    and the Cossacks 243
    and the Russian Orthodox Church 255
    and the Stroganovs 247–8

Tavernier, Jean Baptiste 221–2

technology
    and the beginnings of sustainable imperialism 116
    and the British Atlantic empire 172, 191, 192
    and imperial expansion in Russia 241–2
    and Portuguese ships 199
    and Spanish conquest of the New World 123–4, 125, 152
    see also maritime technology

Tenochtitlan, Mexica city state 137, 138, 139, 140, 142–3
    rebuilding of as Mexico City 143–4

Teutonic Knights 232, 234

Thistlewood, Thomas 101–4, 105

Thomas, H. 141

Thornton, A.P. 98

Tibet 55

Titu Cusí Yupanqui 147, 148, 149

tobacco, and the British Atlantic empire 157, 161, 190

Tobolsk, Siberia 236, 251

Tocqueville, Alexis de 89

Tordesillas, Treaty of 170

torture, and the Amboyna massacre 6, 8

Towerson, Gabriel 6, 8, 10

Tracy, J.D. 218

trade
    and the British Atlantic empire 172
    and chartered companies 51–2
    mercantilist system of 64
    as a motivation for imperialism 116
    and the Navigation Acts 190
    and oceanic empires 67–8
    and the Portuguese empire 195
    Russia 246–9
    and seventeenth-century empires 25
    see also fur trade; spice trade

trading outposts 9, 10, 51, 52, 157

transoceanic empires 22–3, 67–8, 69, 187, 190

transport
    and imperial expansion in Russia 241–2, 245
    see also ships

tundra, and Russian territorial expansion 236

Tunisia 30, 50

Tupaia, Polynesian priest 17, 18

Turkey 37

typologies of empire 46–60, 74–5, 117, 158–9, 180
    maritime trading empires 194
    and Siberia 239

United Provinces *see* Dutch Republic

United States
    as an imperial power 34–5
    and definitions of empire 42, 45
    and the Philippines 56–7
    population growth 68–9
    and power projection 72
    and Russia 258
    world map of military base requirements 33, 35

Utrecht, Treaty of (1713) 25

Vaughan, Robert 176–8

vecinos, in Santo Domingo 132

Velázquez, Diego 135, 136, 141

Venice 115

Vernadsky, G. 244, 245

Verrazano, Giovanni da 180

Versailles, Treaty of (1919) 32

viceroyalties, in Spanish America 153

viceroys 52

Victoria, Queen 41, 42

victuals, and Elizabethan exploration 166

Vietnam 95

Vilcabamba, neo-Inca state 148, 149, 151

Vinland colony 122

Virginia
    and the British Atlantic empire 52, 159–61, 183
    Smith's account of 176–7
    and White's paintings of Amerindians 174–80

Virginia Company 190

Vladimir, grand prince of Kiev 254

VOC *see* Dutch East India Company (VOC)

voevoda (Russian local military commander) 240, 241, 256

votchiny, in Russia 250

Waldseemüller map 14

Walker, Vernon Lee 105–6, 107–8

Walsingham, Sir Francis 171

War of Spanish Succession 25

weaker states, and definitions of empire 45–6

weaponry
    and the Russian army 250–1
    and the Spanish conquest of the New World 123–4, 152

West Indies 24, 27, 69, 126
    and the British 'first empire' 82
    see also Caribbean Islands

White, John, paintings of the New World 173–80

world economy, and American bullion imports 151

world maps of empires 38, 39
    early twentieth-century 29
    eighteenth-century 25–6
    and frontiers 19
    and government of empires 19, 20
    land and size 19
    nineteenth-century 29
    post-First World War 32
    seventeenth-century 24
    sixteenth-century 20

Xavier, Francis 212

Zheng He (Cheng Ho), Admiral 53